DOUBLETALK

THE STORY OF SALT I

DOUBLE TALK

BY THE CHIEF AMERICAN NEGOTIATOR

GERARD SMITH

UNIVERSITY
PRESS OF
AMERICA

LANHAM • NEW YORK • LONDON

Library of Congress Cataloging in Publication Data

Smith, Gerard C.
  Doubletalk: the story of SALT I.

  Reprint. Originally published: Garden City, N.Y.:
Doubleday, 1980.
  Includes index.
  1. Strategic Arms Limitation Talks—History.
I. Title.
JX1974.75.S62   1985   327.1'74   85-6222
ISBN 0-8191-4676-5 (alk. paper)
ISBN 0-8191-4677-3 (pbk. : alk. paper)

For my wife Bernice Latrobe
whose encouragement and love
contributed so much
to my SALT work

ACKNOWLEDGMENTS

I would like to acknowledge a debt to Richard Asplund, who as research assistant labored long and skillfully in the production of this book. In addition to combing through a large number of files he made a substantial contribution to the book's structure and content.

I acknowledge the assistance of individuals who read various drafts of the manuscript and provided most useful comments and proposals for changes—all of whom are good friends and many of whom played an important role in the SALT venture described in this book. Lieutenant General Royal Allison, USAF (Ret.); Harold Brown, now Secretary of Defense; Zbigniew Brzezinski, now Special Assistant to President Carter for National Security Affairs; Philip Farley, retired Foreign Service career minister; Ambassador Raymond Garthoff; Ronald J. Greene, Wilmer, Cutler & Pickering, Washington, D.C.; Benjamin Huberman, Associate Director, in the White House office of Science and Technology Policy; Spurgeon Keeny, Deputy Director of the Arms Control and Disarmament Agency (ACDA); Ambassador Henry Owen, Special Representative of the President for International Economic Summits; J. Graham Parsons, retired U.S. ambassador; Albert Carnesale, Professor of Public Policy, Harvard University;

Paul Nitze; William Bundy, editor of *Foreign Affairs* magazine; John Thomas Smith, partner, Covington and Burling, Washington, D.C.; Lawrence Weiler, former counselor of ACDA; Burke Wilkinson, author and former Deputy Assistant Secretary of State for Public Affairs; and Wendy Jacobson of Doubleday for her expertise in editing. While their aid was invaluable in the book's preparation, they share no responsibility for its content, which is entirely the author's.

I would also like to acknowledge a substantial debt to Mrs. Janice Parrott for her long labors in typing thousands of pages of manuscript.

Finally, I want to thank a number of friends who encouraged me to look backward into the history of SALT to try to illuminate this historic negotiation from a personal point of view while memory and energy were adequate to the task.

CONTENTS

PREFACE   1

YEARS OF PREPARATION   5

GENESIS   15

THE CAST   37

PART I PROBING

1. First Encounter   75
2. The Home Front   108
3. The Negotiation Begins   121
4. "The Great MIRV Mystery"   154
5. A Season of Frustration   179

PART II THE ARRANGEMENT

6. ABM Only   201
7. Back Channel   222
8. A Long Summer   247
9. First Agreements 1971   280

PART III WORKING IT OUT

10. Radar Restraints   301
11. The Summit Approaches   319
12. Last Round in Helsinki   351
13. Bullshit   370
14. Final Helsinki Days   379
15. The Moscow Negotiations   407
16. Aftermath   441
17. Retrospective   446
18. The SALT I Agreements   453
19. Lessons Learned   465

APPENDICES

1. Two Alternative Approaches for
   Comprehensive Limitations   477
2. First Memorandum to President Nixon
   Regarding MIRV Ban   479
3. Second Memorandum to President Nixon
   Regarding MIRV Ban   481
4. Program for Interim Agreements   483
5. President Nixon's Letter Regarding ABM Ban   485
6. ABM Treaty   487
7. Interim Agreement and Protocol   503
8. Accidents Agreement   517
9. Revised Hot Line Agreement with Annex   521

   GLOSSARY   529
   INDEX   539

A cup of science
A barrel of wisdom
A sea of patience
   St. Francis de Sales

FOREWORD
to the
University Press
of America Edition

Thirteen years have now passed since the events described in *DOUBLETALK* culminated in the Moscow agreements on defensive and offensive forces of 1972. Limits on nuclear arms then accepted by the superpowers have significantly advanced international security, although exaggerated expectations of their improving Soviet-American political relations have been disappointed.

Perhaps the most convincing evidence of the utility of arms control for the nation's security is that the agreements have not only survived bitter official criticism in the United States, but even increased the public appetite for more controls. President Reagan has repeatedly stated his commitment to pursue more extensive arms reduction agreements. On the day after his overwhelming electoral victory in November 1984, the President pledged that arms control would be his first priority. The most extreme example is the President's offer to engage in a grand design aimed at eliminating the threat of all nuclear missiles. While this program seems illusory to many scientists and experts, it nonetheless amounts to a tribute to arms control accomplishments of the past.

The maintenance of the international arms control regime has been no small accomplishment—especially in the climate of the troubled Soviet-American political relationship which has developed since 1972—the Soviet invasion of Afghanistan, the shoot down of the Korean airliner, the non-ratification of SALT II, the Soviet walk-out on the INF and START negotiations. Four American and four Soviet presidents have wrestled with strategic arms control problems; the SALT I ABM Treaty stands as the single ratified accomplishment.

The thirteen years since SALT I have also seen a significant change in the sophistication with which Congress considers arms control matters. It now exercises leverage on the Executive branch, not only by withholding or reducing funds for weapons programs, but by delivering strong messages to the President through resolutions expressing its opinions. A new Congressional role in negotiations is reflected in the large delegation of members who descended on Geneva before the resumption of talks this year.

Since SALT I, the attention paid by academia to arms control has likewise increased. Many students now study national security issues, including arms control, as a central part of their education. Public foundations are pouring millions of dollars into grants for projects involving international arms control. Grass roots movements supporting a variety of arms control measures have proliferated. Religious groups have made the achievement of security through agreements a key part of their apostolate.

It seems fair to say that SALT I was followed by an immense national preoccupation with somehow putting an end to the "mad momentum" of the nuclear arms race. The public concern continues to pressure Presidents and Congress alike for progress.

Much of *DOUBLETALK* recalls the story of the negotiation of the SALT I anti-ballistic missile (ABM) Treaty. The ABM Treaty outlawed nationwide defenses as are now anticipated by the U.S. in its "Star Wars" program—the Treaty even went so far as to ban development of space-based systems which are the heart of the Strategic Defense Initiative (SDI), as the Star Wars program is officially called. The basic premise of the ABM Treaty was that an arms race in defensive systems would not only increase the risk of nuclear war, but generate a need to build and maintain additional offensive nuclear forces and result in lessened security for both superpowers. This was a difficult concept for the Soviets to accept, since they had historically placed a great deal of emphasis on the territorial defense of their homeland. But from the very start of the SALT I negotiation in 1969, the Soviet delegation accepted this line of argument, which followed from conclusions reached in the Johnson Administration. This basic premise remains valid, in my judgement.

Yet, how quickly the strategic orthodoxies of one decade become the heresies of the next! In 1972, the Soviets acquiesced in American arguments that a missile defense would be both destabilizing and dangerous. With the Star Wars plan, however, the United States has reopened the debate by declaring establishment of a nationwide anti-missile system to be our prime strategic goal—or as Secretary of Defense Caspar Weinberger has said, "our only hope." The Administration's approach has been to publicly and somewhat piously deplore the erosion of the ABM Treaty at the hands of the Soviets while at the same time, pursuing research and development to prepare for actual deployment of a defensive system, banned by the Treaty's provisions.

The ABM Treaty has twice been reviewed by the parties, in 1977 and 1982, and reaffirmed to be in our national security interests. This record indicates the significance the Treaty has come to have for our national security. Before the ABM agreements were signed, the U.S.S.R. was put on notice that if a treaty limiting offensive strategic weapons was not reached by 1977, the supreme interests of the United States could be jeopardized, warranting American abrogation of the Treaty. But even following the 1980 withdrawal of the SALT II Treaty, which would have provided greater limits on offensive weapons, the U.S. continues to honor the ABM Treaty.

the restrictions on large radars imposed by the ABM Treaty. While these actions may not have a present military significance, they put into question the reliability of the U.S.S.R. as a treaty partner. The asymmetries in the capabilities of the two sides to monitor and verify that commitments are being met is also a large obstacle for the future of arms control.

Prior to the Reagan Administration, however, questions of Soviet compliance with the SALT provisions were handled in channels created expressly to address them—especially the Standing Consultative Commission (SCC). In negotiating SALT I, both sides were keenly aware that weapons technology was evolving rapidly and that conditions conducive to arms control during one decade might well be inadequate for the next. To hedge against this contingency, the SALT Treaties included clauses permitting treaty amendment, review and termination clauses.

The SCC has now been in successful operation for over a decade, discharging the tasks assigned to it successfully and confidentially. Primarily, the SCC performs the vital tasks of implementing the SALT agreements and considering developments which may bear upon their viability. Consequently, it serves as a model for future international bodies, even those dealing with subjects other than strategic arms. While the United States has turned to the Commission to voice charges of violation in the years since 1981, the Reagan Administration appears to have given little consideration to its continuation.

Any realistic assessment of where the SALT process stands in 1985 must come to a gloomy conclusion. Existing agreements seem to be crumbling. Both sides have embarked on programs inconsistent with the ABM Treaty. The Reagan Administration has accompanied its program for defenses with trumpets and drums, announcing the ultimate arrival of a new day when nuclear weapons will be eliminated. The Soviets' silence about their anti-missile defense programs is no less obvious for the fate of the Treaty. In the background, charges and counter-charges of cheating seem to be but preparations for the termination of agreed limitations, marking the return to the unpredictable arms competition of the pre-SALT era.

Thus far, neither the U.S. nor the U.S.S.R. has judged the charges of treaty violations to be sufficiently serious to warrant termination of the agreements. Later this year, however, sea trials are scheduled for our latest missile submarine. At that time, the U.S. will surpass the SALT II ceilings on warheads unless some of its other missiles are decommissioned. Within the Administration, voices have already been heard questioning whether such limitations serve the interest of national security. It is impossible at present to determine whether these voices will prevail.

It is too soon to conclude that *DOUBLETALK* chronicled what was merely a passing phase in superpower military relations, but the evidence points in that direction.

Gerard Smith
Washington, D.C.
April 1985

DOUBLETALK

PREFACE

President Nixon put a high priority on agreements to limit strategic arms. Credit is his for the success achieved in the first SALT negotiation (SALT I for short), which lasted from 1969 to 1972. It is an irony of American history that the only man who ever resigned the presidential office was the first President who succeeded in making significant strategic arms limitation agreements.

Henry Kissinger deserves well of his country for a number of accomplishments, not least his steadfastness in pursuing a policy of strategic arms control when some circumstances and individuals were working in a different direction. For years he preserved the conviction that improved Soviet-American relations were most important for the nation's security and that this required agreement limiting strategic arms. Some of the means Kissinger felt he had to use are criticized in this book, but not his objectives.

International control of strategic arms goes to the heart of America's security. The SALT agreements and the way they were reached are complex matters on which American leaders and people are still incompletely informed. There is a need for a more thorough account of the first SALT negotiation. The process of

YEARS OF PREPARATION

This is the story of SALT I—the Strategic Arms Limitation Talks—which President Nixon called one of the most momentous negotiations ever entrusted to an American delegation. I will try to tell how it went, what it was like to work with Soviet diplomats and military officers for some three years in a partially successful effort to structure American and Soviet strategic forces by agreements in restraint of competition. I hope that this story, while lubricated with personal reminiscence, will make a contribution to history.

In 1931, at age seventeen, I wrote a naïve schoolboy article on the first Soviet five-year plan, predicting that it would not work. The Russian, I thought, was a dreamer, not a doer. During a recess at SALT, I mentioned this to the head of the Soviet delegation, Deputy Foreign Minister V. S. Semenov,[1] my opposite number. He recalled that about that time he had observed a plowing contest between a horse and a tractor. Naturally the tractor won —but onlooking peasants shook their heads. "You can feed the horse hay," one said, "where do you get that stuff the tractor drinks?" That still seems a pertinent question. Semenov added

[1] Pronounced Sem yawn ov.

that at that time the U.S.S.R. had one tractor factory. Now the U.S.S.R. has all the instruments of modern technology, industry, and warfare. I have fewer illusions.

Almost forty years after this first interest in Soviet affairs, Secretary of State William Rogers in January 1969 told me that President Nixon wanted me to be director of the Arms Control and Disarmament Agency. I had been working for about twenty years on national security matters, nuclear weapons and arms control problems in the Atomic Energy Commission, the State Department and as a consultant. These years were, to an uncanny degree, preparation for arms control responsibilities. I had wrestled with issues which in one form or another were central to strategic arms limitation—missile launchers and missile submarines, overhead reconnaissance to monitor Soviet armament, American nuclear delivery systems based in Europe and the Far East, the nuclear programs of allies, the Moscow–Washington Direct Communications Link, the "Hot Line." I was involved in almost every arms control negotiation of that twenty-year period. Nuclear strategy and Soviet-American relations in general were major preoccupations. I had also struggled with marginal success with the Russian language.

Five years after Hiroshima, shortly after the North Korean invasion started and thinking it better "to light one candle than to curse the dark," I went to work in the Atomic Energy Commission as assistant to one of the five commissioners, the late T. E. Murray. More than anyone I have known, he daily lived with the great moral problem presented by the incomprehensible explosive power of atomic energy. The only other person I knew who really allowed the horror of nuclear weapons fully to enter his psyche was a White House consultant who after being briefed for the first time on nuclear weapons effects went home and was ill for several days. A somewhat less noble witness was given by a politician watching a nuclear explosion. He turned to me and said, "Where is the nearest bar?" Murray's conscience drove him to maintain positions which the accepted wisdom scorned. Ban the testing of large thermonuclear devices, he urged, years before test limitation was generally seen to be a way to start controlling nuclear weapons. But Murray was no dove. He favored a test ban because he felt U.S. nuclear weapons were as powerful as they would ever need to be. He urged that the U.S. program should not be dependent exclusively on one laboratory, Los Alamos, and more than anyone else was responsible for the establishment of the Livermore Laboratory. He had cultivated strong anti-Communist sentiments. I am not sure he would have approved of SALT.

At the Atomic Energy Commission I worked with Captain Hyman Rickover, now admiral and the recognized father of nuclear propulsion in the United States Navy. In 1954 I watched the launching of the submarine *Nautilus*, the world's first nuclear-propelled vessel. It would have taken a wild imagination then to foresee that the Polaris/Poseidon fleet of forty-one nuclear submarines would be the most reliable element of American strategic forces—only fifteen years later. Limiting submarines and their missile launchers were to be the stickiest points in the SALT negotiation.

Observing nuclear explosions in the Pacific convinced me that control of nuclear weapons was the most important business in the world. (Another observer at the second of these test series was newly elected Senator Henry Jackson, who played an important role in the congressional phase of SALT I.) There is no better way to begin to understand nuclear weaponry than to see and feel the effects of nuclear explosions. If a million American and Soviet citizens had been able to do this, I think the two superpowers would now be further along in the quest for international control of nuclear weapons.

When working at the State Department I tried several times to persuade John Foster Dulles to observe a nuclear test. "It's like having a look at hell," I said. He gave a surprisingly un-Presbyterian answer: "I'm not sure I believe in hell." He did not observe a test. One of his assistants told me that Dulles felt it might affect his political judgment. Later I urged him to try to persuade President Eisenhower to observe a nuclear test. I doubt that he tried. He felt that the publicity would mar the President's image as a man of peace.

During one informal talk with Minister Semenov, I suggested that the only negative effect of the 1963 treaty limiting nuclear tests to underground explosions was that people no longer could see what a nuclear explosion was like. I asked if the Soviet leadership had observed nuclear tests before they were banned, except underground. He assured me they all had.

As the years pass, fewer people will have any firsthand feel for what nuclear explosions really amount to. People working in the nuclear weapons field, weaponeers, politicians, bureaucrats, academicians and journalists speak of megatons, blast, heat, radiation, tactical weapons. . . . They speak of adequate deterrence being a capability to retaliate by killing 20, 30, 40 per cent of the population of another nation. But we really don't know what we are talking about. To persist in this work one must become callous to horror. Too often this leads to blindness, as dangerous a condition as favoring nuclear disarmament at any cost, supported by "better red than dead" or "peace at any price" advocates. Perhaps the time of greatest danger will be when a new generation somewhere in the world, having no memory of how nuclear weapons were actually used in a war and with nothing but a metaphysical notion of nuclear explosions, may try again to solve international problems with these weapons.

Even more dangerous than the Soviet-American strategic arms competition is the fact that more countries are or probably soon will be developing nuclear weapons. In the first thirty years of the nuclear age six nations developed this capacity. In the next thirty years it may be twenty-five. By the end of the century the 1960s may appear in retrospect to have been peaceful, a secure decade when the atom was under relatively close control. One aim of SALT I was to fulfill the commitment in Article VI of the 1968 Treaty on the Non-Proliferation of Nuclear Weapons, committing the United States and U.S.S.R. to "pursue negotiations in good faith on effective measures relating to the cessation of the nuclear arms race." Some feel that the United States and the U.S.S.R. are in violation of at least the spirit of this commitment.

The first Atoms for Peace Conference in 1955 was an extraordinary meeting of the minds of nuclear scientists and engineers from around the world. As chief political adviser to the U.S. delegation I had opportunities to see and sense the common interest of Americans and Soviets in advancing the peaceful uses of atomic energy. It left a strong impression that if such men, coming from radically different social and economic systems, could so cooperate in the peaceful uses of atomic energy they could, when the time was ripe, do just as well in the greater task of controlling nuclear weapons. During SALT I the work of scientists and engineers on both sides added substantially to the progress made.

Next was the negotiation to set up the International Atomic Energy Agency, a device proposed in Eisenhower's 1953 United Nations address to advance and safeguard the peaceful uses of atomic energy. Ambassador James J. "Jerry" Wadsworth headed the U.S. delegation. I was his deputy. The U.S.S.R. appeared to have little interest in the Atomic Energy Agency or the nuclear proliferation problem. It was still helping the Chinese nuclear program, a policy it later regretted. The Soviet representative, Ambassador Zaroubin, was a dour diplomat who let us carry the burden of arguing for controls and spent a good part of his energies siding with India and other nations which wanted to keep to a minimum any international safeguards over their atomic programs. India wanted to be free to develop nuclear explosives; it exploded its first nuclear device in 1974. This negotiation, lasting many months, was a great lesson in patience. As the dangers of nuclear spread began to be more alarming, the U.S.S.R. took greater interest in the International Atomic Energy Agency and this agency is now assuming greater importance. Its safeguards are a key element in controlling proliferation.

At the London Disarmament Conference in 1957 I was Foster Dulles' aide. Harold Stassen, chief U.S. disarmament negotiator with cabinet rank, had been head of the U.S. delegation. Stassen went beyond his Washington instructions and Dulles took over the negotiation with some brusqueness. The resulting Dulles-Stassen schism was a setback for arms control. Stassen was an able and powerfully persuasive individual with an unmatched zeal for disarmament. But in this case his zeal outran his discretion. I never forgot that lesson.

One of my SALT responsibilities was to brief congressional committees. In 1957 I had been State Department liaison officer to the Senate Foreign Relations subcommittee on disarmament matters. I once reported to Senator Lyndon Johnson that it seemed possible that a disarmament agreement was in sight. Johnson said, "Don't tell any other senator—they'll all start packing their bags to be in London when agreement is reached."

During SALT, I frequently briefed congressional committees. A few members even packed their bags and visited Helsinki and Vienna. Senator John Sherman Cooper was the most helpful.

In the fall of 1957 I became Assistant Secretary of State and director of the Policy Planning Staff. One of my predecessors had been Paul Nitze. Twelve years later he was to be one of the principal SALT delegates.

In 1959, as Foster Dulles was dying, a four-power conference on Berlin was held in Geneva. This meeting was held against the background of a Soviet ultimatum of November 1958 in which the U.S.S.R. threatened to change Berlin's status unilaterally if some agreement was not reached in six months. Secretary of State Christian Herter headed the U.S. delegation and I was chief planner. The United States proposed a disarmament program called the Western Peace Plan. It made no impression on the U.S.S.R. We listened for eleven weeks to long harangues by Foreign Minister Andrei Gromyko. One reason that I felt the Soviets were serious at SALT was the entirely different style used by Minister Semenov. He was serious and businesslike. The day Dulles was buried, the Soviet ultimatum expired without incident. Khrushchev made a junket to America and the beginnings of détente became visible with the spirit of Camp David.

Each year from 1957 through 1960 we worked on a document for President Eisenhower called "Basic National Security Policy." This set out the nation's strategic concept, which for years had centered on the idea of massive retaliation. As the Soviet strategic forces increased in size and quality a number of officials in the State Department and the Joint Chiefs of Staff believed that the concept was becoming obsolete. My predecessor as director of the Planning Staff, Robert Bowie, made a major effort to so persuade the Secretary of State. I continued it. Dulles was very difficult to convince that a change was either needed or indeed possible without demoralizing our allies. Finally he agreed. In November 1958 I accompanied him to the Pentagon where all the hierarchy from Secretary of Defense and chairman of the Joint Chiefs on down had assembled. Dulles, in a most solemn manner, recalled that he had been the father of the massive retaliation doctrine— it had served the nation well, he said, deterring aggression for years. But he had reluctantly concluded that it was a wasting asset. With increasing Soviet nuclear forces, it would become less credible in the foreseeable future and the U.S. military should start preparing plans and weapons systems for alternative strategies. This was more than ten years before Washington officials would say that the days of United States strategic superiority were over. Strategists for more than twenty years have been searching for some rational strategy for the use of nuclear weapons. The "new" strategy initiated in 1974 by then Secretary of Defense James Schlesinger, and now being implemented by the Carter Administration is the latest, but surely not the last, in this probably hopeless quest.

The trend in American strategic weaponry in the 1960s was toward smaller-volume missiles. Taking advantage of American breakthroughs in solid fuels and electronic and nuclear miniaturization, the second generation of ICBMs, the Minuteman, was much smaller and more efficient than the first-generation Atlas and Titan. The U.S.S.R., lacking such breakthroughs, necessarily pursued the opposite approach and produced large-volume missiles which as early as 1969 were seen as a potential threat to the Minuteman force. One of the main U.S. aims at SALT I was to moderate this threat and a major effort was made to get a limit on what were called MLBMs—modern large ballistic missiles. It was not very successful.

During these years in government I worked closely with military leaders and developed, I believe, the confidence of a number of chairmen of the Joint Chiefs and the chiefs of the armed services. For several years after 1957 I met each week with then Director of the Joint Staff General Earle "Bus" Wheeler to consider the significance of national security developments. He subsequently became chairman of the Joint Chiefs. I was pleased to hear him say when I advised him of my Arms Control appointment, "This is good news."

A SALT I agreement was practical because national means of verification had been developed to a high state, especially photography from satellites operating in outer space. During the negotiation I thought back, while listening to Soviet insistence that national means of verification be used to monitor fulfillment of SALT commitments, to that May day in 1960 when an American U-2 photographic reconnaissance plane was shot down by the Soviets. The U-2, so maligned by critics of the Eisenhower Administration, was a forerunner of the technology that has made SALT possible. No such comforting thought crossed my mind during the rather nasty congressional hearings about the U-2 shootdown—hearings in 1960 for the management of which Secretary Herter had given me responsibility.

The U-2, in turn, was partially an offshoot of the Open Skies arms control proposal made by President Eisenhower at Geneva in 1955. He proposed to Khrushchev and Bulganin that each country open up its skies to legitimize reconnaissance so as to reduce concern that a surprise attack might be planned. Khrushchev told Eisenhower that this proposal was a "bold espionage plan" but later said that anyone who wanted could photograph the Soviet Union from satellites. The Open Skies proposal was an example of a decision made with extreme secrecy and almost totally excluding the bureaucracy. In a way it was part of the long process that led to SALT, an effort to get around the Soviet refusal to agree to any arms control proposals that called for on-site inspection.

Failing to get agreement on Open Skies, the United States had conducted successful intelligence operations with high-performance aircraft. Information obtained permitted the United States to structure its strategic forces at a lower level than if it had been completely in the dark about Soviet strategic forces. Armed with this information, the Eisenhower Administration knew that the missile gap charges of the opposition in 1960 were unfounded and that additional U.S. missiles were not needed. Now photography of missile launchers is a key to verifiable limitations on strategic forces.

During the May 1960 Paris summit meeting, shortly after the U-2 shootdown, I was in Paris with Ambassadors Charles Bohlen and Llewellyn Thompson. (Thompson was one of the principal SALT delegates until his death in 1972.) Khrushchev insisted on an apology—which he didn't get. The closest I got to the meeting was to stroll in the garden of the Élysée Palace while Khrushchev was ranting at the President. On returning to the embassy, Eisenhower's first words were, "You might have thought we'd done a Hungary."

As for my negotiation with the Russian language—I started in 1948 as if unconsciously anticipating a responsibility twenty years later. During SALT, I could follow Soviet statements in Russian and so had some advantage in timing replies. I was pleased to hear a report that a Soviet official had observed after I had read one U.S. paper in Russian that "Smith's use of Russian was a demonstration that he did not regard the negotiation as a one-shot affair." I am indebted to a fine Russian teacher in Washington, Madame De La Cruz of the Foreign Service Language School, who through many foodless lunch hours brainwashed a mind far from its schoolday flexibility.

During my years with the Atomic Energy Commission and the State Department I tried to find some moral basis for the use of and even for planning to use nuclear weapons. I could not reconcile my understanding of Christian belief about justifiable use of force and my knowledge of the blast, heat and radiation effects of nuclear explosions. I finally gave up the effort, suspended judgment and kept my conscience quiet with the conclusion that there was no alternative. A world in which the U.S.S.R. had nuclear weapons and the United States did not was unthinkable. I am persuaded that nuclear weapons cannot be done away with until radical political changes occur all over the world, changes which seem little nearer now than in 1947 when the Soviets refused to accept the Baruch plan for banning nuclear weapons. Recently I was asked to lecture on the moral use of nuclear weapons. I declined. I knew of none.

What then should be done? I felt that the best thing was to try to improve relations with the U.S.S.R., by practical moves in the common interest and not by rhetorical flourishes, to work for feasible arms controls, to halt or moderate the spread of nuclear weapons production capability, to guard against diversion of fissionable material from peaceful uses, to ban deployments in environments where nuclear weapons so far had not been placed—all the while maintaining strong, reliable and survivable American deterrent forces.

Before accepting President Nixon's appointment to be director of the Arms Control and Disarmament Agency I called three friends for advice. Douglas Dillon, former Secretary of the Treasury. Undersecretary of State and Ambassador to France, said I should take it on, adding a thought which left me in some doubt: "You have the necessary idealism." Admiral Rickover snorted and asked how many fields I had worked in. "It's time you settled down. If you take the ACDA job, be prepared to work on it for twelve to sixteen years." Senator "Scoop" Jackson advised me to accept, saying perhaps I could succeed in getting some control over ABMs.

So it was, after these years of preparation, having worked on arms control under Presidents Truman, Eisenhower, Kennedy and Johnson, that I found myself one day in February 1969 in a cathedral-like office in the State Department from which John Foster Dulles had for many years presided over the foreign affairs of the United States.

After some six months in office, as I returned from taking part in a Geneva conference on disarmament, the ACDA officer meeting me at Dulles Airport advised that the President wanted me to head up the SALT delegation. I don't recall having any special reaction. I guess I had assumed from the first that SALT would be among my responsibilities. It would certainly have been very disappointing if another had been chosen.

GENESIS

"And at the end looming ever clearer
lies general annihilation."

EINSTEIN

How did it come about that in the late fall of 1969, some twenty-four years after the atomic bombing of Japan, Americans and Soviets gathered at a table in a small palace at Helsinki, Finland, to begin strategic arms limitation talks?

For most of those years informed Americans and Soviets had realized that if it came to general nuclear war both nations and their political systems would be finished. President Truman concluded in his last State of the Union message in January 1953 that an all-out war would "destroy the very structure of civilization." In March 1954 Soviet Premier Malenkov stated that a thermonuclear war would result in a "new world slaughter . . . would mean the destruction of world civilization." While his views were then disputed in Moscow his successors adopted his conclusions. The declaration issued at the 1963 meeting of the Communist Party of the Soviet Union included the sharp reminder that "The atomic bomb does not adhere to the class principle."

Soviet-American strategic parity is widely thought to be a relatively recent development but in one meaning of "parity" it is old. Twenty-three years ago the chairman of the Atomic Energy Commission, Gordon Dean, in the preface to Henry Kissinger's 1957 book *Nuclear Weapons and Foreign Policy* wrote:

For all practical purposes we have in terms of nuclear capabilities reached a point which may be called "parity." We have long known that such a time would come. It is now upon us. I do not mean necessarily parity in numbers of large bombs. Numbers become less important when the point is reached where both sides have the capability to annihilate each other.

Although American officials agree that strategic parity does not require equivalence in numbers of weapons—for some it seems a good thing to have for psychological purposes.

Under the weight of instincts inherited from prenuclear ages, the two superpowers have continued to respond to urges to try to catch up with the superior elements of one another's forces or to mount superior forces of their own. Stimulated by the promise and the dangers of a fruitful technology, the nuclear rivals continued to increase and modernize their strategic forces long after they had the capability to destroy each other. It was as if they feared that they would lose this capability unless they kept the treadmill in motion.

This mindless and macabre rivalry was increasingly questioned by thoughtful leaders of the two sides. But in 1969 the two, while perhaps no longer malevolent scorpions in a bottle, as Robert Oppenheimer had called them, were continuing to engage in a dynamic weapons competition that required a significant investment of their technological and industrial resources.

The United States was proceeding with major strategic weapons programs inherited from the Johnson Administration, the anti-ballistic missile (ABM), and programs to replace the nuclear warheads on strategic missiles with multiple warheads—multiple independently targetable re-entry vehicles (MIRVs).[1] The ABM program was supposed to provide some defense against the prospective Chinese threat and to protect the American ICBM force, believed to be the prime target for a Soviet attack. MIRVs were largely justified by a belief that the United States needed to multiply its missile warheads because a large-scale deployment of Soviet ABMs was expected, and American retaliatory forces needed

[1] A re-entry vehicle is that component of a missile which re-enters the atmosphere carrying the nuclear explosive.

an ample and demonstrable capability to penetrate such a defensive screen if their deterrent effect was to persist.

The U.S.S.R. was building ICBM launchers and missile submarines at a fast rate, with no end in sight. Their small ABM system around Moscow was unfinished, and one could not tell whether it would ever be completed. The Soviets did not deem it necessary to state what the missions of their forces were.

The time now seemed right for Soviet-American cooperation to reduce the risks and costs of this rivalry in strategic arms. Even in the 1950s farsighted officials, including President Eisenhower, had begun to realize and to be resigned to the fact that the most likely outcome of the strategic technology race was stalemate. Eisenhower's experience with world war combined with his great common sense drove him to the quite unmilitary conclusion that Americans and Soviets must find a safer way to carry out their competitive coexistence. His attitude toward arms control encouraged those of us working in the field in the 1950s to feel we were on the right track—even if in those days it was a very lonely stretch of track. Eisenhower in a real sense was a father of SALT. Technology had proved no answer to escaping from an escalating competition. That would have to come from international politics whose prime technique is talk.

For years there had been arms control and disarmament proposals from each side. These proposals were perhaps motivated by modest hopes of providing an acceptable basis for a negotiation, but in good part they were intended to demonstrate to world opinion a sense of superpower responsibility to work toward avoiding World War III and a willingness to end or reduce the economic toll that nuclear weapons and their delivery systems were exacting from needy countries both developed and developing. This tentative grappling with nuclear arms controls had led to the 1963 Test Ban Treaty, which reduced the radiation overburden that nuclear testing in the atmosphere had built up, but it did little to reduce the pace of improvement in the design of nuclear weapons and nothing to reduce their numbers. Treaties had been agreed on in 1960 to ban military activities in Antarctica, and in 1967 to ban weapons of mass destruction in outer space, as well as the establishment of military installations on the moon or other celestial bodies. These agreements did not limit weap-

chance for such a radical solution had passed. The superpowers settled for the time being on a mild remedy, the Non-Proliferation Treaty (NPT), negotiated over the period 1965–68. They and the U.K. (but not France and China) agreed not to transfer nuclear weapons or their technology to countries not having nuclear weapons. Many of the non-weapons states agreed in turn not to undertake nuclear weapons programs, but a number of nations which are technically the most capable of producing nuclear weapons did not. The treaty committed the United States and the U.S.S.R. to negotiate for disarmament. It was hoped that SALT would be taken as some earnest of good intentions to fulfill the commitment. The day the NPT was signed, July 1, 1968, President Johnson announced an agreement to start the SALT negotiation "in the nearest future."

SALT was ready to go that summer of 1968. United States Government agencies worked out an agreed package of proposals. Johnson approved the American position while he pressed the Kremlin for a summit meeting in Moscow or Leningrad to initiate the talks. On August 19 Soviet Ambassador Anatoly Dobrynin informed the White House that his government agreed to a SALT summit on September 30. The next day, August 20, Soviet-led forces invaded Czechoslovakia. Johnson was forced to cancel his SALT date.

A legacy from this false start was informal agreement on a document called "Objectives and Principles." These were drafted in Washington for the aborted September 1968 summit and later passed to Dobrynin. The objectives for SALT talks would be:

- To achieve and maintain a stable U.S.-Soviet strategic deterrence by agreed limitations on the deployment of offensive and defensive strategic missiles.

- To enhance the credibility of forces to prevent the destabilizing actions of other nations by demonstrating U.S. and Soviet willingness to limit their strategic missile forces.

- To provide assurance to each that its security will be maintained while at the same time avoiding the tensions and uncertainties and cost of an unrestrained continuation of the strategic arms race.

- To improve Soviet-U.S. understanding in establishing a continuing process of discussion of issues arising from the strategic situation.

The Soviets responded in November with a draft that essentially accepted the U.S.-proposed objectives. They also suggested certain additions, stressing the interrelationship between offensive and defensive systems, providing that limitation and reduction should be "so balanced that neither side could obtain any military advantages and that equal security should be assured for both sides," and proposed study of "steps to rule out the accidental appearance of conflict fraught situations involved in the use of strategic arms." These "Objectives and Principles" reappeared during SALT. They were never issued as an agreed document because of strong concern among the NATO allies that agreement to a continuing process of discussion in conflict fraught situations might lead to superpower collaboration against their interests.

On the first day of the Nixon presidency, January 20, 1969, the U.S.S.R. Foreign Ministry issued a statement of its willingness to start SALT. "Not so fast" was in effect the Nixon reply. The new administration would have to review the military posture of the United States before determining what if any strategic arms limitations might be acceptable. The President was later to say that "For the first time in history we have considered the shape of our military programs and policies in parallel with possible arms control alternatives." This cautious reaction was designed to signal that the new administration was not about to be carried along on the momentum of the Johnson SALT positions of the previous year. The Soviets apparently found this tempo suited their need to avoid appearing more eager than the Americans to start talking. But there was never much doubt that the Nixon Administration would go ahead with SALT.

After an election campaign in which he argued for American strategic superiority, President Nixon took office determined to prospect for better Soviet-American relations. His interest in improving relations with the U.S.S.R. grew as the ugliness of the Vietnam deterioration became more apparent. Perhaps Nixon saw in SALT the best way to reduce Soviet-American tensions—just as

President Johnson had seen the value of the Non-Proliferation Treaty and SALT in the earlier period. Nixon felt that even though the two superpowers were ideological adversaries, they were in a sense being driven to cooperate. He sensed that our national power, thought to be gained through the possession of more and more weaponry, could not be converted into advantage over the U.S.S.R.—and the effort to achieve it could in itself lead to catastrophe. But he was not sure the Soviets shared these convictions.

President Nixon knew it was politically and economically impractical for his administration to mount major new strategic programs. Demands from the civilian sector made decreases in defense spending more likely. He calculated that, even if a return to strategic superiority was technically and financially obtainable, an effort to regain it might well trigger a much tougher arms competition, harm U.S.-Soviet relations and perhaps even increase the risk of war. That did not fit at all into his image of an era of negotiation.

President Nixon also was confident that he had what it took to reach a Soviet-American arms control agreement. He told me that because of his anti-Communist record he believed he could bring the country to favor Soviet-American arms control to a degree not possible for any Democrat President. Later, at the May 1972 Moscow summit, he was to say to Kosygin, "You know me as an anti-Communist." "It is a well-deserved reputation," was the reply.

By 1969 American strategic forces had reached maturity. Ballistic missile launchers were deployed on land and at sea. Strategic bombers which, from World War II until the end of the 1950s, had alone constituted the strategic force were being reduced in numbers. No clear military requirement existed for increasing the numbers of offensive missile launchers in the U.S. strategic forces. It now appeared that the United States could afford to enter commitments with the U.S.S.R. not to increase strategic forces and perhaps even to reduce them. It was obvious that the Soviets would not agree to settle for strategic inferiority. That meant that the United States would have to learn to live with some sort of strategic parity.

In fact, looking at projected rates of Soviet missile launcher construction in the light of the absence of any such U.S. programs, the Nixon Administration realized that there was no way, save by an arms limitation agreement, to prevent the U.S.S.R. from achieving numerical superiority in offensive ballistic missile launchers. There was no inclination in the Pentagon to increase the number of then current weapons, which had been designed in the 1950s. If strategic forces were to be increased, they should be the last word in weaponry, and new missile systems then required about eight years from first testing to complete deployment. Even if the United States promptly started new programs it would be years before we could have significant additions to the numbers of launchers. Thus the situation in 1969 was that more weapons were unnecessary except for appearances and bargaining leverage. Adding to existing classes of strategic weapons would be doubly senseless.

The Administration soon rationalized away the 1968 election slogan of strategic superiority and adopted a doctrine of sufficiency. This doctrine actually had been introduced thirteen years earlier by the Eisenhower Administration in response to projections of a strategic "bomber gap" and Democratic calls for American superiority in air power. President Eisenhower refused, as one writer commented, "to make the maintenance of American superiority a continuing requirement of policy." Secretary of Defense Wilson told the House Subcommittee on Defense Appropriations in 1955 that "the quality of our retaliatory force is now becoming more important than its size." Donald Quarles, Secretary of the Air Force and one of the most knowledgeable and sensitive American officials who ever dealt with nuclear strategic issues, in a speech entitled "How Much Is Enough?" in February 1956 argued that U.S. officials "must make a determination of sufficiency." Neither the United States nor the U.S.S.R. could prevent the other side from maintaining the capability to inflict catastrophic damage on its homeland, Quarles said, and such a situation could exist "even if there was a wide disparity between the offensive and the defensive strengths of the opposing forces." The nation needed only to maintain a force capable of inflicting a destructive level of damage on the U.S.S.R. "Beyond a certain point the prospect is not the result of relative strengths of the two opposed forces. It is the absolute power in the hands of each and . . . the substantial invulnerability of this power to interdiction."

Early in his first administration President Nixon approved a set of criteria of sufficiency:

- maintaining an effective strategic retaliatory capability to deter surprise attack by any nation against the United States;

- preserving stability by reducing the vulnerability of U.S. strategic forces and thereby minimizing the Soviet Union's incentive to strike first in a crisis;

- preventing the Soviet Union from being able to inflict considerably more damage on America's population and industry than U.S. forces could inflict on the U.S.S.R.; and

- defending the United States against small-scale nuclear attacks or accidental launches.

This acceptance of the Eisenhower doctrine of sufficiency was the key doctrinal basis for SALT. If the United States or the U.S.S.R. expressly or tacitly has strategic superiority as an aim, SALT agreements have no chance of enduring. I wrote Secretary of State Rogers in May 1969 "if either side is striving for or appears to be striving for an effective counterforce first strike capability, then there is no hope for strategic arms control."

If there was to be success at SALT, I felt that the two sides would to some extent have to pursue a similar strategic doctrine, that the prime (but not necessarily sole) purpose of strategic nuclear weapons is to deter the use of such weapons by the other side through maintenance of a clear threat that such use would lead to intolerable damage to the attacker. This in simple terms is the doctrine of "assured destruction." Harold Brown (then president of the California Institute of Technology, former Secretary of the Air Force and soon to be one of the SALT delegates) suggested in an influential article in 1969 that "our principal criterion for judging an agreement to limit strategic arms should be whether the resulting balance of forces assures us of possessing as much or more certainty of deterrence as we would have in its absence. . . . An agreement should be such as to help insure that if one side strikes first it will not gain and preferably will lose in relative military strength."

Most of the theorizing about the Soviet-American strategic relationship has come from Americans. It was fashionable for pundits to speculate about what makes for strategic instability in a crisis and what causes instability leading to an escalating weapons competition. Many American experts had written on such preternatural notions as degrees of deterrence, nuclear war fighting, and damage limitation capabilities. Soviet views were unknown. The Soviets seldom take up their strategic pens to try to rationalize the irrational. They for the most part restrict their rhetoric to propaganda against American military power. SALT seemed to offer a virgin field to cultivate a better understanding of Soviet concepts of how our strategic relationship could most safely be managed.

Was curbing the strategic arms competition a necessary condition for improving Soviet-American political relations, or did such better relations have to come first? Whichever was the case, Nixon knew that the two were intimately related. Progress in SALT and planning for a Soviet-American summit meeting having a broader agenda were to go hand in hand during most of his first administration. This was a latter-day version of the conventional Western wisdom of the 1950s that disarmament must go hand in hand with political settlements. Then it was said in Washington and Allied capitals that there could be no progress on disarmament in Europe unless there was parallel progress on German reunification.

The SALT situation in 1969 was complicated by this inclination of President Nixon toward what was called "linkage." It seemed to me that this concept assumed the Soviets wanted strategic arms controls somewhat more than the United States and that, in order to get them, the Soviets might make concessions on other international issues. Perhaps Soviet help could be enlisted in winding up the Southeast Asian war. A few days after his inauguration President Nixon said at a press conference, "What I want to do is to see to it that we have strategic arms talks in a way and at a time that will promote, if possible, progress on outstanding political problems at the same time—for example, on the problem of the Mideast and on other outstanding problems in which the U.S. and the U.S.S.R., acting together, can serve the cause of peace." Although he was to back off somewhat from this explicit connection of SALT with other problems, Nixon considered "linkage" a fact of life and it was never entirely downed.

The Soviets quite expectedly did not subscribe to this "linkage" concept and said so at SALT on numerous occasions. That would have made it appear that they had a superinterest in SALT which could be leveraged by the United States with profit. Both sides, they said, had an equal interest in curbing the arms race—neither more nor less. When the negotiation continued unharmed by the Cambodian incursion of 1970 and the Haiphong bombing of 1972, it seemed that we were in a vacuum—acquiesced in by mutual consent.

Kissinger later believed that progress in SALT I was accompanied by advances in solving political problems. Briefing congressional leaders in June 1972, he said, "The President was convinced that agreements dealing with questions of armaments in isolation do not in fact produce lasting inhibitions on military competition because they contribute little to the kind of stability that makes crises less likely. In recent months major progress was achieved in moving toward a broadly based accommodation of interests with the U.S.S.R. in which an arms limitation agreement could be a central element." Present-day doubts about this last conclusion do not justify doubts as to the advantages of arms control agreements. It was too much to expect that curbing the military competition somehow meant that Soviet-American crises were a thing of the past.

Although the time when an arms control agreement is reached may well be a good occasion for concluding other agreements, a useful arms control agreement should not be made conditional or "linked" to progress in other areas. Such a "linkage" concept may find support in history but in this nuclear age, when rival nations live under the threat of almost instant destruction, a chance to reduce that threat has independent value. Adversary nations should grasp any such opportunity even though their other relations are not improving.

Although American civilian leaders were interested in making a serious start on curbing strategic forces, some military leaders had been wary of getting on a slippery slope. Once committed to a negotiation, they could not foresee a positive end to the process. They sensed that as long as negotiations held some hope of success congressional support for military appropriations might be inhibited. They were concerned that if we entered serious arms control negotiation there would be some letting down of our guard. The influence of military leadership was at a low level in 1969, however, in the backwash of repeated disillusionments in Southeast Asia. General Wheeler, chairman of the Joint Chiefs of Staff and an army officer with long experience in national security matters, was persuaded that strategic arms control could be in the national security interest. By dint of long hard argumentation in 1968 he had brought the Chiefs around to this point of view. General Wheeler deserves a good deal of credit for the progress made in SALT. His courageous advocacy of a policy that was unwelcome to his military colleagues was an outstanding example of placing the national interest above perceived advantages for the military services. Since then the Joint Chiefs have in general supported SALT, although at times with less than great enthusiasm.

One reason why the time seemed ripe for SALT was a recognition by the military in the United States and perhaps by their counterparts in the U.S.S.R. that, no matter what strategic concept a side might adopt, a level of some two thousand strategic offensive launchers of different types would be more than ample, especially as multiple warheads (MIRVs) were being developed. Merely adding offensive launchers would give no advantage unless widespread ABM defensive systems were to be deployed. So even to the military a limit on launcher numbers seemed tolerable —as long as it was high enough.

Weaponeers' minds then tended to concentrate on improvements in weapons performance rather than increases in launcher numbers. Throughout SALT, the military on both sides agreed that strategic arms limitations should not prevent modernization, and this was the root of a major dilemma for U.S. strategic planners. Then and now, their central concern has been the possibility of a Soviet attack on American fixed, land-based intercontinental ballistic missiles (ICBMs). How could this threat be moderated if Soviet missile improvements were to proceed unchecked? How could continuing replacement of aging Soviet missiles be allowed except under agreed conditions designed to moderate this threat to U.S. ICBMs? The dilemma was not solved and criticism of the SALT interim freeze agreement on offensive launchers reached in 1972 stems in part from this failure.

It did not help the logic of the U.S. position favoring SALT to have Secretary of Defense Melvin Laird state in 1969 that the Soviets were clearly going for a first strike capability. If that were true, I thought we had no business negotiating to limit our strategic arms. Perhaps he hoped that after a SALT agreement Soviet strategy would change or, if it did not, at least a severe limitation on ABMs might reduce Soviet capabilities to implement a first strike strategy. But freezing levels of arms by agreement is one thing and changing a nation's strategic concept is quite another. It struck me that, with the Department of Defense apparently not sharing the view of other government agencies that a first strike strategy was no longer feasible for either side, seeds of SALT confusion were being sown.

I sensed that civilian scientists and engineers in the office of the Secretary of Defense were more influential with Secretary Laird than professional military officers. These men would never have to be users of nuclear weapons. They were not members of military services with experience in fighting wars, but a kind of elite which knew or gave the impression of knowing the new secrets of the nuclear missile age. Their argumentation was refined and sometimes seemed as concerned with proving abstract analytical points as with the merits of the case in a strategic military sense. Nuclear strategy has become an exciting intellectual realm for some Pentagon civilians, and their speculations sometimes affect weapons decisions as much as or more than professional military advice.

Imbedded in our general concern about the Soviet Union's nuclear build-up, fed repeatedly by photographic evidence of more and more Soviet ICBM silos and submarine construction, was a special worry about very large Soviet missiles, the SS-9s, assumed to be targeted not on American urban industrial areas but on Minuteman missile launchers out West. It is a wonder of the nuclear era that the American people carry so lightly the fact that they may be destroyed in a few minutes while at the same time responsible officials are mainly concerned about the vulnerability of some missile launchers.

This concern was a major factor in SALT. American positions constantly reflected it. It seemed possible to some that a SALT agreement could so moderate this ICBM vulnerability as to make new U.S. strategic launcher programs unnecessary. SALT had a number of positive results. This was not one of them.

Although they have hardened their silos and are developing mobile ICBMs, the Soviets do not seem as concerned about this ICBM vulnerability problem. During SALT the Soviets were to say in effect, "What are you worried about, you have large strategic forces other than ICBMs," referring to our relatively invulnerable submarine-based missiles and less vulnerable heavy bombers. They continued to increase the numbers of their fixed ICBM launchers until a puzzlingly large percentage of their overall strategic force is now in this, by American lights, potentially vulnerable force. This apparent difference of view about the fact and significance of ICBM vulnerability plagued the SALT negotiation. The Soviet failure to feel as we do and to respond to our concerns about ICBM vulnerability is a main source of some Americans' apprehension about the whole SALT process.

Nothing concentrated the minds of American leaders on the advantages of SALT as much as the clear and present danger of one-sided arms control in the form of congressional cuts in U.S. defense budgets. The changing popular and congressional mood about strategic arms was not lost on such an astute politician as Secretary of Defense Melvin Laird. His interest in SALT was, I thought, in good measure based on a concern that in the absence of agreed limitations the Congress would go for some unilateral limitation. His was not an idle concern. In 1967 President Johnson had calculated that he had to propose an ABM program to Congress, even though no strong military case could be made for it, lest a phenomenon like the "missile gap" of the 1960 election campaign hurt the Democrats in the 1968 election. But the ABM program never had a broad constituency, and its multiple and shifting rationales drew justified criticism. Technical evidence of the Johnson ABM system's unfitness for its mission to defend ICBMs was persuasive to politicians and people alike. Only two years later, in 1969, congressional support had shrunk to the point that the ABM authorization vote was evenly divided. The measure carried only with the tie-breaking vote of Vice-President Agnew. After that the ABM program became more of a negotiating bargaining chip than a military asset.

Obviously concern about the firmness of national support for weapons programs is not the best basis for international bargaining about their control. This was not the only time that the United States had tried to make arms control capital out of domestic considerations. In the 1960s, after a decision to phase out the B-47 bombers, the United States proposed the so-called "bomber bonfire" plan in which the Soviets would match decommissioning of B-47s with removal of an equal number of their medium-range bombers, many of which are still in service. And in the early 1970s, when pressures in Congress were building up for a reduction in U.S. forces in Europe, we sought a "mutual balanced force reduction" arrangement in good part as an effort to get matching Soviet reductions.

President Nixon, well aware of this risk of congressional nonsupport, felt that the SALT negotiation was perhaps the last chance for bargaining with the Soviets from a level of equality. Strategic arms control suddenly took on new seriousness and respectability. While supporting SALT in public, Secretary Laird's more important responsibility, as he saw it, was to make Americans aware of the continued Soviet strategic build-up and to work on the Congress to fund strategic programs. After SALT agreements were reached, he conditioned his approval on congressional support for a revised budget for strategic arms, including new programs included as bargaining chips for future SALT negotiations. The same phenomenon was apparent in the SALT II ratification process.

A final factor favoring SALT in 1969 was improvement in reconnaissance capabilities. Until recently it had been thought that verification of Soviet commitments to limit arms would require on-site inspection in the U.S.S.R. The Soviets would not accept inspection, except, they said, if there were general and complete disarmament, hardly a likely prospect. Development of so-called national technical means of verification changed that. These are intelligence-gathering systems, popularly thought of as reconnaissance photography from satellites operating in outer space and as remote detectors of various kinds. Using them, some kinds of arms limitations could be adequately verified. One would not have either to "trust" the Soviets or to have on-site inspection. You could tell whether or not they were staying within agreed limits. An important condition for getting on with SALT was the willingness of the CIA to certify that these systems could be relied upon for arms control verification. During much of the 1960s the intelligence community was concerned that use of technical means of verification would draw Soviet charges of illegal practices. High confidence is now placed, and properly so, in these technical means of verification.

And so from the American point of view a widespread belief that the time had come to try to put limits on strategic arms, combined with concerns lest Congress legislate unilateral disarmament, made SALT attractive. The prospect that the Soviets might field a nationwide ABM system to neutralize our retaliatory missiles made SALT urgent and important. Worries that first-line ICBMs would become vulnerable to the threat of a strike by Soviet offensive missiles made SALT of interest as a possible device for reducing that vulnerability. Finally, improvement of technical intelligence techniques made SALT practical.

Why did the Soviets agree to enter the negotiation? We do not know for sure.

After the Cuban missile crisis of 1962 the U.S.S.R. had decided "never again" to find itself strategically inferior in a crisis. Only with equal forces could it gain the prize of recognition that it was on a strategic par with the United States. Only at a time of perceived equality of the rival forces would an arms control agreement be possible. In 1969 the U.S.S.R. was still "catching up" in the strategic arms competition, but a relationship of rough equality in numbers of strategic missile launchers was not far off. The Soviets knew that if necessary they could prolong the negotiation. The relative levels of missile launchers would continue for some time to improve for the U.S.S.R. since the United States had no launcher construction programs under way. Nineteen sixty-nine must have seemed a good time for the Soviets to start the strategic bargaining.

An important reason for the Kremlin's support of SALT was the prospect of an unwanted competition in ABMs. The Soviets had been first to start a modest defensive system, around Moscow, which we called "Galosh." It was never finished. They knew it was not effective, but they must have thought it had some deterrent effect on any Chinese temptation in a crisis to try to destroy Moscow. There was no specific evidence that they planned to deploy a regional or nationwide ABM system, although U.S. intelligence estimates included predictions of large-scale deployments. Certain American officials also had concerns that the Soviets could improvise such a system by increasing the capability of their very numerous anti-aircraft missiles (SAMs). This problem was called SAM upgrade and it was often discussed at SALT.

In February 1967, at the time of President Johnson's SALT initiative, Soviet Premier Kosygin told a London press conference that ABMs were not a cause of the arms race but a means of saving lives. That June, at the Glassboro, New Jersey, summit meeting, McNamara had tried to persuade Kosygin of the burdens and dangers of a competition in ABMs. Reports have it that Kosygin was unconvinced, confident in the traditional belief that defense of the motherland could in no conceivable way produce a bad result. This Soviet view was to change. More than anything else, recognition of the paradox that while offensive forces could keep the peace defensive forces might threaten it opened the way for Soviet participation in SALT.

The Soviets learned well the McNamara lesson that ABMs were not an unmixed blessing. The day of Soviet boasting—that they could hit a penny in space—was over. Their land- and sea-based missiles could be neutralized, at least for a time, by an American nationwide ABM system. They knew that American technology was and likely would remain superior to theirs. During SALT I, we sensed that Soviet concern about American ABMs was as great as American concern about Soviet large ICBMs.

The Soviet leaders must also have been concerned lest it be widely thought by their peoples that an effective ABM system was practical. Soviet experts must have advised them that ABM systems would be far and away the costliest kind of strategic hardware and could ultimately be neutralized by major additions to the American offensive missile forces. But popular urges for defense run deep in the traditions of their people. A high Soviet official told me that his father, a simple man, a plumber, told him he was crazy to consider negotiating away a missile system to defend the Soviet Union. This layman's view was anticipated by Henry Kissinger, writing in 1957, "A nation may be willing to forgo the offensive uses of nuclear weapons but it will be most reluctant to give up its defensive applications, e.g., anti-missile defenses." Surprisingly, the reverse proved to be the case in SALT. Sharp limitation of defensive strategic systems was reached. Similar limitation of offensive weapons still escapes us.

The Soviets undoubtedly appreciated the significance of the MIRV systems which the United States was testing in 1969. They must have seen that much of what they had gained in quantity of missile launchers they were about to lose to the multiplication of American warheads. While the Soviets were already doing research and development work on MIRVs, they realized it would take perhaps a decade before large-scale Soviet MIRV deployments would be possible. They must have been searching for ways to stop or slow down the American MIRV deployments while not stopping their own MIRV development. They probably calculated that prospects for unilateral constraints on the American MIRV program might be improved once SALT negotiations got under way. Perhaps Moscow estimated that while SALT was taking place any new American strategic programs would have harder going in the Congress. As for the American ABM program, if that could not be stopped by SALT agreement, the Soviets must have had some confidence that the SALT process would at least slow it down since they have some influence on American decisions through skillful propaganda.

A primary SALT goal of the U.S.S.R. was formal registration of strategic equality. Having been in second strategic place during the whole nuclear era, the Soviets were careful to avoid appearing to want a SALT agreement more than the United States. During SALT I Soviet delegates often pointedly observed that neither side had a greater need than the other for a SALT settlement. A SALT agreement would go far toward granting the U.S.S.R. that status of strategic and political equality with the United States which for a quarter century had been a main thrust of its foreign policy. With codification of strategic equality the Soviet policy of

tests, defense budgets, and alarms about missiles, bombers and submarines. More than twenty years ago I asked the world-renowned nuclear physicist Professor I. I. Rabi how this greatest weapons race in history would end. "When people get bored with it," he said.

At the same time, it was far from clear in 1969 that SALT would lead to anything concrete. Secretary of State Rogers indicated how tentative was our commitment and how modest our expectations were in an address on SALT in November 1969, in which he said: ". . . we begin these negotiations knowing that they are likely to be long and complicated and with the full realization that they may not succeed."

THE CAST

Although close and continued negotiation with Soviet officials on a wide range of subjects including arms control, trade, grain sales, naval maneuvers and science exchanges are now commonplace, when the SALT negotiation started in November 1969 it was not a normal thing for either nation and few officials had any experience with it.

The SALT delegates were all veterans of years of rough relations between their governments. The rules of the game had included bugging of embassies, entrapment and blackmail, inducement of defections, the whole dreary record of uncivil relations shrouded over by that apparent correctness which mutual diplomatic recognition had initiated more than a third of a century before. Although overall political relations had mellowed slightly in the 1960s, American and Soviet SALT negotiators were under no illusions that they were involved in anything but an adversary relationship, representing two superpowers tentatively searching for a less risky and costly way to maintain the balance of nuclear terror. Security of persons, documents and communications was at all times an important consideration.

SALT work required close Soviet-American contact, sometimes on a daily basis. There was more consultation on political/military matters between the two SALT delegations than ever had been the case between the American Embassy in Moscow and the Soviet Ministry of Foreign Affairs or the State Department and the Soviet Embassy in Washington, at least since the collaborative days of World War II. American and Soviet officials met hundreds of times in Finland and Austria. Even when they were relaxing, SALT was never far from their thoughts. This constant process resulted in Soviet and American delegates getting to know each other fairly well in spite of strong political, cultural and language barriers. I think these people grew to respect one another. Their work, while terribly time-consuming, had to be done in a painstaking way. In the end the United States delegation was satisfied with the product of its efforts, which for the most part were reflected in the ABM Treaty. (While the delegation devoted much time and effort to limitation of strategic offensive arms, the main parts of the 1972 interim freeze agreement were engineered by Kissinger and other Soviet officials and not by the SALT delegations.)

A bizarre aspect of SALT was that military men of both sides were talking to each other for many months in a civil and, in time, even friendly fashion. Men who in their military careers had been involved in one way or another in planning and training for nuclear strikes against each other found themselves working and relaxing together in a way unimaginable a few years before. The respect they developed for each other should be something of an asset in the long process that will be required if real improvement in Soviet-American relations is to occur. That will not come about from any rhetoric of "détente." It will come when the superpowers see that nuclear weapons have placed them both in a common jam, escape from which can only come with cooperative action based on a recognition of their common humanity.

What was it like to have this long talk between graduates of cold war antagonisms? Who were the people who left other tasks of diplomacy and defense to negotiate with representatives of the other camp? In this chapter I will try to give something of an answer.

Picking the principal U.S. delegates had not been difficult. I wanted Philip Farley, my deputy at the Arms Control Agency

(ACDA), to be alternate chairman of the delegation. The President agreed. Ambassador Llewellyn Thompson and Harold Brown had had a good deal of experience with problems of arms control. The White House quickly agreed to their being delegates. On the chance that I would lead the SALT delegation I had sounded out Thompson even before accepting the ACDA post to assure his availability. Secretary Rogers told me that Mel Laird would like to be represented by Paul Nitze. I was pleased to have him. The chairman of the Joint Chiefs of Staff wanted Royal Allison as his designee. Allison, a major general in the Air Force, received an additional star just before we arrived at Helsinki. As soon as the SALT team members were announced by the President, we started to meet in Washington to consider and help coordinate our agencies' positions for the negotiation.

One of the assets I inherited was that all the other delegates had been involved in SALT matters for some time. I don't know if the Nixon White House realized it in 1969, but these men had been involved in the SALT preparations during the Johnson Administration and probably would have been on the SALT delegation if the talks had begun as planned in 1968. Here was an invaluable element of continuity. We got off to a running start. This was not the case with the Soviets, who formed their delegation in 1969 shortly before the talks started. Its leader, Semenov, told me that he had come aboard "after the train was moving," as a substitute for his Foreign Ministry colleague Kuznetzov, who had been diverted from SALT to the Sino-Soviet negotiations in Peking. This last-minute switch may have reflected Soviet priorities in 1969 between SALT and China.

Ambassador "Tommy" Thompson had been, with Charles (Chip) Bohlen, one of the leading American diplomats in the field of Soviet relations. Incidentally, he was a crack bridge player, a talent often employed during the long winter nights in Helsinki. He was the ideal of the Foreign Service. "What does Tommy think?" was a question at least four Presidents had asked when Soviet-American problems arose. I sensed that the Soviet leaders also valued his judgment. Thompson had been slated to lead the SALT delegation had the talks started in 1968.

Most unfortunately, his health failed and he had to leave the delegation in 1971. He died a year later, just before the final round of the talks in Helsinki. President Nixon said of Tommy Thompson that he truly gave his life to the cause of peace.

Harold Brown was equally at home with science and technology, international politics, and managing large affairs. While continuing his responsibilities as president of Cal Tech, he served at SALT for weeks at a time during each session—running his university at long range and at the same time contributing mightily to the SALT process. He was a strong factor for stability on the delegation, combining firsthand experience with nuclear weapons and a conviction that strategic arms control was in the security interests of the United States. His civilian voice backed by extensive experience in defense matters was invaluable. Usually he came down on the side of issues that seemed sensible to me. His powerful mind exercised a strong influence on his fellow delegates. He was highly respected by the Soviet delegates.

Paul Nitze came to SALT after a long and impressive career in government service. It began in 1942 when he left an investment banking firm to join the Board of Economic Warfare. He was closely associated with Secretary of State Dean Acheson for many years and served as the director of the State Department's Policy Planning Staff. He was National Security Adviser to President-elect Kennedy and was his Assistant Secretary of Defense for International Security Affairs. He then became Secretary of the Navy and Deputy Secretary of Defense during the Johnson Administration. Nitze's talents and great experience made a major contribution to the SALT delegation's work.

I wonder if in working on SALT I Henry Kissinger recalled that Paul Nitze in a 1957 review of Kissinger's book *Nuclear Weapons and Foreign Policy* had written: "The only people whose doctrinal and strategic ideas are referred to with approval by Kissinger are Lenin, Stalin, Mao, Hitler, and Napoleon, though I do not mean to suggest that he endorses all their views." Nitze told me that Kissinger subsequently had written some 165 pages of rebuttal but then gave up the effort.

Nitze took some of his frustrations out on his piano, which one could hear every evening as he patiently practiced to perfect his technique. Often he rode horseback. Some forty years earlier on a walking trip in Finland he had inadvertently crossed the Soviet border, and I got a kick out of telling the Soviets how this SALT delegate had thus violated Soviet territory. But Nitze was too young then to have been an on-site inspector.

Lieutenant General Royal Allison had been a fighter pilot in World War II and later served alternately in tactical aviation and in the Pentagon. He was broadly experienced in operational planning, long-range strategic planning and politico-military affairs. His most recent duty before SALT had been director of plans and operations for the Commander-in-Chief, Pacific. In 1968 he became Assistant for Strategic Arms Negotiations to the chairman of the Joint Chiefs of Staff. His work for General Wheeler in 1968 in the Johnson Administration and with Wheeler's successor, Admiral Tom Moorer, in the Nixon Administration was invaluable in assuring understanding of and support for SALT at high military levels. General Allison's steady, quiet assertion of the nation's military interest as seen through his own and the Joint Chiefs' eyes exercised a positive influence on the delegation's work. The Soviets, including military officials, seemed to have great respect for this man at arms.

Naturally differences of opinion and tensions arose at times between people working and living in relatively close quarters away from home over long periods of time. Paul Nitze seemed under the most strain. He realized that the numerical ceilings on offensive missile launchers, which were the most that the offensive side of SALT was likely to produce, would do little or nothing to reduce the Soviet advantage in missile "throw weight," that is, the weight of nuclear explosives or "payload" that can be delivered to targets. As construction of very large throw-weight Soviet missiles continued and the throw-weight of the American missile force decreased (a result of the MIRV program), Nitze worried about the long-run effect of this process on world-wide perceptions about the Soviet-American strategic balance. He was concerned about increasing vulnerability of American Minuteman ICBM silos to attack by these large Soviet missiles whose accuracy would improve over time and which could soon be MIRVed. He tended to grow less sanguine about SALT prospects. He constantly pushed in Washington and probed while abroad to see if the scope of the negotiation could not be increased to include controls over throw-weight. I sensed that he had less than great enthusiasm for so controlling ABMs as to prevent their effective use to reduce the vulnerability of ICBM silos. But in spite of these concerns, Nitze worked long, hard and well, helping negotiate the ABM Treaty. He hammered away at the necessity for ABM radar controls and his argumentation and persistence resulted in more, and more precise, controls over radar than had been generally expected by the delegation or by Washington agencies. And he fully supported the SALT agreements during the delegation's appearances before congressional committees in 1972.

General Allison did not agree that throw-weight limitation would be in the interest of the United States. He believed that the Soviet advantage in throw-weight was not a driving factor in the competition between the United States and Soviet strategic forces. He argued the position of the Joint Chiefs that throw-weight limitations should not be sought because they could not be verified; because they would be too complicated for an initial agreement; and because they would be unnecessary as long as the United States continued to modernize its forces. His forthright advocacy of this position did not endear him to certain influential politicians. General Allison consistently pressed the military's preference for simple arms control arrangements for a starter, simple to understand, simple to negotiate and not difficult to implement or to verify. This meant to him that initial SALT agreements should be limited to ceilings on numbers of launchers. Limitations on the characteristics of weapons were less to Allison's liking but he worked hard for them when Washington so directed.

Allison had a difficult balance to maintain in his relations with Nitze. His principals, the Joint Chiefs of Staff, are charged with advising the President directly on military matters, but they are also part of the Defense Department under the direction of the Secretary of Defense. At SALT Nitze was Secretary Laird's man. Allison and Nitze seldom if ever lost their tempers or their patience. I felt that the advice of these Pentagon representatives benefited from their somewhat competitive relationship and differing approaches.

I wrote two letters to the White House in the summer of 1971 urging that General Allison be promoted to four-star rank. I said that I could conceive of no one single military post on which

American security was more clearly dependent or more directly involved than that of chief military adviser and principal delegate to SALT. Having had the privilege of working for more than twenty years with general officers in our military services, I could say with confidence that Allison stood professionally, intellectually and in terms of human relations at the top of his profession. His deserved promotion would demonstrate the depth of military commitment to strategic arms control and, I thought, might even better the prospects for success of the talks. Washington did not act on my proposal.

After Ambassador Thompson became ill, Ambassador James Graham "Jeff" Parsons represented the State Department. A highly experienced professional, ambassador to Sweden for seven years, he also had held important posts in the State Department and in the Far East. He got along well with American military officers. Before SALT he had served as deputy commandant of the Industrial College of the Armed Forces. He knew more than all the rest of us together about running a mission abroad. Except when Philip Farley was with us, Jeff Parsons acted as deputy chairman of the delegation. He had only a modest claim to expertise in strategic arms control. But his understanding of international relations in general and U.S. foreign policy and diplomacy in particular was of a high order. At times, I suspect, he was not comfortable with the bluntness which marked some of our exchanges with the Soviets—and he spared us troubles by toning down some of our rougher prose. He had a major responsibility for working out the September 1971 Accidents Agreement which will be discussed in a later chapter. He and his State Department associate, the late Jack Shaw, an expert in Soviet affairs, had a substantial hand in drafting the ABM Treaty language. The result was an international agreement of great precision on a number of weapons matters never before contained in a treaty.

Although Philip Farley was abroad for only a short time his strong hand in Washington was a great help. His major contribution was to "broker" the exchanges between the delegation and Washington. A Backstopping Committee which he chaired was not unlike a second delegation in Washington and as might be expected rather tense relations sometimes developed with the delegation abroad. Farley had worked on nuclear matters from the beginning of the atomic era, having served with Paul Nitze on the U. S. Strategic Bombing Survey studying the effects of bombing on Germany and Japan. He drafted the official report on the bombings of Hiroshima and Nagasaki. He was my deputy in the State Department from 1954 to 1957 and my successor there as Special Assistant for Atomic Energy and Disarmament. He served as acting director of the Arms Control and Disarmament Agency during my long absences abroad. Farley had a unique career in the Foreign Service with unmatched knowledge and experience in military and nuclear matters. His early retirement in 1973 was a great loss to the government. He subsequently did an additional stint as my deputy 1977/1978 on non-proliferation matters.

Some critics have asked whether the head of a government agency should also be chairman of a negotiating delegation, the inference being that such an individual would be handicapped by his dual responsibilities. Admittedly there is a problem here although my predecessor as director of ACDA, William Foster, faced it successfully during the protracted negotiation of the Non-Proliferation Treaty. Obviously an individual cannot run a Washington agency on a day-to-day basis and also be in charge of a negotiation abroad for many months at a time. Fortunately Phil Farley ran ACDA with rare skill in my absence. I never felt that my responsibilities to ACDA were in conflict with my responsibilities to the delegation. I had a direct responsibility to the President, both as director of the agency and as his designated chairman of the SALT delegation. Also I had a special responsibility under the law directing the Arms Control Agency to work under the policy guidance of the Secretary of State. Ideally, a SALT-type delegation should have a full-time chief, reporting to the Secretary of State. I doubt that in falling somewhat short of this ideal the first SALT negotiation was prejudiced. Other departures from the ideal were more significant.

On the whole the U. S. SALT delegates had close friendly relations. I had had the good fortune to work with Tommy Thompson and Jeff Parsons in the State Department in the late 1950s. I had known and worked with Phil Farley for almost twenty years. I had held the same position in the State Department as Paul Nitze and known him for over ten years.

The American delegates could hardly be considered idealistic "arms controllers": three had had extensive service in the Defense Department and one of the three had had large responsibility for nuclear weapons design, two had held high offices in the State Department with responsibility for political-military affairs and nuclear weapons matters, one had unique experience serving in the U.S.S.R., the other was a very senior Foreign Service officer with rather conservative views. These men had no illusions about their adversaries at the negotiating table or the ideological chasm separating the two political systems which found themselves at bay in the face of a common nuclear threat. And while the delegates held different views on a number of major issues, the surprising thing was the degree of harmony that existed between these personalities who had long been used to "running their own shops," whether it was a weapons laboratory, a military service or a major embassy. They were all senior to me in terms of service and I appreciated their working with a will under my leadership. I think we will never forget the five hundred SALT days we worked together in Europe.

The principal delegates were supported by a skilled, experienced, loyal and overworked group of people in Washington agencies and abroad—advisers and experts, secretaries, communicators and marines, while abroad the delegation had about seventy members. They wanted and got little recognition or thanks from their government for extraordinary efforts under difficult conditions. Many who served in Helsinki and Vienna were away from their families for a year or more in the aggregate. For some this was about their last duty as a purblind White House on the crest of the 1972 election success decided that it could do without their further services.

Who were the Soviet representatives?

Vladimir S. Semenov was a senior Deputy Foreign Minister. Before SALT he had specialized in Central European and Middle Eastern affairs. He is now the Soviet ambassador to the Federal Republic of Germany. Semenov joined the Foreign Service in 1939, after graduating from the Moscow Institute of History, Philosophy, and Literature. He was counselor in Berlin during the Soviet-German Non-Aggression Pact years 1940–41. He returned to Berlin in May 1945 as a political adviser, then served as high commissioner and finally as Soviet ambassador. He attended numerous international conferences on European problems during the postwar period. He became chief of the Foreign Ministry's Central European Division in 1954 and Deputy Foreign Minister in March 1955. His involvement in Middle East policy dated from this period. In 1966 he became a candidate member of the Central Committee.

Semenov is a good conversationalist, interested in art, classical music, philosophy and history—more of this later. He is co-author of a book, *A History of Diplomacy*. He often chose philosophical and historical analogies to make his points in informal conversations. He speaks German well and apparently understands English, although he speaks it only a little. While he was said to have heart trouble, he was quite active during SALT and I did not notice that health problems curtailed his activities. He continued to be chief of the Soviet SALT delegation until 1979.

Colonel General Nikolai Ogarkov was the official number two man in the Soviet delegation for the first three SALT sessions. He was principal military adviser, representing both the chief of the General Staff of the Soviet Armed Forces and the late Defense Minister Grechko. Ogarkov was first deputy chief of the Soviet General Staff. He had attended the Military Engineering Academy before World War II and held responsible positions in army engineering units until 1946. He began a rapid rise in the military in the 1950s, advancing to chief of staff of the Belorussian Military District in 1961, to commander of the Volga Military District in 1966, then first deputy chief of the General Staff in 1968—all this in eleven years. In party affairs he was elected to candidate membership in the Central Committee in 1966 and to full membership in 1971. Ogarkov is a forceful individual. A Soviet diplomat characterized him as bright and intellectually strong and "by no means a run-of-the-mill army officer." Ogarkov was listed as a principal Soviet delegate for the Vienna and Helsinki rounds of the talks in 1971 but did not attend these sessions. Presumably with his pressing military staff responsibilities he could no longer give time exclusively to SALT. But we were told that he continued as a member of the delegation and kept up his interest in the negotiation. He is now marshal of the Soviet Union and Chief of Staff of the armed forces.

Aleksandr Shchukin is an authority on defense research and one of the U.S.S.R.'s elite academicians. He was said to be deputy chairman of the Committee on Lenin Prizes for Science and Technology and chairman of the Scientific Council for the Propagation of Radio Waves. At SALT, he indicated that he had worked on missile accuracy and guidance systems, and that he had a staff in Moscow working in these areas. He displayed a good knowledge of radar and ABM systems. He had worked on submarine communication problems.

Born in St. Petersburg in 1898, he was somewhat older than the other delegates. We were told that he was the son and grandson of professors at the University of St. Petersburg. He was fluent in French, which he had learned as a child. He had been a telegrapher in the Red Army during the civil war. He was a pleasant and thoughtful person, a cultivated man who conversed on a wide variety of subjects in literature, music and the arts. He was a constant concertgoer. His serious, pert wife often corrected my efforts to speak Russian. "She is a pedagogue," said he. Once he alluded to his somewhat advanced years by saying that we should get on with SALT if agreement was to come in his lifetime. Despite two heart attacks he was reported to be a good cross-country skier.

Shchukin impressed American officials as an able and careful thinker with an understanding of strategic matters and knowledge about American strategic thinking unexcelled in the Soviet delegation. He struck me as a man used to authority. He seemed to recognize the absurdity of uncontrolled competition in strategic arms. As a major general in the reserves, he knew the military bent of mind that tends to think of weapons in the ways of past wars. He once spoke of people who thought of nuclear weapons in terms of a needed number of wheels of artillery per kilometer of front. Shchukin and Paul Nitze conversed regularly in French. These cautious dialogues were helpful to our understanding of Soviet positions. The two enjoyed jousting intellectually. After several American objections to Soviet proposals, Shchukin told a Russian peasant proverb to the effect that, if seeds did not sprout because of poor conditions, the only thing to do was to keep on planting until conditions improved. After that, General Allison occasionally referred to Shchukin as a seed-planting fox.

Petr Pleshakov was Deputy Minister of the Radio Industry of the U.S.S.R. and is now Minister. This ministry is responsible for the production of electronic equipment in the radiotechnical field, a large percentage of which is for the military. Pleshakov is a specialist in radar and radio engineering. He appeared to have a close relationship with General Ogarkov. He smoked more cigarettes than all the other delegates together!

Colonel General of Engineering-Technical Services Nikolai Alekseyev was a principal Soviet delegate at the first four sessions, then was appointed Deputy Minister of Defense, apparently with responsibilities for weapons research and development. Reportedly, he continued to be involved with SALT problems in Moscow. One Soviet official gave him especially high marks as an electronics specialist, and another characterized Alekseyev as a technician rather than a soldier. World War II wounds caused him at times to limp perceptibly.

Ambassador Georgi Korniyenko was a principal delegate at Helsinki in 1969. He has been chief of the U.S.A. Division of the U.S.S.R. Foreign Ministry since 1966. From 1960 through 1965 he served at the Soviet Embassy in Washington, where he was known as the embassy's best-informed man on disarmament. Korniyenko attended meetings between Soviet Premier Kosygin and visiting American officials. While Tommy Thompson was ambassador in Moscow he and Korniyenko knew and respected each other for years. Their friendly relationship eased the stiffness of the early days in SALT. Unfortunately, both became ill during the negotiation.

Oleg Grinevsky, one of three deputy chiefs of the International Organizations Division of the Ministry of Foreign Affairs, served as Foreign Ministry adviser to the delegation at the first two SALT sessions and then replaced Korniyenko as a principal delegate in November 1970. In March 1971, at the beginning of the fourth round, Grinevsky became seriously ill. He had been slated to become acting head of the Soviet delegation during Semenov's absence for the April 1971 Communist Party Congress in Moscow. Before his return to active participation in SALT, Grinevsky reportedly worked on the arms talks "at the other end"—at Foreign Ministry headquarters.

Grinevsky speaks English well, is personable and outgoing. He headed a fourteen-man Arms Control Section in the Foreign Ministry and is highly regarded by American officials for his expertise on the subject. He was probably the most knowledgeable Soviet delegate on arms control efforts of the 1960s, including the 1963 Limited Test Ban Treaty, the 1968 Non-Proliferation Treaty, and numerous sessions of the eighteen-nation Disarmament Conference in Geneva and other international conferences. Grinevsky had worked in the past with Lawrence Weiler, the counselor of the Arms Control and Disarmament Agency, keeper of its conscience and one of my closest SALT advisers. Grinevsky communicated easily with Americans. At SALT he helped prepare for compromises and had a large responsibility for drafting, especially in connection with the ABM Treaty. Much of this work was accomplished in informal sessions with his colleague Kishilov and Americans Garthoff and Weiler. Grinevsky is now chief of the Near Eastern Countries Department, Ministry of Foreign Affairs.

Roland Timerbayev, another senior Foreign Ministry official with a considerable background in disarmament matters, replaced the ailing Grinevsky as a principal Soviet delegate at the fourth and fifth rounds of the talks in the spring and summer of 1971. He became acting chief of the Soviet delegation during Semenov's absence in Moscow in April 1971. Americans who have known English-speaking Timerbayev since he was first assigned to the United Nations in New York in 1950 consider him a well-rounded, experienced diplomat, who seldom engages in propaganda and is a skilled negotiator. When Grinevsky returned to SALT, Timerbayev resumed his duties at the Foreign Ministry.

Lieutenant General Konstantin Trusov became a principal Soviet delegate at the Vienna session in March 1971, replacing General Ogarkov and General Alekseyev as the representative of the Ministry of Defense. Trusov served on the Soviet General Staff with responsibilities for advanced weapons research and development and early warning aspects of strategic defense. He stated that he had been involved in the Soviet ABM program. He was mild-mannered and skilled at using lengthy explanations to avoid saying anything concrete. General Trusov was an active spokesman for the Soviet military at SALT. In 1976, still at SALT, he was promoted to colonel general.

The "point" men who maintained frequent contact between the delegations were the general secretaries, Raymond Garthoff and Nikolai Kishilov. Semenov referred to them as "the wizards." Garthoff speaks Russian well and has written a number of books on Soviet military and political matters. He is the most knowledgeable officer in the Foreign Service on Soviet-American relations and one of the youngest to be made a Class I officer. He retired in 1979 after having been U. S. Ambassador to Bulgaria and is now with the Brookings Institution. During most of SALT I until 1973 he continued to be deputy director of the Bureau of Politico-Military Affairs in the State Department while also serving as senior State Department adviser on the delegation. He had the respect of both delegations. I suspected that some of the U.S. military members did not especially like Garthoff, in good part, I thought, because he knew so much about their business. Garthoff in effect was our chief of staff—an unusually difficult job in this multi-agency delegation. In addition to coordinating the work of the delegation, he spent a great deal of time keeping it on the same track as Washington officials, no mean feat. He also carried a good deal of the load of informal probing and negotiating with Kishilov and Grinevsky. Garthoff's work was invaluable. In 1972 he received for his contribution to SALT the State Department's highest recognition, the Distinguished Honor Award.

Nikolai Kishilov, a diplomat with a military intelligence background, served throughout SALT as general secretary and an adviser to the Soviet delegation. Since 1966 he had been first secretary of the International Organizations Division in the Foreign Ministry, apparently concentrating on disarmament matters. He was an attaché at the Soviet Embassy in Helsinki from 1954 to 1957, when he was declared persona non grata by the Finnish government for attempts to recruit Finns. Lest eyebrows be raised about Soviets' use of former intelligence personnel, it should be added that the U.S. delegation was not without people of a similar background. From 1960 through 1965 Kishilov was secretary of the Soviet Embassy in Bonn. He speaks English well but did not have the background in strategic weapons that Garthoff had. Semenov seemed to rely on him heavily. Garthoff and he handled the mechanics of the conference, arranged for meetings, unsnarled tie-ups. And, under positive control by the chiefs of delegation, they prospected informally for areas of agreement and broke much of the ground for the ABM Treaty.

Both Finland and Austria bolster their neutrality by being hosts for international conferences—calculating, I suppose, that this form of internationalization is worth a number of army divisions. At SALT we were the beneficiaries of a rivalry between these two friendly nations to see which could be the best host. From security to symphonies to junketing around these countries, the SALT delegations were splendidly taken care of. In Lapland and Carinthia and many other places, the sight of their Soviet and American guests must have given some hope to Austrians and Finns as they saw that the superpowers at least were talking to each other.

Our home in Helsinki for more than eight months was the Kalastajatorppa Hotel, the Finnish term for Fisherman's Hut. The quarters were not sumptuous, but there was a pool and sauna. It was pleasant in the summer, but in November and December it could be depressing. The hotel is situated only a few feet from an arm of the Gulf of Finland, usually ice-covered in winter. Seagulls screamed much of the night, which started in midafternoon. During the early days of SALT, for security purposes the U.S. delegation took over the whole place. That later seemed too expensive for the slight increase in security. In those Helsinki days we not only worked SALT but ate, drank and lived with it around the clock. At Vienna things were somewhat more civilized as the U.S. delegation was scattered around a number of hotels.

Our life in Vienna was enriched by the extraordinary hospitality of our ambassador, John Humes, and his wife Jean. It's no fun for an ambassador to have visiting negotiators, especially those who stayed as long as we did, but Ambassador Humes's attitude was consistently more than friendly. In Helsinki Ambassador Val Petersen and his wife filled us with turkey during our far northern Thanksgivings and in other ways helped the morale of the delegation.

All the principal American delegates had the good fortune to be accompanied by their wives and when it became evident that SALT was not to be the usual kind of conference lasting but a few weeks or months I decided that arrangements should be made to permit some other members of the delegation's wives to accompany them. At first the State Department said that would be impossible. A little persistence and pointed suggestions that security risks would increase with men away from wives for many months convinced the department to make an exception. For most of SALT, the delegation had the pleasure of being accompanied by a number of ladies who made a substantial contribution to our well-being and morale. They cheerfully sacrificed their normal lives for hundreds of days of relative boredom of hotel life. It is a compliment to their humanity, good will and common sense that they lived for so many months at such very close quarters and kept their good cheer. They were an important part of the SALT effort.

Marines drawn from a number of embassies in Western Europe guarded our offices around the clock, aided by a battery of electronic sensors, with television maintaining surveillance over the perimeter of the premises. It must have been tedious duty for these young men, but I heard no requests for duty in Vietnam. One night some marines practiced survival technique while venting their spleen by writing HELP in huge letters in the snow in front of our Helsinki hotel. Sometimes I felt the same way.

Sensitive matters could only be discussed by Americans in special quarters designed to prevent penetration by electronic measures. Small and not well ventilated, they seemed to me like the inside of an electric light bulb. These cells were to be our working quarters for hundreds of SALT hours. One might as well have been in an ICBM silo. One of our delegates smoked cigars and pipes incessantly in these unpleasant cocoons. I semi-jokingly observed that a doctor had advised me—a non-smoker—to give up the habit. The hint had no effect. The room remained smoke-filled till the end.

My wife and I assumed that our hotel rooms were bugged, but early on we decided to forget about them and let eavesdroppers get a dose of normal Smith conversation. Our offices were routinely checked for bugs and other types of sensors.

At Helsinki there was little evidence of Finnish security measures although I was sure they existed. But in Vienna things were different. From the time of our first arrival at the airport until our final departure we were conscious that the Austrian government was watching out for us. I guess that this was mostly out of concern lest something untoward happen to a Soviet official. It had been only a few years since the Warsaw Pact invasion of Czechoslovakia. Under a policy of equal treatment for both sides, I received the same security as Semenov.

From the Vienna airport we rode into town behind a motorcycle police escort. As the SALT delegations drove to one another's embassy for meetings they were always preceded by motorcycle policemen. Since the traffic rules in Vienna sensibly require motorcycle policemen to stop for red lights, I never understood the purpose of this display. At the Hotel Bristol there were a number of plainclothesmen at all times. One was stationed outside our hotel room. I heard that the sewers beneath the hotel were searched periodically. Several police agents must have thought they had again become patrolmen as they walked behind me each morning for the two miles separating the hotel from the SALT office. Aside from detouring me around a red-flagged May Day demonstration, the only instance I recall of their intervention was when it started to rain. I was then handed an umbrella!

Semenov joked about our "tails." Once in a while when we met in restaurants or hotels and he wanted to talk SALT, he would wonder aloud if the premises were secure, and then say, "Well, both of us are here, it must be secure." We realized that bugging was a fact of life. He once jokingly lamented about how much easier diplomatic life must have been when Napoleon and Tsar Alexander met on a raft at Tilsit in 1807. "There were no bugs there."

Rumor had it that Soviet delegation security was exceedingly tight. While Americans used cars and drivers supplied by the Austrian and Finnish governments, the Soviets used their own. During the Vienna sessions the Soviet delegation was housed some fifteen miles south of the city, in the resort town of Baden, which had been the postwar site of Soviet army headquarters. It was said that except for Sunday breakfast the Soviet delegation took their meals at the Soviet Embassy in Vienna. They went back and forth from Baden in buses, although I doubt that Semenov did. More relevant to intelligence than security, each weekday morning a copy of the Paris *Herald Tribune* was placed at every Soviet delegate's door. They probably leafed through this

paper each morning in search of leaks about possible U.S. negotiating moves, weapons developments and other juicy bits of information. Would that we had had a similar source of information!

We needed and had the best available communications facilities
with Washington—a number of direct, dedicated and secure telephone lines and cable links for encoded messages. When a number of U.S. agencies are represented at an international conference, the question of separate communications usually arises. I
knew that the Joint Chiefs of Staff and the Department of Defense wanted to maintain direct telephone and cable links with
their representatives and did not try to channel all traffic through
State Department lines, which normally handle such conference
communications. With a few exceptions I was satisfied that copies
of important messages in these separate channels came over my
desk.

Cables even of the highest classification are broadcast much too
widely. I was told that six hundred copies of my SALT messages
to the State Department were distributed by the Joint Chiefs of
Staff to military commands all over the world. So, for most secure
and private communication, especially to the White House, I used
CIA communications. But even here I soon learned that people
without a clear need to know were reading this traffic. I finally
resorted to dictating messages over a secure phone to my office in
ACDA, whence they were delivered by hand direct to the White
House. I think that worked.

Communications must have offered the Soviets no problem
while the conference was in Finland. Practically at Leningrad's
back door, electronic messages could be supplemented by fast
courier-delivered mail and by personal consultations in Moscow.
In Vienna, the Soviets apparently did not put full trust in their
electronic communications. At times Soviet officials would cross
the Danube and drive some forty miles to Bratislava, where
presumably they had available secure conference call facilities
using military systems. It was a sure sign that something was up
when Soviet SALT officials went to Czechoslovakia.

SALT was not what international negotiations are supposed to
be like. There was little bargaining in the normal sense of the
word. International negotiation brings to mind what John Jay or

Benjamin Franklin did far from their home base in time and distance and operating under general instructions. The delegation's situation was quite different. We were in constant, almost instant communication with the White House, State Department, ACDA, the Department of Defense, the Joint Chiefs of Staff and the CIA. We were always conscious of the desirability, while negotiating with utmost seriousness, of making a very complete and persuasive record against the possibility of the talks failing. Since we were dealing with issues central to the security of the nation, we were kept—and properly so—on a very short rein. Except for scouting out possibilities and making recommendations to Washington, we were for the most part acting as instructed agents. "Speaking personally" was a preface sometimes used. In my case, at least, the term was used with confidence that I was on or not far from the line that I knew Washington had taken or was about to take.

Formal interdelegation meetings were held in the conference rooms of the two nations' embassies. The U. S. Embassy in Vienna was then the only American embassy in the world with a men's room sign in Russian! In Helsinki the contrast between the embassies was sharp. The American building of Georgian style was of modest proportions with a very small conference room. The Soviet Embassy was palatial with a conference room giving evidence of being used also as a theater.

A delegation would arrive, some twelve strong, at the other's embassy, usually at ten o'clock in the morning. There would be four or five delegates on each side, the executive secretaries, interpreters and other officials whose specialties were to be discussed that day. One ritual followed from the first to the last day of SALT was shaking hands. Each official of one delegation shook hands with all members of the other on arriving and on departing. Most Americans learned at least to say *"Dobroe utro* [Good morning]" and most Soviets could say "Good morning." It seldom varied. The chief of the visiting delegation would make the first statement, reading a twelve- to fourteen-page paper. Then the other side would present a statement. After the readings a date for the next meeting was set and the plenary session was over. Occasionally there would be a few questions. This was the rite of making a record. It was not negotiation.

After each meeting Semenov and I would move to a separate

room where with interpreters we would comment on each other's statements, ask questions, probe for possible movement in each other's positions. At the Soviet Embassy in Helsinki, Semenov and I always had these private conversations in a room containing a picture of Lenin surrounded by smiling children. The other officials would engage in small groups in a similar process of informal exchanges. This usually lasted an hour or more. Then the visitors would solemnly file out. SALT was in good part stilted business, but we were working in an area of highest political and national security interest for both sides and a number of powerful officials in both capitals wanted to be involved at every step.

The delegations generally met formally twice a week, alternating between embassies. This may sound like a moderate pace but in our case it took hundreds of man-hours to prepare statements. Over twenty high-level officials would work on each one. There would be some five or six drafts screened through all elements of the delegation. This process involved constant communication with Washington. General Allison has a flair for precise drafting—a talent that is not widespread among ranking military officers, who usually are willing to leave such chores to their juniors. His red-penciled insertions in drafts or statements and documents left many a mark on the negotiation. Paul Nitze also has a gift for language and a keen sense of nuance. The draft statements were checked to determine that they contained no classified information. After the statements had been read in the plenary session they would be exchanged to assure accurate translation of the English and Russian. It used to take our interpreters four to eight hours to produce a final translation of a Soviet plenary statement in which they could be sure that all the shadings had been properly rendered in English. And the informal exchanges involving about twelve people on each side had to be carefully recorded and transmitted to Washington.

The atmosphere at SALT meetings was hardly a trusting one. In the first days you could almost smell suspicion. The Soviet military especially seemed uneasy about starting down a road whose end they could not foresee, and one that required Soviet civilians from the Ministry of Foreign Affairs to get involved in weapons matters from which they had largely been excluded in the past. Some may have felt it almost indecent to be sitting around a table with American military officers, whose leaders for years had spoken so often about their capacity to destroy the Soviet Union, representatives of what they considered to be a military-industrial complex, reflecting the worst aspects of the capitalist system. But they seemed to get used to it, and after a while the military on both sides recognized that they were doing international business with human beings.

In plenary session the Soviets courteously noted space flights by the United States. In April of 1970 when the Apollo 13 mission was in trouble after an explosion 200,000 miles from the earth snuffed out almost all the command module's oxygen and power supplies, Semenov opened a plenary meeting by saying, "We would like to say that in these hours we share the general concern regarding the flight of the Apollo 13 spaceship and express our hope for a successful return to earth of the courageous astronauts, Lovell, Swigert, and Haise." By the same token, after three Soviet cosmonauts perished in an accident in June 1971, I expressed condolences and asked to have that message transmitted to their families. Semenov thanked us and said our condolences would be passed on. He later reported that the families had expressed appreciation.

The United States' first negotiating approaches were complicated, involving a number of possible ceilings on missile launchers and heavy bombers. To demonstrate these various possible force levels, one member of the U.S. delegation, Richard Ladder, designed an ingenious device something like a slide rule which was presented to the Soviet delegation. It caused interest and some amusement but not acceptance of any of the approaches. I believe it was the first time such a mechanical aid was ever used in a diplomatic process. Probably ours were the most complicated arms control proposals ever made.

Several times I read plenary statements in Russian, to give a little variety to the process of our making speeches at each other. Paul Nitze once jokingly (since he had a copy of the statement in English) said as I finished, "Now tell us what you said." My Russian is limited and with these few exceptions I always used an American interpreter. With an American interpreter one was assured of an almost verbatim record of all conversations. Unfortunately, when the White House engaged in SALT negotiations in

Moscow, Soviet interpreters were relied on and thus no comprehensive record exists except in Soviet hands. (I have heard it
said, perhaps facetiously, that the reason for this unusual practice
was that Soviet interpreters, unlike Americans, cannot be subpoe-
naed by congressional committees.) Once a White House official
asked to see a Soviet interpreter's notes. The request was turned
down.

We developed the practice of periodic and quite thorough informal reviews and prospecting of the negotiating situation with
the Soviets, conducted by several American officials in whom I
had full confidence. These authorized but entirely informal
probes gave us better insights into Soviet positions and helped
keep the negotiating process alive. I believe that General Allison
had reservations about this practice, feeling that to get insights
our people had to give similar insights about U.S. positions. This
was true, but on balance I felt we were the gainer, since Soviet
plenary presentations were less precise than ours and without
some sort of scouting mechanism we were often too much in the
dark to make useful judgments about future negotiating possibilities. These exchanges were fully reported to Washington and I
believe helped authorities there to shape sensible policies as well
as to judge the validity of delegation recommendations. One such
exchange that was especially useful was during a weekend trip to
Lapland in the spring of 1972, when Garthoff, Kishilov and
Grinevsky in what came to be called "the Tundra talks" identified
a number of points which were ultimately agreed in the ABM
Treaty.

The U.S.S.R. delegation was highly disciplined. Major positions
set out in plenary statements were dutifully echoed by all their
delegates in subsequent informal exchanges. Rarely did we hear
any uncertain signals. But they seemed better at reacting to U.S.
initiatives than at taking their own. Apparently their problem of
coordinating SALT policy in Moscow was even greater than ours
in Washington. We learned that there was little "lateral" consultation in their capital between the military and political authorities. Issues were separately considered by the several agencies and
coordination effected only at the decisional point, the Politburo.
In Washington there was a free flow of SALT interagency discussion. Long before problems were agonized over in the National

Security Council machinery, agencies had a good idea of the others' staff-level positions, and to the extent permitted by the White House style of operation a good deal of coordination was possible at the agency level. Apparently the Soviets had the same trouble with computers that we occasionally had. One Soviet official said that certain U.S. proposals were being analyzed by computers in their Foreign and Defense Ministries. Unfortunately "they do not always supply the same answers."

At times Soviet delegates informally urged us not to press forward too rapidly, saying that they did not have further plenary presentations prepared. They were working them out as they went along, seeking to judge as best they could the most effective way to advance their proposals. So, of course, were we. One Soviet official said that his delegation was authorized to decide a number of lesser questions on a collegial basis. They drafted plenary statements and did not send them to Moscow for approval. He emphasized the importance of the fact that theirs was a uniquely qualified delegation with unprecedented "balance" in representation from key places in Moscow.

There seemed to be in the Soviet delegation a degree of compartmentalization separating the information to which the civilians and the military had access. The Soviets never disclosed the designators by which they identified various weapons systems. American terminology was used by both sides. Thus we referred to SS-9 and SS-11 missile launchers, to Y-, G-, and H-class submarines. The word we used for the Moscow ABM system, "Galosh," led Semenov to complain facetiously about the American choices of code words for Soviet systems. He said that the word "Galosh" connoted in Russian an old rubber and inferred that it was not limited to footwear.

All contacts between members of the U.S. delegation and the Soviets, except for normal conversations after plenary sessions, had to be cleared in advance. In every case a written report was made of what had been said. Members of the U.S. delegation who had direct contacts with Soviets were experienced officers and no difficulties developed. All hands realized this was very serious business and no individual "excursions" would be tolerated.

Before we set out for the first round of SALT, President Nixon had told the delegates that if offered an invitation to visit the

U.S.S.R. we certainly should accept. After a few weeks at Helsinki, Semenov proposed a visit to Leningrad. That would be fine, I said, but only after the back of our work was broken. That did not happen during the first round. When we came back to Helsinki in the fall of 1970 the invitation was renewed. General Allison was disinclined to lend himself to what he considered an untimely Soviet show of hospitality in view of lack of progress in the negotiation for which we blamed the Soviets. The other delegates, however, wanted to see Leningrad and get a break in the conference routine.

The Semenovs, Shchukins, Smiths, Nitzes, Parsons, Browns and several other officials traveled in style in a special railroad car. We gathered for the customary Russian pre-journey snack and vodka in Semenov's compartment. He was in high spirits. Shchukin also seemed pleased to be returning to his native city. Semenov regaled us with stories about Stalin's work habits and his skills with language. Being guests of the U.S.S.R., we crossed the border during the night without any passport or customs check. It was still dark when we entered the Finland Station, saw the steam engine which had drawn Lenin's train in 1917 from Helsinki to St. Petersburg, then drove through the still dark city to the Astoria Hotel. It looked inside and out as if not a drop of paint had been added since 1917.

Our hosts provided us with a fine mix of sightseeing, walking, good food, opera and ballet—all the usual tourist highlights but under extremely VIP conditions. As we walked past the famous eighteenth-century Admiralty building, Ray Garthoff said, "I wonder what Semenov would say if he knew my wife's grandfather used to be Minister of Marine."

I placed a wreath at the memorial monument at Leningrad's Piskarevsky war cemetery, surrounded by mass graves containing the remains of nearly a million Leningraders who died during World War II. It brought home the horror of that conflict—and the significance of our SALT effort to reduce the risk of a new war which by comparison would make World War II seem a minor fracas.

The Soviet delegation once invited us to view a Red Army propaganda film entitled *Liberation*. It showed a number of World War II battles, largely re-enacted, although occasionally documentary film was dubbed in. It was an unusual experience for arms control conferees to be watching together a film whose purpose was to impress the viewer with the prowess of the Red Army. Semenov's six-year-old daughter sat on his lap during the three-hour film. If the film was meant *in terrorem* it didn't work. It all seemed a little prehistoric—before the days of missiles and intercontinental bombers. General Allison noted aloud that the Red Army apparently had little use for air power. The only planes shown, if I recall correctly, were of a French squadron which served in the U.S.S.R. Semenov knew the names of most of the Soviet marshals in the film, represented by actors bearing some resemblance to the originals.

The movie was shown in two parts. I heard in advance that the second contained a sequence showing Allen Dulles secretly negotiating for the surrender of German General Kesselring's forces in breach of American commitments to the U.S.S.R. I advised Semenov that I had learned this through my "spies," and as Dulles was a good friend, I would not attend a film containing such a sequence. I was assured it would not. It did not. I understand it had been removed.

To liven things up I suggested that we in turn show the Soviets *Cat Ballou* and Garthoff suggested *MASH* but our military advisers thought they would be inappropriate. We showed *The Longest Day,* about the Allied landings in Normandy in 1944. It had a number of actual battle scenes and seemed to make a hit with the Soviets, especially with their military. A number expressed regret when it ended at 2 P.M. on D-Day.

At the end of each Vienna and Helsinki round, the delegations used to exchange small gifts. The Soviets seemed to like to receive American Bourbon as much as we liked Soviet vodka. If caviar came with it, so much the better.

Unlike the tradition of U.S. missions abroad, I conceived of the U.S. delegation as a collegial group. Several of my colleagues had much more experience in diplomacy than I, several knew a great deal more about strategic arms. All were very high-level officials representing departments having a direct interest in SALT. I tried to develop a sense that this was a joint venture in which defense and military officials had the same responsibilities as officials from the State Department and the Arms Control Agency. Any final product of the negotiation would be the outcome of full civilian-military collaboration warranting complete support from both sides of the government.

Our main work was to interpret Washington guidance for the Soviet delegation as persuasively as possible at a time best suited to make it effective, while reacting effectively to points made by the Soviets. This was not merely to make a convincing record if the talks failed in order to prove that we had done our best. It was a process of dialogue designed to extract the most from our negotiating partners and to develop full understanding on both sides of the issues and views of the other. Thus executed, a product emerged from the several minds of the U.S. delegates, filtered through their combined experience leading to a collegial judgment of what was negotiable and how one should go about negotiating it. I believe a somewhat similar process took place in the U.S.S.R. delegation.

This collegial approach worked. After some months the Americans began to look at problems in good part with the same perspective. The delegation felt strongly that as long as it hewed to the policy line set forth in White House guidance, tactical decisions should be left to it in the light of its on-the-spot judgment. The five principal delegates were able to agree on important proposals for changes in U.S. positions. After it became clear that the Soviets were not interested in the first two approaches of April 1970, the delegation proposed a new approach, the Vienna Option. It must have come as a surprise to the White House that the delegation, representing elements as diverse as the Joint Chiefs of Staff, the Department of Defense, the State Department and ACDA, could agree on a specific substantive proposal. As we shall see, its content was largely accepted by the President.

A main purpose of this book is to try to show that this methodical collegial approach is far better than the personal approach used in good part in another phase of SALT. There, Kissinger almost singlehandedly dealt with one or two Soviet officials unaided by individuals having the special expertise of the departments of government involved, uninformed by the experience of other minds or the details of continuing past discussions with the Soviets over a period of many months. I very much doubt that this extremely busy aide to the President had the time or inclination to study the reports of all these lengthy delegation discussions. In the final stages of the negotiations, important details were worked out with a Soviet official whom the American negotiator had never before seen or even heard of.

With a few exceptions, officials on the delegation handled relations with Washington authorities with care to avoid conflicts. But an official seconded by the Department of Defense once took it upon himself to report to Washington that a certain unanimous recommendation of the delegation had in fact not been so, and that although his principal had signed off on the recommending telegram he did not in fact agree with it. This individual either had been misinformed or was just making mischief. This led to quite a brouhaha in Washington and interfered with the smooth operation of the delegation for several days before it was straightened out. An even more troublemaking incident was reflected in the following communication to Washington by this official: "Smith and Semenov have decided that a better way to work than in plenary would be to have private sessions. Therefore the meeting next Friday will be private." The clear inference was that I was trying to circumvent Washington clearance. The message had no basis in fact. No such private meeting had been planned. I so advised Washington and issued a directive to the delegation which included these admonitions:

Recent back-channel communications to Washington giving views different from the official delegation reports have substantially prejudiced the work of the delegation and created confusion and difficulty in Washington.

Any member of the delegation who feels unable to conform to normal standards of loyalty to the delegation should leave it.

I heard of no further such incidents.

The delegation's practice throughout the negotiation was to send proposed plenary statements to Washington for comment. Comments often arrived the morning on which the statement was to be made. We leaned over backward to adopt as many as seemed reasonable, but the many hasty last-minute language changes did not improve the clarity of our statements. The delegation felt that the purpose of the exercise was to obtain comments from Washington which in the discretion of the delegation might or might not be used. Misunderstandings developed as some people in Washington felt that it was their responsibility to approve the exact language of the statements. The greatest source of this difficulty was that certain technically-minded officials in the Department of Defense felt that they knew more about conducting an international negotiation than did the SALT delegation. It was even proposed that the delegation advise Washington as to how it planned to answer questions put by the Soviet delegation. When I pointed out the obvious—that since we didn't know what questions the Soviets were going to ask, we could not get advance Washington approval of the answers—the matter was dropped. If that procedure had been adopted, it would have been just as well to conduct the negotiation from Washington and send telegrams to the Soviet delegation.

After several months of difficulties with some Washington officials about how much freedom of action the delegation should have, I was advised early in June of 1970 that Secretary of Defense Laird had written to the Secretary of State that he believed the delegation was "out of control." Laird cited a plenary statement that he said contained four significant problems, complaining that although instructions were sent to eliminate them the same four problems were contained in the delivered statement. "To gain control of the situation," Laird proposed to limit the delegation to those statements approved in advance in Washington.

Secretary of State Rogers' response was that the delegation was in direct touch with the Soviet representatives and thus in the best position to provide a sense of direction for the negotiations and to work out the tactics and tone of the plenary presentations. The process had been working well. The delegation had stayed within authorized policy and had incorporated a good percentage of Washington's drafting and other suggestions. I soon proved to Laird's satisfaction at a breakfast meeting in Brussels that the delegation was not out of control and that his staff had misinformed him. On June 24, I was pleased to receive a letter from President Nixon.

I want to commend you for the excellent manner in which you have conducted the negotiations thus far. You should know that I consider your performance and that of the entire Delegation fully responsive to my directives. You and the Delegation have my full support in the delicate phase which will soon confront you. . . . I would appreciate it if you would convey my best wishes to all of your team.

When it came to keeping each other informed, there was a double standard for the delegation and the White House. The delegation kept no secrets from the White House. In addition to continuous telephone calls, the White House staff received reports of all formal and informal conversations between members of the delegations. To use a term from the lexicon of the Strategic Air Command, the U.S. delegation was at all times under positive control. We were given few targets of opportunity. All advances beyond our guidance were handled in a fashion to "fail safe," and there were no cases where a delegate exceeded his authority. In contrast, White House negotiating was usually kept secret from the delegation until it was finished and often well after that. Sometimes the delegation was made to look foolish because the White House had kept it in the dark. I had no way of knowing how well Semenov was kept informed of White House/Kremlin negotiations, but at least on one occasion it was obvious that he knew something about planning for a summit meeting about which I had not been informed.

During the negotiation I worked with Semenov for hundreds of hours. I think that although Soviet-American negotiations do not to any significant extent depend on human relations, the fact that he and I respected each other and got along quite well was a small plus. A few vignettes concerning this unusual individual may be of interest.

Semenov seldom spoke of his early years in the Foreign Service. But once he described his chief at the Soviet Embassy in Stockholm, Alexandra Kollontai. He said that in spite of her family's close ties before the Revolution with the Tsar's court she had become a Communist while quite young. She had a lover, a sailor in the Baltic Fleet, and had enough influence to have him made head of the Bank of Russia. She later made such a nuisance of herself that Lenin assigned her to the diplomatic service. While serving with her when she was ambassador in Stockholm, Semenov was involved in the armistice negotiations ending the Russo-Finnish War. In an effort to get me to be more forthcoming, he said it was sometimes important for negotiators to get out ahead of their instructions and told how during these Finnish negotiations he had risked repudiation by his authorities by designating on his own responsibility certain crossing points for Finnish representatives to come over to the Soviet lines to work out a cease-fire. I never felt that he was out beyond his instructions at SALT.

He was proud of his good relations with Soviet military leaders. During World War II he had been political adviser to a commanding general on the northwestern front. He told about receiving this assignment. Molotov took him to see Stalin. Semenov happened to be wearing flashy clothes which Molotov knew Stalin despised. Stalin asked Semenov when he could start for the front, and Molotov quickly answered, "Right now." According to Semenov, that saved the day.

Semenov may have worn flashy clothes when he was younger but he didn't at SALT. He told me his practice was to wear one necktie until it was worn out. Someone decided to have a SALT necktie made up with American, Soviet and Finnish symbols. I learned about this idea when it was too late to stop it. For the rest of the negotiations a number of Soviets and Americans wore the neckties. I did not. Semenov did.

The American and Soviet principal delegates were invited by President Kekkonen of Finland to attend an Independence Day reception at which "black tie" was required. Semenov told me he had never owned a tuxedo and was uncomfortable in the uniform that Soviet diplomats sometimes wear on dress occasions. Would I appear in a business suit if he did? The SALT delegates must have presented a rather bizarre appearance as they showed up in the presidential palace in sack suits when all other celebrants were dressed to the teeth.

Semenov was political adviser to Marshal Konev when Berlin fell in 1945. He told of a Soviet major general who toward the end of World War II sent a railroad car full of German loot to the U.S.S.R. Being against regulations, the car was held up at the border. The major general protested to Stalin, pointing out his heroic war efforts. Stalin telegraphed to authorize the car to proceed but addressed the message to Major, not Major General, X.

Semenov seemed to have a very fresh memory of the destruction and death during the war. He had a real sense of horror about the risk of war. Several times, in stressing the importance of the talks, he said, "If weapons ever talked instead of men, it would be an undesirable evil for both our countries." On a number of occasions he spoke with emotion of twenty-five million war dead in the Soviet Union. Germany was seldom mentioned but I sensed that it often was in his mind. The Soviets, I am sure, believed that a SALT agreement would firm up existing barriers to German acquisition of nuclear weapons.

He was naturally quite proud of the accomplishments of the U.S.S.R. After returning from the Twenty-fourth Congress of the Communist Party, he told of sitting with the delegation from Kazakstan. Among his fellow delegates were physicists, biologists and chemists, and this from a republic which a relatively few years before had been a backwater area living for the most part as it had centuries ago.

I asked if there were any people at this Congress who had attended the First International Congress in 1896. He thought a current attendee named Petrov had been there. He once mentioned Marshal Budenny. I asked if Budenny still thought cavalry was the most important branch of the military forces and a decisive factor in winning wars. Semenov replied that Budenny had held such a view at one time. He recalled that at the Eighteenth Congress of the Communist Party Stalin had kidded Budenny by saying, "Semën Mikhailovich does not know anything at all except horses." Semenov went on to say that Stalin had regarded artillery as "the god of war."

Semenov retained a number of superstitions from his Russian past. He would never shake hands across a threshold. He believed in eating and drinking before starting a journey. Once when his wife and mine flew from Helsinki to Moscow, we saw them off at the airport. He insisted on not leaving until the plane had flown off. When I once suggested that a session begin on April 1 he replied, "April 1—don't trust anyone!"

Although I did not sense that he believed that the ideological differences between our two systems were likely to converge, he felt that the Soviet economy would become as productive as the Western economies and then political gaps between the two systems would tend to narrow. At a dinner attended by his daughter, aged six, and mine, aged twenty-eight, he said that by the time the two were our age the political gap would have narrowed. I thought he gave himself lots of leeway between the time of my daughter's and his reaching sixty.

Semenov's second wife was less than half his age. He once smilingly observed that when he reached a hundred she would be seventy.

During conversation in which I referred to former Secretary of Defense Robert McNamara, I was surprised to hear Semenov say, "We used to scold him a good deal in the press but we respected him."

Treaties, he said, are like children, they grow up into different things from what they were when young. He cited the Nuclear Test Ban Treaty. By this I took him to mean that treaties tend to have a dynamism of their own which may produce unpredictable benefits for the parties.

He once observed that the gap between the developed countries and the new nations was an element of extreme "instability."

Semenov made no claim to expertise in arms control. At a luncheon one day at the Soviet Embassy in Vienna he described having been in charge of cholera control some years before in a southeastern region of the Soviet Union. I observed that I knew he was an expert in music and art and diplomacy but not cholera. He turned to my wife and said, "You notice he didn't say an expert in strategic arms control." But several times I somewhat carelessly suggested that he take counsel with his experts when he seemed to doubt a technical point that I had made. He would react somewhat sharply with, "Oh, I know something about that." He once said that, while sometimes what technicians say deserves attention, they often talk nonsense. These were their drawbacks and that was why they were experts. Otherwise they would be chiefs of delegation!

When discussing one complicated issue he said that if one read

Hegel without footnotes one might miss the structure of his thought and his meaning. There was often more meaning in Hegel's footnotes than in the main body of the text. One must look at the entire picture to judge whether one was seeing only details or the focal point of a work of art. These were his views as a philosopher. He was not pretending to be a specialist on phased-array radar.

Semenov was very precise in his language, written and spoken. He said that negotiating at SALT reminded him of the work of diamond polishers and that the subjects we were dealing with were far more valuable than diamonds. I gathered that he was a stickler for precise drafting. Reportedly, while drafting, he used a Russian dictionary of fifty volumes. He practiced with skill the classical technique of diplomacy by hints. We always scanned his statements many times for semi-hidden nuances suggesting possible changes in Soviet positions—and sometimes found them.

He recalled working for Molotov, when the latter was the Soviet Foreign Minister. He would submit papers which Molotov would blue-pencil throughout and send back for revision. When the needed changes were made, Molotov would chide him for lack of conviction about his original positions and even use Semenov's earlier arguments to make his points!

Early in the negotiation I gave Semenov a copy of an excellent little book, *The Negotiators* by Francis Walder, a fictionalized account of the negotiation between Huguenot and Catholic factions in sixteenth-century France which I thought had some relevance to SALT. Translating it gave his interpreters quite a job. He sometimes referred to it, usually saying, "In SALT we are not negotiating about what religion should be practiced in some French towns."

Semenov liked to quote from the Old and New Testaments, the Koran and Greek mythology—"It is good," he said, to read "the old books." His reference to obscure writings of all sorts led one American to observe that what we needed on the delegation was a cultural anthropologist to advise on the meaning of Semenov's allusions.

Having served so long in Germany, he had a broad acquaintance with its literature and frequently quoted from Goethe.

William Krimer, our chief interpreter, had studied Goethe for years at the University of Berlin and was often enlisted to aid the Soviet interpreter in exactly rendering these quotations.

Once he cited a verse from Pushkin's *Eugen Onegin* to make the point that opportunities in negotiations should be seized lest they be lost. I retaliated by referring to a later verse from the poem which neutralized the earlier sentiment—not adding that by chance I had read it the night before and had no great knowledge of Pushkin.

While my wife and I in rare moments of discouragement felt that we were giving up a good deal, spending so many months of our lives away from home on what might well be a wild goose chase, Semenov must have given the appearance of having an enviable time abroad. Several times Foreign Minister Gromyko said to me, "Semenov is on vacation seeing museums in Vienna." They are good friends and I'm sure the Minister knew that Semenov was more than earning his pay.

Semenov has a highly developed appreciation and knowledge of art. His recreation seemed indeed in good part given over to visiting museums. After visiting the Albertina in Vienna to see drawings by Dürer, he remarked with awe, "You know, they let you touch them!" His main artistic interest then was in furniture. He later showed me with some pride furniture in his flat in Moscow. He may not have liked the Viennese climate but compensated for it by attending many a concert and opera. I told him that I'd heard he had once conducted orchestras. "That was long ago," he said.

In view of his accustomed discretion, I was surprised to hear him say in front of a number of Finns, "We believe that President Nixon will be re-elected in 1972." I thought that non-SALT matter well worth reporting to the White House.

He liked to discuss SALT business at social affairs. During a picnic given by the Finns on a small island in the Gulf of Finland, after swimming, fishing and rather hearty eating of barbecued meats, he suggested review of some SALT issues. We withdrew to a quiet spot in the woods. He drew out a typed script and started in. It began to rain. He seemed unaware of the climatic change and plunged on. I noticed that the ink from the interpreters' notes was beginning to run down the pages and suggested that we take shelter. Reaching a nearby structure, he continued reading. We had taken refuge under the roof of the picnickers' ladies' room and I suggested we find a more appropriate spot. A Finnish Coast Guard cutter was tied up to a nearby dock. Our combined language skills did not register our request to come aboard and continue the work. As I recall, this bucolic talk was never finished—with no apparent harm.

In exchanges between the delegations about a strategy of assured destruction and strategic stability Semenov used the antiseptic terminology of algebra by speaking of Country A and Country B instead of mentioning the U.S. and the U.S.S.R. Following this lead, instead of speaking of China, I referred to Country K—Kitai being the Russian word for China. He got the point.

Going down a gangplank from a Finnish icebreaker under the eyes of the rest of the delegations, I heard him say, "Here go Marx and Engels." Once I wondered aloud as to what Lenin would have thought of the implications of nuclear weapons for his conception of the world's future. Semenov said that sometime he would tell me what Lenin and Stalin had thought of weapons of mass destruction. He never got around to it. One Soviet official once said it was a pity that Marx had known nothing of physical sciences.

Only once during the two and a half years did I see Semenov angry or at least giving a very good imitation of anger. I had read a plenary statement, a part of which was intended to give a slight nudge to the dreary pace of the talks, but it was taken apparently as an insult. After Semenov finished reading his statement very quickly, he cut short the session and, after grim-faced Soviet delegates shook hands with us, we were escorted from the embassy. I could not believe that such a random episode could prejudice an important negotiation, but this was a development for which we had no clear answer or precedent. During lunch I instructed Ray Garthoff to contact Kishilov to see if he could work something out to get things back on the track. I told him I would be willing to speak to Semenov privately to make clear that my remark had no unworthy purpose. A private meeting was set up and I so told him. There were other members of the delegation, Semenov said, inferring that I should express regret at the next plenary meeting. I declined, saying I had no intention of taking such a trip to Canossa. The matter was not pressed and shortly thereafter Semenov volunteered that he had forgotten about it.

I had no illusions that personal relations would significantly affect the substance of SALT. I have read most of the memoirs of Americans who have negotiated with Soviets and am not impressed by claims that they "understood the Russians" and could "get along with them," or that they had some special relationship with some official. I subscribe to Harold Nicolson's advice: "The habit of personal diplomacy is dubious and may be even dangerous. . . . There is nothing more damaging to persuasion in international relations than friendliness between contracting parties. . . . Diplomacy if ever to be effective should be a disagreeable business. And one recorded in hard print."

At the same time, the interrelationships between American and Soviet civilian and military officials that existed on and off for two and one half years are not an insignificant factor in over-all Soviet-American affairs. A process has been started of talking seriously about issues on which the survival of our two societies and the rest of civilization depends. While the product of this first SALT dialogue was perhaps more modest than reflected in the triumphalism which the Nixon Administration resorted to in 1972, it was a good first fruit and a product of which the two delegations can be proud.

Jean Monnet, in his great political effort to integrate Europe, used to say it was important for the negotiating parties to consider themselves seated on one side of a table with the problem on the other—with the negotiators acting not as adversaries but as people trying to solve problems together. Although the SALT delegations could never shake off the adversary roles that history had given them, I felt that at times we were trying jointly to solve problems of strategic arms control. As SALT negotiations continue the trick will be to increase and expand these times.

PART ONE
PROBING

FIRST ENCOUNTER

Helsinki I:
November–December 1969

Monday, November 17, 1969, was just another day at the headquarters of the Strategic Air Command near Omaha, Nebraska, and at the command headquarters of the Soviet Strategic Rocket Forces. The usual number of missile submarines were on patrol and hundreds of intercontinental missiles were trained on targets thousands of miles away. Enough nuclear weapons were targeted on the Soviet Union and the United States to blow them both to smithereens at a signal from their political leaders. Carefully worked out arrangements were in force to prevent accidents or unauthorized use of weapons. If these weapons were ever fired the United States and the U.S.S.R. would be destroyed to such a degree as to make Germany and Japan in 1945 seem untouched by war. November 17 was the day when President Nixon, who had the sole authority to communicate an order for nuclear war to the strategic forces of the United States, directed me to deliver a different kind of message to the opening meeting of the Strategic Arms Limitation Talks in Helsinki, Finland. He said, "I am convinced that the limitation of strategic arms is in the mutual interest of our country and the Soviet Union." Here was the basic premise of United States SALT policy.

In July the President had written me that the delegation would be dealing with a subject of crucial significance to the safety of our country. He said our purpose at Helsinki would be

> to determine whether it is feasible to make arrangements with the Soviet Government that will contribute to the preservation and if possible, the improvement of this country's security. . . . When I speak of this country's security, I fully realize that we cannot expect to return to an era when our country was literally immune to physical threat. Neither our military programs nor any negotiation with our potential adversaries can achieve that. But I am speaking of a situation in which I, as President and Commander-in-Chief, have at my disposal military forces that will provide me with the best assurance attainable in present and foreseeable circumstances that no opponent can rationally expect to derive benefit from attacking, or threatening to attack, us or our allies. I am determined, moreover, to pass on to my successor that same sense of assurance.

President Nixon then outlined his general approach to relations with the Soviet Union and to the strategic arms talks. Here was the foundation on which the SALT negotiations could proceed. He had told the Soviet leaders that both sides' security interests should be recognized and that he was ready for bona fide negotiations. If the Soviets were of the same mind limitations should be within reach.

Just before the Helsinki talks started, President Nixon had written me another letter about SALT.

> I should like to make clear that I view arms limitation talks in the context of our over-all relations with the Soviet Union. While I did not advance explicit preconditions for the opening of the talks and will stipulate none for their continuation, I do believe that, to be meaningful, progress in arms limitation must be accompanied by progress in the solution of critical political problems. . . .

Before leaving for Europe the delegates met with the President for last-minute guidance and photographing during which I asked the President if he had read a new biography of Tolstoy by Henri Troyat. To my great surprise he had. To my even greater surprise his sole comment was on the large stakes Tolstoy gambled for. I then remembered reports that the President excelled at poker during his navy days.

The principal American delegates flew to Helsinki in a military plane—Air Force 2—by way of Brussels where we advised the North Atlantic Council of U.S. strategy for this first SALT encounter. The Soviet delegation arrived by train, as was to be their regular practice, at the same railroad station from which Lenin had left for Petrograd fifty-two years earlier to establish the Bolshevik regime. As I watched the Soviet negotiators on television marching down the platform, grim-faced, I had a sinking feeling about prospects for success in negotiating with these people. Was I the right person for this SALT mission? What was I doing there? Were we in for just a dose of polemic, the kind of propaganda and psychological warfare that had taken place at a number of disarmament meetings in the past, or was SALT to be different? I recalled another picture seen many years before of Trotsky and his associates arriving at a railroad platform at Brest-Litovsk in 1918 to sign a "neither peace nor war" arrangement with Germany. That gave me no comfort either.

In a quite literal sense the eyes of the world were on this Helsinki encounter. Nearly five hundred journalists from all over the world descended on Finland's capital to report on what promised to be a first event of central importance, a serious effort by the superpowers to control the competitive nuclear postures which had dominated and determined their overall relations for a generation. It was the largest press gathering ever in Helsinki, surpassed only once since when the Conference on Security and Cooperation brought thirty-five heads of state or government and fifteen hundred media representatives there in July 1975. (About eight hundred journalists would attend the first weeks of the second round of the SALT talks, in Vienna the following April, but this number was inflated by the many East European correspondents who chose to reside in Vienna rather than on their own beats.) Newspapers were full of cartoons of peace doves having their tails salted. The acronym SALT became a familiar word although few knew that the letters stood for Strategic Arms Limitation Talks.

As the talks proceeded, the press army was to melt away because the delegations wouldn't feed it any information. The standard briefing given after each plenary session by both delegations was that the session had been "serious and businesslike," even though on rare occasions it had been neither. Before the talks started Soviet Ambassador Dobrynin and I had agreed that they would be private and there would be no press backgrounding. The commitment to privacy was respected throughout the talks, with the exception of some notorious leaks out of Washington. This unprecedented ability of Americans to keep their mouths shut did much to convince the Soviets that SALT was a serious negotiation. Semenov said so several times.

How did SALT find its way to Helsinki, after Reykjavik the most northerly capital in the world? (We arrived in Helsinki in a November snowfall.) In the spring of the year I had recommended Geneva or Vienna as possible conference sites, and thinking that the talks would start soon, I threw in as a third possibility summertime in Finland. Secretary of State Rogers put these options to Ambassador Dobrynin. The Soviets naturally pounced on the idea of Helsinki, almost at Leningrad's back door. As time passed and no date for the negotiation was set, I made a nuisance of myself with Rogers and the White House stressing that Helsinki had been my last choice. It was unfit for winter negotiation. I even enlisted security people to point out the danger to the delegation from the many Soviet agents known to be operating in Finland. Some consideration was even given in Washington to holding the talks on Soviet and American warships to be anchored in the harbor at Helsinki, but that didn't seem to be the right psychological image to project. Rogers felt that we had offered the Soviets a choice. They had accepted one and that amounted to a contract. I didn't at all like losing this first trick in the SALT game. Once located in Helsinki, it would be hard to switch. But I was in good measure to blame, and in the event Helsinki proved a fine place to work. Finnish hospitality was splendid. And I did manage to obtain guidance from the White House that the United States would not accept Helsinki as the site for subsequent phases of the negotiation. Later we had to compromise.

This was a formidable job that President Nixon had assigned us. To try to negotiate an agreement with the rival superpower on levels of nuclear arms which are the central security concern of each was unlike any task in the history of diplomacy. But after we started exploration of this unknown area I began to feel more confident. We were well prepared. My associates on the U.S. delegation were the best the United States government had to offer, with large experience in the diplomacy of arms control, in the facts of life of nuclear weapons, in strategic thinking. We had the full support and personal interest of the President. I believed that I was trusted by Rogers and Laird, and that I had the confidence of the Joint Chiefs. Other delegates were trusted by their Washington agency heads. The United States had ample strategic forces clearly capable of deterring nuclear war.

While we at SALT were exploring various arms control possibilities, weaponeers on both sides continued developing new weapons and weapons applications. Tests of new systems proceeded with alternating success and failures. Polaris submarines returned from patrols to begin conversion to the MIRVed Poseidon missile system. Older land-based missiles (Minuteman I) were being replaced by MIRVed missiles (Minuteman III). New Soviet SS-9 heavy missile launcher silos were reported with disheartening regularity. Additional Soviet missile submarines showed up in fitting-out basins at a rate of about seven new boats a year. A new American bomber, the B-1, was on the drawing boards, and we began to see a new Soviet bomber prototype, named the Backfire, having uncertain performance characteristics but which might include intercontinental capabilities.

The strategic force structures and ongoing weapons programs of the two sides were quite different. While the U.S.S.R. was building silo launchers for ICBMs and missile submarines at a fast rate, their ABM program apparently was stopping. The United States had not built any offensive missile launchers for several years but was starting to construct an ABM system. The U.S. MIRVed missiles were a major addition to offensive forces; the Soviet Union would not start MIRVing until some five years later. It was not going to be easy to reach agreement to put these asymmetrical nuclear forces under ceilings acceptable to both sides. And unless ongoing modernization programs could be suspended by some kind of moratorium during the negotiation, uncertainties and problems were bound to increase, making agreement even more difficult. Pressures would grow for new programs to neutralize perceived advantages of the other side. As the delegations gathered in Helsinki, we wondered if it were really possible to bring the dynamic modernization programs under some degree of constraint through an international agreement.

The delegation received comprehensive SALT guidance in documents entitled National Security Decision Memoranda (NSDMs). NSDM-33 with instructions for Helsinki was issued on November 12, 1969. The first round of SALT clearly would have to be an exploratory operation. During this phase of the talks the primary objective was to develop a work program and to obtain Soviet views to help develop negotiating positions. The delegation was to avoid statements that might prejudge future positions.

We knew from earlier exchanges that the Soviets were interested in limitations on offensive as well as defensive systems (ABMs). Beyond that we were in the dark. I learned indirectly that the White House had advised Soviet Ambassador Dobrynin not to expect any specific proposals at this opening round. This White House signal didn't strike me at the time as surprising, but it was to be followed by other undisclosed White House SALT communications with the Soviets of much greater importance.

On November 16, the day before the opening plenary meeting, the head of the Soviet delegation, Vladimir S. Semenov, and his wife Lydia paid a call at my invitation on the Smiths at our hotel. I had in mind a short and informal talk to break the ice. I did not expect any serious exchanges, but Semenov did as was so often to be the case when he used social occasions to make points he or his Moscow authorities wanted to put across. The ladies chatted in schoolgirlish French at one side of our small hotel room while Semenov and I, armed with interpreters, talked at the other side. He started by recalling his previous associations with Americans. He had worked with General Eisenhower and Robert Murphy of the State Department when associated with Marshal Zhukov in Germany in 1945. I said I worked seven years for Eisenhower and had also been closely associated with Murphy for many years.

After a few more personal reminiscences, Semenov pulled out of his pocket a number of cards and read away at some length. This was also to be his general practice. Once he read eighteen typed cards of briefing material—non-stop. Later he somewhat defensively explained that this card technique was a habit developed when he was young to add precision to his thoughts and their expression. I guessed that it was also a record by which he could demonstrate that he had carried out instructions of his centrum, as he called the authorities in Moscow. Semenov first proposed procedural arrangements, then stressed the importance of SALT in the eyes of the Soviet leadership. They were ready not only for general exchanges but for concrete moves. There would be no problem about agenda. The era of the Palais Rose was over.[1] The Soviet delegation had come to Helsinki with serious intentions and planned to conduct business in this spirit. Like many Soviet diplomats, Semenov felt it necessary to develop at great length points which American practice would have compressed into a few sentences.

I responded that President Nixon had asked me to say how important he believed SALT to be and how serious our intentions were. As for procedure, I urged as informal an approach as possible with few speeches. While plenary statements are necessary to assure accurate presentation and recording of official positions in a negotiation, they are a slow and inflexible way of working toward agreement. I persisted in this plea for more informality throughout the negotiation, but we never got entirely away from the dreary process of making speeches at each other. Our authorities in Moscow and Washington wanted to monitor SALT closely and that meant a large amount of "negotiation" by speeches. Fortunately these were accompanied by hundreds of more informal working sessions. Semenov and I agreed that this preliminary session should not last longer than two or three weeks. In the event it lasted five. Underestimating the time required to do SALT business proved to be the rule during the entire negotiation.

As the first Smith-Semenov conversation drew to a close, knowing of Semenov's interest in German affairs, I mentioned my understanding that the Federal Republic of Germany intended to sign the Non-Proliferation Treaty in the near future, and expressed a hope that the United States and U.S.S.R. would ratify it

[1] The four-power conference on Germany held at the Palais Rose in Paris in the early 1950s. It broke up after four months of fruitless wrangling over the conference agenda.

quickly thereafter, perhaps coincident with the conclusion of these preliminary Helsinki talks. He thought this an interesting idea. He noted that Germany's signature was a very important factor for Soviet ratification. In the event, Germany signed on November 28, and the United States and the U.S.S.R. deposited their instruments of ratification in March 1970.

Our first exchange had been a good rehearsal for what was to come. Though it took lots of patience, I developed a healthy respect for Semenov, and our wives had a pleasant relationship over the SALT years. Semenov knew what his authorities wanted him to do and he did it in the manner of his profession. If it took much longer than Americans would have taken, that did not concern him.

The formal opening session of the SALT talks was held at the Smolna Palace—small but beautiful. It had once been the official residence of the last Tsarist Governor General, one Nekrasov, before Finland gained its independence in 1918 when the Russian Empire collapsed. Finnish Foreign Minister Karjalainen welcomed the delegations. Semenov followed with a brief statement thanking the Finns for giving SALT a home and greeting the American delegates. He stressed again how important the Soviets considered SALT, paying the usual obeisance to Lenin. The brevity and serious tone of his first statement made a good impression. I then read a message from President Nixon. "You are embarking upon one of the most momentous negotiations ever entrusted to an American delegation. . . . Today . . . you will begin what all of your fellow citizens in the United States and, I believe, all people throughout the world, profoundly hope will be a sustained effort not only to limit the buildup of strategic forces but to reverse it. . . ."

During this opening phase of the conference the delegations were photographed by the media a great deal, often when toasts were being offered. One friend wrote, "You are the biggest boozer since W. C. Fields. In every picture you are having a drink." I replied that photos couldn't distinguish between water and vodka. I tried from then on to avoid toasts in public.

Real business started on November 18. A coin was flipped to decide at which embassy the first meeting would be. The Soviets won. We didn't consider this a bad omen. Their embassy in Helsinki is a large pile built by the Finns to Soviet specifications as reparations to replace a building which Soviet bombing had destroyed during the war. On the negotiating table were a number of packages of Soviet cigarettes and bottles of soda water. Just as we were starting, someone opened one with a loud pop. A Soviet general quietly observed, *"Roket,"* which produced a round of nervous laughter. Then we got down to work.

Semenov began by stating that both sides recognized the importance of curbing the strategic arms race. It could only contribute to a general increase in the threat of war. Mountains of weapons were growing, yet security was not improving but diminishing as a result. A situation of mutual deterrence existed. Even in the event that one of the sides was the first to be subjected to attack, it would undoubtedly retain the ability to inflict a retaliatory blow of destructive force. It would be tantamount to suicide for the ones who decided to start war. However, in the Soviet view, mutual deterrence did not entirely preclude nuclear war. Each side has its own understanding and interpretation of the numerous factors and complex interactions of the evolving military political situation. This could lead to major miscalculations. The strategic situation by no means excluded the risk of a nuclear conflict arising from unauthorized use of nuclear missiles from a provocation on the part of some third power possessing nuclear weapons.

Semenov went on to make a point he would often repeat. It was obvious that mutually acceptable solutions should be sought along lines that would insure the security of each side equally rather than through efforts to obtain unilateral military advantages. He rejected any idea that arms limitation be linked to other issues. While concrete results would contribute to the improvement of relations between our countries, the subject matter of our deliberations was so complex in itself that to link it to other international problems would mean directing the matter into a blind alley. He concluded by saying that the Soviet delegation would consider the preliminary round to be successful if, together with consideration of the range of questions to be discussed, we could work out something in the nature of an agenda for the coming negotiations.

Before we left Washington, President Nixon had suggested that I write him personal impressions as to how the talks were going. I sent the President these first reactions:

> Semenov strikes me as a man bent on serious business and intent on getting through this preliminary phase without delay. . . . The Soviet Delegation, though quite heavily larded with intelligence people, includes a few men who act as if they were accustomed to lots of authority and who seem seriously interested in this exercise.

> The first business session this morning went off slightly better than I had expected. Semenov's statement had a minimum of polemic; and although it gives evidence of being designed for public consumption in the event the talks collapse, it also seems clearly intended to lay the basis for a serious exchange of views. . . . He spoke of nuclear war as a disaster for both sides—of the decrease of security as the number of weapons increases—of the costly results of rapid obsolescence of weapons—of the dangers of grave miscalculations—of unauthorized use of weapons—and of hostilities resulting from third power provocation.

It had generally been thought by some American strategists that the Soviets had not developed strategic concepts and doctrines to the sophisticated level that these Americans thought *they* had. SALT would show this to be another American illusion of intellectual grandeur. Kissinger wrote that he had been impressed by the high quality of the Helsinki exchanges. I was pleasantly surprised by a Semenov statement at a later plenary session. He said this was clearly not the place to try to ascertain the reasons for the beginning and continuation of the present arms race or to determine who was responsible for it. "We have our own definite point of view in that respect and you, evidently, have your own." This was some change from the hundreds of thousands of words in the United Nations and other forums pounding away at America's blame for the nuclear arms race. The delegation reported to Washington that the Soviets seemed to be serious about SALT.

But sometimes I had a feeling that we were being exposed

to a mild brainwash. "Repetition is the mother of learning" is a well-known Russian saying, and we did hear some arguments over and over again. From time to time we also were exposed to a touch of standard polemic. Fortunately this kind of "negotiating" was infrequent.

One curious repetition throughout the negotiation was the phrase "equal security," as if to say that the U.S.S.R. after long years of "catching up" was in no mind to strike an unequal bargain in SALT. Since no great nation would make an arms limitation agreement that was unequal, the delegation took these calls for equality as rhetorical flourishes, perhaps designed for home consumption. And equal security is a good starting point for almost any position of any party in any arms control negotiation.

Before sounding the Soviets out on specific limitation possibilities, the delegation tried to get some idea of their views on basic strategic concepts which we considered important for a successful negotiation. While we were not very successful at drawing the Soviets out, bear with me as I touch briefly on American statements about strategic theory. It is a slippery subject, but once grasped it will help one understand what this negotiation was all about.

The primary objective of U.S. strategic forces was to deter attacks on the United States or its allies. Any conceivable incentive to initiate nuclear war by either side would be reduced if there was assurance that the losses to an initiator would be unacceptable under any circumstance. We believed that such a *mutual deterrent* positively reduced the likelihood that a nuclear war would occur, and that a significant SALT agreement could be consistent with and indeed complement this strategy of deterrence. This is the idea of *assured destruction*. Assured destruction capabilities are the basis of mutual deterrence.

The Soviet delegation was in full agreement that war between our countries would be disastrous for both sides—". . . tantamount to suicide for the one which decided to start the war." No American academician could have put the matter in simpler terms.

A second objective of U.S. strategic forces is to defend the United States and our allies if deterrence should fail. While we realized that neither side could expect to escape disastrous damage from a major nuclear attack, we were building an ABM system to defend our land-based retaliatory ICBMs and to defend against the kind of attack which countries other than the U.S.S.R. might be able to launch in the next decade. We also wanted some defense against possible accidental launches.

The United States had two aims connected with *strategic stability. Arms competition stability* would result from a strategic force relationship in which neither side saw a need to mount major new arms programs to avoid being placed at a strategic disadvantage. *Crisis stability* would result from the sides having such powerful and survivable forces that in a crisis neither would believe it necessary to strike first lest its retaliatory forces be substantially destroyed by a pre-emptive attack. Nuclear retaliatory forces able to survive a first strike were essential to maintain both kinds of stability. Such weapons systems could be threatened by the development of systems which could destroy them in flight or while they were still on their launchers. We were especially concerned by the threat to our Minuteman missiles from the large Soviet SS-9 missiles, and the Soviets knew it. But they also knew that an effective American anti-ballistic missile system could threaten the capability of their missile forces to retaliate against targets in the United States. ABM defenses thus could be another factor making for strategic instability.

Semenov said at Helsinki that neither side had anything to gain by deploying new systems. Throughout the negotiation, however, the Soviet delegation seemed less concerned than the Americans about the crisis aspect of strategic stability, especially as it focused so much on ICBMs. The Soviets argued that the sides had more than one type of retaliatory force. The important thing was the survivability of the aggregate of the strategic forces[2] rather than that of one component.

This view was in some measure shared by the American Joint Chiefs of Staff and was gaining wider acceptance in the United States, if for no other reason than to rationalize and adjust to the gradually growing vulnerability of our ICBM force. The so-called Minuteman vulnerability danger—the prospect that this compo-

[2] ICBMs, submarine-launched missiles (SLBMs) and heavy bombers—called in the U.S. the Triad.

nent of the U.S. nuclear forces will become vulnerable to a Soviet first strike which would destroy a large percentage of Minuteman ICBMs in their underground launcher silos—was, at that time, I thought, somewhat exaggerated by civilian theorists and engineers in the office of the Secretary of Defense. Our military delegate, General Allison, certainly did not share their oft-voiced analytical early write-off of our ICBMs. There is no doubt that in time a fixed-based ICBM will become vulnerable because of the increasing accuracy of the other side's ICBMs. But such vulnerability did not exist in 1969, and it does not yet, although it is now generally accepted to be not far off. But such vulnerability, to my mind, will not automatically make a fixed-based missile force valueless. While less dependence will be placed on ICBMs to deter attack and fixed base ICBMs may have to be supplemented with more survivable systems, I believe they will still have some life expectancy as a significant contributor to our total strategic deterrent forces—a judgment apparently shared by the Department of Defense in the 1970s as it continued to modernize the fixed-base ICBM forces.

As we exchanged views on these grisly subjects, I thought that never before had officials of rival nations spoken to each other so bluntly, albeit affably, about their capability to destroy each other and the importance of maintaining that mutual capability. We tried repeatedly to bring home to the Soviets that their huge SS-9 ICBM was a destabilizing weapons system and should be subject to special limitations. I sometimes wonder if our constant harping on this subject was not counterproductive. The Soviets may well have calculated that the best way to deter war would be to deploy weapons systems that the Americans most worried about. This calculation would be based not on any notion of strategic stability or analysis by computers but on an instinctive feeling that if you have the other fellow worried by your weaponry he isn't likely to attack you.

The delegation also stressed in plenary presentations how uncertainties were a main factor in the arms competition. Neither side could be sure what the other's capabilities and intentions would be in the future. Both sides felt some necessity to assume the worst. A Soviet delegate gave a novel image of how the two sides view each other's strategic forces. He said one side looks at the other's forces through the small end of its binoculars and at its own through the large end. It is a regrettable testimony to the persistence of uncertainty in military planning that after ten years of SALT exchanges and agreements the United States and the Soviet Union are still engaged in a dynamic arms competition. Although there has been no new construction of silo launchers for missiles by the U.S.S.R. and the U.S. since 1971, missile modernization continues and previous generations of missiles are being replaced with new ones. The United States is now well along in building a new fleet of very large missile submarines—the Trident class—and is making a start on a new class of ICBMs, the mobile M-X. The Soviets have deployed a number of new types of large ICBMs and continue to build modern submarines.

On November 24, in an effort to bring the talks down to specifics, we tabled a paper entitled "Illustrative Elements." These were carefully labeled as not being proposals. Rather they aimed at extracting Soviet reactions without committing the United States to any position. I told Semenov that, as in the case of any new process, they should not take too literally these Illustrative Elements presented to get the strategic dialogue started.

I introduced these Elements by suggesting that certain characteristics of individual weapons systems should be considered in deciding what could be controlled. Limitations on a particular system should be attempted or not depending on their effect on crisis stability, on the arms competition and on the strategic balance, the complexity and verifiability of these limitations, and their relationship to third-country concerns. A strategic arms limitation agreement might include the following elements.

- The aggregate number of launchers for fixed or mobile land-based ICBMs and for sea-based strategic offensive ballistic missiles would be limited to the total number presently operational. Within that over-all numerical ceiling, each side could vary the combination of these types of launchers as it chose.

- Other strategic offensive missile launchers, i.e., fixed medium range and intermediate range ballistic missiles (MR/IRBMs) and submarine-launched cruise missiles (SLCMs), would be limited to those presently operational. Mobile MR/IRBMs would be prohibited.

- There would be agreed limitations on ABM systems.

The right to vary the combination of types of launchers by replacing one type with another became known as freedom to mix. In addition to their intercontinental range and their submarine-launched missiles the Soviets had about 600 launchers for medium-range and intermediate-range ballistic missiles (MR/IRBMs) targeted on Western Europe: the United States no longer deployed MRs or IRBMs. Mobile ICBM launchers would be permitted but not mobile MR/IRBM launchers because they would make verification of the number of mobile ICBMs more difficult under a treaty. Submarine-launched cruise missiles (SLCMs) were also deployed in Soviet naval forces at that time. These are like pilotless "drone" aircraft, fly in the earth's atmosphere and resemble somewhat the V-1 "buzz bombs" used by Nazi Germany in 1944 and 1945. Cruise missiles seemed like a peripheral problem in 1969. Their control mushroomed into a central issue in the SALT II negotiation. The United States is developing them and plans to deploy major strategic cruise missile forces. (Here is a bitter example of how volatile a mixture makes up the strategic balance of forces.)

The control of multiple independently targetable re-entry vehicles (MIRVs) was not mentioned in these Illustrative Elements. The fact that MIRVs were not mentioned must have told the Soviets something about the degree of U.S. interest in that major issue.

The Illustrative Elements were a useful negotiating device. They offered reference points for most of the discussions over the next month and served to identify major problems. They foreshadowed the SALT agreements reached in 1972. They called for ABM limitation, and ABM limitations became the subject of a treaty. They called for a freeze with freedom to mix on SLBMs and ICBMs, and the interim freeze of 1972 so provided (although at different levels for the Soviets than existed in 1969). The Elements did not include aircraft; neither did the 1972 interim freeze. MIRVs were ignored in 1969 and in 1972. The only two parts of the 1969 Elements not covered in the 1972 agree-

ment were cruise missiles and launchers for medium- and intermediate-range Soviet ballistic missiles, neither of which was then
considered central to the strategic balance.

Semenov acknowledged that the Illustrative Elements contained
constructive ideas but said they were deficient. One obvious omission was the intercontinental bomber, and the Soviets quickly
noted that the United States had a much larger heavy bomber
force than the U.S.S.R., almost 600 against 150. We argued that
bombers could not be considered a first-strike weapon system.
They were not causing the strategic arms competition. We stressed
that it would be very difficult to define what kind of bombers
should be limited. There was a wide variety of performance
characteristics of the aircraft at the disposal of the United States
and U.S.S.R. and it would be difficult for both sides to agree on a
definition of strategic aircraft. To include aircraft would also raise
the question of anti-aircraft systems, as well as serious problems
of verification to assure the parties that any agreement was being
fulfilled. It was eventually agreed that bombers could be considered for limitation but that missile launchers should be given priority. Problems in limiting bombers proved a main difficulty in
negotiating SALT II.

The Soviet delegation made much of the apparent inconsistency
in the Illustrative Elements provision permitting mobile ICBMs
while barring mobile MR/IRBMs. Washington was now having
second thoughts about even permitting mobile ICBMs, and the
delegation was instructed to keep open an option to ban them.
Allowing mobile ICBMs in the Illustrative Elements had reflected
U.S. concern about the future vulnerability of ICBMs, which
could be reduced if their launchers were moving or movable
rather than fixed targets. But moving launchers would also be
more difficult targets for verification reconnaissance systems.
Verification soon took priority, and for the balance of SALT I we
were to press the Soviets, without success, for a ban on mobile
ICBMs. To show how quickly perceptions of strategic needs can
change, the United States now is planning on a mobile system
which would not be banned under SALT II.

On November 26 Semenov raised the thorny issue which came
to be known as forward-based systems—FBS. In the early days of
SALT, these systems were referred to as lighter delivery aircraft

(LDA). Agreements on the basis of equal security, he said, had to deal with threats as perceived by each side. All nuclear delivery systems which could be used to hit targets in the other country should be covered in SALT, regardless of whether their owners called them strategic or tactical. A Soviet city could just as well be bombed by U.S. fighter bombers based in Europe or on aircraft carriers as by an ICBM launched from the United States. (A Soviet general told of being bombed while lying wounded in a hospital during the war. It had given him no comfort that the bomb had been dropped by a fighter bomber rather than a heavy bomber.) This principle should define which weapons systems were strategic and to be limited. Weapons systems that could not hit targets in the other country should not be included. Thus the 600 Soviet MR/IRBMs trained on Western Europe should not be included.

Although White House guidance was that tactical nuclear weapons should not be limited in any agreement, the way the Soviets inserted the FBS issue into SALT came as a surprise. As I rose from the plenary table, Ambassador Thompson whispered advice that I promptly tell Semenov that raising this issue would ensnarl the conference in extraneous political and military problems that would block any SALT agreement. I did so as soon as Semenov and I sat down for a postplenary conversation, pointing out that the Soviets had for years unsuccessfully tried to roll back American forward bases in Europe and the Far East. These forward-based systems were indispensable elements of the security of America's allies and it was a bad omen for the talks that this matter had been raised. But there FBS was and there it remained through hundreds of hours of argumentation.

The Soviet delegation played skillfully and often on this FBS theme. We heard more about it than any other subject. The Soviets often questioned the logic of our proposing to limit their MR/IRBMs not having the range to reach targets in the United States while at the same time we did not want to limit U.S. aircraft clearly capable of reaching targets in the Soviet Union. I thought our best argument was that the arms competition was driven by additional missile launcher construction, not by lighter delivery aircraft, which were not increasing in number. We were not calling for limits on Soviet medium bombers which had some intercontinental capability. I stressed the definitional problems in limiting FBS aircraft. Even transport aircraft could carry nuclear weapons with some efficiency. There are many ways of delivering nuclear bombs—from modern rockets to railroad trains, automobiles and even light aircraft like a Piper Cub. Where could the line be drawn? Semenov's only response was that that could be "objectively determined."

What did the U.S.S.R. expect to gain by raising this issue? Did the Soviets really believe that FBS were so significant to the strategic balance as to require limitation in a first SALT agreement? Or was FBS more of a ploy to keep a safe negotiating position until it could be seen more clearly where SALT might lead? Perhaps they calculated that the United States might concede something significant to remove this unexpected block. Certainly they appreciated the potentially divisive effect on our North Atlantic and Pacific allies of this claim to include U.S. aircraft committed to forward defense and to exclude the Soviet missiles threatening Western Europe and the Far East. But if this was the Soviet motivation it was frustrated. For over two and a half years we kept in close consultation with our allies, briefing them during each of the seven SALT rounds, and usually before and after. The allies were briefed twenty-two times in all. FBS naturally was the issue in which they took the most interest, and our discussing it frequently and frankly seemed to give confidence to the allies that their most immediate interests were being protected.

As the Soviet position evolved, it appeared that they considered FBS a real American strategic advantage. Semenov put it this way —if one looked at a map of Europe and Asia one would find many bases, air force, naval, and other military bases, each of which contained large stockpiles of American nuclear weapons; thus, in a discussion of strategic force considerations, how could one fail to take this situation into account? There was a certain logic about his position, from the Soviet perspective, faced as they were by thousands of U.S. nuclear warheads deployed outside the United States. The Soviets insisted that this advantage be withdrawn or the U.S.S.R. somehow be compensated for it in a SALT agreement. One Soviet official noted that the megatonnage deliverable by U.S. FBS was greater than that of the Soviet submarine missile force. The Soviet leadership perhaps recalled that the first U.S. nuclear threat to the U.S.S.R. in the 1940s was from B-29 bombers stationed outside of the United States. Later the forward-based B-47 bombers made up a major part of our strategic forces. On a number of occasions Soviets informally recalled how sharply the United States had reacted in 1962 when the Soviet Union tried to deploy a forward-based missile system in Cuba.

Failure to settle this question finally blocked a comprehensive SALT I treaty limiting offensive arms. Even the interim offensive freeze of 1972—a device to get around the FBS block —to some extent reflected FBS considerations. The architect of this freeze, Kissinger, justified the Soviet advantage in numbers of missile launchers in part by pointing to the United States advantage in FBS. In briefing congressional leaders on the SALT agreements, Kissinger recalled, "It was decided to exclude from the freeze bombers and so-called forward-based systems. To exclude, that is, the weapons in which this country holds an advantage. . . . We urge the Congress to keep this fact in mind when assessing the numerical ratios of weapons which are subject to the offensive freeze."

Aside from criticizing the omission of heavy bombers and introducing the FBS position, the Soviet delegation did not comment at length on the U. S. Illustrative Elements or offer a set of counter "elements." I told Semenov this was regrettable.

I then sent President Nixon some further impressions.

The general tone of the sessions continues to be serious, but cautious. . . . The level of Soviet propaganda is much lower than I expected. I made it clear today that a two-way exchange here was important for a realistic basis for later talks. I expect they will move into somewhat greater specificity in the next few sessions.

Unfortunately, lack of specificity turned out to be the standard and very frustrating Soviet negotiating style.

The Soviets quickly disclosed their general thinking about defensive systems. They had changed their minds. When ABMs were first developed they thought them extremely humane instruments to preserve man-made values and protect man himself. Later it was found that they could stimulate the arms competition and contribute to the danger of offensive weapons by casting doubts on the inevitability of retaliation by missile forces. The Soviet Union now realized that ABMs could destabilize the strategic balance. Suspicions that a first strike was being prepared would arise. A nation, believing that its population was adequately protected, might be less concerned about nuclear war than if it believed such war would be a total disaster. Semenov suggested three alternative levels for limiting ABMs: a complete ban, a light deployment (presumably such as the ABM system deployed around Moscow), or a heavy defense of a wide area. The Moscow deployment of 64 launchers for interceptor missiles was described by a Soviet official as "experimental."

Soviet statements at Helsinki seemed to discourage but did not rule out a complete ban on ABMs. They acknowledged, although informally, that that would require dismantling the Moscow system. A ban would leave the third-country issue, by which I think they meant primarily protection of Moscow from a Chinese attack, to be solved by other means. One Soviet official pointed out that from time to time their entire leadership assembled in Moscow, presumably a tempting target for a hostile power. As the talks progressed, the Soviet position on an ABM ban was consistently one of "make us an offer," a position which in time proved quite unwelcome to President Nixon. As to the third ABM alternative, Semenov said that a heavy deployment might tempt its possessor to strike in the belief that it was invulnerable. It was apparent from these initial characterizations of ABM alternatives that the Soviet preference was for limiting ABMs to a light deployment which would permit them to keep their Moscow system.

For all its deficiencies, political as well as technical, the U. S. ABM program had the Soviets worried. This system had missions to defend Minuteman ICBMs, to blunt a low-level Chinese attack, and to destroy warheads from any accidental missile firing. But the Soviets must also have perceived its potential for becoming the basis for a nationwide defense system able to blunt Soviet retaliatory strikes if the Americans struck first. Semenov observed that, if one side employed ABMs to defend its strategic offensive weapons as well as other "targets" a considerable distance away, would not the other side feel uncertainty that such a thin ABM system could evolve into a system useful to support a first strike strategy? A Soviet later said that a nation-wide deployment, even if designed only to protect against a third-country attack or against "light" attacks, could not be considered limited. Their military experts had concluded that a nationwide deployment such as contemplated under the full American program (twelve sites) could too easily be converted into a "heavy" defense. The Soviets probably were impressed by the fact that the U.S. development program was making good technical progress. Of twenty-six test firings in 1969 (which the Soviets undoubtedly monitored), eighteen were totally successful, four partially successful, and only four were failures. The Soviet views on ABM levels were much more specific than other Soviet positions. Their comments on the U. S. ABM program gave a clear indication that limiting ABMs was a primary Soviet aim. So did a remark by one Soviet official's wife who described the Safeguard ABM as *America's Biggest Mistake.*

We said that ABM limitation should be supplemented with certain restraints on anti-aircraft missiles and radars. The U.S.S.R. has widespread anti-aircraft missile systems. Some American experts believed that some of them could be given a capability to destroy incoming missile warheads. In fact, some worst-case worriers claimed for years that Soviet SAM systems already had been given such a capability. U.S. intelligence officials discounted this possibility. Washington by and large seems no longer very concerned about SAM upgrade—if for no other reason, because we now have so many warheads as a result of MIRV programs. At Helsinki the Soviets at first dismissed the possibility, saying that SAMs were designed only against aircraft. Later I was pleasantly surprised when Semenov said the matter was of "substantial interest."

At this first Helsinki session there was hardly any discussion of the complications that radar issues were to bring to the ABM negotiations. We told the Soviets that radar controls would have to be an integral part of ABM limitations. Soviet officials said they were not needed. Much of the later ABM negotiation revolved around this complicated and highly technical subject, which I will spare the reader until he is more of a SALT expert It is enough here to note that the ABM Treaty of 1972 included both restrictions on SAM upgrade and on ABM radars.

The Soviets suggested a ban on transfers of ABMs to other countries and a ban on ABMs using airborne, seaborne or mobile land-based launchers. They said that sea-based ABMs in forward positions could be used in an offensive role, presumably by firing missiles from these launchers at targets in the other country. Perhaps this idea evolved from a United States Navy proposal in the 1960s for an ABM force at sea using Polaris-like missiles having known offensive capabilities. These Soviet concerns were eventually covered by specific provisions in the 1972 ABM Treaty.

The Soviet ABM arguments were encouraging. They were fairly specific. We knew they would be of interest to Washington. There was no doubt that the U.S.S.R. wanted to limit ABMs. This information alone made the preliminary round at Helsinki worthwhile.

Semenov spoke of the need to consider a range of questions related to the curbing of the strategic arms race. Several rather unexpected arms control possibilities were touched on, some of which would develop into intense and fruitful subjects of negotiation. The American delegation concentrated on what might be called hardware problems. The Soviets at this time were interested mainly in principles and political questions and third-country problems and stressed their aim to broaden the scope of the negotiation as I have said.

China was never mentioned by name in plenary sessions but it often seemed a specter at the table. Semenov said privately that nuclear conflict might occur as a "consequence of a premeditated provocation on the part of some third country possessing nuclear weapons and means for their delivery." In the 1950s American scholars had speculated about what was called "catalytic" or "provocative" attack, a very unlikely scenario involving a third country trying to embroil the United States and the Soviet Union in hostilities by a nuclear attack on one or both. After the United States and the U.S.S.R. had destroyed each other, the wily third country would inherit the earth—radiation and all. Not much stock was put in this theory. But the U.S.S.R. apparently did not put it past its former fraternal socialist country, China, or perhaps in the longer future, Germany, to scheme in some such manner.

Semenov, elaborating on the provocative attack idea, said that a third party possessing a minor nuclear potential could, for the purpose of creating conflict between our countries, resort to a provocation involving the use of nuclear missiles. For example some third country could strike the territory of one or both countries with missiles launched from a submarine. Each side would evaluate this situation in its own way. Could not such an incident result in a conflict? It seemed useful to discuss the question of actions by our two countries in the event of a provocative use of nuclear weapons by a third country. At the next round of SALT the Soviets were vigorously to pursue this provocative attack matter.

The U.S.S.R. delegation expressed concern about the possibility of transfers to third countries of the weapons limited by a SALT agreement. Where would it lead, they asked, if one side, while observing the agreed levels of its own strategic weapons, were to transfer similar weapons in excess of such levels to third countries, or were to render other countries technical and other assistance in the development of such weapons? There would be a further stepping up of the arms race, an increase in the risk of a nuclear conflict and international tension. The Soviets remembered that in 1957 the United States had offered to make ballistic missiles (but not their nuclear components) available to its NATO allies, including the Federal Republic of Germany; the U.S. multilateral force proposal of 1963; and that the United States had provided Polaris missiles and related technology to the United Kingdom. We replied that issues affecting third countries were beyond the scope of SALT. I stated at a plenary meeting that the United States was not about to prejudice interests of allies in order to reach an arrangement with the U.S.S.R. Obviously if a party to a SALT agreement were to upset an agreed strategic balance by substantial transfers of weapons, that would remove the basis for the agreement.

I wrote the President:

The one subject that I think might qualify as a "surprise" to us was the Soviet reference to the possibility of some sort of supplement to the Non-Proliferation Treaty in the form of an agreement not to transfer strategic weapons delivery systems to other countries. I told them that this was beyond the scope of our talks, but I predict that this will be a real problem if we get down to serious negotiation. I think what they have in mind is the danger to them if an agreement was reached with us to freeze certain US/USSR weapons systems but leaving us free to then transfer similar weapons systems (retaining custody of the nuclear components) to third countries—or transfer entire strategic delivery systems to the British. At first glance, it seems to me that in theory this is a "Loophole" that will have to be given a good deal of thought. Of course, it has for the Soviets the advantage of being potentially a divisive issue between the U.S. and its allies—especially if the Soviets press for definition as strategic of certain delivery systems which we have supplied our allies, *e.g.,* fighter bombers capable of striking targets in the USSR.

Another Soviet concern was the possibility of accidental or unauthorized use of nuclear weapons. Even if the sides succeeded in reducing the risk of war by an agreed limitation of these weapons, they said, the risk of their unauthorized use would remain. Accidents involving nuclear weapons might occur regardless of a SALT agreement. Semenov noted that large numbers of people were involved in handling nuclear weapons. One could not ignore the fact that manning of existing arsenals involved a certain risk of unauthorized use with all of the dangers and consequences ensuing therefrom. The Soviet delegation suggested that some unspecified technical and organizational measures be agreed upon to reduce these risks. One official mentioned privately that a "hot line" circuit could be used to signal immediately that a third-country or accidental launch was not the beginning of a super-power attack.

They appeared to take this range of contingencies quite seriously. We recalled that their main interest at a conference in 1958 on reducing the dangers of surprise attack had been nuclear accidents. Their concern, they said, stemmed from the physical and organizational difficulties of command and control by political and military leaders over the large number of weapons now in the strategic arsenals. We argued that accidental and unauthorized use could be discussed in relation to the size and qualities of strategic forces, but not if the discussion was to touch upon political questions involving third countries. We offered to have reciprocal exchanges regarding safety precautions covering nuclear weapons, but the Soviets in effect replied that their safety precautions were just fine. Soviet seriousness on this point was sufficient, however, to make me wonder if they had not had a close call of some sort. The United States, it will be recalled, has had several accidents involving nuclear weapons but without nuclear explosions. Two agreements relating to the "accident" problem were concluded with the U.S.S.R. in September 1971.

Semenov now made two specific proposals. One, of an earlier vintage, would have put restrictions on the ocean areas in which missile submarines and aircraft carriers could operate. A second was to limit flights of nuclear-armed aircraft to national air space. He argued that nuclear armed practice flights beyond national air space were not militarily significant. SALT, we said, was a negotiation about limitations on weapons and not about the operations of ships and planes. The United States no longer conducts such flights but might want to at some time in the future.

"Can it be verified?" That was the first question that came to mind when we considered possible limitations. United States positions for SALT were considered by an interagency group called the Verification Panel to give verification issues special treatment in response to concerns expressed by military officials. President Nixon had stressed verification in a letter to me:

> . . . I will accept limitations on our forces only after I have assured myself of our ability to detect Soviet failure to implement limitations on their own forces in sufficient time to protect our security interests. . . . I am determined to avoid, within the Government and in the country at large, divisive disputes regarding Soviet compliance or non-compliance with an understanding or agreement. Nor will I bequeath to a future President the seeds of such disputes. . . . Any agreed limitations must therefore meet the test of verifiability. I recognize that this may not be obtainable with 100 percent assurance; but the margin of uncertainty must be reasonable.

A major asymmetry in SALT was in verification requirements, specifically, the degree to which the sides would have to rely on national technical means of verification. National means of verification are space satellites for photography and other remote electronic detection devices. The asymmetry arises because the U.S.S.R. has access to an enormous flow of information about U.S. nuclear weapons programs in open literature. Our political system precludes, at least in peacetime, secret weapons developments. The Soviets remain suspicious of inspection as an intrusion which they say is designed to discover weakness and sow dissent. Because of our open society and information I don't believe the Soviets are seriously concerned that the United States would fail to fulfill any arms control commitment. However, because the U.S.S.R. is a secretive closed society, the United States had to be much warier—even if Lenin's aphorism that treaties are like piecrusts, made to be broken, was made in reference to arrangements between domestic political factions and not to international obligations. I put this difference in verification needs to Semenov. He often spoke of objective facts. While the verification asymmetry was not sufficient to prevent agreement on arms limitations, it was an objective fact that the Soviet Union would need to rely much less on national technical means than the United States would. I don't recall any disagreement on his part.

The Nixon Administration, as SALT started, believed that national means of verification could be relied on to monitor a number of possible limitations, especially ceilings on numbers of missile launchers. But if limits were also to affect characteristics of weapons, some form of inspection in the Soviet Union (and for mutuality in the United States) might be necessary. Early in the first Helsinki round Semenov raised the flag of national technical means of verification as the primary technique for monitoring fulfillment of any agreement. He stopped short of saying that no other techniques should be permitted. I agreed that national means of verification would have a central role, but pointed out that some other methods might also be needed. Although national means may be satisfactory for some limitations, they alone might be insufficient for others. Cooperative arrangements to aid verification in addition to national means might be desirable.[3]

---

[3] E.g., a side could inquire about facilities or activities that raised questions of compliance and the other side could give answers that would provide additional reassurance. Procedures could be agreed on to verify that replacement of one kind of launchers with another was being carried out

Well, it was a start. But the negative attitude about inspection was obvious. We wondered if Semenov had left the door slightly ajar only to avoid a breakdown of SALT in its preliminary stage over this issue which had torpedoed so many arms control conferences in the past.

Our primary objective now was to develop a work program for the subsequent negotiation. The delegation was well aware of the tangles one can get into in trying to draft a conference agenda with the Soviet Union.

We proposed that there be no formal agenda. Either side could raise any strategic arms question at any time. Consideration might be given to the following weapons systems, including their launchers and other component parts: ABMs and anti-aircraft systems (SAMs), ICBMs and any other systems of intercontinental range, MR/IRBMs, SLBMs, SLCMs, and strategic bombers and defenses against them. Various methods of limitation should be considered, for example, restrictions on numbers or on deliverable payloads. After the exchanges over the status of lighter delivery aircraft (FBS), we stated that this was the reason the term "strategic bombers" had been chosen without further defining the type of aircraft.

It was decided to have the work program discussed in a group of four advisers. The Soviets quickly agreed on the purpose and nature of the work program and that it should remain private. But they maintained that the ideas proposed took no account of Soviet views, which opposed limitations on air defenses, IR/MRBMs and SLCMs. They also wanted to include FBS. Given the U.S. definition of "strategic," the "strategic bomber" category was too restrictive for them. They did not see how restrictions on payload could be verified without intrusive inspections. The U.S.S.R. wanted to add five items: (1) "principles for determining strategic systems"; (2) "measures to reduce the outbreak of war"; (3) "accidental and unauthorized launches

---

according to the agreement. We raised the idea of selective direct observation, which was essentially on-the-spot inspection, to provide insurance which could not otherwise be had. The best reaction we could get from the Soviet delegation was that these suggestions could be discussed. They repeated the position that national means alone were sufficient. Semenov said that additional techniques to supplement national means could make verification itself a source of uncertainty and distrust.

and third-country provocation"; (4) "restrictions on submarine patrols"; and (5) "non-transfer." We objected to the first and fourth items. They urged that we reconsider a non-transfer provision. The working group finally recommended a compromise deleting all references to specific weapons systems.

We then formally tabled a draft work program, not meant to give either side a procedural advantage in later talks or to prevent either side from raising any relevant items at any time. Neither side would be committed to include any items in the final agreement. Substantive differences would be settled in later negotiations. The weapons systems section of the new work program was greatly simplified. It could cover various components including "launchers, missiles, boosters, radars, penetration aids, MIRVs, MRVs, chaff,[4] and decoys." We interpreted limitations broadly as either a freeze or upward or downward adjustments in weapons levels. There would be discussion of verification, "including national means and possible means for providing additional reassurances." We emphasized that verification should be discussed in connection with specific proposals rather than in the abstract. We would agree to have an omnibus paragraph incorporating Soviet proposals include accidental launches or unauthorized use and problems involving a threat from a third nuclear power.

Semenov thought that the Illustrative Elements had envisaged a quantitative limitation on launchers, but other U.S. statements apparently suggested limiting the total payload of missile forces. He asked if this "dual approach" would not complicate the problem. Dealing with individual components and characteristics would involve the parties too deeply in the nuances of control. Some on the Soviet delegation seemed to consider the Illustrative Elements a formal U.S. proposal. One Soviet said that the Illustrative Elements were not difficult to understand but the U.S. desire for limitations by components was a completely opposite approach. The delegation repeated that the Illustrative Elements were in fact illustrative and not proposals. Soviet responses indicated these points were helpful in understanding the U.S. position, but they continued their attack on "components."

The exchanges over the U.S. suggested work program showed

4 Techniques for neutralizing radar systems.

that we could expect continued opposition to on-site inspection. One Soviet official recalled an American's offer at an earlier U.S.-Soviet academic conference: "You can come and look at our missiles and see for yourself." Such an approach was impossible for the Soviet Union. It was contrary to the principle of not prejudicing the interests of either side. A Soviet general noted that any verification of missiles or their components as opposed to launchers would require on-site inspection. Limitations could be verified only by taking the missile apart, putting it on a test stand, or perhaps by witnessing test launches. All of this would require the physical presence of verification personnel. Another Soviet asked how we proposed to verify restrictions placed on component parts; specifically, how would one verify a ban or limitation on chaff and decoys? He answered his question. It would be necessary literally to open up the warhead of a missile. That would be against the security interests of either side and incompatible with an agreement. The delegation advised Washington that we probably had not dispelled Soviet concerns over the verification problems that they believed were associated with the inclusion of components parts. The Soviets might connect the question of U.S. seriousness of purpose with our proposal to get into issues involving missile "components."

Semenov then presented a Soviet draft for a still more general work program, saying that, since differences could not be resolved until the later talks, he saw no need to reflect them in the work program. This draft was the basis for the finally agreed work program, which in effect merely provided that each side could raise any subject at any time.

All that remained at Helsinki was to agree on the time and place of the next SALT session. As Christmas approached, it was obvious that both sides had had their say and that the time had come for Washington and Moscow to take stock and plan for another round. We now engaged in some unpleasantries. The Soviets proposed a vague resumption date, sometime from March to May 1970. I questioned this recess as too long. Semenov believed that much homework had to be done. We were told that their delegation had prepared for only two or three contingencies at Helsinki; they would have to prepare for eight or ten at the next session. Moscow's position on the resumption of SALT had been influenced by a recent NATO communiqué on a European security conference and a recent statement by Secretary Rogers was called by one Soviet "the toughest yet." He and some others in Moscow recognized that favorable times for successful SALT did not occur often and would not last indefinitely. He pointed out that Semenov was new to disarmament and one of his main activities before Helsinki had been preparing a European security conference. The Soviets were also interested in getting the two parts of Germany starting to talk to each other.

After much grumbling we settled on April 16. The question of where to resume work was even more prickly. Our proposal drew a rough reaction. Vienna was absolutely unsuitable to the Soviets. Helsinki had worked out well and we should plan to return there. I guessed that the Soviets thought that Vienna presented too much of a security risk. Thousands of Czech émigrés had settled there after the "beloved enemy" Warsaw Pact invasion of Czechoslovakia in 1968. Semenov probably had participated in Soviet policy making for that affair.

Thinking, I suppose, that the American urge to be home for Christmas would lead us to go along with the Soviet preference, Semenov procrastinated, coming back several times with reports of new instructions from Moscow calling for a return to Helsinki. We then heard that the Soviet delegation had reluctantly recommended Vienna to their Moscow authorities. I contacted the White House and advised Semenov that the President personally had decided that Helsinki was not suitable and that he preferred Vienna. Semenov then proposed to leave open the site question for later decision. Prospects for substantive agreements would not seem bright, I said, if we could not even agree on a place to negotiate. Finally, with a nudge from the White House and the wisdom of Solomon, it was agreed on our last day in Helsinki to alternate future meetings between Vienna and Helsinki. For the next year we went against the grain of the season, spending wintry months in Finland and summer months in Austria. Later, with better meteorological foresight, that was corrected.

Although things had been going reasonably well at Helsinki, the delegation was aware of the price being paid for the passage of time. Our report to President Nixon pointed out that, given the continuing Soviet deployment of ICBMs and SLBMs, the interval proposed by Moscow before resuming in Vienna would tend to strengthen the Soviet bargaining position. The relative numbers in the strategic forces were changing and I never stopped worrying during SALT about the Soviets possibly using the negotiations to mask deployment of a much larger missile force than the United States.

We had not started building any ICBM and SLBM launchers since 1967. The Soviets had been adding 250 ICBM launchers a year since 1967, building up from 300 in 1966, to 1,300 by 1970. Of these, some 240 were the giant SS-9s which some considered a special threat to U. S. ICBMs. And then there was a steady stream of pictures showing Soviet nuclear missile submarines being added to their strategic forces. The Soviets in 1969 began building seven or eight strategic submarines with 112 to 128 missile launchers each year—the annual addition being equal to the size of their SLBM fleet in 1968. There was something especially sinister about those submarines, which memories of World War II and half memories of the Great War made more real to me, while the ICBM silos, concrete cylinders in the ground, contained a force in being never before put into the earth.

Each time photographs from satellites were flown over to us abroad and we saw the relentless build-up of ICBM silos, the delegation wondered when the Soviet build-up would stop. My concern about what the Soviets are aiming for has never been entirely dispelled. It was clear that they wanted to stop the ABM but what else? Even after the SALT I agreements, one could entertain not unreasonable night thoughts as to where the strategic balance could be in another decade. The SALT II treaty is aimed at reducing this uncertainty. Neither side had any illusions that SALT I would be a final solution for the nuclear rivalry. Both sides continued weapons construction programs. At least ABM defenses are now under close wraps—and SALT II could put real constraints on offensive forces.

The preliminary Helsinki round ended December 22. In the closing statement I said that the relative absence of polemics had been a source of satisfaction. It was not easy for governments to communicate satisfactorily with each other on complicated questions involving issues central to their national security. Our exchanges in Helsinki and the opportunity for the various members of our two delegations to become acquainted with each other had been helpful in starting a process of better communication and greater understanding.

The first encounter had been a success. Both sides felt that continuation of the negotiation was assured. Semenov told me how important Helsinki had been in persuading his leadership that this was a serious negotiation well worth pursuing. Both sides had talked hardware as well as strategy and international politics. The delegation's report to the President noted a surprisingly broad area of comparability in statements of general concepts: on mutual deterrence; on ABM-related instabilities; on the interrelationship between offensive and defensive weapons and the need to limit both; and on the absence of political preconditions for SALT progress. The delicate problem of how to detect possible violations had been considered. Members of the delegations had met and measured each other and realized that they were well matched.

In a final personal report to the President I noted:

> My hunch at this very early stage of the talks is that Soviet purposes are a mix of at least three possible main ingredients: a) To see if an arrangement can be negotiated that would improve their prospects, or stabilize the strategic balance at lower cost; b) To "cover" their ICBM/SLBM buildup and hopefully to defer, if not defeat, a U.S. reaction; c) To advance their general arms control image as well as their specific non-proliferation interests by appearing to meet the obligations of Article VI (NPT).

The delegation concluded that the Soviet commitment to proceed with the negotiations probably had been made only after the Helsinki talks were well under way. Several Soviets had emphasized the importance of their decision to continue the talks. After the final plenary, one of their advisers said that, while "old hands" knew that discussions were possible between the United States and the U.S.S.R., a very important result of the session was that others now had this impression.

The delegation had a number of specific questions for Washington to resolve. Should qualitative controls as well as quantitative limitations be attempted? Should we seek controls on MIRVs? At what level should ABMs be limited? What was the real danger of SAM upgrade? Should there be limitations on strategic bombers? How should equal ceilings for offensive forces and the forward-based systems issue be dealt with? Should mobile ICBM launchers be banned or put under a ceiling with fixed-base ICBMs? Should we insist on limits on the Soviet IR/MRBMs? Could we monitor an agreement with national technical means of verification only? Should we pursue agreements covering accidental and unauthorized use of nuclear weapons and the provocative attack problems? There was a lot of work to be done in Washington and our four-month recess would not be much of a rest.

All the issues of importance considered later at SALT were discussed at Helsinki—ABM levels, offensive missile launcher limits, forward-based systems, provocative attack and accident controls. Positions and perceptions stemming from this first encounter shaped the rest of the negotiation. Working habits and negotiating styles were established. The Soviet approach of stressing principles persisted well into the negotiation.

The U.S. approach to these preliminary talks had proven to be well designed to ferret out the coincident and conflicting interests of the United States and the Soviet Union. Whether the common interests were substantial enough to lead to an agreement remained to be seen.

THE HOME FRONT

Washington SALT planning, the preparation of instructions to the delegation and the oversight of the day-to-day negotiation were under direct White House control to a greater extent than in any other international negotiation I had ever been involved in. Policy making for the SALT segment of the international relations of the United States was carved out of the normal sphere of the State Department and handled largely by the White House.

This was accomplished in the so-called "National Security Council system." It gathered the lines of SALT policy making into the White House, where they were worked on by a staff headed by Kissinger. This staff drafted policy papers for consideration by the Verification Panel and the National Security Council. After a presidential decision the Kissinger staff drafted guidance for the Washington agencies and the delegation.

The key committee was the Verification Panel, chaired by Kissinger. I had suggested in June 1969 that it be set up, to focus —as its name suggested—on matters involving verifiability of proposals. It quickly took on much broader responsibilities. In addition to Kissinger and myself its members included David Packard, the Deputy Secretary of Defense, Admiral Tom Moorer, chairman of the Joint Chiefs, Elliot Richardson and later John

Irwin, Undersecretaries of State, Richard Helms, CIA director, and John Mitchell, the Attorney General. Working groups under the Verification Panel generally included representatives of all these agencies except the Justice Department.

A working group of the Verification Panel assigned studies to staff analysts or to working groups throughout the bureaucracy, monitored this work, wrote the initial summaries spelling out conflicting agency views, and submitted papers to the Verification Panel. This working group was chaired by Laurence Lynn and later by K. Wayne Smith, Kissinger's NSC staff deputies for analysis.

Day-to-day liaison between the Washington agencies and the delegation was handled by a Backstopping Committee which cleared instructions to the delegation. Chaired by Phil Farley, this group functioned smoothly as a coordinating mechanism throughout the negotiation. Conflicts that arose (as earlier described) were kept to a minimum.

The effect of this system was that all policy papers were handled under Kissinger's guidance, and those that reached the President contained several options with arguments spelled out pro and con. Proponents of the system believed that it ensured that conflicting agency positions were clearly laid out for the President and not lost in compromises negotiated at a lower level. Development of SALT policy was cited by the Administration as a model of how the National Security Council system worked best. In the words of one NSC official, it was "a model process for analyzing issues for the President and putting everything on a firm, factual basis."

A serious flaw was that Kissinger, as the assistant to the President for National Security Affairs, director of the NSC staff, and chairman of the Verification Panel, had too much influence. I must say that he had us all buffaloed. Nothing could go forward without his approval, be it a press release, a briefing of the North Atlantic Council or an interagency study on a major aspect of the negotiation. Time and again meetings he had called were canceled and set for a later day. It got to be a joke—but not a very funny one. At times, he seemed to be the only one in the cast of SALT characters who was free to take initiatives. Presumably he was at all times consulting with the President and merely passing on his wishes, but it seemed quite clear that Kissinger was often acting as a principal, not an agent.

The National Security Council itself is less potent than folklore would have it. It is not a decisional body. The President merely consults with its members. Often it seemed to me during attendance at some seventy meetings from 1957 to 1972 that much of this consultation was pro forma. Often the main motivation for an NSC meeting appeared to be to provide against the need for an affirmative answer if something went wrong and a question was raised in the Congress as to whether the NSC had been consulted.

SALT was discussed in the National Security Council at least ten times from 1969 through 1972. Quite noticeable was the difference between the knowledge of SALT issues of the professionals and that of the politicians around the table. I was often uncomfortable hearing cabinet officers' views so at odds with what the SALT bureaucracy took for granted.

Secretary of State Rogers sometimes seemed to be trying to get me to avoid advocating specific measures at NSC meetings, telling me once that the President did not like to have personal confrontations between his defense and diplomatic advisers at such meetings. I had difficulty reconciling this with the President's stated policy of wanting to hear all differing points of view before making decisions.

As I believe had been the case with his predecessors, Nixon seldom made SALT decisions at National Security Council meetings. They were taken, with Kissinger's counsel, before or after NSC sessions, then circulated as National Security Decision Memoranda (NSDMs). These memos at times were very complicated, combining substance with negotiating strategy and tactics. They were drafted by NSC staff members who, although quite well informed, did not have the technical background in strategic arms and their control that a number of officials in the agencies and on the delegation had. Often NSDM instructions had to be revised when errors and inconsistencies were pointed out. Questioning SALT guidance seemed to anger White House officials. Such guidance was supposed to have an ex cathedra nature. But as SALT continued several officials from the delegation became members of the NSC staff and the situation improved.

Even at the Verification Panel, exchanges were hardly scintillating. They consisted for the most part of relatively wooden statements, of agency views spoken almost "by rote," mostly by officials whose exposure to SALT issues was only sporadic. Some Panel members had neither the time nor the inclination to read detailed papers prepared for these meetings. Their knowledge of the issues being considered seemed to be based largely on one- or two-page memos, sometimes beefed up by a last-minute briefing session by knowledgeable middle-level officials.

Kissinger used the Verification Panel to inform and prepare himself to brief the President and to guide NSC meetings in the direction he deemed desired by the President. He obviously was a high-ranking student in this class, worked the hardest, and had the advantage usually of being able to reserve his opinions for his principal, the chief magistrate. Kissinger usually put on a show. He was invariably late for meetings—sometimes half an hour behind time—keeping a half dozen top government officials twiddling their thumbs. A Harvard colleague of his told me that Kissinger had told him he deliberately came late to all classes that he taught. That let the students know who was boss. Panel members seemed to regard him with amused admiration mixed with hostility, puzzlement and chagrin. Having insight as to how the President's mind was assessing any given issue, he generally was well ahead of the other Verification panelists. He enjoyed baiting military and intelligence professionals and demonstrating to diplomats and arms controllers his large command of the theoretical bases for strategic arms limitations. A standard feature of Verification Panel meetings was a note passed to the chairman, his abrupt departure and absence for up to half an hour during which many top government officials wasted time in small talk. Then a hurried return after presumably an urgent presidential session of great import. Usually the break in the SALT discussion was followed by a short resumption and a quick adjournment as it became clear that Kissinger had some different preoccupation weighing on his mind. My impression on leaving Verification Panel meetings was that they were perfunctory and made little contribution to solving problems, but rather were recitals of departmental positions fairly well known to all hands before the meeting. The bureaucracy had a highly developed interagency intelligence system to keep track of the status of various SALT possibilities at all times.

To get views across to the White House, I depended more on memoranda to the President and to Kissinger. This did not conform with the multi-agency committee approach that the White House preferred. But a decisional system depending on positions orally expressed in committees is far from the best way to generate precise, responsible advice about an international operation as complicated as SALT. I suspect that a thorough investigation of agency positions as put through the NSC machinery would draw many a blank.

SALT as a general proposition was of great interest to the Congress but in hearings before four committees—the Senate and House Armed Services and Foreign Affairs Committees—I got the impression that few members found time to do the "homework" needed to get a confident understanding of the major issues. Many members were ready to sign resolutions urging various SALT moves. But few took the trouble to visit the SALT negotiations in Europe and talk to the delegates at length about issues and prospects. Senator John Sherman Cooper of Kentucky was an exception. He steeped himself in SALT, visited the delegation abroad a number of times and was of great help in assuring the Congress in 1972 that it should support the agreements. Congressman Clement Zablocki was the most persistent overseer of SALT in the House—and a strong supporter during and after the negotiation. Senator Jackson of Washington had by far the best technical grasp of the subject matter but a deep suspicion of the Nixon Administration's ability to negotiate firmly with the Soviets. I sensed that he was dubious about the good faith of the Soviets. He tended to feel that, if they did not accept American proposals for curbing increases in numbers of launchers for large missiles or for reducing forces, they somehow were not acting in good faith. For him, American adjustments in position in the negotiating process were signs of weakness reflecting a failure to understand that the Soviets were aiming for strategic superiority. Jackson also had been convinced during the ABM debate of 1969 that unless ICBMs were given protection by defensive missiles they would soon be vulnerable to a sudden Soviet strike, and he wanted any SALT agreement to have a relatively high ABM limit to allow for such defense. He correctly concluded that the very low ABM limits that the Administration tended to favor were militarily meaningless. He told me on several occasions that he preferred a ban to such low levels. So did I. Senator Jackson carried the additional burden of suspecting that those who did not agree with him were soft-headed, woolly thinkers—"arms controllers." And he exaggerated their influence.

Although SALT policy was made through the NSC system, the parochial interests of the agencies in good measure shaped the final product. Secretary of Defense Laird was concerned lest certain assumptions with which he did not agree be taken for granted. At an NSC meeting he listed them: (1) that some arms control would be better than none; (2) that both sides had the purpose of merely keeping a retaliatory capacity; (3) that Soviet interest in SALT paralleled our own; (4) that the Soviet economy could stand a new round in the arms competition and was not feeling a great pinch at the present time because of defense requirements; (5) that the United States had a capability to calculate the present and prospective balance of forces; (6) that performance of a SALT agreement could be monitored with ease and confidence. I did not know where he had got these ideas. Neither the State Department nor ACDA relied on such assumptions. However, they were useful straw men in the skillful hands of the Secretary of Defense.

As I was taking over the directorship of ACDA, I had paid him a courtesy call. He asked if "they" had told me that he wanted me to be Assistant Secretary of Defense for International Security Affairs (ISA). That had been news to me. The ISA job had been a key position in previous administrations. Unfortunately, from 1969 to 1973 ISA did not have a major role in SALT, which was largely handled in the office of the Secretary of Defense by more technically oriented officials. Even in the Pentagon arms control matters should be staffed to some extent by people having special responsibility for them rather than be left for the most part to the mercies of people whose major responsibilities are for the development of weapons systems.

In ACDA there were a number of officers having as much if not more experience negotiating with the U.S.S.R. than anyone in the government. They took a pragmatic, realistic view of the limited possibilities of a first strategic arms negotiation. Our purpose was making a start on bringing the competition under some control. Certain Department of Defense officials who were relatively new to arms control work thought that more could be obtained in the way of limiting strategic weapons characteristics. They wanted not only to stop the numbers competition but also to moderate the growing threat to our strategic forces from very large Soviet ICBMs. They felt that if the Soviets were serious they should be willing to agree to treaty provisions having this purpose. But these officials did not support the one measure that would have accomplished this purpose, a MIRV ban. Instead they concentrated on ideas for limiting the payload of Soviet ICBMs and reducing the number of their launchers. This in effect was an effort to restructure the Soviet missile forces to more nearly resemble the American force structure. Although a highly desirable goal, this seemed to me an impractical proposition.

The Joint Chiefs did not appear interested in this approach, and the split of opinion between officials in the office of the Secretary of Defense and the military views expressed by the chairman of the JCS most likely eased President Nixon's task of making decisions for SALT agreements. While leery of any arms control agreement, the Chiefs were persuaded that a simple first agreement placing ceilings on offensive launchers and ABMs could be in the United States' interest. Had the Chiefs supported the positions of the civilian officials in the Defense Department, I doubt that the 1972 SALT agreements would have been reached.

Most officials in ACDA felt that the best we could do to limit offensive systems—once a MIRV ban had been abandoned (as will be described in Chapter 4)—was to try for a ceiling on offensive launcher numbers, which would be a move toward reducing the first strike danger. Although there was a strong interest in some form of ABM limitation, our civilian friends in the Defense Department were of two minds. They recognized that a widespread defense by ABMs could be destabilizing, but they also wanted to deploy an ABM system to defend ICBMs from the projected Soviet threat.

CIA officials seemed reasonably sanguine about the capability of U.S. intelligence to verify fulfillment of any SALT agreement that appeared at all negotiable. Doubts on this score were raised by officials in the office of the Secretary of Defense whose enthusiasm for a SALT agreement was less than great. There seemed to be a direct relationship between an individual's attitude toward an arms limitation agreement and his confidence in its verifiability. I suppose these opponents felt that proponents of SALT tended to give the benefit of the doubt to American verification capabilities.

There were a few officials—and I respected their opinions—who felt that strategic weapons could be safely brought under control if the United States would only adopt less unyielding positions. These people seemed to me to perform a useful balancing function in countering the inclination of many government officials to think that American negotiating positions are always right and Soviet positions wrong. This minority may be more idealistic than most officials but such idealism is a useful ingredient in preparing for an arms control negotiation. Such individuals never had undue influence in the Nixon Administration. By any standard except that of anti-Communist ideologues, the United States SALT delegates were hard-nosed cold war veterans.

SALT delegation officials, both military and civilian, believed that neither the Soviets nor the United States were under any overriding need to reach a SALT agreement. Most of us felt that a modest first agreement was probably all that was possible. While we hoped for success, we would not have been chagrined at failure. SALT seemed like a long shot but one worth pursuing. We saw SALT as a protracted process which could at least lead to better understanding and hopefully to restraints in the common interest.

It was some ten months into the first Nixon administration before the negotiation started. During this period there was plenty of time to construct what Kissinger called "building blocks," products of problem analysis which identified possible limitations and preplanned possible changes if progress in one direction proved impractical. Some of us thought that the trumpet was somewhat overblown when the White House boasted of this preparatory work. Hear this from the President: "The fact that the agreements were signed only two years after the first specific proposals were introduced by the United States testifies to the value of that approach . . . we wanted to ensure that when deadlocks did occur, they would not be over technical issues, and carefully analyzed alternatives would be ready for my immediate decision." We will see that sometimes the alternatives chosen were neither analyzed nor immediately decided. I don't recall the delegation's ever having need to examine a "building block" as it went about the work of trying to find mutually acceptable limitations. Nor did the three White House interventions into the negotiation seem to have been guided by any building block of which I was aware. But the overall negotiation was well prepared. A large amount of Washington analysis preceded and accompanied it. Too much, some thought, as they worked all through many a night to produce papers they knew would not be read by high officials.

A good deal has been written about the several optional approaches used by the U.S. delegation in the early stage of the negotiations. Here is a quick subsurface glance at how they came about. In March 1970, as the President was deciding on the United States negotiating position for Vienna, I wrote him personal views. At this early stage of the negotiations I felt that national security interests would be best served by trying to reach comprehensive limitations rather than a simple agreement freezing numbers of missile launchers. A limited agreement would not resolve a number of concerns about the sufficiency of future U.S. strategic forces. It also might leave unchecked a costly, risky competition in areas left unlimited. We should fully test the nature and depth of Soviet interest in arms control.

While recognizing that a first SALT agreement would have to be somewhat experimental because of its sensitive and unprecedented nature and the risks and uncertainties involved, I argued for a MIRV ban and very low levels or even a complete ban on ABM deployments. "If a MIRV ban and low or zero ABM levels can be negotiated with the conditions which have been worked out in the Verification Panel, and for a short term of perhaps five years, I think that United States security would be subject to no greater risks than obtain under the present uncontrolled situation." I recalled that the General Advisory Committee of the Arms Control Agency had reached the same conclusions.

I also advised the President of some political and tactical reasons why we should attempt to reach comprehensive limitations.

From an international as well as domestic political point of view, it strikes me that if a posture is adopted of not trying for controls over MIRVs or for ABM levels less than the full Safeguard program (12 sites), there will be heavy psychological costs. . . . If SALT fails, Congressional support for strategic weapons programs in the future may depend in good part on the nature of United States SALT offers that the Soviets would not accept. . . . I believe from the negotiation point of view that it would be preferable for us to put forward proposals for comprehensive SALT arrangements at Vienna. This will help us to take control of the negotiation process. We would, of course, retain the option of agreeing to simpler quantitative arrangements if that proves to be all the Soviets are interested in or all they will agree to on our conditions.

At an NSC meeting on March 25, 1970, most of the members did not flatly oppose a MIRV ban. They would be for it if . . . I added up the "ifs" to point out to the President what a heavy burden the conditions proposed by his other advisers would place on a MIRV ban. They were: (a) ABMs must be brought under control; (b) all other parts of the SALT package must be suitable; (c) the Soviets would have to destroy substantial amounts of radar; (d) testing restraints on MIRV-like objects would have to be agreed; (e) there would have to be on-site inspection and (f) reductions in offensive arms. I wondered if such a proposal would look serious. Just as we were worried about the Soviets upgrading anti-aircraft systems, they must be concerned about our upgrading MIRVs to make them a threat to their ICBMs. I was surprised when General Wheeler agreed with this idea. MIRV was our only ongoing program in offensive weapons. Unless they were put on the table we would be proposing no restraints on existing American programs while asking the Soviets to stop all of their strategic missile launcher programs.

The President was in good humor. He said to his officials, Speak up, don't be afraid to be later proved wrong. Everybody was for an agreement. It was only a question of whether such an agreement was possible. The Department of Defense, he added, had been forthcoming and flexible. Naturally, they looked at things more from a military security point of view. ACDA and State looked at things more from an arms control point of view. Some people in Washington had gone overboard at both ends of this spectrum. That was not the case with anyone at this meeting.

President Nixon seemed intrigued with the possibilities of negotiating reductions in strategic forces. Paul Nitze outlined the case for reductions but admitted that their negotiability was marginal. He assumed that we must keep MIRVs and that meant the Soviets would soon have them, and that meant that Minuteman would soon be vulnerable, and that would lead to crisis instability. He felt that we could not deploy new submarines before 1978 and it would take some fifteen years to replace the Minuteman ICBM force with sea-based missile launchers. He did not sound very optimistic. It seemed to me by the meeting's end that with the exception of one or two uniformed military officers all believed our ICBMs were something of a wasting asset.

I told Secretary Rogers I thought the discussion indicated that we were about to put together a classical non-negotiable proposal. I reminded him that some years before we had tabled at the Geneva Conference on Disarmament a proposal for a 30 per cent reduction in strategic nuclear delivery vehicles as part of a general and complete disarmament program. I felt that if we continued in this way we would get the worst of both possible worlds— no SALT agreement while failing to convince Congress that we had really made an effort.

After the meeting the President directed that four alternate SALT approaches be prepared which in addition to limiting offensive missile launchers would have the following features: (A) would permit a relatively large number of ABM sites (twelve) and permit MIRVs; (B) would ban ABMs or limit them to one site apiece to defend capitals, and permit MIRVs; (C) would either ban ABMs or limit them to one site apiece and ban MIRVs; (D) would require substantial reductions in ICBM launchers but permit MIRVs. He set a deadline of two weeks for the job.

Rather than following the usual practice of designating an agency to prepare the paper, Raymond Garthoff of the State Department, the delegation's executive officer, was asked to prepare a draft. Three days later, after a virtually non-stop effort, he came up with an 82-page document. The paper was put in final form three days before the President's deadline. It proposed that each side's missile launchers be limited to the then U.S. total of 1,054 ICBM launchers and 656 SLBM launchers, an aggregate ceiling of 1,710. The United States had maintained this level for some years and there were no plans to increase it. The Soviet Union then had 1,560 operational ICBM and SLBM launchers, and about 400 more under construction. A ceiling of 1,710 would have allowed them to complete roughly half of the launchers then under construction. The paper proposed limiting heavy bombers, Soviet MR/IRBMs, and submarine-launched cruise missiles at their then levels. For the first ABM alternative (A), it proposed 1,000 interceptors (the twelve-site Safeguard program had called for 879). For capital defense (B), 100 ABM interceptors were proposed. Representatives of the Secretary of Defense and the Joint Chiefs proposed that any MIRV ban (C) be conditioned on on-site inspections. The reduction alternative (D) called for cuts of 100 ICBM launchers a year for seven years.

President Nixon must have understood the logic of banning MIRVs if we were able to negotiate a very low level on ABMs. The original primary mission for MIRVs had been to penetrate a dense screen of ABMs—that would no longer be necessary if ABMs were to be limited to a low level. But the President may have calculated that ABM limitation was all the traffic would bear, the "traffic" in this case being the Secretary of Defense, the Joint Chiefs, their supporters in Congress and their constituencies around the country. A serious effort to ban both MIRVs and ABMs might well make serious trouble for SALT. Whatever his reason, the President accepted the military's position that a MIRV ban required on-site inspection.

He also concluded that it was in the national interest to find out if a basis existed for a comprehensive agreement. He wanted the initial discussion to cover as broad a range of issues as possible. The delegation should first present Option C—the missile launcher limit plus the MIRV ban as a framework for this discussion. It was essential that the verification provisions be an integral part of the presentation because he was convinced that a MIRV ban without on-site inspection would create dangerous instabilities in U.S.-Soviet relations. The delegation should also present Option D—the missile launcher limit plus proposed reductions in ICBM launchers. After the discussion of these options, and in the light of any Soviet proposals, the President would judge whether an agreement acceptable to the United States was possible or whether other options should be explored. And so we spent many months at Vienna discussing Options C and D.

THE NEGOTIATION BEGINS

Vienna II:
April–August 1970

The April 16, 1970, opening session of the second round at Vienna was an even more splendid occasion than the start at Helsinki. It was held at the Belevedere Palace, onetime residence of Prince Eugene of Savoy. The delegation cars rolled up to a magnificent entrance behind squads of white-helmeted motorcycle policemen. Oversized American and Soviet flags whipped in the breeze. From the balcony a large part of Vienna was visible stretching out below the palace. The state treaty giving Austria back its independence was signed here in 1955. The American negotiator of that treaty had been Ambassador Tommy Thompson. (Foster Dulles had said as he stood with Molotov on that balcony after signing the state treaty and seeing tens of thousands of joyous Viennese shouting in the gardens below that it was the most thrilling moment of his life.) Little did we think that April day that we would still be at our labors in Vienna in the middle of August. This round was to be the longest of the SALT sessions, lasting 120 days.

The round had three phases. For about four weeks, until mid-May, the delegations presented comprehensive positions. Sharp differences soon became evident. Then for two months, until late July, they attempted to break the impasse by discussing issues on an item-by-item basis as permitted by the Helsinki Work Program. The plenary record was filled with tens of thousands of words. This was making a record to persuade authorities in Moscow and Washington that the positions favored by the sides were not negotiable and that progress depended on their being changed. The third and final phase lasted only a few weeks and consisted of the presentation of a compromise United States proposal, tabled on August 4. We argued its merits and listened to Soviet objections—and went home in mid-August, talked out.

At the start the delegation presented two alternative approaches for comprehensive limitations (set out in Appendix I) which reflected the President's decisions discussed in Chapter 2.

Why did they have to be so complicated? The Soviets seemed puzzled that we wanted to "tie so many knots." Our approaches reflected a number of strategic concerns. One was the worry that the U.S.S.R. might fail to fulfill its commitments, especially if they were vague, a legacy from our bad experience with the Yalta and other postwar agreements.

Many officials believed that the informal nuclear testing moratorium of 1958–60 had been breached by the Soviets. The fact is that before the U.S.S.R. resumed testing in 1961, President Eisenhower had declared the United States no longer bound by the arrangement, saying in a press release on December 29, 1959, "We consider ourselves free to resume nuclear weapon testing." The Soviet Union, as far as this writer can tell, except for several technical violations which it soon corrected, has lived up to its arms control commitments to the United States.

A number of our provisions were intended to ease the verification problem and to deter any possible Soviet attempts to evade SALT limitations. Much of the complexity of the U. S. ABM proposals reflected concern that the Soviets might use their massive anti-aircraft missile system for anti-ballistic missile purposes.

Targets of special American concern were launchers for modern large ICBMs (MLBMs).[1] In volume some eight times greater than the U. S. Minuteman ICBMs, their SS-9 missile can deliver a great weight of warheads. Some defense analysts believed that a sufficient number of MIRVed SS-9s could in time threaten the

[1] Then defined as a missile with a volume exceeding 70 cubic meters.

Minuteman force, even in hardened silo launchers. We aimed to limit the number of Soviet MLBMs to a level near the then Soviet force of 222 launchers operational (with 60 more under construction) at which the potential vulnerability of our ICBMs would still be tolerable. Even if attacked by a Soviet ICBM force of 280 SS-9s, it was calculated that enough Minutemen would survive to be an effective retaliatory force.

ICBM survivability was considered by many American officials an essential condition for strategic stability. They thought that the whole structure of balanced, stable deterrence might be weakened if the Soviet Union achieved a capability to destroy a substantial number of ICBMs and so might have some incentive to strike the United States first in a crisis. An MLBM limit of sorts was to prove negotiable in the May 1972 freeze, but it was porous and ICBM vulnerability is still a major anxiety of American force planners.

A central American concern was to assure that a stable state of mutual deterrence continue indefinitely to keep the risk of nuclear war as low as possible. New technology must not be allowed to erode the deterrent. Presenting the two U.S. approaches in the first weeks at Vienna, the delegation constantly stressed their advantages for ICBM survivability and strategic stability. The MIRV ban alternative would improve ICBM survivability by choking off the prime threat to ICBMs. The threat to the Minuteman force would come only after SS-9s were modernized with MIRVs (a fact that should have received more weight in Washington consideration of MIRV controls.) Reductions, we argued, would also strengthen stability by lowering the number of potentially vulnerable ICBM launchers and their percentage of the overall strategic forces. This reduction would diminish the possibility that either side would think it could gain advantage by a first strike.

The Soviet delegation tabled a document entitled "Basic Provisions for Limiting Strategic Armaments." Although Semenov called it a plan for concrete measures it was simple and in general terms. It called for limitations on strategic offensive armaments, defined as those capable of striking targets within the territory of the other side, regardless of where these armaments were deployed. Forward-based delivery systems in a geographic position to strike such targets should be destroyed or moved out of range. An unspecified aggregate total would be established for land-based ICBM launchers, ballistic missile launchers on nuclear submarines, and strategic bombers. Replacement of units of one type by those of another would be permitted. The *production* (but not testing) of multiple warheads of any kind and their installation in missiles would be banned. Limitations would be placed on ABM launchers and certain associated radars. Verification would be by national means only. No on-site inspection.

This was essentially a political document setting out principles. I wrote President Nixon that it was quite typical of Soviet practice in arms control negotiations. While their proposal contained much that was not in our interest or that of the North Atlantic Alliance, it was not just a propaganda device. It reflected the logic of their definition of what a strategic weapons system was. It seemed to be a typical Soviet comprehensive approach from which they might fall back if the Americans did not want to go as far in arms control as the U.S.S.R. This was the pattern they had followed during negotiations on General and Complete Disarmament, the Nuclear Test Ban, the Non-Proliferation and Seabeds treaties. They were staking out a maximum bargaining position, ostensibly based on reasonable principles and allowing great flexibility. Permitted levels for offensive systems were not specified. The Soviets never budged from the position that numbers would be disclosed and discussed only after agreement on principles. But we were assured that the fine print would pose no real problems.

What were the Soviets after? Apparently they were still undecided. Was SALT for real or not? They wanted to make a good record in case the talks collapsed. They introduced proposals from an earlier day, such as withdrawal from foreign bases and "no first use" of nuclear weapons. The Soviets no doubt hoped to bring influential elements of the U. S. Congress to their viewpoint and to encourage American unilateral disarmament.

But one clear Soviet objective was to bring ABMs under control. They knew that in a technological competition the United States could outrun them. Another main interest was to register superpower equality in offensive nuclear weapons. For a generation they had lived under the superiority of the American strategic forces. The U.S. missile submarine fleet had a substantial advantage in forward bases at Holy Loch in Scotland and Rota in Spain. The Soviets must have considered the U.S. programs to MIRV land- and sea-based missiles as a dynamic addition which they could only match, at least for some years, by having substantially larger numbers of missile launchers. This meant continuing launcher construction programs, which U.S. proposals aimed to stop. The Soviets did not want to appear to be opposing a MIRV ban, but if there was to be one, it must allow them to develop and test MIRV technology.

In retrospect, it looks as if the U.S.S.R. wanted an agreement that would stop the U.S. ABM program, with its potential for triggering a full-scale ABM competition, and one that would register American acceptance of strategic parity. They wanted an agreement permitting deployment of a new generation of ICBMs that we later learned they were developing. And they wanted no inspection in the Soviet Union. Added targets of opportunity were U.S. bases in Europe and the Far East and a long-shot possibility of halting or slowing up U. S. MIRV deployments.

The United States' specific approaches and the Soviet general provisions represented differing interests and attitudes of the sides. With our verification concerns, we wanted to "button up" many points and leave as few as possible for the future. The Soviets wanted a simple, political-type deal. They did not have to worry about detecting possible American cheating. They must have been fairly confident that any weapons programs inconsistent with a treaty would not get congressional support. The Soviets apparently did not share our deep concern about the future vulnerability of ICBMs. Unlike the U.S.S.R., we had no large-scale anti-aircraft systems which might be upgraded to an ABM capability. And Moscow had no problems with getting legislative approval of any agreement that might be reached.

The Soviets showed no interest in phased reductions in land-based missile launchers. They said this would disadvantage the U.S.S.R. by reducing weapons important to it—ICBMs—while not affecting systems where the U.S. had the advantage—SLBMs, bombers and forward-based systems (FBS). This was true. The U.S. approach would have required phasing out of half of the Soviet SS-9 force. As one American delegate said, we "overloaded" the reductions approach. The Soviet position was that limitation must precede reduction. Semenov said the Soviet approach could "eventually lead" to reductions. Later it was said that their approach could admit of reductions in the process of establishing agreed ceilings. Since at SALT I we never learned what the proposed ceilings were, this was not very enlightening. We surmised that Semenov might have had in mind either setting aggregate ceilings low enough to require some dismantling of existing launchers on both sides, or some unilateral reduction in United States forces to compensate the U.S.S.R. for American FBS. In any event, a negotiation for reductions never started.

The main Soviet objection to the American approaches was that they made no provision to limit FBS—those U.S. fighter bombers at bases in Europe and the Far East and carrier-based aircraft. It will be recalled that Semenov had raised this subject at the Helsinki preliminary round. While supporting aggregate ceilings based on the principle of equality, the Soviets insisted that any agreed balance must take into account this alleged United States advantage. Until there was a common understanding as to what forces were to be limited, we could get nowhere. This was the central United States objection to the Soviet approach—lack of specifics—and a circular argument followed. Until we knew the specifics, particularly proposed aggregate levels, progress could not be made. This impasse was clearly registered in a few days but, as usual in arms control negotiations, positions were stated again and again so that even the hopeful maximalists back in capitals would get the point.

Even though the two American packages at first glance appeared to be proposals, and President Nixon's letter to the opening session had referred to "proposals," they actually were not. White House guidance carefully characterized them as alternative "approaches." The delegation was instructed that only after a full exchange of views would the President decide which alternative best served U.S. interests or whether a third approach should be tried. It will be recalled that such a third approach, called Option A, had been under consideration in Washington. It called for a very narrow agreement: a freeze of offensive missile launchers and a high limit on ABM launchers (1,000). As things turned out, the President was spared any difficulty of choice. Neither U.S. alternative proved of interest. Instead of falling back to the third option, the delegation tailored a new proposal, the so-called Vienna Option, which was the basis for the first unconditional American offer, made on August 4, 1970.

When tabling the Soviet Basic Provisions, Semenov said that a mutually acceptable agreement "must provide for a radical solution of the question of bases beyond the limits of national territories"—that meant the total withdrawal of U. S. FBS out of range of the Soviet Union and destruction of their bases. The Soviets said that, as congressional hearings showed, there were hundreds of American forward-based and carrier aircraft, and these systems could deliver thousands of nuclear weapons. The existence of American bases on the territory of foreign countries near Soviet borders and on carriers gave these aircraft the same capabilities as strategic systems. He argued that the flight times for forward-based aircraft were comparable to those of ICBMs, thirty to forty minutes. There were some 500 U.S. aircraft in Europe alone that could be used for nuclear strikes against the U.S.S.R., he said, and similar bases in Asia, and more than half of 1,500 U.S. carrier-based aircraft were nuclear capable. Semenov said these systems together could deliver as many weapons as the American ICBMs. They obviously were "of paramount importance." When making his case one day Semenov went so far as to say that the real danger in the strategic balance was the forward-based systems. I told him that was an extravagant and implausible statement.

The U.S. position against taking FBS into account never changed. The delegation maintained that they were not in the same category as strategic bombers and ballistic missiles, because they did not have the same effect on the strategic relationship. The United States did not propose to limit the hundreds of Soviet medium bombers which could be used to attack American territory. It was both more sensible and more urgent to concentrate on weapons systems central to the strategic relationship. We stressed that U.S. tactical aircraft deployed abroad involved vital political commitments to our allies, and it was essential to avoid getting the negotiation entangled in political matters. Soviet insistence on bringing in the FBS issue was a form of "linkage" which the sides had agreed to avoid. I concluded one formal statement by saying flatly that the United States would not agree to include FBS and that my instructions on this point were firm.

The Soviet delegation then went through the motions of adjusting their position, no longer calling for a "radical solution." Semenov now proposed partial withdrawal plus compensation in the form of a higher ceiling on ICBMs and SLBMs for the Soviet Union. He said that, while the Soviets still favored total FBS withdrawal, we might find the new formula preferable for political reasons. Neither of these proposals could have been advanced by the Soviets with any expectation that they would be accepted. I soon advised him that the United States would not agree to any such compensation. Perhaps the Soviet aim was to try to leverage some other American concession of a nature never disclosed. And a tentative note was added when we were advised that this FBS proposal was advanced "for the present stage of the talks."

These FBS systems had some strategic capability. There were about 850 U.S. airplanes capable of reaching Soviet territory from U.S. aircraft carriers and European and Asian bases. A few years earlier carrier-based bombers had been considered as part of our strategic forces. Some military analysts believe that the present structure of the Soviet navy is in good measure responsive to their concern about U.S. carrier-based aviation; that their shipborne cruise missiles, attack submarines and Naval Air Force were designed with a primary mission of strategic defense to sink the carriers in wartime before or when their aircraft were in range of the U.S.S.R.

Most U.S. fighter bombers are only capable of one-way missions and would have to fly mostly at high altitude and subsonic speed to reach Soviet territory. These one-way FBS missions may present a credible threat to Soviet planners, given the need to take off before their bases were destroyed. But at high altitude and subsonic speed, there would be long warning time and they would be vulnerable to SAM anti-aircraft missiles. This call for U.S. withdrawal from foreign bases had been pressed for the past two decades. The Soviet delegation never made entirely clear what they wanted in the FBS matter. It was even said that FBS inclusion was not a condition precedent to reaching agreement. FBS should be "taken into account" in some fashion. Even vaguer was the suggestion that it be taken up "in the context of easing of tensions."

The U.S. delegation never reached any conclusion as to how serious Soviet FBS protestations were. But there was clear negotiating advantage in the Soviet stance. They insisted on agreement in principle first as to which systems were to be limited, and only then would they give details. By raising this unacceptable condition, they could go on talking, hoping the United States would disclose its positions, weak points as well as strong, while the Soviets disclosed little or nothing. Once the U.S. case was clearly understood, the Soviets could move to shape a settlement. It is possible that one Soviet motive for making such an issue over FBS was to prepare the ground for their later proposal that a first SALT agreement contain no limits on offensive launchers—but on ABMs only.

The Soviets objected to what amounted to a separate ceiling for heavy bombers in the United States approaches, saying it would freeze a large American numerical advantage. We argued somewhat unpersuasively that the effect of bombers on strategic stability was quite different from that of missiles, and opposed inclusion of them in a single aggregate as the Soviets proposed. Later we were to change this position.

The Soviets adamantly opposed a freeze on their European-targeted shorter-range IR/MRBMs. These missiles did not have enough range to strike the United States. They were needed for defense against third countries. The Soviet delegation seemed nonplused when we pointed out that there were Soviet IRBM launchers deployed on the Chukotsk Peninsula in range of Alaska, our largest state. Under their theory, that proved that IRBMs should be limited. They quickly assured us that the Chukotsk-Alaska matter could be handled by a special provision. With a constructive approach to the whole problem, it would not be difficult to agree on this particular question. About a year later the Soviets dismantled these launchers.

As predicted, the FBS issue was a bad omen. It became the central block to progress. All Soviet-proposed solutions—withdrawal, destruction, or compensation—were equally unattractive. No agreement was reached on what offensive systems should be limited. With no common understanding about the extent of the agreement, it is no wonder that progress was not made. A temporary expedient was reached only at the eleventh hour in May 1972.

In the face of our emphasizing the need to limit MLBMs, the SS-9s, the only formal Soviet reaction was that it would be "unfounded to single out missiles of this type as some kind of special category." But they seemed to be taking care to avoid any flat refusal.

The Helsinki Illustrative Elements had suggested unlimited freedom to vary the mix between ICBM and SLBM launchers. This mix concept was in one form or another in all U.S. approaches to limit offensive systems. The Vienna mix proposal would permit replacement of one type of launcher with another— e.g., an SLBM launcher could replace an ICBM launcher, within an agreed total. Both sides wanted to retain flexibility to modernize and vary forces for an unknown future of indefinite length. A major difference in the mix provisions of the United States and Soviet positions at Vienna became a significant point of contention. The U.S. approaches now called for a limited or one-way freedom to mix, from ICBMs to SLBMs, a switch considered to improve strategic stability since sea-based SLBMs are much less vulnerable than fixed land-based ICBMs. The Soviet Basic Provisions called for full freedom to mix within an aggregate ceiling on ICBMs, SLBMs and heavy bombers, which had been the case in 'our Helsinki Illustrative Elements. Full freedom to replace SLBMs with ICBMs, while unlikely to be exercised, would have allowed the Soviets to increase the threat to our Minuteman force. That did not seem like a good idea.

As for cruise missiles, our two approaches would have prohibited testing of land-based cruise missiles of intercontinental range as well as deployment of launchers for such missiles. Submarine launchers for cruise missiles would have been limited to those currently operational. The idea of air- and surface-ship-launched cruise missiles apparently was not then taken seriously. Semenov analogized cruise missiles to prehistoric animals of the Triassic period. I recalled that a Soviet Ambassador Tsarapkin had argued at the Geneva Conference on Disarmament as early as 1964 that all bombers were obsolete, but now the Soviets were placing great stress not only on heavy bombers but also on lighter delivery aircraft (FBS). If Semenov was right their FBS position was really an attempt to summon up ichthyosaurs. Semenov closed out the conversation by saying, "A nightingale to one is an owl to another." Now the Soviet owl has become a nightingale, and in the SALT II negotiation they pressed very hard for limitations on cruise missiles.

As at Helsinki, there was some measure of agreement about limiting ABMs. Reflecting the apparent Soviet preference for a low level, both U.S. options would permit one ABM site for defense of the National Command Authority (NCA) at Washington and Moscow with 100 interceptors and launchers at each site, as well as radar and SAM upgrade constraints. The Soviets quickly agreed to the proposed site level, too quickly in fact, as Washington already was beginning to have second thoughts as to the wisdom of this opening move and soon tried to neutralize it by instructing us to add as an alternative a complete ABM ban, sometimes referred to as a zero-level limitation.

While accepting an NCA limitation, the Soviet side made clear that they were agreeing only to the proposed level and not to the details of the U. S. ABM controls, which were as complex as our proposed offensive controls. The Soviet Basic Provisions referred only in general terms to agreed limitations on anti-missile defense systems in accordance with the principle of equal security. We learned that they favored limits on ABM launchers but not on ABM interceptors. They asked why the U.S. proposed to limit both ABM interceptors and launchers while for offensive systems only launchers would be limited. Each side had to determine for itself what kind of interceptors and what numbers it needed for the defense of its capital. The specific U.S. constraints on ABM radars also did not suit the Soviets. ABM radars, they said, should be limited geographically to a circle with its center in the capital, within which all components of the ABM system would be located. A geographical limit was all that was necessary no matter how great the range of interceptors or radars. If all elements of the systems were located in a limited area around the defended target, they could not be used for an effective defense of other regions.

The Soviet delegation lost no time in challenging our proposed ban on upgrading SAM anti-aircraft systems to give them an

ABM capability. This was only a hypothetical possibility, they argued. If a side wanted ballistic missile defenses, it would have systems especially designed for that purpose and not use a redesigned anti-aircraft system. It was difficult enough to develop a genuine ABM system. One official said even an automatic rifle could once in a very great while shoot down an airplane, but that did not make infantry small arms potential anti-aircraft defenses. Semenov went so far as to state that it was "impossible" to use air defense missiles against ballistic missile warheads. Limits on air defense were beyond the scope of the talks, and this attempt artificially to expand the definition of stragetic defensive systems could sidetrack the negotiation. In a private conversation, he went off on a philosophical tack. One had to deal with the sphere of the possible, he said, because the sphere of the unlimited easily led one into the sphere of the impossible.

The delegation was to learn over the course of the negotiation that Soviet technicians evidently believed that upgrading SAMs for an ABM role was not a realistic possibility, and that some Soviets, especially the military, were suspicious that our SAM-upgrade provisions were an attempt to use SALT to restrict Soviet anti-aircraft systems.

It is not generally appreciated that the Soviet military sees a much greater need for large-scale air defenses than we do. The Soviet long-range bomber threat to us in 1970 consisted of some 250 rather dated aircraft, 160 of which were propeller-driven, and another 45 to 55 were tankers. In view of the great vulnerability of the United States to Soviet intercontinental missiles, the air threat seems only a marginal addition. This is why U.S. air defenses consisted of only 1,400 SAMs and 600 interceptors in 1970;[2] at this writing our SAMs have been phased out and U.S. anti-aircraft defenses consist of some 300 interceptors.

The Soviet military had to consider the capabilities of an effective United States heavy bomber force which in 1970 was composed of more than 500 B-52s; 850 U.S. forward-based aircraft, which the Soviets argued were capable of striking the U.S.S.R.; and 350 British and French bombers earmarked for strategic mis-

[2] As opposed to almost 10,000 Soviet anti-aircraft missiles (SAMs) and over 3,000 interceptor aircraft.

sions or having the range to reach the U.S.S.R. A good fraction of the more than 500 fighter bombers deployed by other NATO countries also had sufficient range to reach the Soviet Union. From a Soviet military perspective, if NATO were to launch a first strike, these aircraft could not be destroyed on the ground. They could all be airborne, en route to targets in the Soviet Union, or at least avoiding destruction by Soviet strikes.

To replace the B-52 the Nixon Administration had recently requested another $100 million to continue development of a more efficient advanced manned strategic aircraft, called the B-1 (later canceled). And Soviet air defenses had to counter the potential bomber threat from the People's Republic of China. A very large Soviet SAM system might even deter the Chinese from investing in a modern bomber force.

Admittedly, this may seem like exaggerated worst-case analysis of air threats to the U.S.S.R., but such a perspective may help one to understand the Soviet interest in air defenses and their arguments that the proposed American ABM restraints were aimed at restricting them. This concern no doubt was sharpened by the fact that the U. S. MIRV-ban provisions called for on-site inspection of SAM sites as well as offensive missile launchers. But in spite of these concerns, during this first Vienna phase we learned informally that there would be no serious Soviet objection to a prohibition on SAM upgrading, even though it was thought to be "superfluous."

After a while we began to recognize that the Soviets were using certain words and phrases in a special sense. The word "superfluous" was apparently a signal that the Soviets were likely to agree in the end to some limitation. When Semenov said that something "can and must be done," it was a sign that they were moving toward some sort of agreement on that issue. The Soviet side repeatedly used the phrase "to curb and limit." They explained when questioned that "to curb" meant stopping new systems from coming into existence, "to limit" referred to existing systems for which ceilings should be established.

At Helsinki we had broached the idea that if an agreement was reached there should be a "continuing dialogue" to make it more viable. Semenov now wanted elaboration. The two U.S. Vienna approaches specified that this dialogue should take place in a standing consultative commission. It was described as a forum where the parties could raise questions about compliance with any agreement reached. It would have no power of decision but would serve as a clearinghouse for exchanges of information to prevent misunderstandings. Perhaps in response to our Helsinki suggestion, the Soviet Basic Provisions also envisioned "continuing consultations." They soon accepted in principle our proposal for a standing commission. It is now operating effectively.

The Soviets also agreed with a U.S. idea that the sides take a commitment not to interfere with the other's national technical means of verification. But they objected to a provision to aid the verification process by banning covered facilities for submarine construction. They said that weather conditions at submarine yards required workmen to operate under cover in wintertime. We assured them that this provision was aimed at possible new methods for fitting out and berthing submarines and would not require changes in current practices. The 1972 agreements prohibit deliberate concealment as well as interference with technical means of verification.

We also raised the possibility of ad hoc, on-site inspections, on a "request" basis, called selective direct observation (SDO). The Soviets objected. They had no trouble with the concept of inspection if a nation invited it, but they were concerned with the political consequences of denying inspections requested by the other side, even though it would be understood that this did not constitute a violation of the agreement. Nothing came of this attempt to take a small first step toward on-site inspection.

In late April, Semenov initiated, perhaps inadvertently, an interesting exchange about a concept known as "launch on warning," slangily called "use before you lose." Speaking of our concern about ICBM vulnerability, he said that the American concept of crisis stability seemed to assume that fixed land-based missile launchers at "precisely established coordinates" were the only strategic systems in existence. But there were also missile-carrying submarines and early warning systems which were continuously being improved. Silos containing ICBMs might be empty at the moment when the enemy attempted to strike them, with the ICBMs already in flight.

I expressed concern lest such a "launch on warning" doctrine be Soviet policy. Did we understand this statement to suggest that a government should plan to launch its ICBM force solely on the possibly fallible reading of signals from its early warning systems, and before it had any further evidence that an attack was in fact under way? The United States had had some experience with warning systems which had indicated that they were indeed fallible. This procedure might be a good way to stumble into an accidental nuclear war. One reason for the U.S. emphasis on survivability was precisely to avoid having to resort to such a "launch on warning" policy, which would be very dangerous and would increase the risks of unwanted war.

After the meeting the senior Soviet military delegate told his American counterpart that the reference had been to operational training doctrine described in U.S. manuals. This information, he said, was readily available in publications. While training manuals describe a variety of concepts they do not express policy. The delegation advised Washington that any such impression should be corrected, noting that Soviet misapprehension of a U.S. "launch on warning" doctrine might explain their lack of readiness to accept at face value our concern over ICBM vulnerability. The next day at a private meeting with Semenov, I presented him with a copy of Secretary of Defense Laird's testimony of the previous day before the Senate Armed Services Committee. A passage about launch on warning was underlined. *This strategy that has been advocated by some to launch our missiles on warning I believe is a very dangerous strategy and should not be followed by our country. . . . I would hope that that kind of a strategy would never be adopted by any administration or by any Congress.* I assured Semenov that, although our communications with the Defense Department were excellent, the Secretary could not have received word of our discussion in time to include this passage in his testimony.

We repeated Secretary Laird's statement at a plenary session a week later, adding that we would welcome having a similar statement by the Soviet Minister of Defense. But in response to efforts to draw them out, members of the Soviet delegation merely repeated that they had been referring to statements by American officials. Shortly thereafter the Soviets said the matter was closed and was not an appropriate topic for SALT. The "launch on warning" episode suggested that SALT could be an important educational channel.

One American delegate thought that perhaps the Soviet view about "launch on warning" resulted from our emphasis on the Minuteman ICBM's vulnerability to first strike attacks. The Soviets appeared to believe that the vulnerability of any one segment of the forces would not destabilize the strategic balance so as to increase the chance of nuclear war. How could one speak at all of this possibility, they had asked, when both sides possessed other retaliatory forces beyond land-based missiles? The U.S.S.R. proceeded from the premise that each side possessed its own chosen mix of strategic armaments. Their deterrent power consisted of the sum total of all these forces, which complemented each other, and consideration of one weapons system only would lead to wrong conclusions. This Soviet statement about the interaction of strategic offensive forces comes close to paralleling the U.S. military view about the importance of what is called the Triad—heavy bombers, ICBMs and SLBMs. In fact this strategic view goes further, crediting the Triad with a capability consisting not just of the numerical aggregate of these three strategic components but of a force weight greater than the numerical sum owing to the synergism among the three forces. In any event, Soviet understanding of mutual deterrence seemed based on a view that outbreak of nuclear war would be determined more by political factors than by an analysis of the other side's weapons vulnerabilities.

On the evening of April 30, President Nixon announced that United States forces were entering Cambodia to destroy Communist sanctuaries. Naturally we were concerned that the Soviets might suspend SALT. A contingency statement was prepared against this possibility. But, at a press conference on May 4, Premier Kosygin merely said, "Of course, negotiations are built on trust and at a time when international documents are being treated in a highhanded manner, then this puts us on our guard. I must say that this action by the U.S.A. does not in the least strengthen trust between our states, and without trust negotiations are very difficult."

At the next SALT meeting Semenov cited this statement and

expressed doubts about American intentions. He than gave a hard-line review of Soviet objections to our two approaches, saying, "We would not be frank if we failed to say that the American delegation's proposals taken as a whole evoke a feeling of serious dissatisfaction." After the meeting I told him that I regretted that he had brought up matters outside the scope of SALT. My first reaction had been to make a formal reply but I had decided against it because I did not think it would have advanced the purposes of the talks. Semenov said that his comments related to the purposes of our talks, without reference to any outside developments. This was the only time the Cambodian operation was mentioned at SALT.

Since President Nixon had announced that the Cambodia incursion would be limited to ninety days, a parallel suspension of SALT must have appeared to the Soviets as an attractive opportunity to add to the generally unfavorable world-wide reaction to the escalated U.S. involvement. Perhaps concern over possible American reponses to a SALT suspension prevailed in Moscow. I wrote to President Nixon that the Soviet reaction to the Cambodia incursion was the minimum that one could expect. I thought it evidenced continued serious Soviet interest in reaching some sort of SALT arrangement. While it still might be possible that the Soviets were in SALT primarily for psychological purposes, in particular to influence U.S. public and congressional opinion, their post-Cambodian SALT stance suggested a real negotiating purpose.

The Cambodian episode coincided with a change at Vienna to a new negotiating approach which would be followed for the next two months. After the initial exchanges I advised the President that it seemed clear that the U.S.S.R. was not interested in either of our two approaches and that the Soviets' approach was unacceptable to us. There was some evidence that the Soviets were preparing for a new phase of the talks. Semenov shortly thereafter summed up the opposing positions of the sides in general terms. More detailed criticism of the U.S. approaches and defense of Soviet positions continued in informal conversations. I suggested to Semenov that we review the negotiating situation in a private meeting.

This two-hour session was a lively affair, reflecting our basic disagreements. I welcomed Semenov to my office in the Strudelhof Gasse and pointed out a wall plaque which said that in that room, "In a secret meeting of the Cabinet under the chairmanship of the Imperial and Royal Minister of Foreign Affairs, Count Leopold Berchtold, the final version of the ultimatum to Servia was adopted and therewith the first world war started." I expressed the hope that we would do better.

Semenov then brought out a nine-page typed brief. One month had passed and still we could not see the outlines of a possible accommodation. Each of the two U.S. approaches seemed to be designed to give unilateral advantage to the United States, in heavy bombers, in vast forward-based arsenals, by limiting Soviet MR/IRBMs. I noted that, while I did not entirely understand certain parts of the Soviet position, their proposals appeared to permit a brisk continuation of the arms race. If our assumptions were correct, they would allow switching freely between a number of different weapons systems. Semenov had said that some U.S. proposals were completely unacceptable to the Soviet side. I was sure he would understand that we also found a number of their positions completely unacceptable.

He charged that the American approaches contained irrelevant elements, which reminded him of the Greek philosopher Empedocles' theory that biological evolution took place by random combination of legs, arms, torsos and other organs that had previously existed independently. Empedocles called these whimsical combinations a totality, a "package," but this hypothesis certainly was inapplicable to political matters. He topped off this philosophical sermon by his standard complaint about hawkish remarks of Secretary Laird.

It had been a long time, I said, since I had read Empedocles, and I was not certain whether these comments were meant in praise or ridicule of our position. It would not do for Semenov to be too critical. At least we had completely disclosed our positions while the Soviet approach was still fully draped. As for Laird's views, I would send him copies of some of Laird's speeches which supported SALT. He would surely find them pacific in comparison to those of any Minister of Defense of the Soviet Union.

Semenov rejoined that he would gladly send me copies of recent statements by Marshal Grechko, and thus would not remain in my debt for the Laird material document for document. (I sent him the Laird statements. I did not receive those of Grechko.)

But after this skirmishing a new procedural approach was settled on. Since we obviously had not succeeded with our respective comprehensive approaches, Semenov proposed that we turn to the Work Program on which we had expended considerable effort at Helsinki. By considering the items listed in the Program one by one, some points of congruence might be developed, while leaving others to the future. I agreed, saying that the Helsinki Work Program had been something of an orphan up to now. If it was understood that the two American approaches were not being atomized, I concurred that this new framework could usefully be employed to search for acceptable limitations. We agreed to begin the next week, without dropping previous positions.

I repeated that we were still in the dark on important parts of the Soviet position. Progress depended on Semenov providing some light. He responded that absolute light was the equivalent of absolute darkness, and existed only in man's imagination. Thus man was never in complete darkness. While I would leave absolute light to the heavenly vision, I replied, just a little light would be most helpful. Semenov asked if we were looking for light at the end of a tunnel. It was agreed that we both were in a tunnel and should seek light at its end. This exchange was typical of a great many SALT hours spent trying to get some light on Soviet positions. Regretfully, the new negotiating approach did not prove fruitful. Real enlightenment was more than a year away.

The most interesting part of this round involved the question of possible provocative attack by a third country. Semenov had followed up earlier Soviet mention of the provocative attack danger with a specific proposal. He saw a danger from adventurous circles in certain countries that wanted nuclear war between the U.S. and the U.S.S.R. Suppose, he suggested, such a country had a submarine which launched a "volley" of missiles against one or both countries and that one of them incorrectly identified the source of the strike. This could lead to irreparable consequences. It would be in the interest of both countries to agree on necessary organization and technical arrangements against this possibility. They were required also to reduce the dangers and damage from accidental and unauthorized launches of missiles.

Steps could be taken, we said, to identify any provocative third-country attack. Both sides should be in a position to know if a nuclear detonation had actually occurred and to identify the source of the launch and the cause of the detonation. We might exchange information on the general character of national capabilities for detecting and analyzing nuclear detonations. This exchange would permit decisions about any needed improvements. There should be rapid and reliable exchange of information after any such nuclear detonation. This would supplement national capabilities for identifying the nature and source of a nuclear detonation and avoid misunderstanding.

As for accidental and unauthorized use of nuclear weapons, I suggested we engage in a discussion of the precautionary measures each side then employed. We should consider ways to improve communications facilities between us. The Direct Communication Link, or Hot Line, established in 1963 could be upgraded. Such emergency measures also were applicable to provocative attack dangers.

Considerable attention was given by both sides to measures to guard against "automatic outbreak of hostilities." A group of experts met three times during the summer to discuss measures to be taken against the possibility of an accidental or unauthorized launch. A year later, in September 1971, two SALT-related agreements emerged. This phase of the negotiation is further considered in Chapter 9.

On the question of provocative attack Semenov observed that, while the United States seemed to regard it as technical, the Soviets considered it a political matter with technical aspects. The question boiled down to whether the two sides were ready to work toward an agreement on jointly coordinated measures to lessen the danger of the outbreak of nuclear war. Although he declined to explain what he meant by a political approach, I surmised and reported to Washington that he was hinting at some sort of superpower agreement having major political import to deter possible nuclear dangers coming from third countries.

Later he went on to say that the possibility could not be excluded that in some country forces could come to power who would attempt to seek advantage by organizing a military provocation to cause a nuclear conflict between the United States and the U.S.S.R. It was all right to discuss technical measures as proposed by the United States. But it was necessary to discuss also questions of action to be taken by the U.S.S.R. and the United States in the event of an actual provocative use of nuclear weapons by a third country. Agreement on procedures to be followed in the event of such provocation would be in the interests of both countries and of strengthening international security. The Soviets were convinced that such an agreement in itself would constitute a serious deterrent to those who might plan this sort of provocative act.

One night, at an intermission during a Rostropovich concert, he passed me a note proposing a bilateral agreement providing for joint retaliation against any country that launched a provocative nuclear attack. He proposed that we discuss specific actions by the U.S.S.R. and the United States in the event of such attack. If facts about a provocation under preparation were obtained the sides should inform each other in timely manner. If necessary, measures could be taken to prevent provocative use of nuclear weapons. Both sides would obligate themselves to take retaliatory action if a third country committed such aggression. Consultations should be held to prevent an automatic start of nuclear war in the event of provocative use of nuclear weapons.

I wondered what lay behind this proposal. Did the Kremlin expect that a SALT-originated strategic parity with the United States could be escalated into some new Soviet-American relationship? I told Semenov that the United States appreciated the seriousness of this proposal. It would be studied in Washington. To prepare him for a turndown I warned that our position might well be negative. There were many complications. Semenov said that, whatever the American reaction, the fact that the Soviets had made this proposal had great significance, especially for the long run. Neither country needed this kind of arrangement more than the other. He would be surprised if the sides could reach an understanding on strategic arms limitations without coordinating their positions on provocative attack.

The delegation thought there were a number of possible moti-

vations for this unique Soviet proposal. It could be an effort to
reach a U.S.-Soviet understanding bearing on China, or an indirect means of interfering with U.S. nuclear weapons arrangements
in NATO or any attempt to create a European nuclear force. The
Soviets seemed to have a real concern over the possibility of inadvertent nuclear war. They might want to establish an appearance
of a Soviet-American nuclear cartel. Pehaps they believed that a
SALT agreement based on parity would tend to so regularize the
U.S.S.R.'s relationship with the United States that it would become important to extend it somehow into a nuclear relationship
in respect to other countries, inhibiting as far as possible the use
of nuclear weapons, whether strategic or tactical and wherever located. The delegation advised Washington that the provocative
attack proposal was primarily political, that it must have reflected
a high-level decision, and that the manner in which it had been
presented suggested that the Soviets considered it to be an important initiative. We recommended that Washington not accept or
reject it offhand.

The authorities in Washington realized that this move presented central and sensitive issues for the United States and its al-
liances. It had clear implications for our evolving relations with
the People's Republic of China. Washington advised the delegation that the Soviet approach contained in its most extreme elements what amounted to a contingent "alliance" that could be
regarded as directed against China and other possible future nuclear powers. This was counter to many lines of U.S. policy and
could have highly undesirable political implications. There was
considerable skepticism about the Soviet approach. We were instructed to tell the Soviets that the subject would require more
thorough analysis.

Privately Semenov made a further strong plea. If either side
had reason to believe in a treaty to prevent the proliferation of
nuclear weapons, it should certainly agree to a provocative attack
arrangement. It would be universal, not aimed at any particular
country. If countries A, B and C had no desire to attack, the
agreement would not apply to them; but if unreasonable leaders
came to power in country X and plotted provocative attack, it
would apply to that country. There were no hidden meanings or
conditions.

The chances of accident, it seemed to me, were greater than the chances of provocative attack. Semenov cited the example of Nazis who would have blown up the whole world in the last phase of World War II when they knew they had lost. Suppose a country felt that its civilization would remain if the United States and the U.S.S.R. destroyed each other. I observed that the resultant radiation would not leave any provocateur healthy.

I advised the White House that the Soviet preoccupation with the possibility of a provocative attack arrangement was a curious phenomenon. They likely saw some possibility that in a strategic arms limitation environment they could float a nuclear superpower grand design to achieve global political aims going beyond arms limitation. They gave the appearance of having an emotional commitment to this notion which, though Russian, seemed un-Soviet-like to me. At a luncheon at the Soviet Embassy, Semenov told a fable about a man who tried to sell gold for a fraction of its value. Suspicious potential vendees passed up the opportunity. He had also referred to a line from Pushkin's *Eugen Onegin*—"And happiness before it glided away was so near." And later, when referring to the offer, he said, "Well, we have sung our song, we will sing no more." I concluded in this report that perhaps the strong Soviet appetite for something on provocative attack could be leveraged into our getting the United States a better SALT agreement.

No more was said about provocative attack at Vienna. Before the next round at Helsinki the delegation was instructed—if the Soviets renewed the proposal—to reject it. When that round was drawing to a close without the Soviets again raising provocative attack, the delegation requested authority to close out the matter. In December 1970 the following statement was recorded.

The United States Government has carefully studied the Soviet proposal—concerning measures to deal with the possibility of a provocative attack involving the use of nuclear weapons by a third country calculated to cause nuclear war between the U.S. and the USSR. In the context of accidental or unauthorized use of nuclear weapons, the U.S. delegation has made and will make specific proposals for the exchange of information on events considered to increase the danger of unintended war between our two countries. These arrangements should be adequate to deal with an exchange of information that a third-country provocative nuclear attack is occurring. Diplomatic and other communication channels are available for other discussions and clarification should either side believe a provocative nuclear attack was imminent . . . the United States is not prepared to enter into an agreement or an understanding for joint action as proposed by the Soviet representative.

So ended this extraordinary attempt to use SALT for a purpose other than arms limitation. In June 1973, President Nixon and General Secretary Brezhnev signed an Agreement on the Prevention of Nuclear War. It commits the two countries to consult whenever there is a danger of nuclear war. The U.S.S.R. seems thus to have achieved a part of the aim behind their provocative attack proposal made three years earlier.

The Soviet Basic Provisions dealt with another third-country problem which had been broached at Helsinki. Transfers to other countries of offensive and defensive strategic armaments or technical assistance in developing them should be prohibited. The Soviet delegation argued that transfers to allies would offer an easy way for a side to evade the limitations of an agreement. The U.S.S.R. has never provided nuclear weapons assistance to its allies except to a limited extent to China. When they stopped helping the Chinese in 1959, the rift between the two deepened. Moscow had watched for years as the United States moved to share nuclear responsibilities with its NATO allies. Although the American-proposed NATO multilateral force (MLF) had never come into being, a NATO atomic stockpile had been established. Thousands of U.S. tactical nuclear weapons are deployed in Europe for delivery by U.S. and allied forces, and the Soviet Union and the Warsaw Pact countries have long considered this arsenal a major military threat. Although in the American view these are tactical nuclear weapons, we have seen that they also give concern to the Soviets because they might be employed on strategic missions.

In addition the Soviets face the British and French strategic forces, which when completed will be composed of, in addition to bombers, more than 9 SLBM submarines. While some Western defense analysts consider these two European nuclear forces of questionable utility, Soviet military planners have to take a different view. The British and French strategic missile forces in 1970 totaled 84 SLBMs, with 100 to 125 more launchers to become operational in the next few years. By the Soviet definition of strategic systems, which included lighter delivery aircraft, the two U.S. allies then had 375 strategic launchers and some 250 more under construction or planned. If ABMs were to be strictly limited, the British and French missile forces would have a substantially greater penetration capability than if the Soviets could have widespread ABM defenses. And unlike the NATO tactical nuclear stockpile, which can only be released by order of the President of the United States, these allied weapons are not under U.S. control. In fact one rationale given for the French nuclear weapons had been that their use would trigger U.S. strategic forces into action during a European conflict if the American President hesitated to commit them.

The British force of 4 Polaris submarines was almost entirely dependent on United States supply—for the missile delivery system, including some of the technology for the warhead, for the submarine nuclear propulsion system, and even for the steel used in the hulls. The French nuclear program was almost entirely independent of American assistance, but U.S. policy might change to give France the same accommodation given the United Kingdom, for political as well as military reasons. America's ability and willingness to assist could facilitate allies' decisions for sophisticated nuclear weapons systems. Such considerations must have led to the Soviet conclusion that there should be a ban on the international transfer of strategic systems (and their technology) limited by a SALT agreement.

The Soviet delegation analogized this transfer problem to nuclear weapons proliferation and the 1968 Non-Proliferation Treaty. They talked of the negative consequences that would come from the proliferation of strategic systems. Third-country possession of such systems would be prejudicial to the security interests of both sides. Since the Soviet definition of strategic arms included shorter-range delivery systems capable of striking the Soviet Union, this could have the effect of prejudicing NATO nuclear arrangements. The Soviets had emphasized that they would expect obligations under a SALT agreement to override obligations under other international agreements.

I tried to handle the transfer problem by saying, as at Helsinki, that any attempt to circumvent a SALT agreement through substantial transfers would remove the basis for the agreement. But one could not tell what a substantial transfer was, they said. Although they later seemed to accept this general formula, they argued that it should be given "concrete expression."

As the prospect for a comprehensive limitation agreement on offensive arms receded, the Soviets ceased to press this nontransfer position. The ABM transfer question was not so difficult, since none of our allies had expressed interest in having ABMs. A "no transfer" provision was included in the 1972 ABM Treaty. The offensive launcher interim freeze agreement said nothing about the problem. At its conclusion the Soviet side made a unilateral statement that if U.S. allies in NATO increased the number of their SLBM submarines the U.S.S.R. would have a right to a corresponding increase in the number of its submarines.

After discussing the Helsinki Work Program for some weeks the American delegates concluded late in May that there was no prospect for agreement unless a different approach was taken. Several Soviet participants informally confirmed this, urging that we needed to get away from both sides' formal "package" approaches. Some hinted that a less comprehensive route might be fruitful. After long and lively discussion among the principal American delegates, we succeeded in drawing up a proposed new approach which later was called the Vienna Option. It was sent to Washington on June 15 with the delegates' conclusion that neither of our two tabled approaches was negotiable. A new move was necessary if the impasse was to be broken. The proposed Vienna Option called for an initial agreement on ABMs and on the three central strategic offensive systems: launchers for ICBMs and SLBMs and heavy bombers. Limits on MR/IRBMs and on cruise missiles would be deferred in exchange for the Soviets' agreeing that American FBS not be included. After a first agreement was concluded, efforts would be made to reach more comprehensive limitations, including other offensive arms. The

Vienna Option became the basis for a new American position—labeled with the date on which it was tabled, August 4.

While Washington was considering this delegation proposal, the U.S.S.R. made a major ABM move. With great secrecy the Soviet leadership proposed to President Nixon that the combined offensive-defensive limitations approach be abandoned and that a separate ABM treaty be first negotiated. I heard about this move after midnight on the Fourth of July. The CIA station chief in Vienna, whom I did not recall having met, telephoned that a message for me from the White House was then being decoded and offered to drive me to the SALT office. I had told the Austrian security officers that my day was finished some hours before. As we drove through the empty streets it occurred to me that it was somewhat imprudent to be going off into the night with a stranger. But in the communications section of the SALT office there was a message from Kissinger at San Clemente.

The President had asked Kissinger to share the following information with me on an exclusively personal basis. No American beyond the President, Kissinger and myself was aware of it. The Soviet leadership had indicated that it would be prepared at Vienna to agree on an ABM limitation coupled with a "broad" agreement on the prevention of accidental or provocative nuclear war along the lines recently proposed to the United States delegation. It would be difficult, they said, to go beyond these two agreements at Vienna. The President on a most urgent and personal basis wanted my reaction before the matter of new instructions to the delegation was decided in Washington.

Never before or after at SALT did I feel such a lonely responsibility. The future of SALT might be at stake. I thought the matter over, then wrote a reply in longhand and gave it to the communicator. I advised that an ABM agreement plus the unknown value of a "broad agreement" on accidental and provocative attack seemed too limited a move to be in the American interest. Any constraint on U.S. ABMs should be accompanied by constraints on U.S.S.R. offensive weapons systems. The desirability of a positive Vienna outcome should not lead us to premature commitment of our strongest bargaining counter, ABM. I returned to the hotel hoping I was right.

A few days later the White House authorized me to put the Soviet proposal to the other principal delegates but only as an "academic question." They all agreed that it would not be acceptable. In reporting this, I added that if for other reasons one were to go ahead on such a limited basis it would be well to make a hard try for a unilateral Soviet stand-down of its ICBM deployment program. For some unknown reason my subsequent request for authority to disclose this Soviet ABM initiative to the other SALT delegates was refused.

It seemed clear from this July 4 episode that the U.S.S.R. would now move at SALT in the direction of an initial agreement limited to ABMs. The U.S. August 4 proposal for a narrow offensive-defensive treaty proved of less than great interest to the Soviets. Their central objection, or pretext, was the continued absence of any United States move to meet their FBS position. Five months later the Soviets were to propose formally a separate ABM agreement unlinked to a provocative attack understanding. It was followed by Soviet-inspired leaks designed to stimulate congressional and public pressures in the United States to support a quick ABM solution. Bait was attached to this hook. An initial ABM treaty, it was said, would open the way to offensive arms limitations. And some less formal offensive measures might even be coupled with an ABM treaty. This latter approach was the SALT formula agreed upon by the White House the next year.

In July 1970 we watched with some concern the debate in the Senate on the Safeguard ABM program, judging that a congressional setback to Safeguard would take steam out of the ABM negotiation, by reducing any Soviet disposition to make concessions. I told Kissinger I was willing to have my views about the effect of a negative Senate Safeguard vote passed to one or two key senators. I pointed out that there was risk involved and that I was not soliciting senatorial calls. But if the President thought it would be useful, I would be willing to take the risk.

By August 10, I was more wary and sent Kissinger a further message. It was important that the delegation not appear to be lobbying for the ABM program and that the SALT negotiation not appear to be leverage for ABMs. Accordingly, I suggested a classified message might be made available as an alternative to open telephone calls, saying:

The delegation believes that Senate action having a "tread water" effect on the Safeguard program or evidencing a significant split between executive and legislative branches would prejudice prospects for SALT agreement.

Kissinger wired that the White House was pleased with this approach. He proposed to show the text to certain senators, with the added comment that they were at liberty to call me should there be any question. He said the President was most grateful for my efforts in his behalf.

Several senators subsequently telephoned me in Vienna. With their assurance that these were confidential conversations, I advised them of my views as to the effect of a negative Safeguard vote on SALT. To my disgust, several days later I read in the New York *Times* that my written views had been given to certain senators. One even referred to my message on the senate floor. I complained to Kissinger about this breach of confidence, but the best I could get from him was that somebody in the White House had goofed.

This was the last time I ever got involved in lobbying for an arms program while negotiating for its limitation. I was advised later by Chief of Staff of the Army General Westmoreland that this intervention had swung enough votes to preserve the ABM program, which survived a key challenge with a 52–47 tally. When I briefed the Senate Foreign Relations Committee the next summer, a few weeks before the 1971 vote on Safeguard, one senator expressed the hope that Senator Jackson would not at the last moment come up with a letter from me that he could use to support the ABM in the forthcoming debate. Touché.

On July 9, five days after I was advised of the Soviet ABM-only proposal, the President instructed the delegation to draw up a specific proposal along the lines of our Vienna Option calling for an initial agreement on ABMs and on the three central offensive systems. In general terms it provided that

- ICBM and SLBM launchers and heavy bombers would be limited to an aggregate total of 1,900. (Bombers were included in the overall aggregate to meet the Soviet objections to separate and unequal bomber limits.)

- There would be a missile launcher subceiling of 1,710 (the aggregate of our ICBM and SLBM launchers) and a subceiling of 250 launchers for heavy missiles (MLBMs).

- Two alternatives having equal standing could be agreed for ABM limitations, one site for capital defense (NCA) for each side or a complete ABM ban.

- Limitations on MIRVs and submarine-launched cruise missiles (SLCMs) as well as reductions were left for future negotiations.

- Verification would be by national means, supplemented by corollary restraints. Provisions retained from the April comprehensive approaches included restricted freedom to mix, a prohibition on new MR/IRBM silos, restrictions on ABM radars, and a ban on SAM upgrading.

I was authorized to tell Semenov that the United States would soon present a new position but told not to provide any specifics until after consultation with the North Atlantic Council.

Later we received additional guidance that the United States must also have a right to 250 MLBMs, which had not been the case under our earlier approaches. This U.S. quota was solely for purposes of symmetry. We had no plans to build MLBMs.

By now the Soviets were showing a strong inclination to end this Vienna marathon. In mid-June some had asked how we would feel about stopping early in July and resuming in Helsinki in November or December. The delegation recommended that the Vienna Option be promptly presented and suggested that some parts could be elaborated informally even before a plenary presentation of the entire package. We wanted to get a preliminary Soviet response at Vienna to lay the groundwork for the next round. We then presented the new proposal to the North Atlantic Council in Brussels. It approved one week later. I informally outlined its details to Semenov on the twenty-third of July. This was record speed for the SALT machinery.

Semenov thought we might adopt a more concentrated work schedule. We agreed to hold in addition to the formal plenary sessions "miniplenaries," working meetings of three or four delegates from each side omitting long prepared statements. "Mini-plenaries" were to become the standard forum for getting on with SALT business.

The U. S. Proposal for an Initial Strategic Arms Limitations Agreement was tabled at the August 4 plenary. It was clear by then that the Soviets were homesick. Several of their delegation were ill. I was told that frequent changes in atmospheric pressure during the Vienna summer were rather hard on people with heart trouble and high blood pressure. One Soviet admiral suffered a massive heart attack. A Soviet general was indisposed. It was relatively late in the summer. The Soviet leadership was out of Moscow vacationing in the south and their delegation had no new instructions. I wondered if we would not have done just as well by holding off this new proposal until the opening of the next Helsinki round. But the timing did give the Soviets a chance to study it carefully during the latter part of the summer and in the autumn.

Their initial reaction was reserved. They asked a number of technical questions and made a few rather predictable objections, promised to study the proposal, and informally called it positive. Semenov still insisted that FBS would have to be taken into account and that the SAM upgrade provision continued the American attempt to limit the Soviet Union's air defenses. They said they would analyze both ABM alternatives. They stated they did not favor the "superfluous" idea of a separate missile launcher ceiling or the MLBM subceiling. Some seemed concerned that the new provision allowing both sides 250 MLBMs foreshadowed a change in U.S. strategic doctrine. They objected to any constraints which would limit modernization.

As a final thrust at the last Vienna plenary, Semenov stated that this latest United States proposal did not constitute the basis for an agreement. We assumed that this was primarily "for the record," since in private conversations the Soviet delegation expressed somewhat positive attitudes. Here was an interesting contrast in the style of the two sides. Kissinger was to say in a news backgrounder in September that "in fairness one has to say the Soviet proposals have provided a basis from which one can negotiate." This was just the opposite of what the U.S. delegates under

Washington instructions had been telling the Soviet delegation. The best one can say about this example of double-talk is that it must have puzzled the Soviets.

On August 14 the delegations went home.

As we left Vienna, it must have been clear to the Soviets that we were not going to reply to their provocative attack proposal, that we probably would agree to some sort of arrangement on accidental and unauthorized launches. Moscow must have realized by now that we were quite serious about limiting strategic arms, just as after the Cambodian affair we had concluded that they were serious. It now seemed clear that we were not likely to get any comprehensive limitations on offensive arms unless the forward-based systems issue was resolved.

The relatively quick switch of American positions may have puzzled the Soviets. It is unusual in arms control negotiations for only a few months to intervene between major proposals. In this case less than four months had elapsed since the U.S. opening approaches. The U.S.S.R. might have taken this tempo as evidence of U.S. eagerness.

The Soviet delegation also may have been confused by the plural United States approach to ABM limitation. After they had accepted the U.S. concept of limiting deployments to defenses at Moscow and Washington (NCA) we had proposed the alternative of a total ban on ABMs. Where did that leave things? Our position was that the earlier ABM approach had been part of a total package including offensive arms limitations, which the Soviets had not accepted. That sounded legalistic even to us.

The hardest job I had that year was to try to understand Washington's reasoning on the ABM negotiation and to explain it to my Soviet opposite number. This plural approach by the United States was to complicate the SALT negotiations for a long time. It was bad enough to offer two alternative limits. Later we would have three proposals on the table at once, without anyone in the delegation and probably not even in Washington knowing which was the preferred United States position. People in the delegation compared this somewhat irreverently to a shell game, with no one knowing under which shell the pea was—or whether in fact there was a pea. This naturally was for American "ears only."

Back in Washington, the delegation reported to the President

The United States delegation, November 1969 (L-R: *Farley, Thompson, Brown, Nitze, Allison, Smith*)

*Semenov leaving the United
States Embassy in Vienna
with* L-R: *Shchukin, Alekseyev,
Pleshakov)*

*The opening ceremony in Vienna, April 16, 1970, at Belvedere Palace.
United Nations Secretary Kurt Waldheim is speaking at the rostrum.*
Courtesy, USIS Vienna

Semenov and Smith end a SALT session after signing a communiqué (L-R: *Alekseyev, Pleshakov, Shchukin, Kishilov, Garthoff, Allison, Nitze*)

Smith reports to President Nixon on the Vienna II round, August 19, 1970, as William Rogers looks on. Courtesy, U.P.I.

President Nixon hands Smith instructions for SALT talks at the White House on March 11, 1971. Courtesy, U.P.I.

we were now convinced that the Soviets were interested in reaching a SALT agreement. They had shown some slight willingness to adjust positions. They had exercised restraint during the Cambodia incursion. They showed understanding of the concept of mutual deterrence but were apparently not yet disposed to improve mutual deterrence by emphasizing strategic stability, at least not by limiting large missile launchers. The Soviets were concerned about the prospect of a 12-site ABM program. This was evident from their quick acceptance of a single-site ABM limitation and by their apparent readiness even to consider a total ban on ABMs. There lay American bargaining power. We had taken the initiative by providing concrete approaches with details and numbers. But there was disadvantage in tempting the other side to choose what it preferred and reject what it did not. The Soviets apparently wanted a simple arrangement that did not have all the interlocking conditions of the American proposal. The delegation did not expect to reach agreement in 1970, but perhaps in the first half of 1971.

The August 4 proposal was the first U.S. major move in SALT. It remained our basic position until May 1971. In moving toward a narrower agreement and away from likely non-negotiable issues, the new approach laid the groundwork for the 1972 agreements. SALT could have broken up had there been too prolonged an impasse, with attitudes hardening and each side beginning to manipulate international opinion toward the view that the stalemate resulted from the other's unreasonableness.

But the August 4 proposal abandoned efforts for MIRV control, reductions, and comprehensive offensive arms limitations. We will never know if they eventually would have been negotiable in SALT I. Each side apparently wanted to improve overall relations with the other, and SALT was a key element. The talks were not taking place in a political vacuum. The stakes were rising. But moving to a simplified proposal may have extinguished some important arms control opportunities.

"THE GREAT MIRV MYSTERY"

"I may authorize a MIRV ban."

RICHARD NIXON

In retrospect, the weak effort to ban MIRVs was a key aspect of SALT. It was considered by some knowledgeable people as the leading lost opportunity of the negotiation. While the United States and the Soviet Union negotiated to limit the numbers of their strategic launchers they were increasing or preparing to increase their warheads manyfold. It is far from sure that even if we had made a more reasonable offer on MIRVs the Soviets would have accepted it. It seems somewhat doubtful that they would have locked themselves into a MIRVless condition, and it is most unlikely that the United States would, while stopping U. S. MIRV deployments, have permitted the Soviets to develop them through the testing stage. While there may have been an opportunity missed, it was not a clear one.

MIRVs were originally designed in the United States as a hedge. Their purpose was to assure that, even if attacked, the United States missile retaliatory forces would be able to penetrate a Soviet dense ABM defensive screen which it was assumed would exist by the late 1970s. With their striking power thus MIRV-multiplied, the potential of American missiles surviving any attack would be seen by the U.S.S.R. to be so great as to make such attack irrational. The integrity of our retaliatory forces would thus be preserved even if the Soviets deployed major ABM defenses. The SALT ABM Treaty of 1972 sharply reduced the likelihood that such ABM systems would ever be built. But MIRV programs persist.

Some MIRVed missiles can have more than a dozen nuclear warheads. MIRV multiplication of nuclear destruction is enormous. Without MIRVs, one United States strategic submarine could deliver warheads to 16 targets. With MIRVs, assuming only 10 warheads per missile, that submarine could launch attacks against 160 targets—more than all German and Japanese urban industrial areas bombed by the Allies in World War II. Small wonder that MIRVs were a key issue in any effort to control strategic arms. Great wonder that the issue was treated so cavalierly.

The major difficulty in trying to structure American and Soviet offensive strategic forces by international agreement rather than by unilateral decisions of each nation lies in the differing composition of the two forces, owing to historical, geographical and technological developments. In 1969 when SALT started, the Soviets were rapidly increasing the number of their missile launchers. The United States was not. The United States had a much larger and better intercontinental bomber force. In SALT the U.S.S.R. was to claim that the United States had a substantial advantage in fighter bombers forward based in Europe and the Far East and in the strategic submarine forces of its allies, England and France.

But the most important asymmetry of this period was in MIRVs. The MIRV capability to have a large number of warheads independently guided to separate targets was the most significant nuclear weapons development since the ballistic missile itself. It may well be that, although the Soviet position on American FBS was the ostensible cause of the failure to reach a treaty limiting offensive arms in SALT I; the real reason was that the United States was years ahead of the U.S.S.R. in MIRV technology. We were actually deploying MIRVed missiles during the negotiation. The Soviet Union had not even started to test them.

To many American officials, it was a very unattractive proposition to give up this great advantage, no matter what counterconcessions the Soviets might make. It was equally unappetizing to the U.S.S.R. to consider locking itself into an international commitment banning a fundamental new weapons system whose technology it had not yet mastered. Planners for a nation's security have to consider what the strategic balance would be if an arms limitation arrangement collapses. It is one thing to agree to stop construction of ICBM silos which could be resumed without much delay if the agreement was terminated. It is quite another to give up development of a major system which one's rival already has in stock. That is what the MIRV ban proposed by the United States in April 1970 would have required of the U.S.S.R.

One of our main purposes was to stop Soviet ICBM and SLBM launcher construction programs. The Soviets must have asked themselves what weapons programs the United States was proposing to stop in return. None. MIRVs were the only programs that the United States had to bargain with for Soviet stoppage of launcher construction programs. When it became clear that the United States was not willing to trade with them, the prospect of treaty restraints on Soviet offensive launchers dimmed. In a June 1969 letter to Secretary of State Rogers, I had written:

> It may be that our giving up MIRVs would be the only quid pro quo that the Soviets would be interested in for their halting deployment of ICBMs, SLBMs, ABMs. I believe that a strong case can also be made that in the long run it is not in U.S. interests to see MIRVs enter U.S. and Soviet arsenals. Certainly it will bring increased instability.

The failure to reach a MIRV ban foreshadowed the slushiness of the interim freeze on Soviet ICBM and SLBM launchers finally reached in May 1972. Although cast in terms of mutual obligations, the freeze (which left out MIRVs) did not constrain any United States programs. As Henry Kissinger said to the press at Moscow after the freeze agreement was signed, we were not in "the most brilliant bargaining position I would recommend people to find themselves in." That was because we had not been willing seriously to negotiate for a MIRV ban. MIRV was the decisive asymmetry which ultimately prevented reaching meaningful controls over offensive forces in SALT I. Seven years after SALT's start, when the U.S.S.R. had mastered MIRV technology and was deploying MIRVed missiles, it agreed in SALT II to a limit on offensive strategic launchers including those for MIRVed missiles at equal though high levels. But SALT II remains in un-ratified limbo in 1980.

The United States military had no interest in giving up MIRV programs in any SALT I settlement. They saw them as America's alternative to building more launchers and as a great boost to the effectiveness of ICBMs and SLBMs. They had worried for some time about the so-called SAM-upgrade problem. In a MIRVless world with many fewer American warheads for the Soviets to cope with, this problem could become much more serious. Their Soviet counterparts apparently also had little interest in blocking themselves off from this most fruitful weapons development. The Soviet military perhaps saw the U. S. MIRV programs as provoca-tive after the U.S.S.R. would have stopped its ABM program at the unfinished Moscow defense. In both capitals, political author-ities would have to take and sustain extremely difficult positions vis-à-vis their military if MIRVs were to be controlled, positions which could undermine crucial military support for the entire SALT effort. This common military interest in letting MIRV run free went a long way to spoil chances for a MIRV ban.

Given this state of affairs, how did the two nations handle the issue? At best only halfhearted efforts were made. Both said they favored a MIRV ban. Neither expressed disappointment when no ban was agreed upon.

The case for banning MIRVs was strong. They would increase the threat to both sides' fixed-based ICBMs. They would unneces-sarily expand the cost of weaponry. United States MIRV pro-grams cost about $14 billion. There is no reason to think the So-viet MIRV programs are much cheaper. MIRV would vastly expand the destructiveness of a general nuclear war. MIRV mul-tiplication of destructive nuclear power would be enormous, from around 2,000 to perhaps 10,000 nuclear warheads on each side, all substantially more powerful than the atomic bombs used in August 1945.

The prime need for MIRV control was reflected in the United States SALT objective of minimizing the prospective vulnerability of its ICBMs. Soviet MIRVs would increase the threat from their large ICBMs to American ICBMs especially as large missiles be-came more accurate and able to deliver many and large-yield warheads. Dr. Harold Brown, a principal SALT delegate, wrote in 1969: "Accurate MIRVs would tend to lessen the chance of land-based missiles surviving an attack since one first-strike missile with accurate MIRVs would destroy several deterrent missiles in their silos. . . . Clearly an agreement to ban the deployment of MIRVs would be desirable in order to forestall erosion of the capability to deter." Because of failure to ban MIRV, the threat to our ICBMs has not been significantly reduced in SALT. The United States for some years sublimated this danger, learned to live with it. But it won't go away. The SALT II agreed ceilings on MIRVed missile launchers are so high as to give only modest relief in the view of those analysts who project a high degree of ICBM vulnerability.

The Johnson Administration left an important arms control legacy to President Nixon. Had it not been for the invasion of Czechoslovakia in August 1968, SALT would have already started when President Nixon took office in January 1969. United States SALT positions prepared for that expected start in 1968 called for control of ABM systems and land- and submarine-based offensive missile launchers, the three systems which ultimately were included in the 1972 SALT agreements. But no ban on MIRVs was then included. The 1968 Pentagon had been opposed, and proponents of a MIRV ban didn't want to take on the Department of Defense in a MIRV fight right at the start. They feared that the Pentagon could have stopped SALT cold before it even started. They hoped that the dynamics of the negotiation would gradually bring the two governments to realize the advantages of MIRV control and the weakness of an agreement that did not ban them.

If there was a possibility of MIRV control, the asymmetries in the sides' programs suggested that it would have to be agreed early in a negotiation before U.S. deployment programs were far along. I believed that the United States should take the lead in proposing a ban. We were testing MIRVs as the Nixon Administration's SALT preparations got under way. In order to verify a MIRV deployment ban adequately, it was thought that MIRV testing would also have to be banned. In the absence of intrusive on-site inspection, it was thought to be impossible to determine with high confidence whether or not a deployed missile contained MIRV warheads. Some felt that even with on-site inspection this would not be possible. MIRV flight tests, on the other hand, would be observable by national means. If the sophisticated MIRV hardware could not be developed through flight testing, the chance that MIRVs would be produced and deployed on a large scale was small. Still, some U.S. officials argued that a MIRV test ban alone would not be adequate assurance. Even to its advocates a MIRV ban looked practical only if agreed on before a significant amount of testing had been done. Strategic analysis based on computer runs had shown that suspension by the United States of MIRV testing for as long as one year would not prejudice U.S. retaliatory capabilities during the mid-1970s.

Although there had been proposals for deferral of U. S. MIRV testing, it does not seem that serious consideration had been given to them during the Johnson Administration. By the winter of 1969 an early decision about stopping or continuing MIRV testing was clearly needed. Should it be suspended for a time to permit efforts to ban MIRVs before either side was in a position to deploy them? Unless something was done soon after the Nixon Administration took office, the option to pursue a MIRV ban could be closed out. During the winter and spring of 1969, I argued the need for a ban and emphasized the relationship between U.S. testing and the likely timing of SALT. I tried to capitalize on the President's known aversion to having his options closed out by actions of the bureaucracy, as in a memorandum I wrote him on May 22, 1969, which appears in Appendix 2.

I repeated my concern to Secretary Rogers on June 6:

Your press conference statement that continuation of MIRV testing would not prevent a successful SALT negotiation is, I understand, the "party line." In fact, at some point in the MIRV testing, the development of this new weapons system will be sufficiently advanced as to make a verification of its non-deployment an impossibility without on-site inspection of such an intrusive nature that we, let alone the Soviets, would probably not be willing to accept it. That will mean the most we can expect is a SALT agreement which permits the deployment of the many thousands of new warheads which a MIRV deployment would produce. What is involved here is for the United States, for example, an increase in nuclear warheads from 2,600 to between 7,000 and 9,500 by 1977. This is hardly a way to limit strategic arms.

My MIRV ban proposals soon merged into a broader position called SWWA, "Stop Where We Are," which involved not only stopping MIRV testing but cessation of Soviet ICBM and SLBM launcher construction programs. This proposal stemmed from a suggestion made by an Arms Control Agency official, Sidney Graybeal, who was a member of the SALT delegation and later the U.S. commissioner on the Soviet-American Standing Consultative Commission set up by the 1972 agreements. SWWA was based on a simple concept that the way to stop arms competition was to stop strategic construction programs on both sides. Both now had sufficient strategic forces to deter nuclear war. Instead of trying to elaborate agreed levels for strategic forces and other complex arrangements, why not just freeze things at the 1969 level? At the suggestion of Henry Owen, a former colleague on the Policy Planning Staff of the State Department and later its director, I recalled for the President the world-wide support which the United States received when Charles Evans Hughes proposed such a plan for strategic naval forces at the Washington Naval Conference in 1921. It was not at all clear that the U.S.S.R. would accept such a proposal, but by proposing it we could take the "high ground" psychologically and, if necessary later, move to something more modest if that was the most the Soviets would accept. I considered SWWA the best way to start the negotiation.

During a number of NSC meetings in the spring of 1969, I made the SWWA case for a moratorium on construction starts on all strategic systems, emphasizing the need to preserve the President's option to try to negotiate a MIRV ban. At this time Secretary of Defense Laird was publicly stressing the growing vulnerability of American ICBMs in the face of the threat posed by large Soviet missiles, especially as they came to be MIRVed. Owing in good part to his concerns, the Administration seemed unclear as to whether the Soviets were much further along on MIRVs than the intelligence community thought. The U.S.S.R. was testing multiple warheads, called multiple re-entry vehicles or MRVs, which were not capable of being independently targetable as are MIRVs. Laird said on a number of occasions, "I don't make the distinction between MRVs and MIRVs." All other U.S. military and intelligence officials did. In fact, MIRVed Poseidon missiles to be fitted into launchers on U.S. strategic submarines were to replace Polaris missiles with three warheads (MRVs). It was surprising to me that Secretary Laird was not more of a proponent of a MIRV ban, which would have moderated the prospective Soviet threat to American ICBMs. Laird used this threat to point up the dynamics of the Soviet missile programs and generate support for U.S. strategic programs but did not advocate the best way to avoid that threat—a MIRV ban.

The Joint Chiefs of Staff under Nixon were as adamantly opposed to a MIRV ban as under Johnson. Their SALT representative, General Allison, argued that the United States should not and in fact could not stop the march of technology. A first SALT agreement, he said, should be simple, easy to fulfill and to monitor, limited to quantitative ceilings and not affecting modernization programs such as MIRV. America's greatest military advantage was its technological superiority. That advantage could be maintained. Yes, the U.S.S.R. would someday deploy MIRVs, but who could tell when? Even if ABMs were to be limited or banned, MIRVs would still be needed for greater target coverage capability and as insurance against a sudden ending of an ABM treaty. It was a strong case, but not as convincing, I thought, as the argument that a MIRV ban was of central importance if the strategic arms competition was to be significantly curbed.

In June, I was encouraged by Secretary Laird's statement before the Senate Foreign Relations Committee that "MIRV is certainly something that is negotiable as far as any arms limitation talks are concerned." But civilian officials in his department then joined with some military analysts to elaborate rather obscure techniques which they said the Soviets could use to develop and deploy MIRVs without full-range testing. By 1970, Laird had lost his stomach for a MIRV ban if he ever had one. Kissinger advised me that Laird was now opposed.

The President seemed to think SWWA was intended as proganda. But he said he would give it serious consideration, perhaps as the basis for a speech—a speech he never gave. I felt and still do that such a mutual stop in strategic construction programs would have been very much in the United States' security interest.

Strategic offensive missile forces of the sides in 1969 were more nearly equal than in 1972 when a freeze was agreed upon. The Soviet large ICBM launchers were less numerous.

There was a good deal of public support for a SALT effort at MIRV control. MIRV received much more public and congressional attention than any other offensive weapon program. Its only competition for public attention during the early days of SALT was the ABM program. The notion of a many-headed missile monster lent itself well to cartoon criticism and those within range of the Washington *Post* were bombarded with cartoonist Herblock's visions of MIRV in many ugly versions.

Ideas for SALT were now proliferating in Congress and the press. Some called for unilateral suspension of MIRV testing by the United States. Counselor Vorontsov of the Soviet Embassy in Washington told the Tenth Strategy for Peace Conference at Warrenton, Virginia, in October 1969, that "the Soviet military want MIRV because the U.S. is developing it." He added that if the Soviets were convinced that the United States had stopped work on MIRV, stopping the Soviet military from MIRVing would not be difficult. "A sense of the Senate resolution which would halt MIRV development may be sufficient to halt Soviet MIRVing," he advised.

By July 1969 some 113 members of Congress had sponsored MIRV moratorium proposals. A subcommittee of the House Foreign Affairs Committee after extensive hearings reported that MIRV deployment would pose a substantial threat to the nuclear balance; that deployment by either side would make control agreements difficult and could lead to a vast new round in the arms race; that the opportunities for control decreased as testing continued; and that certain collateral agreements were necessary to enforce a MIRV limitation. The subcommittee said that the MIRV problem should be handled through SALT. Its conclusion was that "the executive branch should give high priority to obtaining a MIRV freeze during the forthcoming SALT negotiations."

In July I suggested another MIRV move to the White House:

We could approach the Soviets with a suggestion for a joint moratorium—say for a few months—until we had had a chance to explore initial positions in SALT. Alternatively, we could take the initiative and announce we were not going to test for a specified period of time so long as the Soviet Union did not test MIRVs or MRVs.

Since the MIRV ban agitation in the press paralleled the effort in Congress to block the ABM program, I tried to relate the two. In an effort to interest the Administration in a political move, I wrote Secretary Rogers in August urging that certain senators who favored a MIRV ban and were lukewarm about the ABM program be told that if they would back ABM, which was then in serious trouble, the White House would work for a MIRV testing moratorium. Nothing came of it.

On August 12, Senator Hubert Humphrey wrote Rogers that during a recent visit to the U.S.S.R., he had heard a leading Soviet academician, Millionshchikov, say that he saw no obstacle to an early agreement to ban multiple warhead testing. Humphrey urged an immediate U.S. unilateral declaration of suspension of further MIRV tests to last as long as the Soviets also refrained from such testing. He wrote that, in his judgment, "this issue dwarfs in importance the ABM question which has been so hotly debated in recent weeks and months." Senator Humphrey got a rather dusty answer that a moratorium on MIRV testing "in connection with any arms control agreement [is] a possibility we are considering."

I did not favor unilateral U.S. test suspension. When the SWWA approach was not accepted, I pressed for a negotiating moratorium covering all new missile launcher starts, including initiation of new ABM deployments and flight testing of MIRV/MRVs. Such a negotiating moratorium would exchange Soviet restraint on ICBM and SLBM launcher construction for U.S. restraint in ABM and MIRV programs. The White House was not responsive.

"Moratorium" later became a dirty word. The President ordered a ban on lobbying by officials for any kind of pre-SALT stoppage of construction. The order was in fairly rough language. "Any, repeat any, individual who gives any, repeat any, encouragement to this kind of speculation should be first reprimanded and then discharged." Lest there be doubt as to the emphatic nature of this command, I was advised "last sentence of text with emphasis is handwritten."

The White House, throughout SALT, had the incorrect impression that the Arms Control Agency had an influence with Congress out of all proportion to its size and budget (less than $10 million).[1] Although it is impossible to stop executive branch people from expressing views to members of Congress, especially if their views are solicited, I made it clear to ACDA people that they were not to engage in lobbying. This direction was carried out with few exceptions. I doubt if other agencies could say the same.

Still, White House doubts about ACDA people persisted. President Nixon was allergic to arms controllers as a group. In ACDA there were not only some officials who had worked in the Johnson and Kennedy administrations, but they were "arms controllers" to boot, a tribe that President Nixon and some of his staff suspected of some vague disloyalty to the Administration. Even though ACDA people played a major role in the Administration's fine arms control record—the Seabeds Treaty, the Biological Warfare Convention, and SALT—a number of these officers were rewarded after the election of 1972 by, in effect, being fired. The sting from this treatment must have lessened somewhat as their tormentors in the White House got worse treatment very shortly thereafter.

Summertime in 1969 came and went and no date had been set for the start of the negotiation. It was by now clear that the President was interested neither in suspension of MIRV testing nor in proposing a negotiating moratorium on all strategic programs. But he understood the importance of MIRV for the strategic forces of both nations as well as for the impending negotiation. On July 21, in his general guidance for the first SALT round, he wrote that he might authorize an effort to ban MIRV. That was an encouraging signal. It did not fly for long.

When I had finally received specific guidance in November for the opening Helsinki round, this July reference to a possible MIRV ban was expressly canceled. No explanation was given. Perhaps the President was concerned lest we prematurely fore-

[1] A smaller figure than the then cost of the Public Information Center in the Department of Defense.

shadow to the Soviets U.S. interest in MIRV control before he further settled the matter in his mind.

White House MIRV guidance for the opening round at Helsinki was sparse. In the interest of exploring Soviet attitudes, the question of MIRV might be included in a work program. The delegation could discuss it only after consideration of limitations on defensive systems, and within the context of the verifiability of (a) limitations on defensive systems and (b) possible bans on MIRV flight testing and deployment and constraints associated therewith. The President would judge the feasibility of restraints on MIRV in terms of their strategic consequences and their verifiability. Showing how sensitive the White House was about a moratorium, the guidance also forbade any discussion of this issue. Before engaging in any talk about a moratorium or even agreeing to a work program, the delegation was to seek further instructions from Washington.

The day SALT began we requested authority to explore Soviet views if they raised the issue of a MIRV test moratorium. We proposed only to ask some questions for clarification. Our MIRV programs were in large part a response to concerns about Soviet ABM deployments and the possibility of the Soviets making antiaircraft missiles capable of intercepting warheads from ballistic missiles (SAM upgrade). We would like to know whether any Soviet proposal for a MIRV test moratorium would be in the context of a moratorium on ABM deployment and a ban on SAM upgrading. MIRVs would mean more re-entry vehicles. So would additional ICBMs and SLBMs. Would a MIRV test moratorium include a freeze on ICBM and SLBM deployments? What kind of assurances and verification would the Soviets suggest for providing confidence that a MIRV test moratorium was being observed? Would MRVs be included? Should the Soviets propose a MIRV deployment moratorium in addition to a testing suspension, we proposed to ask how necessary confidence could be obtained that deployment was not taking place. The delegation would state that the United States believed this would pose difficult verification problems requiring discussion of some on-site inspection.

Washington's response was negative. The delegation was not to raise the subject of any type of moratorium. If Soviets did so, we were to respond that the United States believed that the general scope of SALT should be explored before discussing a moratorium. White House skittishness was reflected in a final caution that hardly could be called bold diplomacy. If the Soviets presented a specific moratorium proposal, the only thing the delegation was authorized to say was: "We will refer the matter to Washington."

After a few weeks at Helsinki, I reported to the President:

> After five meetings with some five or six to go under present scheduling, the "great MIRV mystery" is, I think, worth noting. Neither side in the full meetings or in private exchanges has so much as mentioned MIRV. I have no clear idea to offer as to the Soviet reasoning. My hunch is that they calculate that there is sufficient Congress/public pressure to cause us to raise MIRV and that they will not, therefore, have to take whatever small loss in bargaining power may go along with being first to raise MIRV. And it may be that, feeling behind in the MIRV competition, they sense that they would be showing weakness by raising the subject and so prefer to wait us out.

It soon became clear that the Soviet delegation expected the United States to raise the MIRV issue, probably in the context of ABM limitation. Finally, on December 10, the U.S. delegation, armed with fresh guidance from Washington, backed into the MIRV matter in a gingerly fashion, by tabling a list of "components" that could be considered later in the negotiation. It included "missiles, boosters, radars, penetration aids, MIRV and MRV, chaff, and decoys." This was the only formal mention of MIRVs at Helsinki.

Our MIRV performance must have been especially puzzling to the Soviet delegation. Since the United States was about to deploy MIRVs and the Soviets were not, MIRV was "our subject" as one Soviet later put it. In early December we heard privately that the military members of the Soviet delegation were suspicious of our avoidance of MIRV. I was sufficiently concerned to write President Nixon about MIRVs on December 3. I recommended that the MIRV issue not be left in limbo, pointing out that Soviet MIRVed SS-9s would offer the greatest threat to our ICBMs. I amplified this view at length as set out in Appendix 3.

As we have seen, Semenov and the Soviet delegation wanted no part of the "components" approach. They interpreted the components list as an indication that the United States would seek controls on weapons characteristics requiring on-site inspection. In limiting elements other than launchers, Semenov argued, it would be necessary to resort to controls beyond national means and this would affect the most sensitive aspects of the national security of both sides.

MIRVs were not included in the agreed Work Program. But it was understood that the general provisions of the program would permit MIRVs to be discussed. Thus MIRV, which was central to the strategic balance, was given very low-key treatment at Helsinki. In subsequent sessions it fared no better.

The Soviets may have given a signal at Helsinki that we failed to notice. In criticizing our list of components, they spelled out all the other components that we had proposed for consideration but failed to mention MIRV, leaving this term perhaps covered with a vague "et cetera." Was this negative pregnant with a possible interest in pursuing a MIRV ban? During an informal exchange, a Soviet official said that their objection to the components approach did not apply to MIRV. Even so, their reception of the idea of MIRV control was hardly enthusiastic. Perhaps this reflected psychological reluctance even to talk about a ban on a weapons system they had not yet developed. But the Soviet delegation was very likely alert to the risk that the SALT record might promptly be published if the talks collapsed. They did not relish the prospect of appearing to oppose any major arms control possibility and especially one that would have been as popular as a MIRV ban. In any event, the possibility of discussing MIRV controls was smothered in general language in the agreed Program of Work for the next round.

I was far from satisfied with the way MIRV had been handled by either side at Helsinki. We had learned little about the Soviet attitude. They were at least as cautious as we. We assumed that it would be very difficult for the U.S.S.R. to agree to choke off its MIRV future when the United States was so far ahead. They obviously were concerned that engaging in an effort to control MIRV would get them involved in on-site inspection. And we did not know what our final MIRV position would turn out to be.

From the Washington record, prospects for approval of a MIRV ban looked poor.

In retrospect, it appears that at Helsinki the Soviets sensed that the United States expected them to raise MIRV, probably in the form of a call for suspension of MIRV testing. They may have calculated that this would have led to a U.S. call for suspension of Soviet construction of launchers for SLBMs and ICBMs and that might have struck the Moscow authorities as a polemic not conducive to convincing them that SALT was a serious negotiation. One Soviet official informally suggested as much. It will be recalled that the delegation estimated after this preliminary round that Soviet agreement to proceed with the talks after the preliminary Helsinki round had been far from a foregone conclusion. It would be time enough for both sides to make specific MIRV proposals at the next round in Vienna.

The U.S.S.R. is sensitive to criticism, by a world yearning for release from bondage to arms, that only a selfish Soviet "closed" policy prevents disarmament. The Soviet delegation apparently considered the on-site inspection issue also a likely subject for an American polemic which would detract from the serious and businesslike approach they apparently were looking for. The Soviets had some reason to believe that the United States was ready to reach limitations that would not require on-site inspection. This was the impression they had gained from exchanges with officials in the Johnson Administration. I think Semenov was anxious to prove to his "centrum" in Moscow that this was to be a real negotiation and not another exercise in propaganda as may have seemed to be the case a number of times in the past.

The "great MIRV mystery" at Helsinki somewhat strengthened the hands of Pentagon opponents of a MIRV ban, who may have felt that they had gained a Soviet ally in the effort to keep MIRV free. The "MIRV" phase of Helsinki left a ban still a possibility. But barely so.

As 1970 started, the issue could no longer be ducked as it had been in 1968 and 1969. The Nixon Administration finally had to step up to it as specific negotiating approaches were developed for the Vienna SALT round due to start in April. Nixon's dilemma now was how to avoid flat rejection of congressional and popular calls for a MIRV ban.

The President had strong recommendations from me for such a ban, in which the Secretary of State joined. I pointed out that, if only launchers were limited and all other aspects of offensive strategic weapons were allowed to be improved, we might not accomplish very much. Kissinger made the same point to a congressional group early that year, saying that an agreement without qualitative limitations was relatively easy but might merely amount to ratification of present military plans. He told me that he favored a MIRV ban "if it could be verified."

I argued at Verification Panel and National Security Council meetings that, in view of the much larger throw-weight of the Soviet ICBM force, not banning MIRVs would in the end give the U.S.S.R. an advantage. MIRVs in Soviet large missiles would be seen as a threat to U. S. ICBMs, and if we wanted to bring this threat under control a MIRV ban was the answer. I wrote the President in late March, "There would be risks in such a controlled environment but I believe that they are calculable, insurable . . . and reasonable ones to run."

On April 9, Senate Resolution 211 passed by a 72–6 margin expressing the sense of the Senate that the President should propose an immediate suspension by the United States and the U.S.S.R. of further deployment of all offensive and defensive strategic weapons systems, subject to national verification or such other measures of observation and inspection as might be appropriate. Supporters of the resolution stressed that the Soviets would not negotiate from a position of inequality and that a suspension was of mutual advantage and the only real basis for a MIRV agreement. Several senators later spoke out against a reported remark by the President that the resolution was "irrelevant."

The Pentagon continued to be flatly opposed. General Allison forcefully presented the negative views of the Joint Chiefs of Staff —and his heart was really in his work. I think he found it somewhat distasteful even to be involved in discussing a MIRV ban conditioned upon on-site inspection—and I know he was relieved when the MIRV control effort was finally abandoned. The military continued to favor MIRV deployment as a hedge against the possibility of the breakdown of any ABM treaty. The argument was also made that U. S. MIRVs were of relatively low explosive yield and therefore "good" and usable only for retaliation, not for a "first strike." This argument ignored important considerations such as their accuracy and large number. These considerations, as seen by Soviet planners, would make them "bad" and useful in a first strike. For SALT to succeed, the President obviously needed support from the military. Later in the negotiation, when agreement was in sight, the White House might be able to take positions somewhat unwelcome to the Pentagon, but not on such a key issue as a MIRV ban and right at the start.

President Nixon finally solved the dilemma by calling for a MIRV ban requiring on-site inspection as part of a larger package of strategic arms control. This came as no surprise. His initial guidance to the delegation the previous year had directed us to raise the flag of on-site inspection if the Soviets proposed a MIRV ban. But he must have known that such a condition had little or no chance of being accepted. A similar condition on American acceptance of a comprehensive ban on nuclear testing had—perhaps with some justification—blocked agreement for more than fifteen years. The Soviet delegation at the 1969 Helsinki talks had stressed that any SALT agreement should be verified by national technical means only. They had reacted strongly against the U.S. "components" approach because they said it foreshadowed on-site inspection. "Such an approach was impossible for them . . . it was contrary to the principle of not prejudicing the interests of either side . . . against the security interests of either side, thus incompatible with an agreement." Methods of verification clearly had been a major concern of the Soviet delegation at Helsinki. U.S. non-insistence on on-site inspection may well have been a sine qua non for proceeding to Vienna.

In the short term, the President accomplished his purpose. A number of pro-MIRV-ban senators, perhaps not realizing the implications of the inspection condition, were very pleased that the President was taking what they thought to be a progressive step. They were soon disillusioned.

In fairness to President Nixon, it should be said that this matter of on-site inspection was not entirely black and white. There had been two slight indications that the Soviets might consider some easement of their past objections. Soviet Ambassador Dobrynin had told me informally, and not speaking specifically about a

MIRV ban, that perhaps in a second SALT agreement some on-site inspection could be agreed on. And Semenov had hinted at Helsinki that some cooperative measures might be worked out to supplement national technical means of verification. Both of these straws in the wind had been reported to the White House. But they were much too slim pickings for President Nixon to have based a judgment on that on-site inspection for a MIRV ban would be acceptable. It is ironic that four years later President Ford at Vladivostok agreed to a ceiling on launchers for MIRVed missiles without calling for on-site inspection. It was then argued that any violation of the MIRV limitation (at the high levels permitted, 1,320) would be much less significant than in the case of a complete ban on MIRVs. And the Salt II treaty contains limits on launchers for MIRVed missiles without any on-site inspection.

There is circumstantial evidence that the U. S. MIRV ban proposal was not serious. During SALT, the White House made much of the great care and thoroughness of SALT preparations, stressing the "building block" approach which was supposed to arm negotiators with preplanned moves for all contingencies. I recall no discussion in the Verification Panel or the NSC of the details of a "building block" for on-site inspection before it was proposed as a condition for a MIRV ban. Although the Arms Control Agency and the Atomic Energy Commission had done some work on techniques for on-site inspection, there was little if any preparatory discussion at high levels about the specifics of such inspection, or, in fact, about what if any advantages it might offer over national technical means of verification. There was little consideration of what such intrusive inspection of American missiles would mean for Soviet acquisition of weapons information. All in all, these deficiencies suggest that the contingency of Soviet acceptance seemed so unlikely as not to be worth much consideration or concern.

Just as we were leaving for Vienna in the spring of 1970, the importance to the President of this on-site inspection condition and the weight of reliance he placed on it was emphasized in a message to me.

It is essential that the verification provisions of that option will be an integral part of your presentation for I am convinced that an agreement on the limitations contained in that option without the required verification provisions would create dangerous instabilities in our relations with the USSR.

The U. S. MIRV ban approach must have been doubly unpalatable to the Soviets when they learned that it also required on-site inspection of their anti-aircraft missile sites, as well as the dismantling of all faces of the large new radars they were deploying to cover potential U.S. missile attack corridors. The first condition was called for because, if MIRVs were to be banned, the strategic risks associated with SAM upgrade would increase. Without MIRVs the U.S. retaliation force warheads would be many times fewer and thus the significance of a missile defense even by upgraded SAM much greater. It was argued in Washington that if the Soviets, by violating the MIRV ban or by improving the accuracy or yields of their single-warhead missile forces, built a first strike force which could effectively destroy a major part of the Minuteman ICBM force they might believe that upgraded SAMs would be capable of reducing to acceptable levels the retaliatory damage which could be inflicted by the non-MIRVed warheads from the surviving U. S. SLBM force. The second condition—dismantling of the radar faces—was necessary because it was thought they would augment an upgraded SAM defense. The depth of military concern over the risk of SAM upgrade in a MIRV ban environment was made evident when Washington was analyzing a MIRV production ban in June 1970. The JSC representative argued then that if a MIRV production ban was to be considered it should be coupled with far more stringent SAM controls even than those provided in the approach just discussed and should include actual destruction of a sizable portion of the Soviet anti-aircraft missile force.

To propose on-site inspection of SAM sites, when we knew the Soviets believed that SAM upgrade was not a realistic possibility and had some suspicion that these provisions were an attempt to restrict their air defense systems, was, to say the least, a bold proposition. It was no surprise when Semenov, after stating that on-site inspection would be tantamount to intelligence activity, argued that they could not but be put on guard by the insistence with which the solution of substantial problems of limiting strategic armaments was made conditional on on-site inspection.

A Verification Panel Working Group eventually did study the adequacy of national technical means of verification and on-site inspection to monitor a MIRV ban. A paper was completed in mid-June 1970, two months after the U. S. MIRV ban proposal was made and just as it was being abandoned. Predictably, there was disagreement between the agencies based on their different views as to the feasibility of upgrading SAMs to give them a significant ABM capability, the degree of Soviet progress in MRV or MIRV testing, and the capabilities of national technical means of verification. The Pentagon argued that SAMs with even modest ABM capability represented a substantial threat which could not be detected by national technical means. Sufficient MIRV testing by the Soviets might already have been conducted, or might be finished before a SALT agreement was ratified. And anyway, flight test restrictions could not eliminate the possibilities of Soviet violations. They might test MIRVs at short ranges, in space, or with numerous other deceptive techniques and deploy them clandestinely. They could complete testing after sudden abrogation of the agreement with a significant MIRV force already deployed. The military concluded that the United States must be able to verify a MIRV deployment ban with high confidence and for that on-site inspection was necessary.

Officials in the State Department, ACDA and the CIA believed that SAMs could not be significantly upgraded without detection by U.S. national technical means, that the Soviets had not yet developed MIRVs, and that if the Soviets conducted flight tests needed to develop them they would be detected. It seemed highly unlikely that the Soviets would replace their existing warheads with inadequately tested MIRVs and even less so that they would rely on such systems to mount a surprise attack. While on-site inspection would have value in helping to deter violations and in supplementing intelligence sources, they judged that a MIRV ban could be safely verified by national technical means alone.

At Vienna an ingenious and disingenuous MIRV mismatch was proposed by the two sides. The American approach would have banned deployment of MIRVs but permitted the United States, with MIRVs fully tested before a treaty was signed, to continue to produce and stockpile them as insurance against collapse of the agreement. The Soviet proposal called for an unverifiable ban on

MIRV production and deployment but would allow them to test MIRVs. Cynics might suspect sub rosa cooperation between two parties unwilling to give up MIRVs but anxious to appear to be in favor of outlawing them.

The Soviets said that there should have been no question in our minds as to whether they would accept on-site inspection. Our proposal, they said, was clearly to meet public relations requirements. The Soviets claimed that inspection of a deployment ban under the conditions proposed by the United States would be meaningless. The United States, being permitted to produce MIRVs which it had already tested, could simply put MIRVed warheads on missiles as soon as Soviet inspectors had left the area. In order to have any kind of effective on-site inspection of a MIRV deployment ban, there would have to be inspectors "all over" on a resident basis, and even then it would not be really effective under the U.S. approach allowing unlimited MIRV production. Soviets also claimed that the MIRV control approach was contrived since the U.S. delegation said that it would also soon be presenting an alternative SALT approach having equal status with the MIRV ban approach.

When asked how their proposed MIRV production ban could be verified, some Soviets conceded informally that it was not possible to verify it but that when major powers are serious about something they expect to take their obligations seriously and others should accept their intention to do so.

Several officials on the U.S. delegation now pressed me to propose to Washington the obvious compromise between the two positions—to offer to accept the Soviet proposal for a ban on production if they would accept the proposed ban on testing. In late May 1970 the delegation wired Washington that unless the United States was willing to consider a MIRV production ban in addition to the proposed flight testing and deployment bans, we did not believe we could usefully probe Soviet interest further. But in making this indirect recommendation, we did not propose dropping the on-site inspection condition. By then we knew the President had made up his mind on this score. Washington did not reply. Later Kissinger told me that if the Soviets had shown any interest in a MIRV test ban the on-site inspection condition would have been dropped. I wonder.

In a private conversation on June 1, Semenov charged bluntly that the U. S. MIRV proposal had been designed to be rejected. The Soviet side had repeatedly insisted that SALT verification must be by national means alone. At almost the same time that the Vienna negotiation began, the U.S. had announced that it was proceeding to deploy Minuteman III missiles equipped with MIRVs. He understood from the press that 18 such missiles had already been deployed and that work was in progress on others. This situation made the U.S. proposal propagandistic.

There was, I told him, no basis for his argument. If the United States took the position that because the U.S.S.R. had continued deploying ICBMs while engaging in the negotiation it was interested only in propaganda, it would hardly be conducive to agreement. His statement amounted to questioning the good faith of the United States. In fact, I felt Semenov's comment was not far from the mark. But the same could be said for the Soviet MIRV proposal.

My state of mind about MIRV control was reflected in a letter to the President on June 3 which started with "SALT is not pouring very fast these days." I reported that the Soviet MIRV proposal still seemed to be for the record and was not indicative of serious interest in a verifiable MIRV ban. Then, on June 9, Semenov privately questioned whether reductions and MIRV control would not be "premature" and "complicate" an initial agreement. Was he suggesting that a first agreement omit a MIRV ban or reductions? He seemed to think so—and mentioned the difficulty of MIRV verification. He remarked that "both sides had spoken about MIRVs" in a way that implied that our duty had now been done. It seemed clear that the Soviet preference was for a limited initial agreement not banning MIRVs. Soviet officials commented to this effect. On June 15 the delegation proposed to Washington an approach to the Soviets which omitted a MIRV ban. This, it will be recalled, was designated the Vienna Option.

That was the end of the road for a MIRV ban. The sides had been quite passive in exploring the respective positions to see if anything could be worked out. Each had made its record. But in the absence of any real pressure from the political authorities, MIRV control withered on the vine. Those of us who favored a ban had finally got the point. Our side did not want a MIRV ban.

Later there were a few informal and intermediate-level indications that the U.S.S.R. was really interested. But this line never was officially surfaced.

Was it the on-site inspection condition or the proposed American MIRV flight test ban that made our approach unacceptable? It may well be that the former was a convenient excuse to cover the central objection to the latter. Several informal probes indictated that even without the on-site inspection condition the Soviets would not accept the U. S. MIRV proposal because it would allow the United States but not the U.S.S.R. to produce already tested MIRVs. Being cut off from testing, they could not develop them. And it was not clear that even if the United States would agree to ban production of MIRVs the Soviets would agree to a test ban, all without on-site inspection.

Only three months after tabling its MIRV approach, the United States, having decided that a comprehensive SALT package was not negotiable, moved to a narrower proposal and jettisoned the MIRV ban. This was a critical turning point. When Kissinger and Dobrynin were negotiating covertly during the winter of 1971, Kissinger asked if the preliminary accord they were working on should state that MIRVs were not included. "That's self-evident," Dobrynin observed in a fitting epitaph for this lost opportunity. And it was about at this time that the first U.S. submarine with MIRVed missiles became operational.

After the United States tabled its next SALT proposal on August 4, 1970, Semenov said it was defective because it contained no MIRV ban. This could not have been a serious observation.

In November 1970, at the next round in Helsinki, a Soviet said that it was our fault that the opportunity for MIRV control had been lost. They had never considered the U. S. MIRV proposal as genuine. The nature of the United States' proposal made it clear that it was a "cheap sop" to appease congressional opinion. This kind of proposal was "preposterous." Although that was his personal evaluation, he said it had also been accepted by the Soviet government. But another Soviet acknowledged that there were deficiencies in both Soviet and American positions.

Later at Helsinki, Semenov revived the Soviet version of a MIRV ban, prohibiting production and deployment but not testing. An American inquired how the United States could verify it, facetiously asking, "Would we read about it in the Soviet press?" They did not push this renewed MIRV proposal. The United States had been the first to give up what at best had been a half-hearted quest. Now the U.S.S.R. also jettisoned the MIRV issue. Semenov said this question must be given appropriate treatment within the framework of an overall agreement and that a "cardinal" solution at SALT must include MIRVs. But by this time both sides were aiming for less than a "cardinal" solution. We were informally advised that the Soviets planned to say nothing more about MIRV unless we raised the subject. After that, with one exception, all was silent on the MIRV front.

In May 1972, when the leaders of the two nations tried their hands at SALT negotiating, they almost stumbled inadvertently into an arrangement that would have been the equivalent of a partial MIRV ban. But that comes later in the SALT story.

I think now that I should have pressed the case for a MIRV ban even after the Soviet rejection at Vienna. Only three months after presenting its MIRV approach the United States abandoned it without any effort to search for a middle ground between Soviet and American positions. That's an unconscionably short period as measured by the usual life of arms control positions. But there seemed no chance of weaning the White House away from the military position that MIRVs must not be outlawed. It seemed time to get on to more negotiable possibilities.

Too late was it realized that no stable agreement to limit offensive strategic arms could exist without stringent MIRV control. Kissinger was asked at a press briefing in December 1974 if he was sorry the United States went ahead with MIRV in 1969. He said, "Well, that's a good question. And I think that is the same question that people faced when the hydrogen bomb was developed. And it raises the issue whether your development of MIRVs or of a weapon produces the development on the other side, or whether by not going ahead you then simply give an advantage to the other side. . . . I would say in retrospect that I wish I had thought through the implications of a MIRVed world more thoughtfully in 1969 and in 1970 than I did."

In the second SALT negotiation, which started in November 1972, the parties agreed on a limit instead of a ban on MIRVs at the level of the MIRVed missile launcher numbers now in the

U.S. strategic forces—which might more accurately be called a ratification rather than a limitation. All that we can do now is to project rather faint hopes that significant reductions in MIRV launcher levels will be agreed in the future.

In considering the pros and cons of a MIRV ban, one should keep in mind that in 1970 we were aiming for an agreement that would limit at an equal level missile launchers of the two sides. By 1972 this equal-limitation concept had been replaced by the idea of a short-term "freeze" at then existing levels when the U.S.S.R. had a substantially higher number of missile launchers than the United States. Under these conditions our MIRV advantage, which would persist throughout the short term of the freeze, looked very good and a MIRV ban no longer seemed advantageous. But this was a short-term perspective. The U. S. MIRV advantage will not last long and, once gone, it will be irretrievable.

President Nixon stated in his 1971 Foreign Policy Report, ". . . our MIRV systems by contrast do not have the combination of numbers, accuracy and warhead yield to pose a threat to the Soviet land-based ICBM force." This was the "good MIRV" argument. But by 1979 American policy was to develop such threatening systems, apparently in order to match the Soviet threat to our ICBMs. And the manifold multiplication of warhead numbers provided by MIRVs was a major stimulus to the new American doctrine of limited so-called "surgical" strategic strikes the adoption of which is taking us into unknowable recesses of the sphere of deterrence. A MIRVless world would have been much safer.

CHAPTER
5

A SEASON
OF FRUSTRATION

Helsinki III:
November–December 1970

After the long second round in Vienna (April to August) the Helsinki third round seemed very short—from November 2 to December 18, 1970—but it was stormy. President Nixon's instructions were to hold the line on the Vienna August 4 position and insist that the Soviets respond to it. "The ball was now in the Soviet court." We were to avoid volunteering any clarification of the U.S. position. Any provision affecting U.S. forward-based systems was absolutely unacceptable.

At first the U.S.S.R. appeared to remain interested in an agreement limiting both offensive and defensive arms, but their most important move was formally to propose separation of the two with an initial agreement limiting only ABMs. The timing and target for negotiations on offensive weapons was left unclear. But Soviet comments suggested willingness to have an arrangement of the kind reached the following year which would link an ABM agreement with some unspecified measures to moderate the offensive missile launcher build-up. The Soviet delegation kept on repeating FBS arguments. It was said that our refusal to consider their views prevented progress on offensive arms limitations. FBS infected the atmosphere and set a discordant note for the whole round. This was the nadir of SALT I.

The session got off to a poor start. The Soviets reacted negatively to our negotiating strategy of standing pat on the August 4 position, which Semenov had earlier said did not constitute a basis for agreement. A series of incidental exchanges and events marred the first week. One was precipitated by Semenov's remarks in his first formal intervention. Attempts to use the ongoing negotiation, under one pretext or another, to justify and substantiate or even to spur the strategic arms race did not correspond to the objectives of the negotiation. The use of methods of this sort created a danger that the talks would be transformed into their antithesis. I told him that I realized we were in the election process in the United States, a time when polemics were often resorted to, but I wondered to whom he was alluding. He was speaking of Secretary Laird, who had made some unfavorable remarks since the talks recessed in Vienna. I again assured Semenov that Secretary Laird was interested in a positive solution of the arms limitation problem and did not oppose the negotiation. He was far too intelligent a politician to make statements intended as pressure on the Soviet Union. He knew that attempts to pressure major powers were likely to be counterproductive. Laird's statements were normal reporting by a Secretary of Defense to the Congress and the American people about what would have to be done in the way of defense programs if a SALT agreement was not reached.

The second American plenary statement was limited to just a few lines, the shortest ever made at SALT, urging that they address our August 4 proposal.

"We have studied your statement at our meeting of November the 3rd and will carefully consider your remarks of this morning. With some of the general observations in the November 3rd statement we agree. We have noted with satisfaction the reaffirmation of the interest of your government in the success of our talks. If, however, we are to achieve success in our talks—if we are able to make progress in our negotiations—the single most important requirement at this time in our judgment is that the Soviet side continue to respond in specific terms to the U.S. August 4th proposal."

This minuscule plenary statement was intended to jolt them into a realization that we were running out of patience, that we felt that the time had come to stop talking in generalities. I recalled for Semenov his statement in Vienna that the U.S.S.R. had sung its song and now would listen. That was now our position. The parties were engaged in a duet, said he, and it was important to listen for new nuances. Other Soviet officials commented informally that this was not an appropriate way for the United States to negotiate. But they got the point.

For the second time in SALT there were interdelegation tensions. A Soviet interpreter rendered in Russian the English word "requirement" in my statement as "demand." The Soviets, especially military officials, were exercised by what they took to be a *diktat*. Semenov reacted immediately by saying there were two methods of presentation, polemic and positive. He preferred the positive. We learned of the mistake at a reception that evening when one Soviet explained that Semenov's sharp reaction to our "polemical" approach had been caused by their interpretation of "requirement" as "demand." Things were smoothed out by pointing to the fact that the English word "requirement" was quite appropriate in the context.

Another irritant was a Finnish press story reporting that the United States had presented a proposal and it was up to the Soviets to accept or reject it. Semenov said that if anyone having anything to do with the SALT negotiation had said that to the press it was a breach of confidence and a biased and disloyal act. I denied that any American was responsible and recalled Foreign Minister Gromyko recently had been told that in no sense was the U.S. August 4 proposal made on a take-it-or-leave-it basis.

An unrelated incident provoked some sharp exchanges. Two U. S. Army generals, Scherrer and McQuarrie, flying a light plane from Turkey, inadvertently crossed the Soviet border in bad weather and were detained on landing. General Allison expressed his feelings with some vigor to General Ogarkov about Soviet refusals to release these men. Ogarkov said he knew nothing about the matter. Soviet Armenia was far from Helsinki and the problem was not related to SALT. Allison asked how to reconcile this action with the need for mutual understanding and cooperation to limit strategic arms. Every problem has invisible strings tying it to other questions and requiring mutual cooperation. Obviously the crossing of the Soviet border had been owing to adverse weather with strong winds. Allison could not understand the need for detention of the two generals and the excessive Soviet delay in their release. Ogarkov then indicated he knew about the episode and he expected it to be resolved quickly. Allison expressed hope that they would be released before the next SALT meeting. The day of the next plenary, the entire American delegation was invited to a Soviet reception commemorating the October Revolution. The generals were still being detained. To demonstrate feelings about the incident, the American presence was minimal, a fact quickly noted by the Soviet hosts. An American officer asked his Soviet counterpart how they could expect us to be voluntary guests when our countrymen were being detained involuntarily. One Soviet said the generals' case was indirectly related to SALT. They would not have crossed the Soviet border had the United States not had forward bases in Turkey. Our people retorted that the U.S. bases abroad were related to political conditions well known to the Soviets and had no relationship to SALT.

Four days later the generals were released. It is quite possible that Generals Scherrer and McQuarrie were detained to underscore the Soviets' FBS objective. A Radio Moscow commentary of October 21 said: "The incident involving the U.S. aircraft once more serves to stress the fact that the proposals made by the Soviet Union for the liquidation of foreign military bases in other countries' territories are completely topical and timely."

On another occasion a Soviet plane fired its guns close to an American Air Force plane flying well away from Soviet territorial waters. General Allison again took umbrage at this reckless move and pointed out to Soviet generals how inconsistent it was with protestations of Soviet interest in strategic arms control. While this sort of confrontation had happened a number of times in the 1950s and '60s, I understand this was the last of these incidents.

The rest of November was uneventful. Most of the time was spent going round and round old positions with old arguments— the need for ABM controls, FBS, limits on offensive arms/ bombers, MR/IRBMs, mobile missile launchers, modernization and silo modification, and non-transfer. There was little new and few Soviet specifics. As plenary followed plenary and we reviewed the August 4 proposal without presenting new material, the Soviets complained that this passivity was not consistent with good-faith negotiation, that we were in effect stonewalling. Soviet tactics were also aimed at stringing out their presentations, which could easily have been made in several meetings, which one Soviet informally admitted.

Just as we had begun this session by saying that progress depended on the Soviets responding in specific terms to the August 4 proposal, Semenov stated that the Soviet side continued to expect us to respond on the question of forward-based systems. Absence of an FBS provision was said to be the fundamental problem with our August 4 position. We were told again and again that, in their strategic significance, these systems were commensurate with so-called central strategic systems. The U.S. side was proposing agreement on the basis of inequality and the creation of unilateral advantages. The United States was said to be increasing the range and performance of its FBS aircraft even as the negotiations proceeded. Informally we heard that FBS had to be "taken into account" in any agreement; that the Soviets could not propose a specific aggregate level of offensive launchers until the United States made some move on FBS; and that if this FBS problem could be resolved, the negotiations would move quickly, since there were no other major problems. There was one straw in this wind to suggest that the Soviet position had flexibility. When one Soviet was told by an American that they must know that the United States would never grant compensation for FBS that would allow the Soviets more strategic missiles and bombers than the United States, the reply was, "All right, then make a suggestion to solve the problem." Later, Soviets repeatedly tried to extract suggestions from us for solving this prickly problem.

Semenov was told that including FBS was absolutely unacceptable. He should not expect any change in our position. In an effort to get him to understand the solidity of our position, I said that after listening to his long FBS statement I felt as I supposed he would if I were to give long expositions on the advantages of on-site inspection. All I got for this analogy was a disquisition on how on-site inspection and forward-based systems were entirely different problems! Each time Semenov or another Soviet repeated that FBS must be included somehow in an offensive agreement, we repeated our insistence that this was not possible. We contended that the August 4 position had already taken FBS into account by dropping limitations on certain non-central weapons systems that had some strategic capabilities. We had now proposed an initial agreement without limits on Soviet MR/IRBMs, which were targeted on Europe and were a counterpart to our FBS, and also without limits on other systems in which the U.S.S.R. had an advantage—submarine-launched cruise missiles and medium bombers. While certain Soviet officials privately indicated that this was helpful in making our point clear, their position did not change. These Soviet systems were, they maintained, not strategic because they did not have the range to attack targets in the United States.

Semenov informally described the American position on FBS as similar to the case of an American farmer who when shown a camel remarked that there was no such animal. But he did not despair of progress on the issue, saying that we were not now in the position of the prophet Joshua, who said that time should stop and the sun not traverse the heavens because the present moment was so beautiful.

The Soviet FBS position seemed to be based on the concern and insistence of their military. They were said to stress the ability of these aircraft to reach the Soviet Union in a short time. They were reported to consider American FBS aircraft more effective in some respect than the B-52 bombers, because their flight time was shorter, they could fly at lower altitudes, and their bomb release system was said to be more effective. We heard that the Soviet military was arguing that if a first-step limitation was to be followed by reductions in intercontinental strategic systems, FBS would become an even more important factor in the strategic balance. It was said that Soviet diplomats had no answer to this argument of their military colleagues. A Soviet again noted privately that the Cuban missile crisis had shown extreme American sensitivity to forward-based Soviet missile systems. The U.S.S.R. now had friendly countries where they could be stationed, he concluded, just as the United States had hospitable European allies.

Secretary Laird was publicly asked about this analogy between the Soviet Cuban missile deployment in 1962 and the forward-based systems question. He said that we would be willing to discuss these systems in the framework of the Mutual Balanced Force Reduction (MBFR) negotiation which was supposed to start in the near future. (While the MBFR talks have touched on some systems that might be considered forward-based, they have not covered FBS in any depth and do not cover forces in any area other than Central Europe.)

The atmosphere of the negotiation was not improved when, in early December, Semenov reintroduced the FBS "compensation" proposal and labeled it as an attempt to compromise on the issue. Since the United States had not found acceptable the "radical" Soviet solution of withdrawal of FBS out of range of the Soviet Union and liquidation of their bases, the Soviet delegation now wished to propose that only some of these systems be withdrawn and for those that remained the U.S.S.R. be compensated by an "appropriate" reduction in the aggregate quantity of U.S. central strategic launchers. This compromise was a non-starter. Without waiting for Washington instructions, I promptly said that it was absolutely unacceptable. Semenov bridled a bit saying that proposals by one side should be considered by the other side with the attention and consideration they deserved. I agreed, with the clear implication that I had already given this new proposal the consideration it deserved. He then asked me to report it to the American authorities. I remained silent, but reported the matter promptly to Washington, where there was no disposition to consider it seriously. In unofficial exchanges, some of our people told their opposite numbers that they must have known this proposal was unacceptable. Why had the Soviets made it? It seemed to us that the proposal was a negotiating step which the Soviet delegation had to take because of pressure from the Soviet military. Their civilian officials must have realized full well that it was not acceptable.

There were two aspects to the Soviet FBS position: existing systems had a strategic capability and should be "taken into account"; if not, the United States could in the future circumvent any agreed strategic balance by increasing FBS numbers and strategic capabilities. We tried at Helsinki to meet these concerns. A majority of the American principal delegates felt that future strategic capabilities of FBS should somehow be taken into consideration, and we cast about for some verbal formula that might remove this stumbling block.

I asked for a National Security Council staff study. It developed six policy options ranging from a categorical refusal to discuss the matter to a proposed assurance that in the future the United States would not make substantial changes in FBS deployments except in response to changes in the forces of the Soviet Union or its allies or increased threats to our security interests. The delegation then (with General Allison dissenting) recommended that an FBS statement be recorded that "no substantial increase of non-limited nuclear delivery systems would be made by either side except when required in its judgment to respond to changes in the general level, mix or deployment of opposing forces, or to increase in the threat to the security interests of itself and its allies." Allison thought such a statement might be interpreted as accommodating the Soviet position. The rest of us argued that such an initiative was necessary to get a full Soviet response to our August 4 approach. We said it was important that the Soviets realize our readiness to deal with the legitimate concern of both sides about loopholes for the circumvention of an agreement. We considered this formula a positive if vague move to "take account of" the FBS problem.

There was considerable division in Washington over any changes in the FBS position. After a Verification Panel meeting, President Nixon decided on what was called the "Helsinki formula." I prefaced its tabling at a plenary meeting by repeating that FBS should not be included in an agreement which limited central strategic systems only. The question was how to take account of a category of systems not subject to specific limitation in an initial agreement. After such an agreement both sides had in mind more comprehensive arms limitations. Once an agreement had been reached they would have an interest in maintaining its viability. Then came the Helsinki formula.

> Only after all the main elements of an initial agreement on central strategic systems have been worked out would we consider it possible to assess mutually satisfactory ways in which actions by either side relating to other nuclear delivery systems could be prevented from upsetting the strategic balance.

The formula was of no interest to the Soviets. One informal comment was that the fact that the United States said it was now "taking account of" FBS was helpful, but not a solution to the problem.

FBS was the SALT problem of the year 1970. In spite of thousands of words the Soviet position remained ambiguous. Even with the earlier radical proposal for total withdrawal of FBS and later the "compromise" proposal for partial withdrawal, Soviet officials in private continued to say that FBS would somehow have to "be taken into account and be reflected in a concrete agreement." To add to our perplexity, there was the formal Soviet proposal for equal aggregate ceilings for the two sides' central weapons systems. A Soviet official stated categorically that the Soviet position favoring equal aggregate ceilings applied not only to the radical FBS solution but also to the compromise solution calling for compensation in the form of an appropriate reduction in other U.S. strategic weapons. We could not figure that out. It may have meant that, under the compromise, a lower U.S. level would be equalized by counting the FBS which were not withdrawn from forward bases. But in the Soviet Basic Provisions and their plenary presentations, FBS were kept separate from the aggregate of ICBMs, SLBMs and strategic bombers.

What is clear from the record is that FBS by this time had become a matter of principle for both sides. The United States for good reasons adamantly and consistently refused to consider any substantive move. We may have underestimated the give in the formal Soviet FBS demands. Soviet officials told us a number of times at Helsinki that they could not explain or discuss the compensation idea further until we made some move agreeing to the principle that a SALT arrangement must somehow take FBS into account.

I ask the reader's forgiveness for the length of this account but that's the way it was—and to understand SALT's evolution one should have some feel of how this subject was drilled into us ad nauseam.

I wrote the President on December 8 that the Soviet FBS compensation proposal could not have been made with any expectation of acceptance. "My hunch is that it was intended to make negotiation of a formal agreement on offensive systems look so unattractive (or at least more distant to us) that by comparison an ABM-only deal at this time would look good." And, referring to offensive arms, I added, "It may also signal Soviet interest in some informal reciprocal measures of restraint which would not be as difficult to reach as a concrete agreement."

By this time, after a year of negotiations, the Soviet and American delegates had discarded their original stiffness and spoke quite directly. For example, on November 24, Semenov spoke about the horrors of nuclear war and the importance of our work. I agreed with his diagnosis and said that I could never understand why the Soviet government preferred to let this terrible situation continue instead of permitting it to be moderated by paying the relatively small price of accepting some on-site inspection. If a plague from outer space should strike the earth, would any nation refuse to permit doctors from abroad to assist in its control? Both countries, if they really wished to reduce the risk of war, should be willing to pay any necessary price to find a way. The subject was dropped.

Semenov later specifically criticized Laird's speech of November 17 foreshadowing new U.S. strategic programs if SALT failed. It seemed to him that Mr. Laird was saying that the United States should have nuclear superiority as in 1962. Laird was not proceeding from the principle of equal security but rather from the viewpoint prevalent in 1962. Perhaps the purpose of expressing such views was merely to get a larger appropriation in the budget, but if these were genuinely Mr. Laird's views, then they hardly corresponded with the realities of life, and they hardly supported the SALT negotiation.

I countered by asserting that Laird did not advocate a principle of nuclear superiority. He had only said that if there were to be no positive results from the negotiations the United States could not stand idle. These views were based on common sense. I suggested a hypothetical trip through the United States. One would see many military bases being closed down due to reduced funds. Unemployment existed due to our shrinking military establishment. I questioned if a visit to the U.S.S.R. would show a similar picture. I concluded that actions spoke louder than words. In looking at the United States, one did not see a military build-up. We did not have parades along Constitution Avenue showing off ICBMs. We did not rattle our weaponry.

It was during this session, over a December weekend, that the trip to Leningrad described earlier took place. We there saw a première of the ballet *Hamlet*. Semenov several times referred in slightly minatory tones to the title of one act—"And after that all was silence." I assumed he was speaking about the possibility of failure in SALT.

During this round the Finnish government invited the delegations to visit Lapland and I received a lesson in Soviet constitutional law. I asked Semenov if he thought such a trip to see reindeer would be a useful application of our limited Helsinki time. He replied that under the Soviet constitution he was not only entitled to relaxation but obliged to take it. He went. I did not.

Although the Soviet delegation remained griped at what they saw as American passivity and continued to object to what they considered pressure to limit the negotiation to our August 4 position, some areas of agreement were identified. The Soviets agreed that missile launchers on diesel-powered submarines should be included in any SLBM limitations. This was a concession from their Basic Provisions, which had proposed a limitation only on "nuclear submarines with ballistic missiles." It is interesting to speculate whether Kissinger recalled this concession when diesel submarines became an important element in the Moscow summit negotiation in May 1972.

The Soviets also conceded that their SS-11 ICBMs targeted not on the United States but on Western Europe would be included. They dropped the claim that U.S. medium bombers should be limited. They agreed to a ban on missile launchers on inland waterway vessels. They agreed to provisions barring special measures of concealment and interference with national means of verification. And they agreed to a standing commission to consider ambiguities in the implementation of an agreement, with terms of reference similar to those proposed by us.

The U.S.S.R. also wanted to ban missile launchers on surface ships. Our original position was to keep this option open, but we now agreed to include any such launchers under an aggregate offensive missile launcher ceiling as well as the missile subceiling of our August 4 position. I heard that one Soviet official mentioned that he once worked as a stevedore in Leningrad and had been impressed by the depth of the holds of commercial vessels. He speculated on the need for a ban on missile launchers on such ships, saying that in the absence of such a ban it would be difficult to know what was in such a vessel.

The Soviet delegation now agreed with our condition that "Testing of cruise missiles of intercontinental range, and the deployment of launchers for such missiles, would be prohibited." It would be in line with the objectives of the negotiations, Semenov stated, to prevent the deployment of types of strategic offensive armaments capable of significantly affecting the further development of the arms race, as well as types possibly not possessed by the sides at the present time, but which, if made operational, could lead to an intensification of the arms race. As for these latter types, banning them obviously did not entail the additional difficulties involved in the destruction of already deployed armaments. The U.S.S.R. delegation considered it useful to prohibit the development and deployment of both land-based and sea-based cruise missiles of intercontinental range. This Soviet position "got lost in the shuffle" of the subsequent negotiations when it was decided that a comprehensive offensive arms agreement was not possible in the first SALT negotiation. Five years later the cruise missile was to become a major issue in SALT II. The United States started development of air- and submarine-launched cruise missiles as bargaining chips after the SALT agreements of 1972 and the Pentagon was loath to let them go. The SALT II agreements do not ban such cruise missile launchers.

Toward the end of this round Semenov privately proposed that when concluding a SALT agreement the parties agree not to be the first to use nuclear weapons. We were now considering how to establish levels for limiting strategic offensive arms. We were thinking in terms of a couple of thousand weapons. (This was the only indication we had of what aggregate level the Soviets had in mind for offensive launchers.) This quantity of weapons would still be so large as to produce annihilation many times over or, as the standard phrase went, to inflict unacceptable damage upon either side in any eventuality. Would it not be advisable to assume a long-term obligation not to be the first to use them? I recalled that this proposal had been made a number of times in the past, that the U.S. position was that it would be inconsistent with defensive commitments to our allies, and that in any event the matter was already adequately covered by the United Nations Charter. But I would report the proposal to Washington. It generated no interest.

The main event of this round, and the second major move in the whole negotiation, now took place. Since we were not making progress on a treaty limiting both ABMs and offensive arms, the Soviet delegation proposed that we try first to negotiate a treaty on ABMs. This was no surprise. The U.S.S.R. had first broached this idea with the White House five months before, as described in Chapter 3. While in Washington I had met with Georgi Arbatov, director of the Institute of U.S. and Canada Studies of the U.S.S.R. Academy of Sciences, a man reportedly having close contacts with one or more members of the Politburo. In the course of an otherwise general conversation he floated the idea of an ABM treaty coupled with some unspecified constraints on the build-up of offensive arms. I was noncommittal and stressed the importance of having a close link between limitations on offensive and defensive weapons. Since academicians in good Moscow standing generally do not stray far from the party line, I took Arbatov's initiative as another signal of the direction we could expect Soviet SALT policy to take.

There also had been hints in Helsinki about the possibility of a more limited agreement than the one we had been trying to negotiate. Being aware of the high-level July ABM overture, it had not taken much prescience for me to advise the President on November 12 that the Soviets had in mind, at least as a target of opportunity, a very narrow agreement—perhaps just on ABMs. Then, one November day, Semenov had suggested that it might be useful to concentrate on individual aspects which might be more rapidly solved rather than waiting for a total solution. I replied that there was a question as to how narrow an agreement could be and still make sense. I told him I had the feeling that the Soviets might be suggesting an agreement limited to ABMs. This was difficult to reconcile with the principle that both sides had accepted that offensive and defensive aspects of the strategic balance were closely interrelated. I could not favor an agreement to limit defensive weapons while the Soviets remained free to continue unchecked expansion of offensive weapons.

On December 1, Semenov made the proposal to single out the question of limiting ABM systems and to attempt to reach a separate agreement in the immediate future. Defensive limits should be separated out because the offensive negotiations were blocked by the FBS impasse. He argued that defensive limitations were less complex and that the sides were in some measure of agreement on limiting ABMs. An initial ABM undertaking would pave the way for progress on offensive weapons. It was important to show concrete progress. Their proposal was motivated by the logic of the negotiating situation and by the need to get control of ABMs while they were still in their infancy.

The ABM-only proposal was said to be a probe of the seriousness of U. S. SALT intentions. Moscow claimed to be puzzled about the inconsistency between Washington proposing a very limited ABM deployment for defense of capitals or even a total ABM ban while pushing in Congress for a widespread Safeguard system for defense of ICBMs. Contrary to some opinion in the United States that Safeguard was not much of a weapons system, U.S.S.R. officials continued to indicate that they took it seriously, especially its potential for a nationwide defense which could eventually neutralize the danger to the United States from Soviet retaliatory missile forces. Semenov even said that an initiative to deploy an expansive ABM system would be an indicator that the side taking it wanted to accelerate the arms race. That permitted me to ask what about a side that continued to build more ICBMs? One American asked what could be expected in the Soviet SS-9 deployment program if the new Soviet approach was adopted. The answer was that Semenov would soon have something "quite important" to say which should help the negotiations.

On December 4 the Soviets tabled a document called "Basic Provisions for an Agreement on Limiting Deployment of ABM Systems." It had few specifics. Much of this package had already been suggested in Semenov's plenary presentations on ABMs.

- The Soviets proposed a single ABM site for defense of national capitals and not a ban.

- There would be limitations on ABM launchers and interceptor missiles, long-range acquisition, tracking, and guidance radars.

■ These systems would have to be deployed within a circle of unspecified radius around the center of Washington and of Moscow.

■ Each side would have an agreed number of launchers and interceptors.

Spaces were left blank for the numbers of launchers and missiles and for the radius of the deployment circle. We were told that the question of "numbers" would offer no difficulty. There would be a prohibition on international transfers of ABM systems. Also included were U.S. proposals to ban mobile ABM systems and rapid reload mechanisms. However, the SAM upgrade problem was ducked by the use of a definition of ABMs as systems "specifically designed" to counter incoming ballistic missiles. And there were no numerical or quantitative limitations on radars. For those who feel that the United States made most or all of the concessions at SALT it would be interesting to compare the final ABM Treaty with these Soviet positions.

Privately we were told how important it was that we not reject the new proposal out of hand. While the Soviet decision to go for a separate ABM agreement had only been reached during the current Helsinki session, it had long been in the works in Moscow and was the result of profound consideration. Specifics would be available if we would merely agree to "consider" the proposal. The Soviet delegation already had guidance including quantitative levels and other numerical specifics for both defensive and offensive systems, but they were under strict instructions as to the conditions under which these details could be disclosed. It was too late to develop a situation at Helsinki in which Soviet proposed ceilings for offensive launcher limitations could be revealed. But it was not too late for specifics of the ABM limitation if we were willing to consider it even without commitment.

The delegation advised Washington that in order to find out more about Soviet thinking on ABM controls we should avoid a flat rejection. While Washington reviewed this new development and our recommendation, we used the time to point out to the Soviets our disagreements with their ideas on radar constraints and SAM upgrade and to complain about the continued non-disclosure of numbers for permitted ABM launchers and interceptors.

President Nixon authorized us to give the Soviets a somewhat ambiguous response. "We continue to believe that, to achieve the purposes of these talks, an agreement should include limits on both offensive and defensive systems. We expect to continue to negotiate towards the objective of limitations on both offensive and defensive forces." This left it open to the Soviets to continue making their case for a separate ABM agreement. In effect it left the matter for the next round in Vienna.

In spite of the ostensible specificity of this new Soviet move the difference between U.S. and Soviet negotiating practice continued. We tabled detailed positions. They favored general formulations and sought acceptance of principles as a condition for disclosure of "fine print." They continued to try to bait the United States into agreeing to "take into account" FBS and to "consider" the ABM-only proposal. Our negotiating position was not to react "in principle" until we knew details. Not much progress could be made as these circular arguments continued.

We still wanted the record to look good. After we had abandoned the MIRV ban and the reductions approach, we continued to state for the record that we would press for them in subsequent negotiations. The Soviets used the same technique.

In tabling their new ABM proposal, the Soviets seemed anxious to lessen American concern that if it were accepted that would mean an end to limitations on offensive arms. They continued to present views on offensive limitations even after tabling the ABM document. Semenov said that discussion of an ABM agreement must in no way slow down the consideration of other questions within the scope of the negotiation. This thought was repeated a number of times. The message was clear. While negotiating for an ABM agreement, the negotiations on offensive systems should proceed, as Semenov said, "in parallel." A Soviet official suggested that during the next Vienna phase both sides should seek individual areas on which they were in agreement. The Soviets had already proposed a separate agreement on ABMs and at Vienna we should see what areas we could reach agreement on in the field of offensive systems. He declined to elaborate, saying that he could not at that time say what these individual areas might be or how agreement would be registered. But he did state that the Soviets would be prepared at Vienna to negotiate toward agreements covering both strategic offensive and defensive arms.

How the ABM agreement would be related to concurrent or subsequent measures on offensive weapons was left vague. But the Soviet delegation spoke informally of an agreement on ABMs along with an "understanding" on offensive systems. Semenov noted the possibility of a concurrent "tacit" agreement on offensive systems. And on December 9 a Soviet asked an American if he recalled what Arbatov had said to me in Washington about the possibility of an ABM treaty accompanied by a moratorium on certain offensive force developments. This was a clear projection of the arrangement reached the following May after months of negotiations in another channel between Moscow and Washington. But at Helsinki the delegation had no authority to encourage this Soviet approach.

I cited to Semenov his use of two different Russian words to refer to agreement, *soglasheniye* (agreement) and *dogovorennost* (understanding), and asked him to clarify the difference, if any, in the meaning of the two words. He replied that, depending on the context, *dogovorennost* was a less formal term, and he observed that sometimes the terms were used in a way intending to convey slight shades of meaning. I then gave him a copy of his December 8 plenary statement and asked whether there was in that context any difference between the terms. He read the text carefully and said the usage had been very precise. The Soviet side believed a "separate" agreement on ABMs was possible and necessary, and it would create favorable circumstances for reaching an "understanding" on other problems. I reported to Washington on December 11 that, taken together with other recent comments by Soviet delegation members, it seemed clear the Soviets wished to signal the possibility of a formal separate agreement limiting ABM systems combined with unilateral restraints, and possibly even with an agreed understanding, regarding certain strategic offensive forces. There it was again, the much-touted "breakthrough" negotiated in the "back channel" in 1971.

As the third round of SALT closed, the United States delegation had developed some important information for Washington. The U.S.S.R. was willing to continue to negotiate a separate

ABM treaty, the U.S.S.R. would agree to parallel negotiations for offensive constraints. These constraints could be either tacit or explicit. The delegation's report to President Nixon concluded that the Soviet tactics were aimed more at a suspension of further deployment of certain offensive strategic weapons than a formal comprehensive limitation agreement. The Soviets, we reported, must appreciate that to achieve this major purpose of deterring a widespread U. S. ABM program some constraints of their offensive build-up would be needed. The Soviet delegation seemed to be limiting its efforts to close the gap between the positions of the two sides in the expectation that a new thrust would soon be injected into the negotiation as a result of high-level political decisions by one or both sides.

Nineteen-seventy had started with good hope of reaching a SALT agreement. We took off from the positive results of the preliminary round at Helsinki in 1969. Both sides wanted to control ABMs while they were still in their infancy. While forward-based systems were a dark cloud in the sky, the prospect for some control of offensive missile launchers and bombers seemed reasonably good. After all, the Soviet delegation was "serious and businesslike." Nineteen-seventy showed how durable SALT was when U.S. forces entered Cambodia. It could have been expected that the U.S.S.R. would have reacted by at least a temporary suspension of negotiations. There had been only a rhetorical slap on the wrist and a quick return to business.

By year's end, however, there were disappointments and frustrations. Positions had been presented by both sides, but the Soviets had insisted for almost six months that American FBS be taken into account in any agreed strategic equation. Nineteen-seventy involved exchanges of maximalist positions and wrangles on abstractions like the composition of forces to be limited. There had been a quick move by the United States in August toward what we thought might be a negotiable position, followed by the Soviet proposal for an agreement on ABMs only. There seemed to have been a dragging out of the talks in the expectation that the political authorities would step in and head the talks in a different direction. That direction was clearly pointed out by the Soviets and accurately reported to Washington. The year 1970 closed with a feeling in both delegations that "something had to give," that a new and top-level political impulse was needed if the talks were to get anywhere in 1971, and an expectation that such a move was in the wind.

All during this year the Soviets seemed to be marking time. Perhaps the Politburo was putting off hard decisions until it had a clearer idea of American foreign policy in general and toward the U.S.S.R. in particular. There was some evidence that United States policy was hardening: the Cambodian incursion and stepped-up U.S. activity in Vietnam, NATO preconditions for considering the Soviet proposal for a European security conference, Pentagon announcements of MIRV and ABM program milestones, and finally our rather rigid SALT position at Helsinki. The Kremlin might have estimated that the United States was also trying to improve its relative position by resuming discussions with Chinese representatives in Warsaw after a two-year lapse, and possibly by Secretary Rogers' peace initiative in the Middle East. If the Soviet leadership perceived Washington in a mood to flex its muscles, they might well have calculated that that was no time to be making a SALT agreement.

In Moscow they were preparing for the Twenty-fourth Congress of the Communist Party, scheduled for late March 1971. It is generally thought that General Secretary Brezhnev there consolidated his leadership and support for a policy of détente. SALT may have had to wait for this priority development. If our assessment of the importance the Soviet military attached to the FBS problem was correct, and their military no doubt were suspicious of SALT in general, an agreement excluding FBS might have been politically impossible before the Party Congress.

The tactical postures of the two sides were not unlike. Both claimed they would prefer a comprehensive agreement, but since this did not seem feasible because of the other's intransigence, a try should be made for a less comprehensive arrangement. The United States, while insisting that its preference still was for one of the two broad approaches featuring MIRV control and reductions tabled in April in Vienna, now urged the practicality and equity of the narrower approach of August 4. The U.S.S.R. as early as July had signaled an interest in going first to an ABM limitation and at Helsinki had made a formal proposal. The Soviet delegation continued to hammer away at the FBS question but made several technical adjustments in their offensive arms positions, supposedly toward those of the United States. Although now pressing for an ABM treaty, the Soviet delegation gave the impression at Helsinki that they were not severing the link between defensive and offensive arms control which both sides had repeatedly acknowledged. In his final Helsinki statement Semenov had said that the interrelationship existing between strategic offensive and defensive arms undoubtedly had to be taken into account in working out a separate agreement on limiting the deployment of ABM systems.

After that, some seven months were to pass before the delegations got back to serious work, although in the meantime they would mark some time together at Vienna in the spring of 1971 while a Kissinger-Kremlin negotiation worked out the accord of May 1971. In light of the many indications of what the Soviet position was in the fall of 1970, it is difficult to understand why it took from January to May to reach a consensus along the lines which the Soviets had suggested so clearly in December 1970 at Helsinki or why this phase of the negotiation was not left to the two delegations rather than handled in the unorthodox style of the Kissinger talks. As will be seen, those talks did not produce any precise mutual understanding, and they left a legacy of confusion.

PART TWO
THE ARRANGEMENT

6

ABM ONLY

Vienna IV:
March–May 1971

The American delegates melded into the Washington SALT community in January 1971 and prepared for the next round, scheduled to start in March. Both sides, through a year of negotiation, had shown an interest in reaching agreement. The United States still favored having both offensive and defensive arms controls. Its August 4, 1970, proposal remained on the table. The U.S.S.R. proposed as an initial arrangement an ABM agreement, but it was willing to agree also to some measures to restrain offensive systems. The parties were closer together on ABM limitations than on offensive arms, where the Soviets were insisting that the American forward-based systems somehow be taken into account. As we started the second year of SALT, we sensed that a new approach would have to be devised if agreement was to be reached.

In a television interview in January, President Nixon gave a signal. "I do not suggest now that we are going to have a comprehensive agreement because there is a basic disagreement with regard to what strategic weapons—what that definition is. . . . But we are now willing to move to a non-comprehensive agreement." General Haig, who then was Kissinger's assistant, called me the next day to advise that the President, after the TV interview, said that he had gone further on SALT than he intended to. Nixon was simply referring to the possibility of an accident control arrangement. Kissinger also called to say he was being deluged with calls from the media about the meaning of a less comprehensive agreement. Four months later we were to learn that the President may have had more in mind than he had told Haig.

I soon sent the President some views about the state of SALT. The Soviet position on ABM was generally known and popular. The U.S. position, offering either an ABM ban or a limit of one site to defend the national capital, was not known to the public. An exception should be made to the rule of privacy. I suggested the President disclose the American position in a major address. I especially wanted the public to know that the United States had proposed a complete ban on ABMs.

The Soviets seemed to be exercising self-restraint by halting new construction starts on ICBM silos and the Moscow ABM complex had been left unfinished. The United States should also be restrained. I urged the President to announce that our ABM program would be continued but not expanded, with deferral of construction on the third site authorized by Congress in 1970. No funds should be requested in 1971 for a fourth site. Research and development should proceed on an improved ABM missile and on a so-called hard-site defense (HSD) system against the chance that a better defense of Minuteman ICBM silos might be needed. To put the Soviets on notice, I would have the President say in his speech, "If after a reasonable period the SALT negotiations prove unproductive, or if the U.S.S.R. resumes land-based ICBM deployments . . . the United States would take whatever steps are necessary to maintain its strategic deterrent, including possibly deployment of a more advanced defense of land-based ICBMs."

As for submarine missile launchers, I wrote that if, after their ICBM program had topped out, the U.S.S.R. continued to build submarines that would look to us to be an effort to gain unilateral advantage and could cost them a SALT agreement. To put the Soviets on notice, I suggested that the President say, "Unless this submarine program halts, a SALT agreement at present levels will become much more difficult, if not impossible."

The President's 1971 Foreign Policy Report to the Congress reflected the state of the negotiations. The section on "Strategic Policy and Forces" took critical note of the continued growth of Soviet forces. Soviet operational ICBMs had increased from 1,109 to 1,440 during 1970, in contrast to the constant U. S. ICBM level of 1,054. The Soviets could be expected to have an SLBM force equal in numbers to the U.S. fleet by the mid-1970s. The report underscored other topical SALT issues. There were repeated references, six in all, emphasizing the prospective Soviet ICBM threat to the survivability of the Minuteman force. But mentioned also was the recent suspension of new Soviet ICBM launcher construction. Its significance was not clear. "If the U.S.S.R. is in fact exercising restraint, we welcome this action and will take it into account in our planning. If it turns out to be preparatory to a new intensification of the strategic arms race, it will be necessary for us to react appropriately."

The Nixon report reviewed the course of the negotiations during the past year. It noted that Soviet positions lacked any specificity to permit firm conclusions. He reported differences on the definition of strategic offensive weapons, the FBS issue, on whether a separate agreement limiting ABMs alone would be in the mutual interest, and on certain verification requirements. He also noted that our ABM approach had alternative provisions—either a limitation or a total ban on ABMs. This statement, buried in a long report, did not give the ABM ban proposal the kind of public emphasis I had in mind.

The review concluded with three policy statements. A SALT agreement "must deal with the interrelationship between offensive and defensive limitations. . . . The strategic balance would be endangered if we limited defensive forces alone and left the offensive threat to our strategic forces unconstrained. . . . To limit only one side of the offense-defense equation could rechannel the arms competition rather than effectively curtail it."

Restraint was essential during the talks. "If the Soviet leaders extend their strategic capabilities, especially in ways that increase the threat to our forces, we would face new decisions in the strategic field." At this stage what was needed were political decisions to move toward an agreement on the basis of an equitable strategic relationship. Nixon rather grandly announced that we had taken this decision. I wondered what this statement meant. Hadn't we taken that decision a year earlier before the United States delegation went to Vienna? Or was this a sign to the Soviets that some new decision had been taken, perhaps one to aim for some kind of "non-comprehensive" SALT agreement such as the President had referred to earlier.

In February, at Secretary Rogers' request, I prepared a detailed program for interim or narrow agreements to "hold" the situation while the negotiations continued (Appendix 4). Rogers did not react. The delegation's instructions for the next round authorized discussing informally a rise in the aggregate to 2,000 offensive launchers; omitting the sublimit for missiles (1,710); and simplifying some of the verification provisions. We should try to find out informally what quid pro quo the Soviets would likely concede in return for these modifications. The trade-off would then have to be approved in Washington. We never got very far into offensive limitations at Vienna. And no consideration was given to my suggestion emphasizing an ABM ban and the possibility of an "interim understanding."

During the winter and spring of 1971 there were strong public and congressional pressures on the White House to accept the Soviet proposal for a separate ABM treaty, overlapped by pressures to end or curtail the ABM program. The President faced hard decisions on the ABM budget. He did not like the idea of a complete ban on ABMs, probably because the U.S. military opposed it and because strong supporters in the Congress might have felt they had been sold down the river after upholding so long the unpopular ABM program at the President's request. He may have felt that the Soviets, although not rejecting an ABM ban, did not favor it, and that U.S. support for it would complicate the negotiations. On the other hand, the Administration's program had survived a key Senate vote in August 1970 by only a 52–47 margin, better than the 51–50 margin in 1969 but not much better. Nixon knew that ABM would have a difficult time outliving the SALT negotiations no matter what their outcome.

Those in the Department of Defense concerned with potential vulnerability of the ICBM force opposed with special vigor Soviet calls for a separate ABM agreement. They wanted to defend ICBMs with ABMs specially designed for that purpose. Our

ABM system had initially been designed to defend "soft" targets such as people and cities. Effective defense of ICBMs called for a system designed to defend "hard" targets like concrete ICBM silo launchers. Such a hard-site defense system had been authorized for development in the 1970 defense budget. Now its advocates were arguing that any ABM limitation should permit deployment of an HSD system. During the final preparations for the 1971 defense budget, I urged the President to confine the HSD program to research and development and give it no public emphasis. I pointed out that if we proposed an ABM limitation permitting a hard-site defense system it might torpedo SALT, as well as the ABM program before the Congress. An HSD construction program was not proposed. But some research and development on this technology continues.

The White House was obviously ill at ease with the American capital defense ABM negotiating posture calling either for banning or limiting ABMs to one NCA site—a type of deployment for which the United States had no plans. It was inconsistent with the Administration's position in Congress requesting four sites to defend ICBM fields out West. A Washington site, while favored by the Joint Chiefs, had no support in the Congress. The Chiefs opposed an ABM ban, as did others who felt that no area of weaponry should be closed out entirely and argued that one could not tell what ABM needs the future might bring. The United States should gain experience in operating an ABM system, even if only at one site of limited military signficance. Secretary Laird was tinkering with the bizarre idea of permitting the sides to have an NCA site somewhere other than at the capital, and he was inclined to favor hard-site defense, which he was told would have a stabilizing effect in the face of Soviet ICBMs capable of destroying hardened ICBM silos.

Pressures for a separate ABM limitation agreement were now stepped up by Moscow. In briefing the Senate Foreign Relations and House Foreign Affairs Committee on February 3 and 4, I followed the Administration line and opposed a separate agreement. These were private sessions, but several days later *Izvestia* described my stand as "strange." It said that the idea of signing an ABM agreement evoked much interest in American political and scientific circles, and the senators listening to me were puzzled at my "extremely negative" approach. Would that we had such a pipeline into Soviet briefings of their authorities!

Domestic pressures for accepting the Soviet proposal now increased. The Federation of American Scientists published a statement arguing that the U.S. position at SALT threatened to sacrifice an ABM agreement for a "sham," i.e., a limitation on offensive weapons that did not cover MIRVs. Soviet ABMs were the only foreseeable neutralizer of the deterrent effectiveness of submarine-launched missiles, the heart of the U.S. deterrent, and the chance to limit ABMs should not be passed up by insisting on an offensive-defensive link. The statement advocated reaching an ABM agreement as part of a two-step process in which continuation of the ABM limits would be conditional on concluding an offensive agreement within a given time.

A New York *Times* editorial of January 17, 1971, urged "an immediate, favorable American response without waiting for resumption of formal talks. . . . It would be self-defeating to endanger a possible ABM agreement by insisting that offensive weapons limitations must be linked to it." The Democratic Policy Council proposed that the United States sign an ABM agreement as part of a two-step process conditioned on a freeze on offensive missile launchers while negotiations continued. Senator Humphrey introduced a Senate resolution urging the President to first agree to ban or limit ABM deployments and then to negotiate offensive limitations. Senator (now Secretary of State) Muskie advocated an ABM agreement as a first step toward a more comprehensive agreement.

One of the mysteries of this winter of 1970–71 was the already mentioned Soviet halt on new construction starts of ICBM silos. On December 16, 1970, about the time when the Soviets were formally proposing a separate ABM agreement and informally suggesting certain parallel offensive arms restraints, Secretary Laird's spokesman said, ". . . there are some preliminary indications that the Soviet Union may have recently started slowing somewhat the level of activity associated with SS-9 missile construction. As a consequence we now believe that the Soviet Union could have somewhat fewer than 300 SS-9s operational (or under construction. There are more than 250 SS-9s operational.)." In fact no new SS-9 starts had been made for some time. This was the most encouraging sign yet. If the Soviet SS-9 force topped out at its then level of 288 silos, it would be less than the number which Defense Department computations showed would make the U. S. Minuteman force unduly vulnerable. This looked like an indication of Soviet intention to curb the arms competition. The United States had at times tried to signal the U.S.S.R. that it was exercising restraint, by speeches and actions. But it would be a rare, if not unique, Soviet action if the SS-9 program in fact had been cut short of what it originally called for. Perhaps the Soviets were trying both to show the United States that ABMs were not needed and to induce the United States to negotiate a separate ABM treaty by this demonstration of continued interest in offensive arms restraint.

In any event, hopes were soon dashed. Before the next Vienna round started, intelligence indicated that the Soviets had again started on new ICBM silos. On March 7, Senator Jackson announced this development and added that the holes being dug by the Soviets were larger than needed for silos for SS-9s. Since Soviet practice is to start constructing silos for missiles even before starting to test the missiles, we had no good idea of what characteristics these new missiles would have. Jackson used this new intelligence to argue against an ABM-only agreement, saying, "This is why I think the President is right. We must do both—to limit just the defensive system makes no sense at all."

Soviet Ambassador Dobrynin visited my office to advise of his government's agreement to have technical groups consider arrangements to reduce the risk of nuclear accidents and to modernize the Washington–Moscow Hot Line. I asked him how one should relate the resumption of new construction of silos to Soviet interest in a strategic arms agreement. He said that Soviet embassies were not informed of such developments. But in keeping with his claim to be the most knowledgeable man in the U.S.S.R. about SALT, after Semenov, he added that he would be informed when he visited Moscow in the near future.

Dobrynin made a strong case for getting on with an agreement limiting ABMs. His people were traditionally defense-minded. They had fresh memories of World War II. If their leaders now told them that defenses were not needed, this would be a clear message that Soviet-American relations were better. ABM controls were urgent. If ABMs were allowed to run free, in ten years both sides would have nationwide systems and the chance for ABM control would have passed. He was sure an ABM treaty could be reached in 1971. He was just as sure, after checking with his leadership in Moscow, that offensive limitations could not be negotiated that year.

Dobrynin also said he felt that the U.S. offer of a ban on ABMs was just for propaganda. I told him that if the U.S.S.R. accepted the offer they would find out that that was not so. Dobrynin speculated that if we would agree to a separate ABM treaty an ABM arrangement allowing the United States two sites and the U.S.S.R. one site around Moscow might be negotiable. He also characterized the American proposal for a MIRV ban as a bluff. "Why don't you call it?" I suggested. That was the last I saw during SALT of this second most knowledgeable SALT expert in all of the Soviet Union! From then on, his negotiating partner in the Administration was closer to President Nixon.

Nixon realized that SALT could not go on indefinitely. The numerical relationship between the strategic launchers of the two sides was changing to our disadvantage. Even if, as we believed for a time, the Soviet ICBM force had topped out at about 1,500, the Soviet strategic submarine fleet was increasing rapidly. The Soviets could have a fleet equal in number to that of the United States in three years. The ABM program was having rough going in the Congress and its questionable fitness for its mission to defend ICBMs was attracting public attention. If congressional support for ABM failed, its value as a bargaining chip would be gone and ABM would really have been "America's Biggest Mistake." And now the U.S.S.R. had started up its ICBM silo construction program again. What was the bitter end of this process? Influential voices urged the President to request funds for a new missile program to let the people see who was more concerned about U.S. security, the President or the Congress.

Nixon felt that the time would quickly pass when the United States would retain equal bargaining power in SALT. He had doubts that the Congress would support a substantial build-up in U.S. strategic forces in the face of apparent Soviet willingness to reach at least a partial arms accommodation. These considerations must have focused his mind on reaching agreement soon, in 1971

—a less ambitious agreement perhaps than the United States had been prospecting for in 1970, but one that at least would stop that build-up of large Soviet ICBMs which Mel Laird was telling him was so destabilizing and in a crisis might bring nuclear war prematurely or unnecessarily because American ICBMs would seem so vulnerable as to invite a Soviet pre-emptive strike. It must be an awfully lonely feeling to be the only human in the country facing possible responsibility for nuclear war. An international agreement having any tendency to make the need for this decision less likely must have been a tantalizingly attractive prospect. In January Nixon announced that he had decided to go for a narrower SALT agreement. He must have made this key decision not in National Security Council assemblies, not after extensive briefings and interdepartmental discussions of building blocks, but alone and probably late at night. No Watergate miasma should prevent historians from saying that this was a courageous and correct decision.

Although the White House did not like to have agency heads submit SALT views directly to the President, but rather to Kissinger as head of the NSC committee structure, I continued to take advantage of the "direct presidential access" promised when I was appointed to office in February 1969. I now sent the President some views on what our position should be for the next round. In light of his recent announcement that he had made a political decision to go for a SALT agreement, our guidance should be progressive and not stick to past positions or, as some would have it, make them even harder. We should avoid appearing to stall for time to develop an efficient ABM/HSD system or a mobile ICBM system. In fact, we should try to ban mobile ICBMs, since allowing them under some limitation level would be difficult to verify; it was doubtful that the Congress would fund a mobile ICBM force even if permitted under a SALT agreement. We should try, in the first instance, for an arrangement of indefinite duration. Anything else would suggest a dubious and short-term American commitment to a SALT regime.[1] Any agreement would contain provisions for review at five-year intervals as well as a short-notice termination clause exercisable if the nation's vital interests were

[1] A change from my 1969 view that at first we should only try for a five-year agreement.

prejudiced by the operation of the agreement. These protections would be about as good as having a short-term agreement.

We should tell the Soviets we assumed they were willing to negotiate either for a separate ABM treaty or for agreements having offensive and defensive limitations. We preferred the latter, and I pointed out that in view of their renewed ICBM construction the Soviets might be hard put to insist that negotiation on offensive controls now be postponed. But any agreement would have to be less complicated than our August 4 proposal. As Secretary Rogers had said, at a recent National Security Council meeting, at the end of a serious bargaining process understandings rather than formal agreements might be appropriate and sufficient.

I again urged the President to support a complete ban on ABMs, arguing that permitting the defense of capitals would require the United States to demolish work completed on the existing system without requiring the Soviets to demolish anything. Only a ban would require both sides to dismantle their ABMs. But if the President would not propose a ban, I said that two sites for the United States with the Soviets retaining their Moscow site was all the traffic would bear.

In closing, I flagged the FBS issue, saying that the delegation might need fresh FBS authorization to introduce a formula along the lines of the general language the delegation had floated recently in the North Atlantic Council. "The agreement would include an understanding that neither side would deploy other types of nuclear delivery systems in an attempt to change the strategic balance between the U.S. and the USSR."

The President was well aware of differing views in the national security community as to how to get on with SALT. The basic question in early 1971 was how far we should go to meet the Soviet proposal that the initial target should be a separate ABM agreement, with parallel negotiations on offensive limitations, and, as Semenov had said, then decide whether to have an offensive and defensive arrangement. As we have seen, Nixon had already given two public responses. He would not approve an ABM-only agreement, but he would accept a less than comprehensive arrangement. Not mentioned during the National Security Council discussions, or at any other time during the Vienna preparations, was the fact that the President had been in contact with the Soviet leadership about a new SALT approach and that Kissinger had been working on it for some time. One can only conclude that the SALT delegates were duped into believing that they were to be involved in a serious negotiation that winter at Vienna.

The earlier presidential decision to take a new approach to SALT was not reflected in the pedestrian guidance given the delegation. It was even inconsistent with the President's earlier statement to the Congress that the basis for an agreement might be emerging. It was not responsive to any of my major recommendations. But, as we later found out, our guidance was not expected or even intended to produce agreement at Vienna. The delegation was instructed to continue pressing for the August 4, 1970, proposal. We were not authorized to negotiate for a separate ABM agreement. We could give priority to detailed discussions of an ABM system for defense of capitals. The ABM ban proposal remained on the table. Until the details of a capital defense (NCA) limitations had been discussed, no choice could be made as to the U.S. preference. There it was again, a shell game. We were to make proposals in the alternative but not tell which we preferred.

But this time we had three shells! "This can't be serious," was my reaction as I read that we were directed also to put to the U.S.S.R. delegation a new concept for ABM control having "equal status" with the alternative proposals already tabled. To Soviets bent on obtaining equality, we were to propose that the United States be permitted four Safeguard ABM sites to protect ICBMs, with the U.S.S.R. having one ABM site to protect Moscow. The Soviets must at times have shared a wonder if there really was a pea under any of the shells as they tried to follow our negotiating sleight of hand. So the fix for our differing SALT and congressional ABM postures was to table yet a third ABM alternative consistent with what the Administration was trying to get the Congress to support, a four-site Safeguard deployment. And, although originally described as having equal status, we would soon learn that this was the White House's chosen instrument—at least for a time.

Not that anyone believed that this new alternative was negotiable. The White House authors must have seen it as a device to permit Kissinger and Dobrynin to work for a season on SALT. It was a kind of "charge of the Light Brigade" mission to keep the SALT delegation occupied. A report has it that the four-to-one alternative was pressed on the White House by Senator Jackson, who believed strongly that one or two ABM sites would be militarily meaningless. The President probably calculated that tabling this four-to-one proposal would not only conform the congressional and the negotiating stances, but also put a little more pressure on the Soviets. He assumed that an ABM limitation was what they most wanted, while a limit on their big ICBM (MLBMs) launchers was what we most wanted. And Nixon's raising the ABM negotiating ante to four to one in favor of the United States may have been intended as a reaction to the recent Soviet renewal of construction starts on MLBMs.

The only gesture in the direction of the Soviet emphasis on a separate ABM agreement was the license to give priority to discussion of the details of ABM controls. On offensive limitations, we were to pursue a slightly adjusted version of our August 4 proposal, which by March 1971 had to be seen as essentially nonnegotiable. The President must have realized that both these offensive and defensive proposals were "fishy" offers which would not be easy to present with conviction to the Soviet delegation. He wrote me during the first week in Vienna to be sure I understood the importance he attached to this new third approach to the ABM problem. He regarded it as having at least the same status as the other two approaches; it was important that in my discussion with Semenov I should be persuasive and reflect the weight of my instructions. All I could think, in effect, was "Theirs not to reason why," and present what was obvious to all—two non-negotiable positions. At times I used to wonder whether it would not be better to let the strategic situation run free—a not very violent competition which we had got used to—rather than try to structure a rather advanced legal relationship between two antagonistic powers. But pessimism passed.

Armed with firm presidential instructions, I met with Semenov at the former Tsarist embassy on Reisnerstrasse. President Nixon had also written me that I was quite right in telling the NSC that the new intelligence of the Soviet's resuming ICBM launcher construction lent urgency to the SALT negotiations. While avoiding any impression that we considered ourselves under pressure of any special deadline or were eager to rush in with concessions, he wanted me especially to get across to Semenov his sense of concern and the adverse impact the apparent new momentum in the Soviet build-up had in the United States. I also was to point out that we had deliberately refrained from public speculation on its significance and had chosen not to take explicit account of it in the 1971 defense budget.

After congratulating Semenov on his sixtieth birthday and on his receiving the Order of the October Revolution, I said I wanted him to know of our concern over the build-up of ICBMs in the Soviet Union and also of the adverse effect that this had on opinion in the United States. The ICBM silo starts could mean that the Soviet leadership was still not ready to reach agreement for improvement of the stability of the strategic relationship.

He must have expected this blast. Reading from typed cards, he assured me that the U.S.S.R. was acting in a restrained fashion. The United States had been modernizing its strategic armaments, and naturally the Soviet Union was doing the same. Our concerns were unfounded. This development had in fact no bearing on the strategic relationship. He interjected that it was completely natural and understandable that the U.S. highest authorities had shown restraint in commenting on it. Indeed, certain steps and statements in the United States could be interpreted as attempts to bring pressures on the negotiations and such attempts could create doubts about our seriousness. After I had rebutted that contention, Semenov said that in the physical sciences this sort of phenomenon was known as an aberration. It was his impression that each side read what the other side was saying with greater attention than that given to statements by its own people, and we could help each other by directing attention to such statements

Given the Soviet push for an initial ABM-only agreement and our guidance to discuss the details of the ABM part of an agreement as a matter of priority to facilitate continuing negotiations on offensive forces, it was inevitable that we would spend most of our time on ABMs. The Soviets opened by tabling a draft treaty. This was a somewhat more explicit formulation of their Helsinki ABM proposal. A few of the blanks had been filled in. It called for limiting ABM systems "specially designed to counter strategic ballistic missiles" to not more than 100 launchers and interceptors, to be deployed within a 200-kilometer radius from the center of the national capitals, with no limit on the number of long-range acquisition and tracking radars deployed within this circle. To give the appearance of linking offensive controls to the ABM agreement, the draft provided that "the Contracting Parties undertake to continue active negotiations on limiting strategic offensive weapons."

"Under instructions" I said that the Soviet draft was not acceptable but that we were willing to consider specifics of ABM limitations. I proposed that the ABM portion of an agreement take into account systems presently under construction. This approach would reflect the two countries' existing ABM programs. Each ABM system could contribute to strategic stability. After an initial comment to the effect that he was "all ears," and after hearing our new ABM approach, Semenov's response was that our proposal for four ABM sites for the United States and only one for the Soviet Union was aimed at obtaining unilateral military advantages. It was not acceptable. A year before Laird had said that the ABM deployment program would not be an obstacle to a SALT agreement, since the deployed ABM elements could be dismantled if an agreement was reached. Now the United States was using the existing deployment to support an alternative intentionally not aimed at solving the problem of limiting ABMs on an equitable basis. Semenov on one occasion even resorted to a rare use of sarcasm. Would the United States be interested in a Soviet proposal permitting them four or five ABM sites and allowing the United States one? If so, he would gladly report it to his government. If not, then the "rule of contraries" should apply. I kept a straight face and solemnly said that if the Soviets wanted to table such a proposal I would duly report it to Washington, adding that his scoffing indicated a lack of understanding of our proposal.

A Soviet delegate said that U.S. talk about a Soviet build-up in offensive missiles could not be taken seriously when the United States was engaged in a very large offensive escalation in its Minuteman and Poseidon MIRV programs. I pointed out that the U. S. MIRV program was quite different from increases in

MLBMs. The Soviet said it was worse. But the main obstacle to working out offensive limitations continued to be FBS. The Soviets must surely have seen FBS as marginal at most to the strategic balance. But this delegate replied that FBS had an important effect on thinking in Moscow. We were told informally that the United States should itself understand this because "when one bloody little submarine goes to Cuba everyone in America goes crazy." We should, therefore, not minimize this problem.

We argued hard for the new "four-to-one" ABM approach, carrying out the President's special instruction that it should be presented persuasively. Considering that most of us thought the proposal to be far from serious, I believe we made a good effort. We emphasized the advantage of the new arrangement. It took into account the realities of the overall strategic relationship between the two countries. Destruction of existing ABM systems could be difficult to agree on. A four-site ABM deployment would not be destabilizing since it would not provide significant protection to the U.S. population, and the sides understood it was population protection that cast doubt on the inevitability of retaliation and thus made ABM systems destabilizing. The protection of retaliatory forces would produce stability, particularly in view of the continued Soviet ICBM deployments.

The ABM systems of the sides would serve different purposes. That of the U.S. would protect retaliatory forces, while the Moscow system defended the national command authority and the capital. Each objective was important, and since different purposes could require different numbers, a simple numerical comparison of complexes was not a proper criterion by which to judge the equity of an arrangement. It was not possible to equate numerically the value of protecting a capital and protecting missile complexes.

Soviet ABM defense would protect Moscow's industry and Soviet political authorities, as well as some ICBMs deployed near Moscow. Our ABMs would protect some ICBMs located in a part of the United States having a relatively sparse population, little industry, and not including our National Command Authority at Washington, D.C. The real measure of strategic defensive systems should be in terms of what was defended and the effect of the resulting defense on strategic stability. On this basis, a four-to-one limitation would not give the United States military advantage.

The Soviet delegation was not about to be persuaded that equality of numbers was unimportant because the histories and purposes of the ABM systems were different. The proposed four-to-one arrangement was "manifestly inequitable." Our ABMs had a more expansive purpose than a limited defense of four ICBM fields and the inequality involved more than the number of sites. U. S. ABMs looked like a long step toward a thick ABM defense and covered a much larger area than the Moscow system. Soviet military experts estimated that four sites could cover about one half of the United States. The Soviets were not worried by those sites alone. They were concerned about their potential effect on strategic stability.

General Trusov told Allison that the Soviets were concerned that they could readily be converted into a thick system which would tempt the United States to make a first strike. Allison disagreed, arguing that the illogical Soviet position against strong controls on ABM radars would result in more capability for expansion than our deployment. I said our proposal would place tighter controls on ABM systems than the Soviet proposal. And, if the Soviets were truly worried about expansion, they should reconsider our alternative calling for a total ABM ban.

A report on the negotiation for radar controls is presented in Chapter 10. At this Vienna session our position that strict radar controls were an essential part of ABM limitations was argued at length. We insisted that both numbers and types of radars must be limited. This was to protect against sudden abrogation of an agreement accompanied by deployment of a large-scale ABM defense. Additional interceptors and launchers could be secretly produced and quickly deployed, while radars required a much longer construction time, so if they were not limited a nation could prepare a base for a large-scale ABM defense. An unlimited radar capability could also increase the potential of anti-aircraft missiles to supplement true ABM systems.

After some weeks at Vienna, I sent along to Kissinger my impression that SALT seemed in suspense. Semenov and General Alekseyev had gone off to the Congress of the Soviet Communist Party. Lack of specifics from Washington on our ABM proposals prevented useful work on this subject and was not consistent with our declared position giving priority to discussion of the details of ABM limitations. How long were we to push three ABM alternatives and maintain that they all had equal status? The Soviets had not specifically rejected the concept that the United States could use ABMs to defend ICBMs while the U.S.S.R. defended its capital, or, for that matter, the possibility that the United States should have more sites than the U.S.S.R. They had rejected the proposed ratio of four to one and also three to one, but had not explicitly rejected a two-to-one arrangement. We could not do much with offensive limitations unless something were done about FBS. There was speculation that with U.S. political pressures for moratoria and acceptance of ABM only, the U.S. position might become more flexible. While assuring Kissinger that things had not reached an impasse, I suggested that I return to Washington, to see if some new instructions could be extracted from the White House. I was advised to plan for a return May 9. By that time things were humming in Washington.

The White House now asked for the delegation's views. After long and sometimes hot deliberation, we advised Washington that the four-to-one ABM offer was of absolutely no interest to the Soviets. Our best bet for finding out if there was any give in the Soviet ABM positions was to concentrate on the national capital NCA alternative. The delegation made a strong pitch to Washington to send on more details on the desired ABM constraints, such as a precise definition of an NCA site and the meaning of a requirement for consultation with respect to ABM radar replacement. This was not the first time we had solicited this data which was vital negotiating information about which Washington apparently could not make up its mind after months of effort.

Our exasperated state of mind was reflected in blunt advice to Washington on ABM tactics. If we were to back off from our offer to consider NCA details, the Soviets would have real grounds for suspicion of U.S. motives. We had described our three ABM alternatives as having equal status. If we were soon again to change our ABM position, the U.S. purpose in SALT would be put seriously in question. If we now withdrew our offer for an NCA limitation it would not be without substantial cost—perhaps even prejudicing the whole negotiation.

The delegation was chagrined but not surprised to be advised in April that the President now favored the new alternative for a four-site Safeguard deployment. The White House recognized the sensitivity of an explicit U.S. switch in priorities. The delegation was to avoid making a further record on NCA which could be used against us. It was a pleasant surprise that this instruction explicitly kept open the possibility of an ABM ban.

This was the beginning of the end of our year-old proposal for an ABM limitation at an NCA level. Very soon, thereafter, the Soviets were given to understand that the United States had lost interest in an NCA-level limitation. They started to consider other limitations. When asked where they thought a mutually acceptable limitation would be found, they merely stressed the need for "equality" and "parity." On a number of informal occasions we heard the term "two to two."

At the end of this Vienna session I formally withdrew the United States NCA offer.

May 4 was my fifty-seventh birthday. Semenov was among the guests at dinner that evening. Afterward he asked if I would discuss some SALT business and pulled out the inevitable sheaf of cards. He had a birthday present of considerable interest. The Soviets were ready now to move on the question of the link between offensive and defensive limitations. He said that at the last meeting I had spoken about a possible temporary suspension of construction of new ICBMs by the U.S.S.R. He thought that at this stage of our negotiation we could achieve a common mutual understanding on such a possibility, with the understanding that the details were to be discussed only after achievement of a separate agreement on limiting ABMs to the defense of national capitals. Such a cessation would not effect modernization or replacement activities. National means of verification would make it possible to differentiate between "heavy" or "light" missiles that would be placed in existing or modernized launchers. To be sure I had understood, I asked our interpreter to repeat his interpretation of the key passage. The evening ended on a happy note.

Semenov returned to the subject of a possible halt in Soviet ICBM silo construction starts a few days later. The Austrian gov-

ernment was hosting a weekend junket for the delegations to
Carinthia, a beautiful region in the southeast. After a fine dinner
at a mountain restaurant on Saturday, Soviet and American delegation members rode back to the hotel in a bus. This was the
only time they turned to song. Each side tried to outdo the other.
This exuberance seemed a good sign that at last progress was in
sight.

The next day our Austrian hosts arranged a picturesque trip on
a steamer around the Wörthersee. Semenov's penchant for mixing business and recreation turned the cruise into a hard morning's work. While the rest of the delegations enjoyed the spring-
time cruise, I listened as he developed his views on the state of
SALT.

Semenov was concerned. The United States proposal of August
4, 1970, was unacceptable. He reviewed FBS arguments for the
nth time. While we might think forward-based systems a normal
situation, to the Soviets it didn't look like equal security for the
United States to continue to have all of these bases and weapons
deployments. And circles in the United States opposed to SALT
were blowing up out of all proportion the continuing Soviet construction of ICBM silos. The United States continued to build up
its strategic forces, he said, citing MIRVs and the proposed new
missile submarine program now called Trident. The Soviets did
not believe the strategic balance was undergoing any genuine
change and there was no basis for the concern expressed about Soviet programs. Next came a rather long passage about the military
industrial complex, opponents of détente and those trying to fan
the cold war. A U.S. policy of "positions of strength" against the
U.S.S.R. had been beaten—"That bet was lost in the late fifties
and early sixties," et cetera.

I denied that there were any influential circles in the United
States working against détente. During my twenty years under
Democratic and Republican administrations I had seen no evidence of responsible people in the United States who opposed improvement of Soviet-American relations. I could not foresee progress in offensive weapons control if the Soviet FBS position
remained unchanged. I saw little chance that the United States
would change its Western European policy by retracting its forward bases. Presumably that policy could be changed in the fu-

ture if circumstances warranted, but not in the context of the SALT negotiations.

In spite of all this, Semenov said, he felt there was a reasonable basis for satisfactory arrangements if both sides had a genuine desire to reach them. For once he apologized for having taken so much time. He thought that what he had to say might be of interest to me because he had heard I was returning to Washington. About this point the boat was due to dock but the captain was instructed to keep steaming. Semenov obviously had not finished.

He now proposed that we turn a new page in the negotiation and concentrate all attention that year on ABM limitations with a view to subsequently engaging in intensive negotiations on offensive systems. For some time deployment of land-based ICBMs could be halted. What would be bad about this? Who would gain and who would lose thereby? Peace would be the beneficiary. Such a halt would apply not only to heavy missile launchers (MLBMs) but also to other offensive systems, although it should not affect necessary modernization or replacement.

I advised him that I had reported his earlier remarks to Washington and had not yet received any reaction, so I wasn't in a position to discuss them further. This reference to heavy missiles was interesting. I asked if it was fair to conclude that his specific mention of heavy missiles indicated a positive disposition to have an MLBM sublimit. He said it was not chance that he had spoken of the fact that modern technical means of verification made it possible to distinguish between heavy and light missiles. Should this question be raised on a more practical plane, we would have to conduct further negotiations. I asked if he had in mind offensive weapons other than ICBMs. He said no. He avoided a commitment on whether these offensive measures would be covered by an informal understanding or a formal agreement, saying that in the history of Soviet-American relations there were cases where agreements had been concluded in two different modes, both of which had equal status.

He stressed that in this part of the discussion he was replying to a question asked by me. I noted that he had said the same thing on May 4. It was not important, but I did not recall ever having raised the subject of a temporary ICBM halt. Still, if it would help him to engage in this line of exchange, I would be perfectly willing to take the responsibility for raising this subject in the first place. Semenov said he believed that we understood each other. There was further talk about a temporary ICBM halt, but he obviously did not want to get into detail. I tried to sound him out as to whether the freeze would apply to all construction and not only to new starts. This would be determined by the duration of the halt.

He was talked out. When we emerged on deck we were cheered. The delegations had had quite enough sunbathing without so much as a beer. Although we had not taken advantage of it, Semenov and I had been working in the ship's bar. We came ashore pleased with the morning's work.

BACK CHANNEL

"If I had thought my coat knew my plans,
I would take it off and burn it."

FREDERICK II OF PRUSSIA

I arrived in Washington on May 10. The first inkling I had had that something was up was when my message reporting Semenov's offer of May 4 to stop ICBM construction starts when an ABM agreement was reached went unanswered. Here was a major negotiating signal and Washington was silent. Philip Farley at ACDA was preparing a paper proposing that we try to consolidate Semenov's "proposal." I should be authorized to tell Semenov that the United States was prepared to negotiate along those lines. He suggested that we press for a communiqué concluding the Vienna talks making public our agreement to negotiate on this basis. Farley's idea was soon overtaken by events.

Nine days later Kissinger broke the news to me at breakfast in his office. He wanted me to have the whole background of his recent direct involvement in SALT. It had started in January in a talk with Dobrynin about how to break the impasse. The whole record would be made available to me. The United States would negotiate an ABM agreement with the Soviets, who would agree to halt new construction of ICBM silos while negotiations for offensive arms limitation continued. My notes of this conversation read "apparently . . . the two would be worked out in parallel (although this is not clear)." The President was to announce the agreement the next day and would exchange letters with Kosygin spelling out the arrangements. I read the draft public announcement.

> The Governments of the U.S. and the Soviet Union after reviewing the course of their talks on the limitation of strategic armaments have agreed to concentrate this year on working out an agreement for the limitation of the deployment of antiballistic missile systems, ABMs. They have also agreed that together with concluding an agreement to limit ABMs they will agree on certain measures with respect to the limitation of offensive strategic weapons.

> The two sides are taking this course in the conviction that it will create more favorable conditions for further negotiations to limit all strategic arms. These negotiations will be actively pursued.

I pointed out that the drafting was imprecise and that the "agreement to agree" procedure would be criticized. I suggested clarifying language but soon realized that changes were not welcome. Under these circumstances, I said I could take no responsibility for this agreement as drafted. Kissinger said he knew who could be blamed if anything went wrong. I was struck by the absence of any mention of SLBMs. Kissinger spoke only of a proposed halt in Soviet ICBM silo construction. He said he had pushed Dobrynin to a more liberal position, Dobrynin having originally proposed only an ABM agreement as a first step.

All through this conversation Kissinger referred to the offensive weapons part of the accord as an ICBM arrangement. He showed little concern that under this arrangement there probably was not going to be a freeze on SLBMs. After I had a chance to review the record, I pointed out to Kissinger that in effect he had agreed to exclude SLBMs. He demurred, saying the record was ambiguous. When I later was instructed by the President to press for including SLBM launchers in the freeze, Kissinger's advice was to make a try for it but not to take much time and not to "fall on my sword" over this issue.

I was told that Secretary Laird would be advised of the agreement at one o'clock that day and the President was just then advising the Secretary of State. I suppose I should have been pleased to be advised before the Secretary of Defense! There was no need for me to tell Kissinger what I thought of his procedure in negotiating behind the back of all responsible Administration officials save the President. But I tried to make the best of it by saying that the product and not the process counted, and I thought the product looked positive. I got the impression that Kissinger was more interested in the major political thrust that this accord would give the negotiation than in its specific provisions. As I left he observed that the only way the White House could have obtained it was through a highly secretive process.

Kissinger suggested that I return to Vienna before the President's announcement. I asked if the President really wanted to have me out of town at this turning point in SALT. He then said he was sure the President would be glad to have me participate in the briefing of the congressional leadership and the scheduled press conferences. He added that the President had been griped by a news story saying that the arrangement had been reached by Semenov and Smith while cruising on the Wörthersee. In backgrounding the press, he planned to make no mention of his own participation in the negotiating process. He would say we had reached this point by negotiations at a number of levels. This, he said, had been a hard decision for the President to make and there had been temptations to go in the other direction and propose new strategic programs to the Congress.

The next day President Nixon resorted to some of the high-flown rhetoric that occasionally was used in SALT. "If we succeed, this joint statement that has been issued today may well be remembered as the beginning of a new era in which all nations will devote more of their energies and their resources not to the weapons of war but to the works of peace." Right after the President's announcement I took part in several press conferences. It was a queer feeling to be explaining an agreement I had not negotiated, the announcement of which was so poorly drafted as to defy clear construction. I was embarrassed by the obvious Russian origin of some of the language. No American would have proposed "They have also agreed that together with concluding an agreement to limit ABMs they would agree on certain measures with respect to the limitation of offensive strategic weapons."

That looked to me like transliteration of a Soviet text. Kissinger said the most important point was that "this marks a major step forward in breaking the SALT deadlock by Soviet acceptance of the principle of linking defensive and offensive limitations." That seemed rather strange since the Soviets had insisted on this from the beginning and had only partially broken away from it in late 1970.

In fact one might characterize this accord as a "breakthrough" back toward the U. S. 1969 Illustrative Elements which spelled out an ABM limitation joined with a freeze on missile launchers but with no limit on aircraft.

But the May 1971 accord was a turning point. The United States in effect accepted that the FBS issue was blocking a treaty setting ceilings on offensive weapons and switched its aim to negotiating a moratorium or freeze approach. This would be a short-term hold to permit negotiations for a treaty to continue while aggregate Soviet missile launcher levels were not increasing very much. The Soviets assured Kissinger, as they had the SALT delegation, that after an ABM treaty had been reached the prospect for a comprehensive offensive arms limitation would improve. However, the move from an agreed ceiling to a freeze concept entailed eventual registration of the Soviet numerical advantage in missile launchers. I doubt that this was fully anticipated in May 1971. Subsequent U.S. proposals that this freeze also provide for approximately equal levels of SLBMs for the sides were brushed aside by the Soviets and the freeze started at a time when missile launcher levels were unequal.

An autopsy may be in order to see how the May 20 agreement was reached. The negotiating record is meager. This back-channel negotiation, as it has been called, followed an entirely different procedure from that which governed the delegation. There were no building blocks, no analytical work, no strategic analysis in the agencies concerned. There were no Verification Panel or National Security Council discussions. There were no consultations with congressional committees or with allies. It was a one-man stand, a presidential aide against the resources of the Soviet leadership. Several times during this subnegotiation the entire Soviet

Politburo considered the issues, a unique phenomenon which impressed that hard-to-impress individual, Kissinger, with the extreme importance of what he singlehandedly was doing. It is not a pleasing contrast—one American (presumably keeping the President informed) ranged against the top Soviet political and technical authorities.

In January 1971, while the SALT community was beginning to prepare for the next negotiating round in Vienna, the President had advised the Soviet leadership that, although he would insist on keeping some link between offensive and defensive arms limitations, he would be willing to have a less strict tie between the two than had been the past U.S. position. It seems likely that the Nixon initiative resulted from the clear signals the delegation had reported from Helsinki that the Soviets were interested in an ABM agreement accompanied by some less formal understanding on offensive limitation measures. The President's message to the Kremlin led to a series of exchanges in Washington between Kissinger and Dobrynin during the winter and spring of 1971.

The dual problem was how to move the U.S.S.R. off its position that FBS had to be taken into account and to move the United States off its position that it would not enter into a separate ABM treaty. (Kissinger had had some doubts as to the wisdom of the decision back in July 1970 not to accept the Soviet proposal for a separate ABM treaty. He wondered aloud to me one day if the Soviets might have been more tractable during the recent Middle East crisis if we had accepted that proposal and reached an ABM treaty.) Perhaps there was a compromise possibility in which an initial ABM treaty could be combined with some constraints on offensive forces. Perhaps the traditional diplomatic asset of time could be capitalized on to postpone the sharp disagreement about FBS to another day. Some interim arrangement might be worked out, perhaps a freeze to give time to negotiate a treaty limiting offensive systems to match an ABM treaty that seemed to be closer at hand.

Kissinger and Dobrynin met in January. Kissinger said that, while there must be some link between defensive and offensive limitations, we were flexible as to form. An agreement to couple an ABM treaty with a freeze on offensive weapons was possible. A separate ABM treaty could be concluded if it was coupled with an undertaking to continue working for offensive arms limitations and an undertaking for a freeze on new starts of ICBMs until the formal offensive limitations were agreed. The U. S. ABM proposal would be based on the existing U. S. ABM program.

The Soviet response was positive. Moscow had "considerable sympathy" for the U.S. notion of coupling an ABM agreement and a freeze.[1] It had "general openmindedness" on whether the ABM constraint should be a ban or a limit of one site for each side to defend its capital or, surprisingly, even three Safeguard sites for the United States and a Moscow defense for the U.S.S.R. The Soviet political leadership favored NCA while their military people had done a study which found merit in the three-to-one idea! Dobrynin said that none of these alternative ABM levels was excluded. The Soviets were prepared to be "very constructive."

Dobrynin had not given up entirely on the forward-based system issue and asked how it would be handled. Kissinger argued that these secondary forces could not upset the strategic balance. FBS could be handled more easily in some sort of tacit agreement not to raise their numbers except in an emergency. (On December 4, 1970, the delegation, with General Allison dissenting, had proposed that this very formula be offered to the Soviets at Helsinki. It had been rejected by the White House in favor of the much less committal Helsinki FBS formula that we would consider ways to prevent FBS from upsetting the strategic balance once the main provisions for limitations on central offensive systems were agreed.)

For a time nothing more was heard from Moscow. At the end of January Dobrynin said he was authorized by the Politburo to state that Moscow wanted a SALT agreement and the earlier the better. He explained the delay by saying that they did not have governmental machinery for lateral clearance short of the Politburo, so important decisions took much longer than in the United States. Dobrynin's admission says a good deal about how the Soviet system and the American system were handling national security matters, in 1971 at least. Early in March Dobrynin ex-

---

[1] Not surprising since this is what it had proposed in December of the previous year.

plained that all the leadership were at their country places—
dachas—which inexplicably was recorded as "Dachaus."

There was some talk of having a Nixon speech after a Kissinger-Dobrynin agreement in principle to surface this idea of trying for an ABM treaty and an offensive freeze, to which the Soviet
leadership would respond positively. But Dobrynin wanted to
have a formal U.S. proposal before the speech was made. He said
it would help things if Kissinger gave him a *note verbale* (a
diplomatic message that is more formal than an *aide-mémoire*
and less formal than a signed note). But it appears that the White
House did not want to be committed to this extent.

Although the U.S. priority on the offensive side of SALT was
for ICBM limitation, because of their potential threat to the U. S.
Minuteman force, we had watched with some apprehension a
stream of photos showing the rapid build-up of the Soviet SLBM
fleet. All our previous SALT approaches had included limitations
on SLBM launchers. By early 1971 the U.S.S.R. had nearly as
many submarines in operation and under construction as the
United States had in operation. Geography benefited the United
States, as did advanced bases, but longer-range Soviet seaborne
missiles which were being developed would soon eliminate a good
deal of this advantage.

Knowing of our preoccupation with ICBMs, the Soviets probably hoped that the "freeze" would apply only to them—and let
submarine construction run free. Their ICBM launcher construction program perhaps was already topping out. The SLBM
matter had been raised by Dobrynin at the first meeting. Kissinger
gave an equivocal answer that maybe the submarines would be
covered but that this issue could be left for the detailed negotiations.

In February Dobrynin had come back to the SLBM question.
Would they be included in the freeze or not? Then came a stun-
ning answer. We would, Kissinger said, be prepared to have it either way. Here, in one sentence, the position which the United
States had pressed for almost a year was changed. There is no evidence to indicate that this major change in SALT policy was
ever considered in advance by anyone except Kissinger—and perhaps not even by him. It may well have been a random answer of
a fatigued and overextended man who did not realize the im-

mense significance of his words. It was to take a lot of effort and expenditure of bargaining power to redeem these words and restore the earlier U.S. position that SLBMs must be included in any SALT agreement. Dobrynin pocketed the offer diplomatically and without appearing to lunge at it. He said that the Soviets were prepared to discuss sea-based systems but preferred not to. So the matter rested in May when the results of this winter's back-channel negotiation were endorsed by the political authorities of the two countries.

The talk turned to the key question of force modernization during the freeze. For the Soviets modernization meant primarily new classes of larger ICBMs then in the development stage. Kissinger said categorically there would be no constraint on modernization. Turning to ABM, he asked if the Soviets would agree to a complete ban. Dobrynin, contrary to his January position, said he now doubted it. The two Washington negotiators then discussed how long the freeze should last. Kissinger opined that eighteen months to two years should be an adequate time to permit negotiation of a comprehensive agreement to replace an interim freeze. The Soviets must have been puzzled when they subsequently proposed just such a time limit and the U.S. delegation, at White House instructions, insisted on a longer term. Kissinger asked whether, if an ABM treaty was agreed upon, it would terminate if an offensive arms treaty did not replace the interim freeze. No, said Dobrynin, it should continue until an offensive arms treaty was concluded. Should the freeze be an oral agreement or in writing? Kissinger said it must be in writing. They agreed to try to work out an exchange of letters.

A first White House draft was dated February 17. Apparently Kissinger was thinking in terms of an agreed document which could be used as instructions to the delegations when they resumed work in Vienna in mid-March. There would be two ABM alternatives: three U.S. sites and the Moscow NCA defense or an ABM ban. There would be no more ICBM launcher construction starts and work on existing ICBM construction would be halted by January 1, 1972. Modernization or replacement of ICBMs would not be precluded.

The draft also had a provision stating that if the freeze was not converted into a treaty in five years either party could terminate the ABM treaty without resorting to the clause normally contained in arms control agreements permitting termination if the parties' vital interests were prejudiced. But Dobrynin argued that the normal clause was adequate. Kissinger remarked, "This would certainly be a fair counterproposal." And after the U.S. delegation, under instructions, subsequently argued at length but in vain for a special withdrawal clause, that is the way it finally worked out.

In March Dobrynin handed Kissinger a draft document proposing that the sides "concentrate in the current year on ABMs in order to conduct, after conclusion of a separate ABM agreement, active talks on controls over offensive weapons." The Soviets were prepared subsequently to discuss "freezing" offensive weapons as proposed by the United States. Concrete details could be worked out after a separate ABM agreement was concluded. Kissinger was disappointed. This was merely a restatement of the maximum Soviet position set out in the Helsinki SALT session late in 1970. He said the only way to make progress was to agree in principle on a freeze and then negotiate the ABM agreement and details of the freeze. All right, said Dobrynin, you try your hand at drafting an acceptable letter.

Kissinger later gave Dobrynin another draft, which called for a major effort to reach an ABM treaty in 1971 and, as an integral part of the arrangement, a commitment to try to reach an offensive arms treaty by a fixed date and a commitment that no new offensive launchers would be completed after a fixed date. The same day, Dobrynin handed him a paper which Kissinger said was unacceptable because it lacked the necessary clear linkage of the continuing negotiations on offensive and defensive arms. Apparently the Soviets still hoped they could inveigle the United States into one of the kinds of arrangements they had proposed to the SALT delegation in Helsinki in 1970, an ABM treaty coupled only with some vague assurance about further negotiations on offensive arms controls. Kissinger wanted to get a flat commitment that the target for the next stage of the negotiation was the simultaneous attainment of two agreements, an ABM treaty and an interim freeze on offensive arms.

The next day there was a new U.S. draft which set out obligations to continue active negotiations to limit offensive arms and to freeze construction of such arms after a fixed date. Replacement by weapons of the same category and modernization of offensive launchers would be allowed if the total number of launchers was not increased. Kissinger and Dobrynin reached agreement on this document.

Then they haggled further over the "sequence" question. Dobrynin asked, Does the freeze have to be negotiated prior to the ABM treaty? No, said Kissinger, they should be handled simultaneously but neither would go into effect until both were signed. In late March the Soviet was still trying to wiggle away from the concept of simultaneity. Dobrynin submitted a paper saying that the details of the freeze would be discussed after the ABM treaty had been worked out. Kissinger tried out a formula that discussion of the details of the freeze would be concluded simultaneously with the conclusion of the agreement on ABMs. Things were getting somewhat metaphysical, but the sequence issue was important. It was not to be cleared up during these talks and plagued subsequent negotiations for months.

Another sequence formula was tried. The United States was prepared in principle to have a separate ABM agreement. The parties would begin discussing the ABM agreement and the freeze "practically concurrently." Dobrynin said it would be very difficult to put in the draft that the freeze would be discussed from the very beginning of the next phase. He proposed that the details of the freeze be discussed simultaneously with the conclusion of the ABM agreement. Although this would not provide clear guidance as to when the freeze would be negotiated, it appealed to Kissinger. "That would be fine. Yes. Something like that would go." But that same day Kissinger called back to say in effect, When we begin discussing an agreement on ABMs, then we want, side by side, to discuss the principles of a freeze. It could hardly be called a meeting of the minds.

Dobrynin then went off to Moscow for the Party Congress and to get his authorities' approval of his work on SALT. On his return, he presented Kissinger a new draft. The U.S.S.R. accepted in principle the idea of freezing strategic offensive weapons, having in mind including in such an understanding questions relating to the composition of strategic offensive weapons as well as to the nature and dates of "freezing." These questions could be discussed before the work on the ABM agreement was complete. Kissinger topped this off by adding, "both agreements to be concluded simultaneously." Dobrynin characterized this formula as conceding most of the U.S. points, except that the U. S. ABM proposal calling for three ABM sites and Moscow NCA was not acceptable. Dobrynin said he had pressed his authorities hard on this score. It seemed that no progress had been made on narrowing the gap about ABM site numbers.

Kissinger pointed out to Dobrynin that the Soviet draft merely said the freeze understanding and its details would be discussed before work on the ABM Treaty was complete. It did not state that it would be concluded with the ABM agreement. He said the Soviets had already agreed to discuss offensive arms. He proposed a statement that the agreement and the understanding would be concluded simultaneously. He told Dobrynin that a capital-defense NCA-level ABM limitation was not of interest to the United States. But he also said it was not definitely ruled out.

Now hope for success began to be mixed with irritation. Dobrynin was playing hard to get, telling Kissinger that the U.S.S.R.'s attitude toward SALT was that "we can take or leave it." He was reminded that the Soviets had pressed for SALT, to which Dobrynin replied that that was with the looser formulas considered in Lyndon Johnson's days and not an arrangement having the precise details now being proposed by the United States.

It was the middle of May. Four months had elapsed since these two gentlemen started this second SALT negotiation. Two months had passed since our delegation had resumed work with the Soviets in Vienna, with instructions quite different from the line Kissinger was taking. It had been set the impossible task of working out a single comprehensive treaty limiting both ABMs and offensive arms, an aim which Kissinger had long since advised his negotiating partner, Dobrynin, no longer to be the immediate purpose of the United States. It would be hard to dream up a more confusing method of handling an international negotiation.

Dobrynin now suggested another sequence formula: "While concluding an ABM treaty certain measures affecting offensive arms would be agreed upon." Kissinger then adopted a somewhat harder line, saying, "We want it explicitly recognized that the two agreements would be concluded simultaneously." Dobrynin said it would not be necessary to state that, it was already fully covered in the draft letter they had been working on.

Kissinger now realized that despite all his efforts he had not succeeded in clearing up the muddled state of the "sequence" matter. The next day he prudently proposed that a new paper be put to Moscow making the sequence matter clearer. Dobrynin demurred, saying that would require another two weeks if Gromyko thought the matter must go to the Politburo. There had already been six meetings of the "whole government." There was no question but that the two agreements would be concluded simultaneously.

The back-channel negotiation finished on this vague note.

What did it accomplish? It led to a very general understanding, formally registering what the President had earlier indicated to the Soviet leadership, that the United States would accept an ABM treaty accompanied by a less formal interim agreement restraining offensive arms until a companion treaty could be negotiated. The letters which Kissinger and Dobrynin had worked out were exchanged by President Nixon and Premier Kosygin on May 20. They covered the same points as the press release but also provided that, during the freeze, modernization and replacement of offensive weapons would not be precluded. This provision was later to take on major importance.

For months the White House had carried out one line of SALT policy while directing the delegation to take another. Was it necessary to pursue such a duplicitous diplomacy? It was known as early as December 1970 that the Soviets would agree to an ABM treaty and probably would agree to certain parallel measures constraining offensive deployments, presumably in a less formal agreement. Why was it that the apparently rather simple task of spelling out this general understanding was handled in this unusual fashion? President Nixon later said that secret personal diplomacy had to be resorted to because of the way the Soviet leadership works. An equally persuasive case can be made that it resulted from his distrust of officials responsible for SALT—the Secretary of Defense, the Secretary of State, the Chairman of the Joint Chiefs of Staff, the director of the Arms Control Agency, and our associates. I thought the whole episode a sad reflection on the state of affairs in the Administration. Kissinger and the President went the Soviets one better. At least in the Soviet Union, the whole Politburo was consulted, on several occasions. The bulk of the American national security leadership was never consulted. It was informed after the fact.

It may be said that, because the May 20 arrangement represented such a sharp change from United States insistence on a single limitation agreement covering both offensive and defensive weapons, negotiating it required the additional secrecy that only back-channel exchanges could afford. In the process, a good deal was lost, not least of which was the confidence of the SALT delegates in the backing they had been expecting from the White House—all of this to reach a procedural understanding which was fully foreshadowed in the previous round of the negotiation proper. I concluded that the May 20 "understanding" would have been much better with less secrecy.

There was no open disagreement with the general concept of the accord. It seemed only sensible to go for an ABM treaty that then seemed attainable and couple it with some arrangement that would freeze Soviet offensive launchers while negotiations continued. That is what we had proposed to the Secretary of State in February of 1971.

The sequence question—whether the ABM Treaty would be fully negotiated first, and when discussions on the offensive freeze would start—was left in a hazy state. No agreement was registered about what forces would be frozen. The U.S.S.R. had been told that the United States would not insist on SLBMs being included in the freeze. Although the Washington negotiators had discussed when the freeze would start and whether it would include missile launchers on which construction had already begun, these issues were left up in the air. The Kremlin had learned that the United States might still accept an ABM capital defense (NCA). They had been told that the United States would consider some sort of tacit agreement on forward-based systems if this issue arose again in the future. The U.S.S.R. had been assured that there would be no constraints on modernization and replacement of missile launchers under the interim freeze. The U.S. negotiator had suggested a freeze duration of eighteen months to two years. And he had indicated that no special withdrawal clause in the ABM Treaty would be necessary. The back-channel negotiation had taken some five months and the United States had now, in effect, accepted the Soviet concept presented in Helsinki the previous December.

When SALT was handed back to the delegations, I was instructed to negotiate some positions quite contrary to those taken by Kissinger.

It seems fair to say that the course of the remaining SALT negotiations would have been smoother if the delegation had simply been instructed in January 1971 to work out a procedural arrangement stating that the sides would try to negotiate an ABM treaty and an interim freeze in parallel and conclude them simultaneously. I do not understand why it was necessary, in reaching some such procedural arrangement, to get into the range of substantive issues that Kissinger and Dobrynin did without reaching agreement but in the process of which things were said which required a long time to reverse.

On pondering the process by which the May 1971 accord had been reached, I compared it with a statement that appeared in President Nixon's Foreign Policy Report a few months earlier. He had said that "at home we are not the prisoner of bureaucratic jockeying to come up with an agreed response." Keeping the bureaucrats uninformed is a good way to keep them from jockeying, even though the price is high.

The delegates were chagrined at being kept in the dark. Their expertise had been ignored at a key turning point in the negotiation which they had been working on for more than eighteen months. The delegation's trust in its Washington authorities was never restored. Afterward we always assumed that other contacts with the Soviets were taking place which we could not be trusted to know about—which proved to be the case. Officials in Washington agencies who had worked for months on SALT analysis, preparation and backstopping now grew cynical at this blatant example of how big business was really done by the intervention of a presidential aide unsupported by a staff save a few White House officials whose military and arms control experience was modest.

In fairness, it should be recalled that Washington in 1971 was a city of leaks. Kissinger believed that complete privacy was the best hope for reaching agreement with the Soviets. They could clear proposals with parts of their governing structure that had responsibility for strategic arms because they do not have uninspired news leaks. Kissinger must have felt that presenting the concerned agencies with a fait accompli was the only way to get business done. It is a sad commentary that "leak" concerns led to one-man governance of such a key part of the foreign relations of the United States.

There were a number of breaches of security of information about the SALT negotiation which I believed at the time prejudiced our negotiating capability. In retrospect I think this concern was exaggerated. But these leaks did lead to suspicions among top SALT officials which soured the Washington atmosphere. President Nixon believed that leaks could seriously limit his freedom of action in orchestrating the congressional aspects of the talks as well as his direction over the national security agencies and the negotiation itself. Leaks were one reason for excessive White House SALT secrecy that deprived it of the know-how of its SALT officials. Public information about the talks and the agreements reached, while not ideal, was, I think, sufficient.

In SALT as in most sensitive diplomatic negotiations in which the United States engages there was constant tension between two highly desirable conditions—negotiating privacy and an informed public. SALT issues were discussed publicly in the context of overall American foreign policy in the President's annual Foreign Policy Reports. Secretary of State Rogers and Kissinger from time to time made either public or background statements about SALT purposes and the general posture of the talks. The Congress was kept well informed by the principal delegates as to the current negotiating situation—at least to the extent of their knowledge. It cannot be said that the public got short-changed. But the SALT agreements while they are certainly open covenants were not openly arrived at.

From time to time privacy was breached by Washington officials in leaks to eager newsmen, much to the concern of the SALT delegates and to the anger of the President. Reaction to past leaks and fear of future ones caused or was used as an excuse by the White House for narrowing access to SALT information so that at times the negotiation proceeded without any technically qualified officials aware of what was going on. It need hardly be said that a price was paid for such a constricted conduct of diplomacy.

When taking on responsibilities for the negotiation it had seemed to me that there would be more of a chance for success if negotiating privacy could be maintained. Flexibility in adopting and adjusting positions would be sharply reduced if the process had to be carried on with the kind of publicity which had generally accompanied "Geneva"-type arms control negotiations of the previous twenty years. Some of my associates in ACDA felt that I exaggerated the need for secrecy and that I did not give enough weight to the need for public understanding.

Although news leaks seemed especially painful to some of us during SALT they have been a common Washington phenomenon for years. I still recall having sharp feelings of regret more than twenty years ago on reading a first-page story in the New York *Times* about what President Eisenhower was going to say in a speech several days after I had briefed a journalist about the Atoms for Peace program. I decided never again to get into such a fix and, according to my friend the late Arthur Krock of the *Times,* I was called a "tomb" by his colleagues.

President Nixon saw news leaks not only as disclosures benefiting the Soviets but also as narrowing his options in making tough decisions, sometimes deliberate on the part of the "source," sometimes inadvertent. He was especially sensitive to leaks that the Administration was to propose a very low level of ABMs or even a ban. He thought that could prejudice the case for continuing appropriations for the Safeguard ABM program. He tried unsuccessfully to combat leaks from government departments all the years of his presidency.

In the spring of 1969, I had raised the SALT privacy matter with Soviet Ambassador Dobrynin. Secrecy suited the Soviets and we agreed that the SALT negotiations would be private. Neither side would seek to gain propaganda advantages by disclosing positions taken in the negotiation. To the Soviets, American interest in avoiding publicity probably signaled a serious negotiating purpose—and an absence of a propaganda motivation. Although this privacy was invaded from time to time I think the Soviets were impressed that the Americans were able to keep their mouths shut as much as they did. The relative paucity of press leaks led Semenov several times to remark on this "positive phenomenon quite unique in his view." He added that his side greatly appreciated the American efforts in this respect.

When during the negotiation the privacy rule was broken the Soviets lost no time in reminding us—in a rather brusque way—that the American side was breaking an agreement. At times they suggested that they might have to engage in a counterleaking campaign. I sensed that some of their complaints were with "tongue in cheek" since it seemed that they could only benefit from news reports spelling out likely future U.S. positions. And when it suited their purposes, the Soviets publicized their position, as in January 1971 when they let it be known that they had proposed that, as a first step, a separate ABM treaty be worked out. Some American journalists and members of Congress normally maintain contacts with Soviet Embassy officials in Washington. Through this somewhat bizarre channel the American people learned about some SALT developments which their own government was trying to keep private.

Leaking to the press inevitably leads to suspicion and distrust. It is not a pleasant feeling to sit in the White House cabinet room with one's colleagues and wonder which one supplied the headline story of the day and what his motive was. President Nixon, with some reason, did not give his official family very high marks for keeping secrets. At an NSC meeting early in his first administration the subject turned to news leaks. He looked at me and said, "And your agency is the worst in the government." This was before any SALT leaks had occurred. After the meeting I asked Kissinger what was the basis for this statement. He somewhat lamely said that the President had not been looking at me at the time. That didn't satisfy me so I asked Secretary Rogers. He said the President was engaged in an operation to stop leaks in all agencies and had given the same treatment to other officials on other occasions. Later Kissinger came back to the subject and said, "The President swears he was not looking at you when he made the remark." I jokingly said I was glad the President was looking past me at the time. Since I was at the end of the table he must have been looking at President Eisenhower's portrait hanging on the wall!

Several times after serious leaks had occurred I called Kissinger to see if there would be any White House objection to my asking for an investigation. On one of these occasions he quickly called back to say he didn't understand the purpose of these "cryptic calls." He said that he was just as outraged as I was and if I thought he had been the source I should write the President. I said that my purpose was to find out if the press disclosure had been authorized. I was not suggesting that it had been he but I didn't want to embarrass the White House by asking for an investigation if the White House had inspired the story.

In a directive of October 31, 1969, President Nixon ordered that measures be taken to maintain the security of SALT information and prevent press leaks. White House NSDMs before each SALT session during the next three years contained the following: "I reaffirm my directive of October 31, 1969 entitled 'Avoidance of Leaks on SALT.' The Chief of the Delegation will be responsible for assuring that all actions dealt with in that directive are conducted in conformity with it." That responsibility made me especially "jumpy" about leaks. I believe the delegation was never the source of a news leak.

As sensitive disclosures about SALT continued, Kissinger, in May of 1970, sent a memorandum to the Secretaries of State and Defense, to the chairman of the Joint Chiefs of Staff and to myself saying:

> Vital national interests are being jeopardized by leaks to the press regarding SALT. No one in the government is authorized to divulge the United States or Soviet positions to the press or to speculate about United States intentions with respect to the negotiations.

When especially concerned by one story which disclosed certain intelligence findings, I had called the director of Central Intelligence, Richard Helms, to assure him that it had not come from ACDA. He laughed and said, "Whenever there is a leak like that I always call the White House first thing!" Helms knew that ACDA was not the culprit. The White House was well aware that the CIA was not above leaking. The President once sarcastically suggested that when CIA leaked the low levels in an estimated range of Soviet missile launchers they should also leak the high levels in the range. At the beginning the President was quite cynical about CIA estimates of the Soviet strategic forces. He felt that opinions about Soviet intentions were being factored into estimates of their capabilities. He directed that if "opinions" were to be given the contrary opinion should be flagged. This cynicism worried me since trust in CIA's verification capability was the keystone of our confidence that a SALT agreement could be adequately verified. I pointed this out to Secretary Rogers and Kissinger. Later the President seemed to give CIA estimates greater credibility.

On July 25, 1970, there was a major SALT leak divulging the upcoming U.S. August 4 proposal. I wrote Kissinger:

> It must be very difficult for the Soviets to bring themselves to believe that this was merely American journalism at work and not an act of the U. S. Government. . . . If the Smith[2] piece was officially inspired, perhaps there are higher purposes of which I am not aware. But looking at it from my parochial responsibilities, it is unhelpful. We have worked hard for months to develop a private channel of communication with the USSR about matters which are central to the security systems of both countries—and then the current product of our discussions is laid bare to see. This will make it more difficult for the Soviets to forgo propaganda type statements and for us to get them to talk in the specifics necessary to proceed with true negotiations.

I was told the disclosure was absolutely unauthorized.

Things became so bad that the President sent the following message on May 21, 1971—the day after the back-channel "breakthrough" which set the course for the second part of the SALT negotiation. It went only to the Secretary of State, the Secretary of Defense and myself.

> I want all speculation or disclosure by officials of the administration to the press or any other unauthorized individual concerning the substantive positions we may take in the SALT talks to cease immediately. I expect that prompt disciplinary action will be instituted against any person found to

2 Not Gerard.

be responsible for stimulating the kind of press speculation on our negotiating position that appeared in the press from [sic] May 21, 1971. A successful outcome of the Strategic Arms Limitations Talks hinges crucially on the utmost discipline within the Administration and on my complete freedom in reaching the substantive decisions required for the further course of the negotiations. Any leaks will be prejudicial to these objectives and must therefore be ended at once.

The Washington leak problem persists in spite of a number of well-intentioned efforts to bring about a more rational government-press relationship. It will continue as long as heads of departments are privileged to pass secret information to the press. Lesser officials then do the same—whether to advance causes, prejudice positions, or merely feed egos. The parties still seem far apart as to where a fair balance should be struck between the needs of official privacy and press freedom—and we still need to find a happier medium between negotiating in a goldfish bowl or in a news blackout. Although SALT leaks didn't make our job any easier and, taken together with other leakage in the Administration, generated an unholy degree of high-level emotion, I now believe that the SALT sources had no intent to harm the national security. Rather the leaks seem to have been efforts to manipulate the press—by officials high and low lobbying for or against positions they favored or opposed.

There was another type of "privacy" which, on balance, did not pay off. News leaks and other efforts to influence U.S. positions caused the White House, which already had a strong disposition toward secrecy and tight control, to distrust department and agency officials. This in turn seemed to justify the highly contained personal method of negotiation resorted to on several occasions in SALT—a method which advantaged the Soviets and is preferred by them since they can then bring all the weight of their pressures, skills and charm to bear on one individual. Although the use of highly personalized diplomacy was rationalized at the White House as responsive to Soviet negotiating requirements, I think the real reason was so that agreements could be reached in total privacy without congressional and above all without that intra-Administration agitation that wider knowledge resulting from normal interagency processes would have engendered. Consider Kissinger's observation as reported in a spring, 1968 essay, a year before he joined the staff of a President:

> Because management of the bureaucracy takes so much energy and precisely because changing course is so difficult, many of the most important decisions are taken by extra-bureaucratic means. Some of the key decisions are kept to a very small circle while the bureaucracy continues working away in ignorance of the fact that decisions are being made, or of the fact that a decision is being made in a particular area. One reason for keeping the decisions to small groups is that when bureaucracies are so unwieldy and when their internal morale becomes a serious problem, an unpopular decision may be fought by brutal means, such as leaks to the press or congressional committees. Thus the only way secrecy can be kept is to exclude from the making of the decision all those who are theoretically charged with carrying it out.

The Special Assistant to the President for National Security Affairs had been a key position for more than twenty years. I had worked with all holders of that post since 1954: Robert Cutler, Dillon Anderson, Gordon Gray, McGeorge Bundy, Walt Rostow and Henry Kissinger. All had different styles. All presumably served the President in the manner he wanted. I think that Kissinger was the only one who as a matter of general practice engaged in diplomatic operations usually handled by the Secretary of State and his staff. The problem with this practice is that the Special Assistant's main function is to see that the President has all points of view. When he becomes a negotiator, he has a personal position to present to the President. In the nature of things, it is bound to take on a different nature than the positions of other government officials not so directly in contact with the President.

In some ways the Kissinger-Dobrynin negotiation was an unfortunate rehearsal for the Moscow negotiations of the following spring. The public and congressional acclamation given to the

May 20 accord must have encouraged Kissinger in the belief that singlehandedly he could negotiate at SALT successfully, and that the delegation indeed was what he came to call them, "technicians," whose function should be limited to converting what he had negotiated into acceptable treaty language.

I had naïvely continued to believe a Kissinger assurance of the previous December. Near the end of the 1970 Helsinki session the delegation had picked up hints about contacts at other levels. I sent Kissinger a message that said, "At best, ignorance can be an embarrassing and even demeaning thing in this business; at worst it can be prejudicial to effective work at the front." He replied, "You can be sure there are no other channels and have not been." Perhaps he would rationalize this deception by saying, "Yes, but I didn't say anything about the future." As George Bernard Shaw said in his preface to *Heartbreak House,* "Truth telling is not compatible with the defence of the realm."

For a few days after May 20, I considered the idea of resigning, a course which I heard Ambassador Thompson felt I should take, although he never said so to me. Being deeply committed to SALT, I decided to see it through even though the White House handling of the delegation struck me as outrageous. Whatever his methods, I felt that Kissinger was seriously aiming for a worthwhile SALT agreement and that it was my job to help regardless of personal considerations.

The May 20 accord was well received by the Congress and the country. After the President had briefed the Cabinet, there was general applause. Nixon said he wished I would come back from Vienna more often because "these fellows had never applauded like that before." A sour note was struck by Senator Jackson, foreshadowing his attitude toward the agreements reached the next year. When I was briefing his Arms Control Subcommittee of the Armed Services Committee, he referred to a provision of the Arms Control and Disarmament Act of 1961: "No action shall be taken under this chapter or any other law that will obligate the United States to disarm or to reduce or to limit the armed forces or armaments of the United States, except pursuant to the treaty making power of the President under the Constitution or unless authorized by further affirmative legislation by the Congress." To propose a treaty for defensive limitations and an informal agreement to freeze offensive arms was to get the cart before the horse. "It was all wrong," he said.

The NATO allies, though informed only after the fact, welcomed the SALT accord. But they were quick to point out its ambiguities. When the United States ambassador to NATO gave the North Atlantic Council on May 20 a copy of the public announcement, five of the Council representatives asked questions about the "certain measures with respect to the limitation of offensive strategic weapons" and their relationship to the negotiation and conclusion of an ABM agreement. What did the "agreement to agree" mean? What was intended for the offensive "measures"? When would they be negotiated—in parallel with the ABM agreement or "together with concluding" it? There were no clear answers.

The first fruits of the imprecision of the May 20 accord became apparent on my return to Vienna. We were to wind up on May 28, to permit preparatory work in capitals for the next round due to start in Helsinki in July. The Soviet delegation gave a dinner on May 26. The May 20 accord naturally was the main topic of conversation. There were some heated exchanges. The Soviet interpretation of the sequence issue was that after an ABM agreement had been fully negotiated the sides would turn to measures affecting offensive arms, and the two agreements could then be concluded together. But we had no interest in completing an ABM treaty, which would probably involve concessions during the negotiation process, until we were much clearer as to what was going to be possible in the way of restraints on offensive arms. Our version called not just for simultaneous conclusion of the two agreements but for parallel negotiations.

The language of the accord—"together with concluding an agreement to limit ABMs they will agree on certain measures with respect to the limitation of offensive strategic weapons"— was so unclear as to permit either interpretation. The Russian word for "together with" ($\pi \rho \mu$) was the main culprit. Apparently neither then nor at subsequent negotiations did Kissinger employ the standard diplomatic practice of having an American expert in the Russian language check a proposed Russian version of a text to make sure that the translation was precisely rendered. In fact, his practice of secrecy went to the extreme of excluding American interpreters. When negotiating in Moscow he relied entirely on Soviet interpreters! This practice of not using American interpreters continued for several years in the second SALT negotiation. It has been reported that at Vladivostok in 1974 a major misunderstanding arose as to whether the agreement being reached covered strategic cruise as well as ballistic missiles or just ballistic missiles. An American interpreter experienced in SALT terminology might have detected this non-meeting of the minds and clarification could have followed.

Kissinger had assured me that as soon as we tabled an ABM position at Helsinki the U.S.S.R. would agree to turn to negotiating on offensive arms. That is not the way it turned out. Many months were to pass before the Soviets turned seriously to the offensive arms problems and the "agreement to agree" began to be implemented.

This dinner dispute almost spilled over into the final plenary session on May 28. I had a statement which explicitly set out the American interpretation of the sequence issue. We learned that Semenov planned to give a different interpretation. That would have been a sour anticlimax to the much-trumpeted SALT breakthrough. I cabled Kissinger suggesting that he tell Dobrynin what was about to happen. Was it possible to get Dobrynin to "straighten out" things to head off terminating the talks on a note of disagreement? Not surprisingly, when Semenov walked into the conference room the next day, he asked to speak to me privately. His statement would not include any interpretation of the meaning of the May 20 document. Could I not do the same? I hurriedly, and somewhat ostentatiously, made a few changes to fuzz up the language in my statement. The dispute was left for another day.

We were not sorry to put this Vienna round behind us. From the start, when we had to propose a wholly unrealistic ABM arrangement, there had been an artificial atmosphere. We surmised that high-level contacts were taking place but had no way of knowing what was going on. Perhaps the May 20 accord would now allow us to conduct serious negotiations at Helsinki.

This agreement to agree was more a political initiative than an arms control agreement. In effect it directed the delegations to go back to work, no longer fettered by either the U.S. objection to a separate ABM treaty or the Soviet position that any offensive limitations would have to take into account the FBS issue. All specifics remained to be worked out—how many ABM sites would be permitted, what other controls on ABM systems would be required, what offensive systems would be frozen, as of what dates, and under what conditions. The delegations faced a busy summer. The U.S. delegation's morale reflected a mixture of disgust at the way it had been deceived during the past winter and anticipation of the summer's work to come.

A LONG SUMMER

Helsinki V:
July–September 1971

As we started our third sojourn at Helsinki, a main American concern was the same as when SALT started some twenty months before: how to stop the Soviet build-up of missile launchers, especially the largest ones. During the twenty months of SALT, the Soviets had completed about 450 ICBM silos and submarines mounting almost 300 SLBM launchers. While it now appeared that they no longer were starting construction of ICBM silos, strategic submarine starts continued at a fast pace.

How should ABM systems be limited? The two sides had different missions, one for capital defense, the other for ICBM defense. The situation here seemed the reverse of the ICBM case, where the Soviets were building and we were not. The Moscow ABM system was about half finished. Except for occasional Pentagon alarms at appropriation time, it appeared that the Moscow deployment had stopped, probably because the Soviets realized that their first-generation ABM technology would not be effective.

Construction continued on our ABM site at Grand Forks, North Dakota, and a second had been started in 1970 at Malmstrom Air Force Base, Montana. No one saw fit to tell us that construction at Malmstrom had stopped owing to a labor dispute in the spring of 1971, when work on major facilities—radars and power plants and interceptor missile fields—was due to begin. The delay was to last for the rest of the year.

The halt in construction at Malmstrom must have come to the attention of Soviet intelligence, probably through local news-papers and satellite photographs, and the Soviets may well have concluded this was deliberate restraint on our part to suggest an American interest in limiting ABMs to one site for each side. Certainly it would have seemed highly unlikely to the Soviet mind that construction of a military facility which the Nixon Adminis-tration claimed was of essential importance would be halted for a year over a labor dispute. In January 1972, when the dispute was finally settled, one Soviet remarked informally that there was renewed activity at the Malmstrom site. He said it would have a bad psychological effect if work really started up again.

The May 1971 SALT accord had settled only one issue. But this signaled a sharp change in American policy. Before that we had been trying to negotiate ceilings on what were called central strategic systems—launchers for ICBMs and SLBMs, intercon-tinental bombers, and ABMs—in one treaty of indefinite dura-tion. Now we were to negotiate a treaty limiting ABMs together with companion and short-term constraints on strategic missile launchers. The United States no longer would insist on a treaty limiting both offensive and defensive arms.

The integrated offensive and defensive limitations which we had been trying to negotiate until May 1971 would have applied equally to the United States and the U.S.S.R. Now the short-term constraints on missile launchers would affect Soviet construction only, since the United States was not building offensive launchers. The United States was engaged in multibillion-dollar MIRV pro-grams, but the Kissinger-Dobrynin negotiations had confirmed the earlier negotiating situation that MIRVs would not be controlled. What was being projected by the United States now was a mora-torium on construction starts of Soviet built land based missile launchers while negotiations continued for a treaty limiting all strategic offensive arms (bombers as well as missile launchers) to match the ABM treaty we hoped to agree on by the end of the year 1971. Not an easy job.

All the other major SALT issues were also unresolved. What kinds of launchers were to be included in the offensive constraints? How long should the constraints last? What was to happen if the interim agreement was not succeeded by a more permanent arrangement? As of what date would the interim agreement take effect? What kind of agreement should it be?

Confusion about what Kissinger and Dobrynin had negotiated arose with the simple question of what form the agreements would take. The White House initially instructed the delegation to table a draft for a single agreement covering both ABM limitations and "certain measures" on offensive systems. This was the opposite of what the May 20 agreement had appeared to call for.

Suspecting that SALT was getting second priority to planning for Kissinger's upcoming trip to South Asia, I gently pointed out this inconsistency to the White House and predicted that we would be sharply rebuffed by the Soviet delegation in what would be a poor start at Helsinki. Tabling such an integral offensive/defensive agreement at the outset seemed absolutely inconsistent with the high-level communication of May 20, which referred to "the agreement limiting ABM systems" and I recalled the Soviet insistence on the modifier "separate." It was also totally at odds with what the President said publicly in his June 1 press conference. While we would try to make the best case for the abrupt switch from the American commitment of May 20, such procedure would lead to a sharp Soviet reaction and, I thought, a legitimate Soviet concern as to the seriousness of the American commitment of May 20. I found it hard to believe in the light of the record that we would not have to recede quickly from this position with attendant embarrassment and psychological setback at the start.

Three days later General Haig wired me in Brussels (where I was briefing the North Atlantic Council on our strategy for the Helsinki talks) to report that Kissinger agreed. It was two agreements, not one, that we should be trying for.

This is one example of the lack of precision of White House staff work on SALT. Another was that our Helsinki guidance would have permitted unlimited increases in the depth and interior diameter of Soviet ICBM silos for modern large ballistic missiles (MLBMs). This would have allowed unrestricted increases in volume for the SS-9 and follow-on classes of ICBMs. We asked for and got instructions to try to get controls over silo dimensions. Kissinger must have also had China very much on his mind. There was no clear blueprint in Washington as to how to implement the May 20 understanding. We were to find out that an ABM ban had not yet been thought through and that there had been hardly any thinking at all on the question of future types of ABM systems. Even the matter of the form of the two agreements was left in the air. Were they to be treaties or executive agreements or what?

As the Helsinki V round started on Thursday, July 8, 1971, the United States delegation was at work preparing drafts of an ABM and an interim offensive arms freeze agreement. Until the drafts were approved by the White House, we were instructed to stick to generalities.

The "sequence" issue filled up most of the early exchanges. Should the sides first try to work out an ABM treaty and only then turn to offensive measures, or should the two negotiations proceed in parallel? We were back to the Kissinger-Dobrynin merry-go-round of the previous winter and spring.

Our guidance was clear on this score. The negotiations on offensive and defensive systems must be conducted in parallel. At my discretion there might be an initial period of two to three weeks when the negotiations concentrated on ABMs. Thereafter, offensive systems must be considered equally and in parallel with defensive systems. The two agreements must be concluded simultaneously. Kissinger assured me that the Soviets had agreed to negotiate and conclude the two agreements in parallel. Ambassador Dobrynin had told him that once we tabled an ABM draft at Helsinki the way would be clear to start working out the "interim freeze."

The two delegations continued to interpret the May 20 agreement differently. Our discussions of the sequence question became more or less a dialogue of the deaf. Semenov claimed not to understand what I meant by "in parallel." He said we should first prepare an ABM agreement as was intended by the May 20 understanding and then we could proceed to discuss the details of certain measures in the field of offensive arms limitations. *Pravda* reported that the Soviet Union still adhered to the understanding that after the conclusion of an agreement on ABMs "some measures would also be agreed on in the sphere of limiting strategic offensive arms." *Izvestia* also ran an article saying that an ABM limitation was basic to the success of the talks. After this crucial matter had been settled, some measures would "also be harmonized in the sphere of restricting strategic offensive armaments." The sides seemed as far apart on sequence as on substance.

On July 29, I again asked the architect of May 20 what his understanding of the sequence issue was. Kissinger reported that Dobrynin's understanding was that the offensive limitations measures would have to be discussed before the agreement on ABMs was concluded. Dobrynin had told him that if the United States insisted on talking about offensive as well as defensive systems right from the start of the Helsinki session we would meet with a stone wall. Dobrynin had offered his personal opinion that this matter would be amicably settled as soon as there was agreement on some aspect of ABM limitation, for example, the number of sites to be permitted. This number was not agreed upon until April of the following year!

I had the impression that we were just repeating what Dobrynin and Kissinger had said to each other months ago. Most of the back-channel negotiation had been devoted to this question of sequence. I read and reread the language of the May 20 announcement, which seemed a classic example of obfuscation. "The Governments . . . have agreed to concentrate this year on working out an agreement for . . . [ABMs]. They have also agreed that, together with an agreement to limit ABMs, they will agree on certain measures with respect to the limitation of offensive strategic weapons." The communication between the heads of state did not clarify matters much. "To facilitate an agreement on limiting strategic offensive weapons, the United States Government favors the idea of freezing strategic offensive weapons in principle and is prepared to reach a basic understanding on this point. The concrete details of this understanding . . . would be discussed before the agreement to limit ABMs is completed."

"Sequence" was not the only aspect of the May 20 accord which led to confusion. A standard Soviet objection to United States substantive positions now was that they were inconsistent with the May 20 understanding. Semenov probably surmised that, as White House secrecy apparently excluded the SALT delegation from knowledge of the backchannel negotiation as it was taking place, the delegates' knowledge of the negotiating record was probably still quite slim. Our efforts to include submarines and their missile launchers under the interim freeze agreement were said to be inconsistent with the May 20 undertaking. So was our proposal to limit ABMs to three ABM sites to defend U. S. ICBMs with one site for the Moscow defense. Finally I advised Semenov I had studied the negotiating record. From then on we heard less of that argument.

Our insistence on parallel negotiation of the offensive and defensive agreements was aimed at using the bargaining power of American concessions in the ABM negotiation to extract concessions from the Soviets in the interim agreement negotiation. This was based on a calculation that the U.S.S.R. wanted to limit ABMs more than the United States did. In fact the Soviets never made a major concession in connection with the interim agreement, as might have been suspected, since its effect was to constrain Soviet but not U.S. programs.

The U.S.S.R., in pressing to complete the basic ABM negotiation before turning to the interim agreement, may have calculated that once the United States had moved to its final ABM position it would have little or no bargaining power left for the offensive arms negotiation. If the Soviets were to get any quid pro quo for halting their offensive launcher construction programs, it would have to come in constraints on the U. S. ABM program, and until they had a fairly clear idea of what the ABM deal was going to be, they did not want to discuss the interim agreement in any detail.

In the end the sequence issue, under the pressure of the prospect of an approaching springtime summit meeting, piddled out into tacit acceptance by the Soviet delegation of our refusal to go further into the key aspects of the ABM limitations without some movement on the offensive agreement. On September 14, ten days before the end of this Helsinki round, Semenov at last acknowledged that the two governments had in mind that specific details of the interim agreement could be discussed before completing an ABM agreement and could be agreed upon at the same time that the ABM agreement was reached.

The most notorious news leak of SALT—"the Beecher leak"—occurred in a front-page article (as most SALT leaks did) in the

New York *Times* of July 23, 1971, headlined "U.S. Urges Soviet to Join in a Missiles Moratorium: Would Halt Construction of Land and Sea Arms and Allow Each Nation Up to 300 Anti-missile Weapons." It laid out the major provisions of the U.S. draft agreements to be formally tabled at the Helsinki talks four days later. The article, by William Beecher, later the Deputy Assistant Secretary of Defense for Public Affairs, also hinted that the delegation had an ABM fallback position permitting dropping from three to two sites for ABMs.

The Beecher leak now appears less prejudicial than it did in the heat of the negotiations. It revealed little that was not known to the Soviet delegation, since we had been presenting in general terms the main provisions of our draft agreements for two weeks since the resumption of the talks on July 8. It did not differ in kind from other major leaks during SALT I. The hint that I had authority for a fallback on ABM levels was rather indirect, and Moscow must have been expecting that move in any event. (I exercised this authority on August 20.) At the time, however, all the SALT principals were quite upset, to say the least.

We were not dealing so much with information which should be kept secret indefinitely (as is the case with cryptographic techniques or weapons design) but with information which had been or shortly would be disclosed to a foreign power as a necessary part of the negotiating process. This sharing of negotiating proposals with Soviet representatives while withholding them from the American people presented a difficult problem of maintaining security of SALT information.

On balance I believe that the degree of privacy that we were able to maintain during SALT paid off. Polemic was kept to a minimum. SALT was a businesslike process. Perhaps public information was less than ideal. Even after extensive publication of the texts and open-hearing congressional cross-examination and debate, the degree of public understanding of SALT issues and the significance of the agreements reached was not high. I trust that this book will make some amends.

On July 15, 1971, President Nixon made a dramatic announcement about another secret negotiation. Kissinger had been in Peking negotiating with Premier Chou En-lai. The warming up in Chinese-American relations went unnoticed in the official SALT dialogue but I was left in no state of uncertainty as to Semenov's views. During a private conversation he told me at great length how shortsighted it would be for the United States to lose out on the long-term gains of an improved Soviet-American relationship just to make short-term gains with the People's Republic of China.

About the time of Kissinger's China trip Semenov also said to me privately that when he last was in Moscow he had been asked whether the United States had any concern about a possible future build-up of offensive armaments by a third country and how in the presence of a SALT agreement the United States would approach this fact. I said that we had faced this question. In working on an agreement, hopefully of long duration, we wanted to provide machinery for change when circumstances changed. The same circumstances that would give one of us concern about being locked into a situation would also give concern to the other. I did not think that any great power would remain in an arrangement after it had concluded that its vital interests would be endangered. But it did not seem to me that prospects for change during the next decade were such as to require any change in the arrangements we were working toward.

We tabled drafts of an ABM and an interim agreement on July 27. This double-tabling was done for psychological purposes, to emphasize the interlock between offensive and defensive arms and to symbolize our intention to keep the two negotiations side by side. Reference was made in the draft interim agreement to the ABM treaty, and a number of provisions were common to both documents. The delegation thought the two were quite well buttoned together—but the Soviets would still only talk about ABM limitation.

The Soviet delegation said they would forward our "freeze" draft to Moscow for study. During most of this Helsinki session they refrained from commenting on it, fending off questions by saying it was still under study. This was an obvious ploy to defer discussion of the offensive agreement until the ABM negotiation was further along. Throughout the summer we kept needling the Soviets to get to work with us on the interim arrangement. The standard reaction was that they were trying to carry out the May

20 understanding, which contemplated first working out ABM arrangements. Moscow was studying the American draft of offensive arms agreement, and they would discuss it in due time.

On the offensive freeze, the U.S.S.R. had given an important signal. Since the May 20 accord, no new starts on ICBM silos had been made. We knew this from satellite photographs. The Soviets knew we knew and even mentioned it privately. They may have thought this self-imposed restraint would be enough to meet the offensive freeze requirement of the accord.

We now had to face squarely the issue of what the ceiling on ABMs should be and what they should defend. As late as May 1971 in Vienna, we had been presenting a triple alternative, either four U. S. ABM sites and one Soviet site for defense of Moscow, or one site for each side for defense of their capitals, or a total ban on ABMs. We did not disclose which alternative we preferred—with good reason—because we did not know.

At the very end of the Vienna session we had finally moved to narrow these alternatives. I told Semenov under instructions that the United States was no longer interested in the defense of Washington. That ABM alternative, which we had argued for during the whole first year at SALT, fell victim to congressional hostility and commitments to our ABM program for defense of ICBMs. This left two ABM options: a limited defense of ICBMs or a total ban. The maximum and unrealistic alternative allowing the United States four sites to defend ICBM fields was now reduced to three. And the White House liberally allowed me to fall back at my discretion to two.

The ABM draft that we now tabled at Helsinki would limit each party to one of two choices—either to defend its capital or to defend three ICBM fields, located west of the Mississippi in the United States and east of the Ural Mountains in the U.S.S.R. This was supposed to be a significant concession from the previous four-to-one proposal, because of its less unequal numbers, and because each side would have a choice as to what to defend.

The choice was artificial and was so characterized by the Soviet delegation. It assumed that the Soviets, with the beginnings of a Moscow defense in their Galosh deployment, would necessarily elect to defend Moscow, and the United States, embarked on the ICBM defense program, would choose the three-site ICBM defense option. The American proposal, said the Soviets, offered no real choice. They wanted to defend Moscow while the Americans, lacking interest in a defense of Washington, would elect to defend ICBMs. Semenov said privately that there was as much chance of the United States electing the second alternative defense of Washington as there was for the Sultan of Turkey to become the Pope of Rome. The Soviet delegation were more correct than they realized. President Nixon had added parenthetically to our guidance that we should make clear that the United States would agree only to the existing Moscow defense and three sites defending Minuteman ICBMs. But at last we had abandoned the shell game and actually made an ABM proposal.

Until this Helsinki round, every American approach had included the alternative of a total ABM ban—although no serious discussion of a ban had taken place. Now the ban alternative had been dropped from the United States ABM proposal. Why? From the very start of SALT, arms control professionals and some other high officials in the government had favored a ban. It was recognized by almost everyone involved that deploying extensive defenses would likely trigger additional offensive missile programs, to assure penetration of these defenses. To permit some ABMs by treaty merely because the sides then had them or were about to have them seemed to some of us to be shortsighted. Present and prospective small ABM forces, while meaningless militarily, could become springboards for a fast build-up of area-wide defense systems if the treaty was annulled.

Often, perhaps too often, I urged the President and Kissinger to support a ban, arguing the case by memoranda and in the Verification Panel and the National Security Council. It would be more advantageous militarily for the United States to have no ABMs on either side than to have ABM systems to defend capitals or even for the United States to have three sites to defend ICBMs. A ban would mean greater Soviet vulnerability to U.S. missiles, and a reduction in the risks of their upgrading SAM anti-aircraft missiles to have a capability against ballistic re-entry vehicles. It would permit easier calculability of assured retaliation requirements. This would outweigh the advantage of a small increase in ABM-defended U. S. ICBMs that would survive a Soviet first strike attack. Politically, since the U.S.S.R. seemed willing to consider an ABM ban proposal, the United States would bear the onus for a failure to have a ban. In this fishbowl world, the process by which a ban escaped us would become public. One proposal then being considered in Washington was for a temporary arrangement limiting the sides to one ABM site apiece. If such a proposal were made, it was almost certain that any limitation arrangement would be on a one-for-one basis. In the last analysis we might have to settle for such an outcome, but if we proposed it I thought we would lose whatever bargaining power we had on the SAM upgrade and radar limitations issues. A ban proposal would not involve such leverage loss.

On the American side, as on the Soviet, there were strong feelings in the military that ABM was an important segment of missile technology in which they should keep a hand, even if it were agreed that present ABMs might be limited to a very low level. The Soviet leadership apparently was convinced that the Moscow defense, unfinished and ineffective though it was, still offered some deterrent to an attack on Moscow, perhaps by the small Chinese missile force of the 1970s. The United States, having started down the ICBM defense road, was equally tempted to retain some minimal defense. You never could tell when it might come in handy. From his talks with Dobrynin, Kissinger had the impression that the U.S.S.R. would not accept a ban. It will be recalled that Dobrynin had told me in March 1971 that our ban approach was just propaganda. I had urged him then to find out that it was not—by accepting it.

After I learned that our formal instructions would probably not permit consideration of a ban, I discussed with Kissinger an informal exploration of the ban possibility with Semenov but received no such authority. I then wrote him that our guidance made no reference to my sounding out Semenov privately. I could not take responsibility for raising the subject of an ABM ban without some further authority from the President. I was glad to receive in Brussels a message from General Haig that Kissinger now "had agreement" that a ban on ABMs could be raised privately with Semenov.

After a week at Helsinki, I broached the idea with Semenov. I understood some Soviet officials felt the United States ban offer had been for propaganda purposes and that we were not serious about it. I was authorized to say the ban was a serious proposal and was instructed to sound him out as to whether the Soviet government was interested in pursuing the matter. Semenov asked if I was prepared to set out our ideas in detail if the Soviets showed interest. Was his understanding correct that this elaboration could take place in a less formal manner than in a plenary session? I told him any forum he liked would suit us. Semenov then went on to say that he already had instructions for just this contingency. He was to listen carefully to the U.S. considerations and determine their substance and real significance. He hoped to get our views in as much detail as possible. I said I'd report his reaction to Washington.

That same day another Soviet official asked an American informally whether the United States had been serious about its proposal for an ABM ban and would raise it again. He stated that Moscow was "now interested" and urged the United States to raise the issue. This was reported to Washington along with the Smith-Semenov talk and with my conclusion that these exchanges strongly implied that the Soviet delegation had contingent guidance for a favorable response if we advanced the ban idea.

The President and Kissinger were now preoccupied with matters Chinese. It was not surprising that for several weeks Washington was silent about the ABM ban. Semenov needled me, saying his instructions were to work seriously with the United States delegation to see if an ABM ban was a realistic proposition. He drew my attention to the fact that Soviet plenary statements had been specially tailored so as not to give any impression of ruling out a ban. I told him that we had noticed that with interest. Another Soviet asked why we didn't make a specific proposal if we were interested in a ban. Again we heard there had been a change for the positive in Soviet attitude.

There was a hint that the military members of the Soviet delegation did not share the alleged interest in an ABM ban. One general said in effect that they weren't about to demolish the Moscow defense. His American counterpart interpreted this as a negative reaction to an ABM ban. Hearing of this, Semenov told me in no uncertain terms that Soviet SALT positions were stated by him and not by any other members of his delegation. The Soviet ABM position was as he had told me, not as the general had been reported to have said. It turned out that the Soviet general had not intended to indicate a negative view on a ban. They were interested in pursuing a ban proposal and were waiting for the United States to make one. (The general, it was later reported, had been arguing that the proposed "choice" to the Soviets of giving up the Moscow ABM defense and opting for three ABM sites to defend ICBMs was not realistic.)

On July 26, after reviewing these events in a message to Washington, I recommended that we promptly table a formal ban proposal, predicting that, while General Allison did not favor it, the other delegates would. I asked for a quick decision, since the tactics of the whole ABM negotiation depended on our knowing the Administration's ban position.

Another week passed with still no answer. Sometimes negotiating with the Soviets seemed to require less patience than negotiating with Washington.

Finally, on August 3, I received a personal message from Kissinger. He was concerned by what appeared to be "the leisurely pace" of the negotiation. It was time to get down to business. We might be pursuing a plethora of esoteric issues on matters which involved the specialized concerns of arms control experts but which in the final analysis were barriers to achieving the kind of momentum we had hoped for. He added that the foregoing was not suggested by way of criticism but was rather an expression of his own personal concern that we might be traveling down too many byways which could divert us from the ultimate goal we all were seeking. Then he referred to the ABM ban. From his talks with Dobrynin, he had believed that it would never be seriously considered by the Soviets because it would require costly dismantling of assets already provided for. He concluded disingenuously, "But I will yield to wiser heads"!

I replied that I shared his concern about the leisurely pace of the talks. But the hard fact was that we had made the Soviets wait for almost three weeks for U.S. drafts of ABM and offensive freeze agreements and our ABM text was even now not complete. The Soviets had had just over a week to study these rather complicated texts. We still had not told them whether we were negotiating for ceilings on ABMs or for a ban. I didn't expect Soviet movement until we could tell them what we thought the ABM negotiations were about. The delegation also was unclear about our ABM position in another respect. Was the arrangement to be a restraint on all ABM systems, including future systems (futuristics), or just a restraint on current type systems composed of interceptors, missiles and radar? We needed guidance on these two issues before we could get down to business.

It has been reported about this ABM ban episode that the White House believed that Americans in Helsinki heard what they wanted to hear. "Those who favored zero heard yes," someone reportedly put it, "while those who didn't want to hear yes from the Russians didn't hear it." This observation might be applied to Kissinger. He had shown his feelings about banning ABMs in a magazine article in August 1969 in which he wrote, "I doubt if the Soviet Union will give up the Moscow ABM system and I doubt I would urge them to."

Kissinger now raised the ban idea again with Ambassador Dobrynin. To assure me that he was taking care not to get involved again in SALT he prefaced his report by saying, "During a meeting on another subject . . ." Dobrynin said that initially the Soviets hadn't taken a ban seriously and now they were confused as to our views. He believed that to table a formal ban proposal at Helsinki would delay and confuse the discussions there. It would be far better to put such a proposal into the Kissinger-Dobrynin channel and get a reply in the same channel. Then, if both sides were definitely interested, the proposal could be tabled at Helsinki, thereby avoiding the loss of momentum that action now at Helsinki would result in.

That struck me as a queer suggestion. To Kissinger's query, "What do you think?" I replied that tabling a ban proposal wouldn't result in any loss of momentum at Helsinki, which indeed was not great. On the contrary, I believed it would speed things up. Diverting the ABM ban exchanges from Helsinki to a different channel would only delay and confuse matters. In a mischievous moment I suggested that I sound out Semenov to see if he confirmed Dobrynin's estimate.

About this time some Pentagon officials saw a tactical opportunity in tying a ban proposal to a new and, I believed, non-negotiable call for reductions in ICBMs. I advised the White House against this move. If, God forbid, the Administration were to accept that notion, I said, I would agree with Dobrynin that the Helsinki forum not be used to float it. The fallout from such a peculiar offer at that late date, some 18 months after the Soviets had rejected a "reductions" approach could be much worse than confusion and loss of momentum.

President Nixon's decision against an ABM ban came on August 12. Knowing of my commitment to a ban, the President wrote a long personal letter giving the reasons for his negative decision. It revealed much about his views of SALT. (See Appendix 5.)

I wired the President thanking him for the letter. I assured him the delegation would fully carry out this as well as all other guidance in letter and in spirit.

The President's August 12 letter ended the matter of an ABM ban, perhaps forever. The opportunity to eliminate a central weapons system from strategic arsenals and from the competition between the two sides was lost. The White House by this time had had quite enough of the subject. In September I would urge that the draft preamble of the ABM Treaty include some pious language to the effect that the parties had in mind as an ultimate aim a ban on ABMs. Even this harmless gesture had to be considered at a Verification Panel meeting and the White House ruled against it.

A few days later I advised Semenov of the President's decision. He diplomatically limited his response to suggesting that our interpreters check their notes against each other's and he said he would report this communication to Moscow. So the cat was walked back. This was not the first time that the United States had pulled back on an arms control approach after the Soviets gave evidence of interest. These on-again, off-again performances must have given Moscow the impression that we didn't know what we wanted. Coming so soon after the ABM "shell game," the Soviets must have wondered about American SALT leadership.

I still fail to see the logic in the President's claim that going for a ban would have required us to seek greater offensive limitations, or why there was any necessary connection between an ABM ban and reductions in offensive arms. That was shown up as a rationalization at the second Moscow summit in 1974. With no such reductions in sight, President Nixon agreed to reduce the two ABM sites permitted under the SALT treaty to one. Later Congress directed that the one and only U. S. ABM site at Grand Forks be "mothballed" even though no reductions in offensive arms have yet been agreed upon. We have in effect imposed an ABM ban on ourselves while the Soviets retain their Moscow ABM defense. It would have been much better to have an international agreement under which both parties forswore missile defenses, once considered humane but then seen to be at best ineffective and at worst a potentially destabilizing strategic factor.

My hunch is that the President's ABM ban decision was really based on three factors. Dobrynin must have been very convincing with Kissinger that a try for an agreement depriving the U.S.S.R. of its Moscow defense might risk the whole May 20 deal.

Secretary of Defense Laird must have pressed the President hard to condition any ABM ban proposal on getting some reductions of Soviet ICBMs. This would have reflected Laird's feeling that unless the Soviet ICBM force was substantially reduced the United States should have an option for ABM defense of ICBM silos. (Department of Defense representatives also argued that in the next stage of SALT negotiations an ABM ban could serve as a bargaining chip to induce the Soviets to accept offensive reductions!)

Perhaps the President's central motivation was to avoid what he thought would be a real fight with Congress over a ban on ABMs. He probably did not want to ask those senators who, against opposition, had stayed with him in the long months of the ABM fight now to agree to dismantle the Grand Forks deployment and completely terminate the ABM program. But I wonder if the congressional opposition would have developed. Senator Jackson, one of the leading ABM proponents, had earlier told me that a two-site ABM limit was "military nonsense." He would prefer a ban to a two-site level. I reported this to the White House. It was not an idle observation. Jackson was to repeat it during the 1972 congressional hearings on the SALT agreements and recall his earlier stand.

The Kissinger-Dobrynin exchanges on an ABM ban seemed to have confused the matter. Semenov had stated categorically that he was authorized to negotiate seriously about a ban. That should have been good enough for us—had we been seriously interested. As it was, we started a process from which we backed away when the U.S.S.R. showed interest. I assured Semenov in a later conversation that he would find us entirely serious about an ABM ban in SALT II. But it should be no surprise that when SALT II started in December 1972 an ABM ban proposal was not part of the agenda. Instructions then were that we should not reopen issues related to the ABM Treaty.

The President at this time also decided another ABM matter somewhat picturesquely called "futuristics." This label referred to as yet undeveloped laser, high-energy-radiation, or other techniques for anti-ballistic missile systems. These kinds of ABM systems might be deployed in the late 1980s. Should the ABM agreement limit only present applications of ABM technology—interceptor missiles, and their launchers and radars—or should it ban possible future methods? It is generally thought that SALT I resulted only in limitations on numbers of ABM systems, not on their characteristics. Not so. The negotiation about future ABM systems was as significant as any part of SALT.

Futuristics was a controversial issue. Harold Brown and I were convinced that the ABM agreement should not permit deployment of future type systems. Paul Nitze also favored banning them, but with an exception for what are called sensors, which could perform the tracking and guidance functions now handled by radars. We felt that not to shut off future type ABM systems would be a clear invitation to weaponeers to try to fill this treaty loophole. Ambassador Parsons and General Allison wanted any such systems to be unconstrained until such time as the technical and strategic possibilities became clearer and one could better judge the effects of a constraint.

A number of us saw in this issue a clear opportunity to stop the inevitable further march of ABM technology. Qualitative limitations are much more difficult to negotiate than quantitative, since it seems to be an article of faith in military thinking that the advance of technology cannot and should not be stopped. Here was a chance not just to limit numbers of ABM sites but also to control characteristics of ABMs. We argued that there was no sense in an agreement which would have the effect of permitting deployment of even a nationwide ABM defense simply because it did not use present types of systems involving interceptors, launchers and radars.

Just before the delegation tabled the U.S. draft ABM agreement on July 27 we were instructed to have a blank paragraph for futuristics pending the outcome of a Verification Panel study. Feeling strongly about the issue, I sent messages to the White House emphasizing the political and arms control reasons for banning futuristics. The general public expectation was that we were trying to limit all kinds of ABM systems, future as well as present. There would be congressional criticism of an approach limited just to existing types of ABM systems. More importantly, if we did not get a ban on futuristics, in a short time there would be a competition in them just like the one we were presently trying to stop. What was the logic of trying to ban the upgrade of anti-aircraft systems while allowing testing and deployment of future types of ABM systems? If we were trying to reach a more stable situation, I argued, it would be foolish to leave the door open for competition in advanced destabilizing systems. It is easier to control weapons before they come into being than after.

If, as had been decided, U.S. security would be improved if both sides could not deploy area-wide ABM systems of present technology, it was hard to understand why the situation should be different regarding next-generation technology. Finally, since research on future systems would not be limited, the United States would have insurance against their possible deployment by the Soviets in violation of a ban.

In August, before the final futuristics decision was made, I wrote the President asking that he consider my personal views. This was a more important issue than ABM levels and radar restrictions. It posed a basic question—did we seek an ABM constraint to provide greater stability by assuring maintenance of retaliatory capability, halting a build-up of defensive systems that could threaten that capability, lessening pressures for unnecessary build-up of offensive systems—or were we looking for just a temporary truce on ABMs until such time as more effective futuristic systems were developed and deployed? The latter approach ran counter to U.S. strategic policy and public statements on the destabilizing effects of nationwide ABM defenses. It could well lead to a race for futuristic systems and merely put off the danger we were trying to preclude in SALT. If future ABM systems were not to be limited, the onus should rest on the U.S.S.R.

I was glad when the President made an affirmative decision and I took special satisfaction in tabling the U.S. proposal: "Each Party undertakes not to deploy ABM systems using devices other than ABM interceptor missiles, ABM launchers, or ABM radars to perform the functions of these components."

Semenov quickly expressed doubts as to the appropriateness of the proposal. But he said his government would study it. I pointed out that there were precedents for banning deployment of future types of weapons in the treaties banning weapons of mass destruction in outer space and on the seabeds. Why should there be an exception in the ABM case? Uncertainty would increase if future ABM systems were not banned.

Soviet military officers thought it was not reasonable or necessary to include a provision covering undefined systems, essentially the same arguments made by their American counterparts. Some Soviets seemed to consider our proposal more a fishing expedition for intelligence than a negotiating initiative. They said a provision permitting review and amendment of the ABM Treaty would be sufficient. We were proposing to limit systems not known to anyone. They said this was not a correct approach. It could refer only to something that was amorphous and not subject to clear determination. I said I had too high an opinion of Soviet weapons designers to agree that they did not have any ideas about possible future ABM systems. Anyone could learn from unclassified literature that there were ABM concepts other than those already developed. Informally a U.S. official referred a Soviet to one unclassified article about future types of ABM systems. We said it would be a cruel illusion for people to think that we had limited ABMs without checking the possibilities of future technology.

The Soviets continued to oppose a futuristics limitation at Helsinki, but the groundwork had been laid for a solution suitable to both sides which was reached the following year.

Throughout SALT, the Soviets had a paramount ABM interest: to retain a system defending Moscow while preventing the United States from having any system that could become the basis for a nationwide defense. One Soviet official argued that it would be a factor for stability if the United States had an ABM defense of Washington. The Soviet delegation stressed two principles throughout the ABM negotiations. First, equality. If one side wanted to have two sites, the other side should have a right to two sites. Second, homogeneity, meaning that each side's defense should have the same mission. If one side had the right to defend its capital, both should. If one side had the right to defend some of its ICBMs, both should. This was logical. And that's the way it finally worked out—but not until many more ABM proposals had been tabled.

We pressed four ABM propositions. First, our task was to limit rather than raise levels of strategic defensive arms. Second, due account should be taken of current programs of the two sides which reflected the different development of their ABM programs. Third, the principle of equality should govern efforts to limit all strategic arms. Fourth, an agreement must prevent creation of a basis for a widespread ABM defense. A widespread regional or national ABM deployment might foster an illusion that sufficient population and industry could be so well protected from retaliation that an aggressor might blunt a retaliatory attack. Commenting on this fourth proposition, Semenov said that the effectiveness of an ABM agreement could be judged by the extent to which it precluded the possibility of creating an ABM defense system which could create an illusion of safety in adventurous circles. We seemed to be in agreement there.

A review of the bidding shows that by August 1971 the United States had suggested six approaches in about ten months of negotiation. On August 20, three weeks after tabling the "three or one" proposal, and after fumbling about with an ABM ban, I used the discretionary authority to offer a choice of two ICBM defense sites *or* one site for capital defense. This move generated little Soviet interest. They clearly were waiting for the United States to surface its final position. They realized that it would be either one or two ABM sites for each nation.

This quick-change performance did not speak highly for the clarity of the U.S. vision on limiting ABMs. The White House seemed to be playing it by ear. It looked a little childish to have so many building blocks. In fact our changing positions had little relation to strategic considerations but were based rather on dim insights into congressional support for the ABM program and on somewhat shallow and probably incorrect notions about the utility of bargaining chips in superpower arms control negotiation.

The American capacity for rapid switches was more than matched by the Soviets, who now proposed four different ABM approaches. We marveled at the speed with which the Soviets came up with new positions. Proposals were made before earlier ones were rejected, leading us to believe that a number of alternatives must have been approved en bloc in Moscow for feeding out as circumstances warranted. The Soviet leadership could not have made separate decisions before each new proffer, especially not during the favorite months for Soviet summer vacations. In any event, this "quickstep" was a good sign that the Soviets wanted an ABM agreement and soon.

At the first Helsinki plenary on July 8, Semenov had "re-affirmed" the Soviet draft ABM treaty tabled at Vienna in March, calling for limitation to one site for defense of capitals, even though he was by then on notice that the United States had no interest in such an arrangement. Semenov then devoted three plenary statements to supporting his March proposal. Finally I told him that I thought it had been made clear both in Washington and in my advice to him at Vienna that the United States would not accept a capital defense solution. Had Semenov thought on the basis of the Washington exchanges between Dobrynin and Kissinger and other information that the United States favored such an agreement? He merely responded that he and I were engaged in negotiations on the basis of instructions from our respective governments.

On August 10, a month after reaffirming their March proposal for capital defenses, the Soviet delegation, in an effort advertised as intended to harmonize the United States' declared need for ICBM defense with the principles of equality and homogeneity, had proposed that each side have an ABM system to defend a so-called "administrative-industrial" site. This terminology was invented to meet the Soviet principle of homogeneity—that both sides defend similar kinds of facilities. The inference was that

Grand Forks, North Dakota, and Moscow could be equated as administrative-industrial sites. In the words of General Allison, we quickly concluded that "that dog won't hunt."

Some days later, probably to meet the U.S. need to have two sites to defend ICBMs, this peculiar offer was followed by a proposal that each side defend two "administrative-industrial sites." At this time neither the delegation nor Washington was interested in any concept allowing the U.S.S.R. to build a second ABM site. Later that was to change. I pointed out to Semenov that under this formula the United States could pick New York and San Francisco for its two sites, providing a clear basis for a future nationwide system. It was just this danger of a nationwide or regional system that made both sides want to put a stop to ABM deployments while they were still in their infancy. Under the Soviet proposal, the bitter end of their insistence on equality in ABM numbers and function would be a doubling of existing forces, a far cry from disarmament. I was aware that a not very different result would have followed from the U. S. ABM proposal for three sites. To reduce Soviet arguments to the absurd, I said that if exact standards of homogeneity and equality were to be met, since the Moscow ABM system would not only protect Moscow but also some ICBMs deployed near Moscow, the United States would have to either move an equal number of ICBMs close to Washington or move its capital to the vicinity of an ICBM field.

Then, calling it a new constructive step, the Soviet delegation suggested in early September that each side have one site to defend its capital and, in addition, the United States could retain an ABM system at one of its ICBM bases where ABM construction had been started, while the Soviet Union could deploy ABM components for the defense of an equal number of ICBM silo launchers. When the Soviet interpreter called this a "proposal," Semenov corrected him, labeling it an "approach." This was probably a reminder of the earlier U.S. practice of presenting ABM "approaches" rather than proposals. As usual, specifics were lacking. Details would be disclosed, we were told, if the U.S. delegation showed serious interest.

A major difficulty with this new Soviet approach was that the U.S.S.R. deploys fewer silo launchers in an ICBM field than the

United States. Defending an equal number of silos would require more than one Soviet ABM site. Even this fact, known to the U.S. delegation, seemed not generally known in the Soviet delegation. One Soviet said that sometimes they were not in an equal situation. An American could tell him that the ICBM fields in the U.S.S.R. contained fewer silos than the ICBM fields in the United States. He could not make that kind of statement because he simply did not know. Another Soviet suggested they might need three sites. I wondered if this reversing of the earlier U.S. three-to-one proposal was a form of Soviet humor. Hoping to find out more, I advised Kissinger that the likely minimum price of admission to Soviet specifics was some suggestion of Washington interest. A definite American reaction must await a much clearer understanding of the proposal.

The White House did not want us to indicate any interest in this latest Soviet move and we were told to stand pat on our August 20 "two or one" position. Helsinki V ended without any discussion of this latest Soviet formula. It seemed to me that Washington wanted to wait until the U.S.S.R. moved to disclose in some detail its views about our draft for an interim freeze on offensive systems.

Perhaps the most important concrete product of this summer's work was Soviet acceptance of the American argument that the SAM upgrade danger had to be taken into account in limiting ABMs. After repeated plenary exchanges, Garthoff and Kishilov spent hours trying to articulate agreed restraints that would meet American concerns as well as Soviet insistence that their anti-aircraft systems not be prejudiced. The following language was worked out, subject to approval by delegation heads and subsequently by governments: "not to give missiles, launchers or radars other than ABM interceptor missiles, ABM launchers or ABM radars, capabilities to counter strategic ballistic missiles or their elements in flight trajectory and not to test them in an ABM mode." This provision found its way into the ABM Treaty in 1972.

The Soviets also made a considerable move to meet American radar concerns by agreeing that the parties would not give ballistic missile early warning radars capabilities of performing an ABM role, would not test them in an ABM mode, and would not deploy them in the future except at locations along the periphery of their national territories and oriented outward. I was surprised that they were willing to take such specific commitments. That augured well for the prospect of an ABM treaty.

While central ABM issues and a number of questions of radar limitation remained unresolved, significant progress also had been made in combining some parts of the draft agreements which the two delegations had tabled. Once the sides had proposed texts, the stage had been set for a joint drafting exercise. A Special Working Group was established, headed by Ambassador Jeff Parsons and Roland Timerbaev. Their job was to convert understandings reached informally into agreed provisions in writing in English and Russian, ad referendum to the two delegations. They would also identify in a joint text those provisions still in dispute, so that the agenda for the balance of the negotiation was precisely understood by both delegations as well as by their authorities. An Ad Hoc Committee was also set up to discuss provisions of special difficulty. These groups produced a so-called Joint Draft Text late in September.

In Article II the Soviet delegation wanted to describe obligations, while the United States wanted to define terms, including radar definitions still unacceptable to the Soviet side. The core of the dispute here was over a definition that ABM missiles and radars were all those either constructed or deployed for an ABM role or of a type "indistinguishable from" those tested in an ABM manner. The Soviets continued to state that the "indistinguishable" criterion was not acceptable because it cast doubt on the effectiveness of national means of verification which they felt could "distinguish" systems designed for an ABM role. In Chapter 10 a fuller report is given on this thorny topic. Article III set out three different proposals for ABM levels and areas of deployment: the Soviet capital defense proposal, the Soviet capital defense plus ICBM defense "approach," and the United States "two or one" proposal.

It was not yet settled whether an ABM agreement would be in treaty form, as the Soviets proposed, or an executive agreement as the United States proposed. Some Washington officials urged that this question of the form of the agreement could be used as a bargaining chip. Assuming that the Soviets wanted it to be a treaty, they argued, we should seek some concession before agreeing to that format. This struck me as nonsense. I saw no bargaining power in this matter and urged the White House promptly to accept the treaty form. I knew that any sounding out of interested senators would have proved there was no alternative. The President eventually decided on the treaty form for the ABM arrangement and a less formal agreement for the interim offensive arms freeze but nevertheless requiring approval by both houses of Congress. Having called so often on his friends in the House of Representatives to support appropriations for armaments, President Nixon told me, he wanted to give them a chance to go on record as voting for an arms control measure.

Semenov said he was pleased at the number of specific points of agreement that had been reached. He reported that some of his friends in Moscow kidded him about his frequent travel abroad with nothing to show for it. The Joint Draft Text, even though still pockmarked with bracketed disagreements, some on major points, would change their minds. A serious ABM negotiation was under way.

Although I had little sense of great progress during this long summer in Helsinki, Washington from time to time put out optimistic assessments reflecting the euphoria that sometimes overcomes politicians. On July 6, at a briefing for news media executives, President Nixon said that the United States was making progress in nuclear arms limitation negotiations with the Soviet Union. He thought that in the future, looking ahead fifteen to twenty years, the United States might have a perfectly effective arms limitation agreement with the Soviet Union which would totally remove the danger of confrontation with that country. Soviet leaders never talked like that. Foreign Minister Gromyko recently had said to the United Nations General Assembly merely that the U.S.S.R. hoped the SALT talks would "eventually" lead to a strategic arms agreement.

I wrote the White House about my concern on this score. From the Helsinki angle of vision, it seemed that any reporting from official sources of SALT optimism did not help our bargaining position. I thought this consideration became especially important as we entered a critical phase in the negotiation. I hoped that the President would direct members of his official family concerned with SALT matters to refrain from optimism—and better still to refrain from any comments at all unless authorized by him. Kissinger wired that he agreed.

But the optimism continued. At an August 4 press conference President Nixon spoke as if a SALT agreement was certain. "We on our part will be having very severe limitations with regard to our defensive capability, the ABM. They on their part will have limitations on their offensive capability, their build-up of offensive missiles." In addition to being overoptimistic, this language made it seem as if the Soviets would not also be subject to limitations on their ABMs. It discounted entirely the invaluable gain for American security that would result from the Soviets agreeing in an ABM treaty to keep their country almost completely defenseless against American missiles.

It will be recalled that shortly after the start of this Helsinki round we had tabled a draft interim agreement for certain measures to limit offensive arms. ICBM and SLBM launchers would be limited to those operational or under active construction at the end of July 1971. Modern large ballistic missile (MLBM) launchers, the Soviet SS-9s, would be limited to those externally completed by December 31, 1971.

This was no simple informal moratorium the United States was proposing but a fleshed-out, though short-lived, formal agreement. The U.S. draft included provisions for verification, a Standing Consultative Commission, withdrawal, a prohibition on using covered facilities to fit out or berth submarines, and a commitment to continue active negotiation for more complete limitations on offensive systems. Apparently the Soviets then had in mind a much less formal arrangement. Kissinger and Dobrynin had talked earlier about a halt of ICBM launcher construction and considered possible cutoff dates, but nothing had been agreed. Semenov at Vienna had spoken of a temporary cessation in new starts on ICBM launchers. He made clear the Soviet position that SLBMs should not be included in any such temporary halt. Our Helsinki draft must have looked to them as if we were departing from the May 20 understanding and going a good way back to our earlier position calling for formal limitations on both defensive and offensive launchers.

But it seemed that if the SLBM launcher issue could be settled the stuff of an interim freeze agreement was at hand. SLBM submarines did not offer anything like the threat to stability that ICBMs did. Submarine-launched missiles did not have the power or the accuracy to menace the U. S. ICBM force in hardened silos. SLBMs are a relatively invulnerable force and their existence presents a powerful disincentive to a nation which might consider making a pre-emptive first strike against its adversaries' ICBMs. Therefore they are considered a "good" deterrent force as opposed to the potential first strike Soviet heavy ICBM force. A freeze affecting a halt of the Soviet ICBM build-up was thus our prime interest. However, the overall increase in Soviet missile forces would be large and rapid if they were to continue to build seven or eight submarines each year of the freeze. Excluding SLBMs would result in the U.S.S.R. having an increasingly substantial numerical superiority, and one that would, in effect, be sanctioned by SALT. Freezing Soviet submarines at approximately the level of the United States SLBM force seemed important to the delegation if the freeze was to lead to an offensive arms treaty based on equal force levels.

Naturally Semenov objected to the idea of including SLBM launchers in the freeze. He said submarines were a new element and their inclusion would scarcely facilitate progress. On the contrary, I argued that they had been discussed during the Washington exchanges, therefore could not be considered a new element. The May 20 announcement had not spoken of one offensive system but of certain measures regarding "offensive armaments." If only one system had been envisaged, the wording of the announcement would have been different.

This initial exchange previewed the basic arguments of the two sides about SLBM inclusion for the remaining months at Helsinki. The Soviet delegation continued to maintain forcefully that an SLBM freeze would be inconsistent with the May 20 understanding. We pressed the Soviets to reconcile this position with their previous insistence upon equality. They liked equality in ABMs but apparently not in a short-term freeze on offensive weapons. The Soviet delegation responded that they were basing their position on a strict interpretation of the May 20 accord. The Americans had expressed a main concern about new construction of ICBMs, which the U.S.S.R. had now agreed to halt, indeed had already halted. The Soviets were on fairly solid ground in this objection. They must have seen confirmation of this in the article by journalist Beecher on July 23, who reported that "the U.S. was on May 20th thinking in terms of proposing a hold on ICBMs only," and "the shift in the administration position toward a more ambitious proposal was the result of extensive study and debate."

Our position, that the wording of the May 20 accord had not ruled out SLBMs, was somewhat legalistic. We kept arguing that the agreement spoke of measures affecting "weapons systems" and so several systems must have been contemplated, not just one as the U.S.S.R. was arguing. Semenov answered that the May 20 reference was not to types of weapons but to individual units. A Soviet general had another explanation for the use of the plural form. The Russian word for weapon system has no singular form!

The Soviets argued that if submarines were included in the freeze there would be nothing other than bombers left for the follow-on negotiations for an offensive arms treaty. To negotiate now for a freeze on SLBM launchers would resurrect the issue of forward-based systems. That problem had not disappeared just because it was not being talked about. Semenov privately predicted that SLBMs would not be included in the freeze.

Another Soviet official somewhat facetiously said that perhaps the Americans were pressing for including SLBMs because the chairman of the Joint Chiefs of Staff was an admiral. He was not far from the truth. The Joint Chiefs after the May 20 accord had reviewed their options. If SLBMs were not to be included, the United States would be free to build more SLBM submarines. But even if the Congress favored new construction all U.S. strategic submarine building yards were busy installing MIRVed Poseidon missiles into Polaris submarines, a job of major reconstruction on thirty-one submarines. Although the Trident class of missile submarines was in the advanced planning stage, none could join the fleet during the freeze even if it lasted as long as five years. Thus the Navy wanted no part of a freeze which left submarines unconstrained. That, they thought, could only benefit the Soviet Union.

The delegation now redoubled efforts to convince the Soviets that SLBM launchers must be included. We pointed out that for nearly two years both sides had shared views on the importance of limitations on SLBM launchers. It was quite logical to include them since the ABMs, which were to be limited to a very low level, defended not only against re-entry vehicles from ICBMs but also from SLBMs. This line of argument was turned around when the Soviets retorted that United States MIRV deployments were continuing despite the prospect of severe limits on ABM defenses. We could only point out that it had been agreed that MIRVs would not be limited in an interim arrangement.

The delegation also tried some ABM leverage. With our present knowledge, all we would be able to say was that we did not know what the Soviet position on offensive arms measures was except that the Soviet side believed it appropriate that the fastest-growing launcher program remain unconstrained for now. That answer would not make any easier the process of negotiating the unresolved ABM issues.

During these SLBM exchanges I expressed personal views more often than at any other time in SALT. I repeatedly told Semenov the United States just could not go along with the idea that a freeze affecting only one type of offensive missile launcher was a sufficient accompaniment to an ABM treaty. I caricatured the current Soviet positions that ABMs be limited to two "administrative-industrial" sites and that submarines not be included in the freeze by saying that as a result of all our common effort for the past two years new ABM systems would be constructed around New York and San Francisco and a new submarine program started by the United States. I argued that the Soviet SLBM submarine program was now the most dynamic part of their force build-up, and it would be quite inconsistent with an interim freeze to leave it unrestrained. In that event, I would not feel that the cause of arms limitation had been advanced. I recalled that they already had more missile launchers than the United States. Semenov seemed incredulous.

As the leaves fell from the trees in the very early northern autumn, the U.S. delegation was still hammering away on SLBMs. In fact, a snow flurry back in August had prompted me to remark to Semenov that the season was advancing faster than we. Washington had no complaints about the vigor of our SLBM argumentation. I have often thought that the Kremlin must have been puzzled by the difference between the winter when Kissinger told Dobrynin that the United States could make an agreement excluding SLBMs and our summertime insistence on including them. There perhaps were some fairly warm exchanges in the Kissinger-Kremlin back-channel to explain the change. The delegation had the uphill task of arguing for their inclusion and at approximately equal levels. We didn't succeed. It took another Kissinger-Kremlin negotiation the following April to walk this cat back and get SLBM submarines and their launchers included in the freeze—but not at equal levels.

The time had come to try to stop Soviet procrastination. The whole negotiation depended now on their willingness to talk turkey on this score. Three days before we recessed, the basic and blunt point of my formal statement was that the paucity of substantive discussion by the Soviet side on the offensive freeze had been the most serious defect of the session. I was instructed to advise the Soviet delegation that the United States considered it essential to have full discussion of the specifics of offensive measures as soon as the negotiations resumed in Vienna. More information must be available to permit simultaneous agreement on ABM limitations and on offensive measures. Simultaneous agreement on the two had now been recognized by both sides to be an objective of the May 20 understanding. Given agreement on a limited number of remaining substantive issues, it should be possible to conclude an ABM agreement soon. It hardly needed saying that such a constructive development hinged directly on what happened in the offensive freeze negotiation.

After this meeting Semenov said he had a matter to raise which he believed essential. The Soviet delegation considered it inadvisable at this stage to include in discussions of a possible temporary freeze the question of limiting SLBMs. That was hardly news to me. I took the occasion to stress SLBMs one last time. I had tried in diplomatic language to get across the solid concern felt in Washington about developments in the submarine field. It appeared that the Soviet submarine program was proceeding at a faster rate than the previous year and there was some evidence that the Soviet Union might be planning even further acceleration. I could not stress too strongly my belief that this question was having a strong effect on people in Washington as they judged the possibilities of limiting strategic arms. When in the middle of the current phase Semenov had categorically rejected the proposal to freeze SLBM launchers, it had caused shock there. I could understand there were some difficulties here for Semenov, but I wanted to state quite clearly that Washington believed SLBMs must be included in the interim freeze.

This Helsinki round did not suit the White House at all. The May 20 accord had not worked out as expected. The Soviet delegation had refused to negotiate on the interim freeze. We had not succeeded in getting parallel negotiations on both defensive and offensive arms. We had fallen back to what seemed to supporters of our ABM program as too liberal an offer to keep just two ABM sites to defend ICBMs, only one sixth of the deployment originally planned. Two hundred defensive missiles to protect 1,000 ICBMs was military nonsense and the White House and almost everyone else knew it. I had pestered the White House with proposals for a complete ban on ABMs and a ban on future ABM systems, posing hard issues which the President could no longer avoid. SALT agreements that had seemed relatively simple in the spring looked complex in the fall.

Like the Vienna round before it, this Helsinki round was a negotiation on ABMs. Including the aborted ABM ban approach, seven different proposals were made by the sides. This rapid-fire propositioning did not constitute negotiation. Rather, it was primarily going through the motions of demonstrating that any approach based on inequality was unacceptable, and, secondarily, to show that any approach which used artificial designations like "administrative-industrial" sites was non-negotiable. Proposals designed so that the United States might say that Grand Forks, North Dakota, was an administrative-industrial complex were nonsense.

The changes which the Soviets offered could hardly be called concessions. Both sides knew by early August that if an ABM treaty was to be negotiated it would call for one or two sites for each side. The speed with which one Soviet offer followed upon another indicated that it didn't make much difference to them. The Soviets were signaling that there was "no way" that the United States could get more ABM sites than the U.S.S.R.

This turned out to be a good thing, in spite of high-level opinion in the United States to the contrary. Some in Washington argued that, since the Soviets now had operational or under construction more offensive missile launchers than the United States, an interim freeze agreement would leave them with an advantage. If the Soviets were to have more offensive weapons, then we should have more ABM sites. This theory seemed to appeal even to President Nixon. The delegation pointed out its dangers. The ABM Treaty supposedly was forever while the interim agreement was for a short time. If there was an inequality in our favor built into the ABM Treaty, it would be very hard to avoid inequality in the Soviets' favor in a permanent offensive arms limitation treaty. Fortunately, the Soviets by insisting on equality in ABMs spared us that problem.

This Helsinki round showed that the prospects for working out the terms of an ABM treaty were quite good while the prospects for working out the interim freeze were not so good. The United States had jettisoned its foolish proposal that it have four ABM sites to one for the U.S.S.R., had proposed three for one and then two for one. The delegation and probably our Soviet counterparts expected the last shoe to drop with a U.S. offer of one for one. Such a formula came but not until SALT I was over. The SALT delegation had told Washington in September 1971 that one site apiece was *the* likely solution. It took two and a half years more to reach it. In any event, it is not far from the ideal of a complete ban which some of us had urged from the beginning.

In spite of all the open issues, I sensed that we were close to a point of no return for both sides—that point in an international negotiation when, even though great issues are still unresolved, political pressures to settle become greater than pressures to break. Kissinger once asked if I thought we would reach an agreement in 1971. I said that I doubted that great powers would get themselves seriously committed to a course of conduct such as limiting their central strategic systems without reaching agreement.

Helsinki laid a foundation. The sides had begun detailed presentations on ABM limitations, sounding out each other's positions and areas of compromise. Helsinki produced the first tangible results of some twenty-two months of SALT negotiations. The

Joint Draft Text of an ABM agreement highlighted basic disagreements but also identified good progress in removing a number of differences which had existed from the early phases of the talks. And very soon signature of the first SALT agreements—on accident control and on Hot Line modernization—were to make new international law.

CHAPTER

9

FIRST AGREEMENTS
1971

Speaking to the Supreme Soviet in July of 1969, Foreign Minister Gromyko said, "There is another aspect of the matter that must not be overlooked in long-range policies of states. This is largely connected with the fact that weapons control and guidance systems are becoming . . . more and more independent of the people who create them. Human hearing and vision are not capable of reacting accurately at today's velocities and the human brain is sometimes unable to evaluate the readings of a multitude of instruments quickly enough. The decision made by a human being ultimately depends on the conclusions provided to him by computer devices."

On September 30, 1971, Secretary Rogers and Foreign Minister Gromyko signed the first two SALT-related agreements: Measures to Reduce the Risk of Outbreak of Nuclear War and Measures to Improve the USA-USSR Direct Communications Link (or Hot Line). The Accident Agreement spells out standards of behavior and communication to prevent nuclear accidents which might lead to unintended war. It is supplemented by the Communications Link Agreement, which provides for Hot Line modernization through the use of space satellites.

The superpowers now recognize the need to keep in touch at all times lest some untoward event trigger unwanted hostilities. It is generally believed that no sane leadership would deliberately start a nuclear war. If it comes, it probably would follow an accident or unauthorized act. When the Soviets showed interest in discussing these problems we were ready to talk.

The Hot Line had been useful in at least one crisis. But it had weaknesses. One link used land lines in Europe. A Finnish farmer's plow had once put it out of operation. It seemed prudent to immunize the link from this kind of interruption. Having been involved in the original Hot Line proposal some ten years before, I was especially interested in this subject.

These two agreements were for the most part overshadowed by the SALT limitation agreements in 1972. But if techniques used under these agreements ever smother a nuclear war risk, these modest accords will be seen as heaven-sent.

Semenov said in 1969 that despite the existence of mutual deterrence dangers remained. The sides should consider technical and organizational arrangements to preclude unauthorized or accidental use of nuclear missiles. We agreed. The Helsinki Work Program referred to "ways to reduce the danger of the outbreak of a nuclear missile war between the USSR and the USA, including ways to guard against unauthorized or accidental use of nuclear weapons."

The White House commissioned an interagency study on accident measures, one of fifteen analytical "tasks" undertaken in preparation for the April 1970 Vienna session. The study concluded that it was axiomatic that the United States was interested in preventing any misuse of nuclear weapons. There were grounds for belief that the Soviets were seeking a serious bilateral investigation of ways to cope with the problem. But in view of the effort to label our forward-based systems as strategic, the Kremlin might also be trying to focus on United States nuclear weapons deployments overseas and on NATO nuclear arrangements, subjects which were clearly beyond the scope of SALT. It would be in our interest to explore further with the Soviets ways to prevent unexpected nuclear events and to reduce the risk of a U.S.-U.S.S.R. nuclear exchange resulting from any such event. The topics of nuclear weapons safety programs and communication capabilities were appropriate for a United States initiative; other possibilities were more complex and were deferred until we had a clearer view of Soviet motives.

Many of the Soviet comments on these issues seemed to parallel those in a book, *Present Day Problems of Disarmament,* published at the time by the U.S.S.R. Academy of Sciences. After discounting for a heavy dose of polemic, the author's views are worth pondering:

The technical systems on which a modern war machine is based are unreliable. Personal characteristics of people who use them and the interaction between men and machines must be considered. Accidental war risks increase with the complexity of war material, the power of the weapons, and the number of people with access to them. While only elimination of weapons could do away with the risks of an accidental war, organizational and technical controls on machines and men could reduce them.

The rapid development of weapons brought about a lag between weapons systems and their control. Because of extensive utilization of computers, their reliability becomes a large factor in that of the whole system. Faults may occur in nuclear missile systems kept in a state of constant readiness.

Occurrences of breakdowns in combat units carrying nuclear warheads are a major danger. (He listed fifteen cases of U.S. bomber crashes.) Modern reconnaissance methods can increase the danger of spontaneous outbreak of war (here he probably had in mind the U-2). There have been cases in which early warning systems gave false signals of attack against the United States. Complexity of reconnaissance and intelligence collection and analysis could produce errors which could lead to wrong judgments.

The United States Air Force had 26,500 officers and over 85,000 enlisted men whose duties were directly related to nuclear weapons. Under the circumstances in which a modern military machine is maintained in a state of permanent high readiness, the uncontrolled actions of individuals, extremist groups and criminal elements become particularly dangerous. Criminal actions with nuclear weapons also may be caused by drunkenness, drug addiction, mental illness. He cited an alleged example of a mentally ill American sergeant who in 1958 tried to fire his pistol at a nuclear bomb. In moments of historical crisis, pressures can become so strong that mental breakdowns might occur.

In the past, weeks and sometimes months of intensive efforts by thousands of workers were required to put a war machine into motion. Now starting it would be only slightly more complex than starting a car. Even lengthy periods of calm and the lack of major accidents represent a certain danger, as do a false feeling that "nothing will happen" and the belief that protective measures, locks, blocks, and safety devices are absolutely effective.

While Soviet discussion of accidents at SALT may have reflected real concern, it could also be useful as propaganda if the talks collapsed. It could support other Soviet proposals for submarine patrol zones and bomber flight constraints. But an agreement in this area would be relatively simple to reach. An accident agreement might add momentum to the SALT negotiations and offer a minor success even if the main negotiation broke down.

When the Vienna phase started in 1970 the Soviets pressed for agreement in the field of accidents. Their arguments were: the development of technology led not only to an increase in range and accuracy; improvements were accompanied by increased complexity of control systems and an increased role for automatic and computer equipment; actions by people might depend on the condition of highly complex automatic control and data processing systems; among such individuals could be some mentally unbalanced; the Soviet Union takes steps to preclude the possibility of accidental or unauthorized use of nuclear weapons; apparently measures in this direction were also taken by the United States, but it appeared advisable to agree on possible additional measures which could be implemented by the two sides individually and jointly. We could also provide for appropriate action in emergency situations aimed at preventing automatic outbreak of war.

General Allison asked General Ogarkov if he would elaborate on some of the proposed organizational and technical measures. Ogarkov replied that more details could be made available later, but the important thing now was for the United States to agree in principle. The usual Soviet ploy.

We proposed two areas for consideration: (1) precautionary

measures each side then employed for preventing accidental or unauthorized nuclear detonations; and (2) steps for improving U.S.-Soviet communications capabilities to minimize possibilities of misinterpretations of a nuclear incident. There had been considerable advance in communications technology since the Hot Line was established. The use of satellites had reached a high degree of perfection. They might contribute to more reliable communication by minimizing the possibility of technical failure and by avoiding the need to go through other countries.

Semenov proposed to split the problem into two aspects: accidental war and provocative attack. He made a four-point proposal for notification and exchanges of information.

- immediate mutual notification using all possible means in the event of unauthorized missile launch or other acts which may lead to the use of nuclear weapons;

- mutual exchange of information in the event of detection of unidentified objects by missile attack warning systems, or signs of interference with these systems and with corresponding communications facilities;

- notification of planned missile launches, if such launches beyond the limits of national territories occur;

- notification of mass take-offs of aircraft from airfields and aircraft carriers.

He said the Soviet side intended later "to discuss another aspect of the problem"—provocative attack. The two were not linked again. The Soviet push for a provocative attack agreement (described earlier) soon began in earnest, dominating the talks for about a week, with only passing reference to the problems of accidental or unauthorized attack.

American statements on the "accidents" problem were carefully drafted to support other United States positions. We used this subject to challenge an earlier Soviet reference to a "launch on warning" doctrine, saying that one of the "pressing reasons why our government placed great emphasis on the ability of its ICBMs to survive an attack is precisely to avoid having to resort to a launch-on-warning policy which would be very dangerous and increase the risks of unwanted war." Risk of accidental attack was also used to argue for a capital defense level ABM limitation (a position we had later abandoned). In the event of an unexpected nuclear attack it would be important that decision makers survive to establish the nature of the attack so that appropriate decisions could be made.

We referred in general terms to measures taken by the Department of Defense and the Atomic Energy Commission to guard against accidental and unauthorized use. Weapons design, procedures, and command and control measures to avoid unauthorized or accidental detonation of a nuclear weapon had been an integral part of U.S. precautions from the beginning of its atomic weapons program. For every nuclear weapon system there were positive measures to prevent accidental detonations, to prevent inadvertent releasing, arming, launching or firing; and to prevent unauthorized access to weapons. All U.S. nuclear warheads were designed so that in the event of an accident (e.g., involving fire or shock) detonation would not occur. Safety precautions for weapons operation included specifications on the positioning of various control switches for each nuclear weapon system and requirements that critical switches be safety-wired and sealed where necessary to help prevent inadvertent operation. Verification that approved safety procedures were being strictly adhered to was obtained by frequent and thorough inspections of all nuclear weapons systems and checking on personnel and organizations responsible for them. Authority to release any U.S. nuclear weapon for use must come from the highest authority. The validity of the order must be authenticated by at least two responsible individuals. Comprehensive human reliability programs for personnel who might have access to nuclear weapons were standard procedure. This program was designed to assure the possibility that an individual with behavioral problems or mental aberration would not get access to nuclear weapons. A two-man procedure is required for any access. We concluded by saying that U.S. experts could engage in reciprocal discussion of precautionary measures if the Soviets agreed. They did not. Probably Soviet hypersecrecy about military matters made our offer unacceptable. Perhaps their military did not even want such information to be known to their civilian colleagues. And the Soviets did not then amplify their four-point notification proposal because of admitted lack of knowledge of its technicalities.

But they quickly agreed that the Hot Line should be modernized. Academician Shchukin saw technical problems in satellite communications. The sides used different frequencies and wave lengths, but he thought this could be worked out.

As for the Soviet proposal for notification procedures in case of some untoward nuclear event, we thought an agreement on immediate notification to the other side if there was an accidental or unauthorized launch of a missile would be useful. The target country, however, might be the first to become aware of such a launch. Unavoidable delay by the country where the missile came from in notifying the other should not be interpreted as confirmation that such a launch was intentional. Other nuclear events subject to notification procedures should be limited to incidents involving a risk of war. We thought that for this notification primary reliance should be placed on the Hot Line. We saw merit in a Soviet proposal for notification if unidentified objects were detected, but exchanges of information should be confined to objects which appeared threatening or where there were signs of hostile radar interference. Each side should decide for itself what was threatening or hostile and notify the other only when it thought it necessary to avoid the risk of nuclear war. There might also be agreement on advance notification of certain missile test launches and mass take-offs of aircraft but we needed more information. What a world this was where both nations had legitimate concerns about such hair-trigger events that could cause war!

A small group was set up to discuss these issues. The question of improving the Hot Line was being studied in Moscow and could not yet be discussed. But Semenov thought a solution employing modern technology would be found.

Five advisers from each delegation met in the waning days of the marathon 1970 Vienna round. The Soviets were not ready to discuss their notification proposals in any depth. Their explanations went little beyond previous statements. As in so many other phases of SALT, they answered our specific questions in general terms. The Soviet formula was complete and broad, fully reflecting the substance of the matter, it was hardly possible to be more specific. They repeatedly asked us to offer alternative formulas or introduce specifics. After a good deal of such fencing we told Washington that the Soviet goal seemed to be to reach agreement in principle that the four points were desirable and to identify "points of contact" between the two sides. Again we faced the standard U.S.-Soviet negotiating posture—general vs. specific.

We tried to focus on a definition of what comprised a "mass" take-off of aircraft. If the United States was to take a commitment to notify the Soviet Union of a mass take-off of aircraft, we wanted to know precisely what the obligation was. How many planes? The Soviets replied that if the U.S. side had numbers in mind, that would be of interest. So we then asked, should each side decide for itself what constitutes a mass take-off? No answer. They asked, did the U.S. side accept the principle of notification in the event of mass take-offs? Did we believe such notification necessary or useful to reduce the threat of war? If there was a general understanding on this score it would be easier to agree on what a mass take-off was. But until we knew what they specifically had in mind we could not answer those questions. It was the usual standoff.

The Soviets then tabled a document summing up the experts meetings, emphasizing statements of American agreement with Soviet proposals. A Soviet stated that the essential difference was that we wanted notification only if a nuclear event was likely to increase the risk of war, while they wanted notification of a nuclear weapon event whether or not there was a war risk.

While vague and circuitous, these exchanges demonstrated that both nations were interested in some sort of agreement. The delegation reported that the two sides were in accord that this was a subject worth pursuing, either as a part of SALT or separately.

During the 1970 fall recess a Verification Panel Working Group developed a concrete position. Agreement to exchange information on events which could have war significance already existed in the 1963 Hot Line accord. This group proposed that the parties act when it was believed that an event increased the danger of unintended war between the United States and the U.S.S.R.—specifically

> to give—immediate notification in the event of an unauthorized missile launch or accidental event involving nuclear weapons;

to have—mutual exchange of information in the event of detection of unidentified objects by attack warning systems, or signs of interference with these systems and with related communications facilities;

to give—advance notification of planned missile launches and strategic aircraft take-offs.

Each party would decide for itself which events might increase the danger of unintentional war and therefore require notification or an exchange of information. It would be too difficult to try to reach specific definitions of these terms. This study concluded that the delegation should continue to treat the "accident" issues in parallel with other SALT matters. This was a middle ground between fully integrating them into SALT limitations and making them the subject of a separate agreement.

The President adopted the Verification Panel's recommendations with one exception. Any "accidents" agreement would have to be part of a strategic arms limitation agreement. A separate agreement on this issue could not be considered. This position was aimed at reinforcing our then primary objective of pressing the Soviets to negotiate seriously on the U.S. August 4 limitation proposal. As a result the accident measures negotiation was caught up in the confusion of the next round.

Early in December we agreed to include in a limitations agreement some arrangements for exchange of information where it would reduce the danger of war. The Soviet proposal for prenotification of mass take-offs of strategic aircraft was not acceptable. (Washington had accepted the delegation's advice that such a provision could be used to challenge U.S. air operations for political or propaganda purposes.)

The Soviets informally welcomed this statement as a positive response to their proposals but they said it came too late and Moscow would have to consider it after this Helsinki phase ended.

During the Helsinki round Semenov noted speculatively that the sides might be missing an opportunity in not paying enough attention to issues at the fringes of the main subjects at SALT. They had intrinsic importance. Suppose a nuclear weapon exploded over a city? What would follow? Apologies? Compensation for damages? The whole thing was unthinkable. I could only agree. But we had to work on ways to make the risk of it happening as low as possible. The "accidents" negotiation and the resulting agreement received little attention—but the delegations knew that they were engaged here in deadly serious business. Though the risk of accident was small the results could be immeasurable.

The Accidents and Communications Link Agreements were worked out for the most part at the Vienna round in the spring of 1971. This was when the Kissinger-Dobrynin talks were taking place in Washington. Who knows? Maybe the "accidents" work may prove the more significant of the two efforts. The Soviets then proposed that a separate accidents agreement or treaty be signed. They urged that we not postpone agreement or link it to the solution of other questions of curbing the race in strategic armaments.

A Soviet draft went a long way toward accepting our proposals of the previous December. We asked for authority to engage in detailed discussions. This could be done without deflecting SALT from mainstream issues. The question of whether an "accidents" agreement should be separate did not have to be decided yet.

The question of whether or not there should be a separate agreement was caught up in the larger issues of SALT. The United States negative position had been taken after the Soviet proposal of the previous July for a quick SALT agreement limited to an ABM treaty. By opposing a separate accidents agreement we were supporting our position that limitations must be placed on Soviet offensive forces.

Moscow probably calculated that a separate agreement would be hard to resist after most of its terms had been agreed. So they merely repeated the case for a separate agreement—these measures were important and could stand on their own. An early accidents agreement would show that SALT was making progress and that Soviet-American agreements were possible. The Americans should not worry about "bringing forth a mouse." The agreement's effect would be positive, especially if coupled with an agreement to modernize the Hot Line.

A Special Technical Group was established in mid-April which met eleven times. Ambassador Jeff Parsons and Roland Timerbaev were co-chairmen. All agreed language and working documents were ad referendum and did not bind governments. Parsons stressed that tentative agreement on language must leave open the question of whether or not the agreement would be part of a SALT agreement. Timerbaev continued to urge that there be a separate agreement or treaty, saying that, despite the fact that both would aim at reducing the risk of war, linkage of accidents measures to a SALT agreement was inappropriate. He quoted Brezhnev's statement to the ongoing Twenty-fourth Party Congress: "We consider that it would be expedient to work out measures to reduce the likelihood of the accidental occurrence or premeditated fabrication of military incidents and their development into international crisis and war." To the Soviets' satisfaction and perhaps surprise we agreed to use their draft as the basis for the Group's work. They agreed to extensive substantive and editorial changes. They had proposed a catchall formula for exchange of information which struck us as much too broad:

> Each party undertakes to act in all other situations involving nuclear weapons in such a manner as to reduce the possibility of its actions being misinterpreted by the other side. Each Party may inform the other side or request information when, in its view, this is warranted by the interests of averting the risk of outbreak of nuclear war.

What did that mean? Timerbaev said that there were two types of exchange of information: mandatory, as prescribed by specific provisions of the agreement; and voluntary, which each side might exchange at its own discretion. The main purpose of their proposal was to provide for information exchange in case of incidents which had a risk of war significance, as the Americans had proposed.

Ambassador Parsons proposed substitute catchall language providing for exchange of information only at each side's discretion.

> In other situations involving the possibility of accidental or unauthorized use of nuclear weapons, each Party may provide relevant information to the other side, when, in its view, providing such information is warranted in the interest of fulfilling the purposes of this agreement.

This didn't suit the Soviets. It narrowed the obligation to avoid actions that might be misinterpreted to those situations which could involve the possibility of accidental or unauthorized use of nuclear weapons. But they adopted the U.S. idea of making it clear that any obligation was limited to fulfilling the purpose of the agreement. There this somewhat abstract issue rested.

Now the Soviets asked about accession by other nuclear powers to such an agreement. We discouraged this idea because of its broad policy implications. China and France would not be parties to treaties in the negotiation of which they had not had a part. The Soviets were well aware of this fact. But Washington wanted to hang loose on this issue.

A curious exchange developed from our question as to why the Soviet proposed immediate notification of a "possible" nuclear detonation and not of a detonation which had already taken place. Timerbaev answered that "a possible detonation" included a detonation which might have taken place, but it would be "inadvisable" to refer to detonations that had occurred. That would lessen the obligations of the sides to undertake precautionary arrangements. Parsons said not so. The sides would continue to make improvements in their safety procedures. Both sides obviously intended to prevent accidents or unauthorized launches, but the agreement would be directed to the remote possibility that such events could nevertheless occur. That was the obvious implication of such an agreement. Avoiding reference to actual detonations could not alter that fact.

Semenov entered the lists at this point, saying that the agreement should assume that there would be no detonations. The very purpose of the agreement was to prevent any detonation. The proposed American language was an invitation to detonate and would legalize detonation. I did not understand why we should have arrangements to reduce the risk of accidental detonation if it was assumed there would be none. That would be like taking out insurance against a non-existent risk. It was not possible to guarantee that there would never be an accidental detonation. Semenov was unconvinced, saying he thought it better to work on reducing the possibility of accidents rather than to admit that such a possibility existed. The language should not convey the idea that the agreement represented an invitation to detonation or that the agreement appeared to legalize accidents. Suppose an accidental launch destroyed a city, he asked, could one simply say, "But that's all right, we have an agreement covering such contingency"? I rejoined that of course the United States was not looking for excuses for destroying cities, then moved the talk away from this fruitless subject. After their continued protests that the U.S. wording could be interpreted as "legalizing" detonations, we eventually gave in to this Soviet quirk. This was perhaps the most extreme case of "ships passing in the night" of the whole SALT negotiation—though fortunately not on a very significant issue.

At the final plenary session in Vienna, Timerbaev reported on the work of the Group and submitted a "Joint American-Soviet Draft Document on Accident Measures." We were making progress.

At this same Vienna round a Joint Technical Group on improving the Hot Line, headed by Clifford D. May, Jr., and V. P. Minashin, worked out the essentials of a satellite communications agreement. May noted that the existing system had been highly reliable in operation but had certain vulnerabilities. The Memorandum of Understanding of June 1963 had set up two communications links, a wire telegraph circuit running between Washington, London, Copenhagen, Stockholm, Helsinki and Moscow, and a radio telegraph circuit with a single relay station at Tangier. Owing to the vulnerability of these links, the two governments had agreed to investigate means of improving them. The United States wanted to have a link independent of third countries and more survivable in a wartime environment, and also wanted multiple terminals rather than a single terminal at each end. We proposed use of communications satellites.

Minashin discussed satellite communications. He then asked why the United States was concerned about terminals which had operated without a hitch. May said that the primary problem was the single location. Since the President was not always in Washington, terminals were needed at other locations. Only one of the multiple terminals would be in operation at a time. The United States was not proposing to change the character of the terminals.

On completing its work this Technical Group recommended a series of terminals, with switching circuits so that only one terminal location would be connected to the communication circuit at any one time, with encoding equipment synchronization affecting only one terminal at a time. The terminal points were to be identified as the U.S.A. and the U.S.S.R., instead of Washington and Moscow as in the 1963 Hot Line Memorandum.

It soon became clear that both sides wanted to change over the Hot Line to satellite circuits. The only major issue was what type of satellite system to use. The Soviets objected to our idea of using the multinational system Intelsat. Minashin maintained that the operation of satellites by a multinational committee of seventy-seven members might reduce the stability and reliability of the system. A third country might change frequencies and create a disturbance. National satellite systems in the control of the two governments would be best and would make the link least dependent on third-country influence.

He suggested using the American Defense Satellite Communications System (DSCS). That, he was promptly told, would not be appropriate. No U.S. military system would be available. They were designed for specific purposes. The United States might want to move them. To then have to duplicate such a system would be very costly.

We pressed for Intelsat. Members of Intelsat had a direct interest in the operations of its satellites. It was unlikely that they would interfere with them. The Soviets had expressed some concern about costs. It would be possible to lease a channel from Intelsat for about $30,000 a year.

Minashin then proposed setting up two channels, using Soviet facilities for one and American facilities for the other. He was thinking about two redundant communications systems, each to be used for transmitting messages in both directions. The Soviets would use the Molniya (meaning "lightning") II satellite then under development and scheduled to be operational in 1972–73, and the United States could use its military system. It seemed to us that the Soviets were more interested in parity and national prestige than genuinely concerned about third-country interference.

May counterproposed a two-circuit system using Molniya II and Intelsat. Each country would be responsible for assuring the reliability of its half of the system and for selecting the means it considered most appropriate. This solution would achieve true parity. The Soviets apparently were somewhat surprised by this proposal. They said that it merited serious consideration if it meant that the use of satellite systems would remain fully under state control. They did not specifically reject Intelsat. May declined to accept "state control" as a condition for a two-circuit system and presented the Soviets with a list of "technical" questions about Molniya II. The United States understood that Cuba and other countries had been invited to use the new Soviet satellite. Would not this raise the same third-country dangers the Soviets feared with Intelsat? Since Molniya II would operate on the same frequencies as Intelsat, would it not be subject to jamming? The United States was not inclined to commit itself to an untried Soviet satellite system which in any event would not be ready for two or three years.

The Soviets quickly agreed to Intelsat as the American half of a two-channel solution. This was not before Minashin made a last plea for his "strong preference" for the Defense Satellite Communications System. He said that in his view it was up to the Group to make the best recommendation to their governments, and the President would surely approve a recommendation from the American members of the Group to use DSCS. Naturally we made no such recommendation.

A document was initialed by May and Minashin on May 19, 1971. Some details remained unresolved, but most of the Hot Line upgrade agreement was finished.

As the Long Summer round began in Helsinki in July 1971 the Accidents and Communications Link Agreements were almost in final form. We continued to favor concluding them when the ABM Treaty and interim offensive freeze as called for by the May 20 accord were agreed on. The Soviets wanted to close out these first agreements at that session. Semenov repeated that measures to reduce the risk of nuclear war were independently important. It would be unwarranted to delay working out an appropriate understanding, the more so since its main provisions had been essentially agreed upon. We replied that we should work to bring our positions into agreement and then give further consideration to the question of separability.

On July 16, the day after the announcement that Kissinger had been to China, I congratulated him on constructive use of his spell "under the weather," the cover story for his China trip being that he was sick in Pakistan. I also stressed the negotiating advantages of early separate Accidents and Hot Line agreements. Recalling his interest in possibly concluding them prior to the limitation agreements, I suggested that they would tend to balance off the U.S. move toward China. Both agreements were probably reachable in a matter of weeks. Communicating a positive decision to the Soviets at an early date would help lubricate Soviet review of other SALT matters. The White House soon authorized us to advise the Soviets that separate agreements were acceptable.

The Accidents Agreement was then concluded. The Special Group had met six times and finished a complete text in August. The White House approved this text for initialing, but without publicity. I was to inform Semenov that we were prepared to sign an executive agreement without waiting for other SALT agreements, but that U.S. signature must await allied and congressional consultations. Shortly thereafter Moscow agreed.

At the last minute the Soviets again brought up the question of third-country accession. Timerbaev informally asked if this might not be handled by joint or individual statements of readiness to conclude similar bilateral agreements with other nuclear powers. We did not agree.

When the agreement was signed, the U.S.S.R. made no appeal to other countries to accede to it. But in 1976 it concluded a similar agreement with France.

Semenov and I initialed the Accidents Agreement at a plenary meeting on August 20. The timing and place of the final signature would be determined by the two governments. I remarked that this success in reaching agreement showed that differing views could be reconciled. It should serve as encouragement in the work ahead. Semenov called the agreement the first major result of the SALT negotiations, undoubtedly a significant international event, a first step which he hoped would be followed by others. In conversation later he said that words were not adequate to express the importance of the agreement. It involved the maintenance of peace for the whole world. He felt the agreement would serve the vital interests of the United States, the Soviet Union, and other countries as well.

The Communications Link Agreement was not completed until September. The main issue left was its form. We proposed that it be an amendment to the 1963 Memorandum of Understanding. The Soviets favored a new agreement. Informally, the Soviets indicated that their leaders attached political importance to a new agreement. One said that a simple amendment would not justify the expenditures needed to buy the Intelsat earth station or adapt Molniya II for this purpose. The technical content of the communications link was completely new, it was argued, and the language of the 1963 agreement did not correspond to the new technical concept. Further, the 1963 framework was inadequate, too narrow to reflect the purposes that the Direct Communications Link would serve in the future or the contents worked out and agreed to at Vienna. After some minor skirmishing we agreed.

The initialing ceremony of the Hot Line Agreement was something of an anticlimax after the Accidents Agreement initialing two weeks earlier, but it made us feel that something concrete had been produced.

Although it had been agreed not to make public the substance of these documents until the governments were ready for signature, word quickly leaked to the press. The Washington *Post* disclosed the Hot Line Agreement on the same day it was initialed in Helsinki. Not so predictably, Moscow revealed the existence and nature of the Accidents Agreement. I could not pass up this unusual opportunity to show a copy of the offending report to Semenov. His reply was that the printer's press was like a tongue. It had no bones and told everything at once. I said that some of the story appeared quite accurate. Evidently someone had put some bones into the flesh.

The two agreements were well received by the North Atlantic Council and the United States Congress. Philip Farley, briefing congressional committees, pointed out that it was up to the notifying party to judge whether an incident created a risk of nuclear war and said the 1966 B-52 crash in Spain would not have required notification since it did not in the judgment of the United States create a risk of war. One congressman noted that the United States had no way of destroying its ICBMs after they were launched, because putting self-destruction mechanisms in the missiles would expose them to enemy counteraction. Farley said the United States interpreted the agreement to make every effort to render harmless or destroy an errant nuclear weapon to mean "do only what is possible." Another question was whether the Soviets might exploit the agreement to aid them in launching a sneak attack on the United States. Farley reported that this question had been thoroughly studied and there was no significant risk. Congressmen asked about the Communications Link Agreement and cryptographic security. They were assured that the United States would control this equipment and procure it *from a third-country* source, and that the kind of coding equipment supplied would not involve any risk to American techniques. One Representative expressed surprise that the U.S.S.R. was willing to provide the United States any access to its most modern satellite technology.

The Accidents and Hot Line Agreements served several purposes of no small importance. They provided useful psychological impetus. They represented progress during an otherwise slack period of the negotiations. Concluding them demonstrated to skeptics and participants alike that SALT could produce something useful.

Although a codification of what the two governments might reasonably be expected to do under such circumstances, the Accidents Agreement is important on its own merits. It establishes in international law obligations that every feasible effort be taken to prevent nuclear war as a result of accidents or the misinterpretation of other nuclear incidents. Establishing agreed standards of behavior and communication provides a useful framework for reducing risks. The Communications Link Agreement as a technical complement to the Accidents Agreement enhances the reliability of communications between leaders in crisis situations. Secretary of State Rogers and Foreign Minister Gromyko put the agreements in good perspective in their remarks at the signing ceremony on September 30, 1971. Rogers considered that "they represent realistic and concrete steps forward . . . hard and realistic and persistent work on a step-by-step basis." Gromyko said, "True, the agreements signed today do not yet solve in any way the substance of the problem of limiting strategic armaments.

This task is still outstanding and participants in the talks should seek ways to solve it. . . . At the same time these agreements are steps in the right direction, since they serve to relax international tensions and reduce the risk of the outbreak of nuclear war."

PART THREE
WORKING IT OUT

RADAR RESTRAINTS

Radar controls are an important part of the ABM Treaty and were a grueling feature of its negotiation. This chapter should help one better to understand the radar negotiations during the last SALT sessions in May 1972. How radar restraints were finally agreed is left for the chapters describing those sessions. In this chapter I will report on differing Soviet and American approaches to ABM radar deployments and proposed restraints— how American insistence on specific controls ran into Soviet concerns that they would limit their freedom to design and deploy anti-aircraft defense systems, and how the United States adjusted its position to meet Soviet concerns. The evolution of the two sides' positions on radars tells much about their respective negotiating styles and how they meshed in SALT. The issue was complicated by the multipurpose nature of radars, an example of a "gray area" in weapons systems that complicates arms control. Radar restraints illustrate what can be done, in addition to limiting numbers of launchers, to put controls on military technology —and how difficult it is.

While these radar considerations may sound complicated they are based on a few relatively simple ideas.

The basic function of an ABM system of which radar is a key

part is to intercept and destroy attacking objects. Radar is the guiding eye of the system. Its capability, together with data processing computer facilities to translate radar input into guidance for interceptor missiles, is a central requirement for an ABM system which must track many incoming re-entry vehicles (RVs) traveling thousands of miles per hour.

The American ABM system had two types of radar—the perimeter acquisition radar (PAR) which locates at long range and tracks incoming objects, and the missile site radar (MSR), which tracks objects at closer range and guides the interceptors to their targets.

To support ABMs around Moscow the U.S.S.R. deploys a different kind of radar system. They have one modern large radar which we called "Dog House," and eight older-type complexes called "Try Adds," each consisting of three radars. A second large radar, designated "Chekhov," was also under construction in the Moscow area. Soviet ABMs require a larger number of radars than planned for the American system because of the greater sophistication of U.S. radars. This asymmetry made agreed controls difficult to reach.

Another serious difficulty was that radars are inherently multipurpose systems. Establishing what purpose they are intended to serve in the U.S.S.R. can be difficult, and determining their capabilities even more so.

The United States wanted to limit the number of ABM radars to those needed to support the number of ABM launchers allowed by the treaty and to constrain other radars which, while not directly a part of an ABM system, had some ABM capabilities. Washington believed that both restraints were necessary for confidence in a treaty. In the absence of such restraints, rapid increases in ABM systems above treaty levels would be relatively easy to make since additional interceptor missiles could be produced and stored covertly and deployed to existing sites. Although ABM launchers using then current designs would require considerable time to deploy—thus giving warning if construction was started at new sites—future designs employing different ABM launchers could reduce construction time substantially. The limiting factor could then be whether sufficient radar was available to support such a clandestinely expanded ABM system. An agreement permitting only a small number of ABM launchers and interceptors would be less meaningful in the long term if a nation could build as many and as large radars as it wished.

The Soviets maintain broad radar coverage of the U.S.S.R. for anti-aircraft defenses against bombers which might come from any and many points around the periphery of their country—their Air Defense Forces have some 5,000 radars—and here again we ran into the SAM upgrade problem. We would have little confidence in limits on ABMs if the Soviets remained free to give anti-aircraft systems a capability to track and destroy re-entry vehicles (RVs) from American missiles. If attacking re-entry vehicles' location in space at a certain time could be predicted accurately, SAM interceptors might be flown to those points and their nuclear warheads detonated to destroy the re-entry vehicles. It was thought by some that a large number of Soviet SAMs might thus be upgraded to have some capability to intercept ballistic missile RVs. But if the U.S.S.R. were planning to use anti-aircraft missiles in an ABM defense role, powerful radars would be essential.

Radar controls were also important because of what was considered their lead-time verification advantage. Modern ABM radars are tremendous in size and make conspicuous targets for satellite photography—some Soviet radars are larger than the great pyramid of Egypt—and they take years to build. A SALT study suggested that the warning time given by a Soviet start of construction of radars of this type would be long enough to permit extensive countermeasures such as the development and initial deployment of wholly new offensive missile systems.

During preparation for the negotiations the U. S. Joint Chiefs of Staff argued against seeking tight radar restraints. They thought that such controls would present negotiating difficulties because they would be hard to define and to verify. They said that a radar's ABM potential would be difficult to establish—even with on-site inspection. They believed that the multipurpose nature of radar systems, the numbers deployed in both countries, the linkage between various types of radars and the computer systems which integrate radar data into firing systems would make virtually impossible any agreement on definitions sufficiently precise to provide a basis for demonstration of non-compliance. They were concerned that with the increasing application of more advanced radars to civilian as well as military purposes—and with the potential for interlocking all this radar data with ABM defense computer systems—the U.S.S.R. could in fact build a widespread radar system adaptable for ABM purposes at a time when the United States would be living up to agreed controls. Finally, the JCS believed that to assume verification lead-time benefits based on current radar systems and technology might lead us down a garden path under an ABM treaty (assumed to be of long duration) because expected lead-time benefits could be eroded by technological developments, for example, the development of very small mobile radars.

While the JCS were thus negative about seeking precise radar limitations, they did not condition their support for the whole SALT initiative on acceptance of their radar views. The President's decision to seek limitation on ABM radars presumably took into account a number of considerations including these views of the Joint Chiefs. On these rather complicated radar issues there was a lot of rough interplay between the Washington agencies which I make no attempt to describe here. In effect the President's decision to seek ABM radar restraints was based on a judgment that it would be preferable to have as precise a set of radar limitations as was negotiable rather than no restraints at all. This we sought to achieve.

We wanted controls both on ABM radars and on radars built for another purpose but which could have some ABM capability. For these latter, U.S.-proposed controls focused on characteristics essential for effective ABM performance and observable by national means of verification to distinguish ABM from non-ABM radars. We wanted to restrain radars *located* so as to contribute to defense against missile attacks. And we especially wanted to limit those with a *phased-array type of antenna.* The electronic scan of phased-array radars provides vastly greater ABM traffic-handling capability than do radars whose scan depends on mechanical movement. A third criteria was their *power-aperture product,* the product of emitted power and the area of antenna from which the electronic waves are sent out. (These waves are reflected back from distant objects and picked up again by the radar's antenna, indicating the distance, direction and speed of the reflecting object.) These three criteria—location, antenna type and power-aperture product—were used to define restraints on radars which might have an ABM capability even though built for some other purpose.

Aside from their Moscow ABM radars, the Soviets had five very large early warning radars in operation and under construction which we called "Hen Houses." Soviet negotiators said that they were not part of any ABM system. However, Hen House locations and performance characteristics gave some of them a potential for acquisition and early tracking of incoming re-entry vehicles. They were phased-array radars with a power-aperture product well above our proposed threshold for presumed ABM capability. Two of these units were located on the northern perimeter of the Soviet Union covering possible U.S. missile attack corridors, and a third uncompleted one near the Black Sea was under flight paths of missiles which might be launched from submarines in the Mediterranean Sea. We believed that these three units as well as Hen Houses constructed in the future might perform significant ABM functions if the Soviets later decided to deploy a regional or nationwide ABM defense.

The radar provisions in the first U.S. comprehensive approaches in April 1970 were quite precise. Existing ABM radars were to be listed by number and type and if an ABM ban was negotiated they were to be destroyed. If a MIRV ban was to be agreed on and the United States thus gave up this great increase in number of warheads able to penetrate illicit ABM defenses (e.g., upgraded SAMs), or ABM defenses constructed rapidly upon abrogation of an agreement, we proposed that the U.S.S.R. dismantle its three early warning Hen House radars covering potential U.S. missile attack routes. To prevent future proliferation of radars like Hen Houses which, while not part of an ABM system, had some ABM potential, there would be agreed criteria for establishing a radar's ABM capability, and future requirements for such radars would be subject to Soviet-American consultation. This was taken to mean a veto power. For example, if the Soviets planned to build a phased-array radar for air traffic control, the United States would want it oriented away from likely missile attack routes. Or if the Soviets needed an outer space radar, other criteria would be applied to rule out an ABM role (such as an elevation angle limiting it to the declared space role).

There was not much discussion on radars during the first three rounds of SALT through 1970. The delegation did not elaborate on its proposed constraints or the nature of consultation for future radars. We did list the Soviet radars—Try Add, Dog House, Chekhov and Hen House—that we considered technically capable of contributing to an ABM system and thus to be included in an ABM limitation. We appreciated that these designations might sound awkward to Soviet ears and suggested that they provide Russian designators. They did not. (Incidentally, one member of the U.S. delegation once asked a Soviet—a former pilot of a heavy bomber which U.S. intelligence designated "Bear"—what the Soviet Air Force called this class of bomber. The Soviet replied unsmilingly, *"Medved"*—the Russian word for bear.)

The Soviets proposed radar limits only on systems "specifically designed" for an ABM purpose, to include ABM long-range detection and short-range guidance radars (presumably in their case those we called Dog House and Try Add). They made it clear that their quick agreement in principle to an NCA capital defense limitation did not include the radar details of the U.S. approaches. But for the time being the Soviet delegation also seemed content to soft-pedal radar problems. Semenov said it was important to have a clear-cut delimitation and attempts artificially to expand the composition of strategic defensive weapons would only lead to additional difficulties and could sidetrack the negotiation.

The radar provisions of the United States August 4, 1970, proposal were essentially those of the April approaches, specifying Soviet ABM radars by type and number, with the United States to be allowed a radar system "roughly equivalent" to the ABM radars around Moscow. The August 4 proposal also introduced geographical limits for ABM radars: engagement radars (American MSRs and the Moscow Try Add complexes) would be restricted to an area within 100 kilometers of the centers of the capitals; acquisition and long-range tracking radars, the Soviet Dog House and Chekhov units and the American PARs, would be limited to an area within a circle of 200-kilometer radius. Hen Houses would be limited to those currently operational or under construction, and the United States would have a right to build additional early warning radars to match Soviet capabilities. There would be an agreement to consult on future large non-ABM radars.

To stress our concern about the ABM potential of the Hen House radars, in accordance with instructions, I directed Garthoff to give Grinevsky and Kishilov the following note: "Since Hen House radars can detect and track ballistic missile warheads at great distances, they have significant ABM potential. Accordingly, the U.S. would regard any increase in the defenses of such radars by surface-to-air missiles (SAMs) as inconsistent with the agreement." Garthoff explained we were no longer proposing dismantling of any Hen Houses. They were not then heavily defended, but their ABM potential would be enhanced if they were to be given increased defenses. Left implicit was the military consideration that high vulnerability to attack would be a severe constraint on their use in an ABM defense role. I confess to having had some uncertainty about thus telling the Soviets that if they wanted an agreement they must keep these radars vulnerable to attack. This statement was included in the list of unilateral statements attached to the ABM Treaty when it was forwarded to the Senate.

Semenov complained that the U.S. radar provisions were unclear. The Americans were trying to obtain irrelevant information and some people wanted to know everything even if it was not relevant. This, I said, was no fishing expedition to obtain information illegitimately. We were trying to get an agreement that was safe for the United States, and I assumed that the Soviet delegation was trying to get an agreement that was safe for the U.S.S.R.

The radar restraints negotiation began in earnest with the fourth session in Vienna in March 1971. This session was devoted almost entirely to ABM limitations. The Soviets were then pushing for a separate ABM agreement. The White House directed us to present a new ABM option permitting the United States four sites to defend ICBMs. The Soviets were refusing to be drawn into exchanges about offensive arms limitations, ostensibly because of the FBS impasse. Their ABM draft treaty provided only that "specifically designed" long-range acquisition and ABM tracking radars be restricted to a circle around the capitals having a 200-kilometer radius. This geographic limit was the full extent of the Soviet proposed radar controls.

It was far from adequate. We stressed the importance of limiting numbers and types of radar as well as their location. Since the prime purpose of a capital defense system was to defend against small-scale or accidental attacks, why was there any need for additional radar support around Moscow beyond the existing units? The Soviet proposal was insufficient in that it failed to limit other ABM-capable radars. To limit only radars "specifically designed" for ABM work presupposed that each side somehow could have knowledge of the intentions of the others' radar designers. While a system might have been designed for a certain mission, it could have other significant capabilities. Widespread deployment of Hen House early warning radars could provide ABM acquisition and tracking support. They would have to be restrained.

On no other SALT issue was the difference so clear between the American preference for specific obligations and the Soviets' for general undertakings. Paul Nitze constantly stressed the importance of sharp and clear definitions for radar limitations. Academician Shchukin told him that the technical details of the proposed American ABM limitations would require 150 pages of fine print. Nitze thought they could be set forth in less than five. Shchukin said that more precise ideas could be exchanged after agreement had been reached on treaty language. The Soviet side would lean over backward not to introduce ambiguities if they entered into an agreement, but he saw no solution to the ABM problem if one tried to anticipate the contingency that ABM components would be widely stockpiled and suddenly installed in breach of a treaty.

The Soviets argued that launchers and interceptors, not radars, determine the capabilities of an ABM system. Numerical limits on launchers and interceptors together with geographical limits on radar would effectively preclude ABM deployments beyond an agreed level; geographical limits would localize ABM deployments, while the numerical ceilings on launchers and interceptors would limit a system's size. As for ABM radars, their range was limited. If they were deployed only within a permitted area, the Soviets maintained, they could not support deployments over a wider area. The prohibition on deployment of ABM radars outside the circle would prevent creation of an ABM radar base in other areas. Their proposal, they said, was quite adequate.

The Soviets took special exception to our proposal that numbers and types of ABM radars to be permitted be spelled out. Each side, they stated, should be free to choose radars on the basis of its own technology. This would avoid seeking impossible coefficients of equivalence for numerical limits on radars. One Soviet argued that it was inadvisable to limit the numbers of radars and their technology because a SALT agreement would be of long duration. Others said radars would be self-limiting because of their expense. Extra radars would only mean "extra trouble."

We said that if ABM radars were unlimited in number they could be used to support increases in ABM capabilities. Radars could be used for various purposes and to be effective did not have to be deployed at optimal locations. The resultant uncertainty could affect the viability of all SALT arrangements. Numerical as well as geographical limits were important to prevent the development of a potential base for a thick area defense, which would be especially significant around Moscow. Both sides had agreed that it was desirable to control radars as well as ABM launchers and interceptors. The U.S. proposal had specific initial limitations and provisions for the future. Both sides had spoken of a joint commission to consider changes in circumstances after the original agreement, and new radar needs could be considered there. This combination, we thought, was an effective way to stand the tests of time.

Against our proposals to freeze Hen House radars, the Soviets argued that the U.S.S.R. had no ABM radars outside the proposed circle of 200-kilometer radius around Moscow, except at test sites. Hen Houses were early warning radars like the American ballistic missile early warning system (BMEWS) radars in Alaska, Greenland and Britain—and should not be limited. They were also necessary for verifying arms control agreements and would exist whether or not there was any ABM deployment. One Soviet flatly stated that these Hen House radars were not capable of performing in a ballistic missile acquisition and tracking role.

The American BMEWS radars were not the latest technology and had little ABM tracking capability but Soviet Hen Houses were suitable for long-range acquisition and were comparable in this respect to our ABM system perimeter acquisition radar (PAR). Asked if they thought Hen Houses should be left unlimited and deployable anywhere in the Soviet Union, they replied that there was no question of large numbers in view of their purpose and cost. They were needed only on the periphery of the country.

The Soviets also said that a number of their new radars would be of the same basic phased-array antenna type as the Hen Houses. They complained that this standard and other U.S.-proposed criteria such as a power-aperture product ceiling would tie designers' hands. If Hen Houses were converted to an ABM role, this would be detected and would constitute non-compliance with the agreement.

But it would not be easy, we said, to distinguish between the large phased-array radars that could perform some role in improving the effectiveness of an ABM system and those that could not. For example, the technology of space tracking or early warning radar was also useful for predicting missile trajectories for ABM purposes. It would be easier to identify ABM radars if the U.S.-proposed criteria were agreed. If these observable characteristics were not acceptable, what critera would they propose?

Here was another instance of a twilight zone—where a system, not clearly designed as strategic, could yet play some strategic role under an arms control regime (like FBS in the offensive sphere).

We later presented some new radar concepts to meet Soviet objections. Instead of limitation by numbers and types, we proposed a new geographical limit called a modern ABM radar complex (MARC) to limit ABM radars and a definition of other large phased-array radars (OLPARs) to control Hen House-type radars.

A MARC was defined as a circular area of no more than three kilometers in diameter in which each party could deploy ABM radars. For defense of its capital each side could have four MARCs; if a party chose the option of defending ICBM fields, it could deploy ABM radars in a total of five MARCs located in these fields (later reduced to four when the United States changed its proposal to allow only two ICBM defense sites). Any number of ABM radars would be allowed in a MARC. In effect we accepted the Soviet principle of geographic limitation for ABM radars, but countered with such restrictive geographical MARC limits that the number of radars also would be limited.

We thought this new MARC concept met the needs of both sides because there would be no prejudice to existing radars. All of their components could fit into a MARC. While MARCs would be large enough to allow a number of ABM radars to be deployed, they would still be restricted enough geographically so that neither side could misinterpret future radar deployments as aimed at supporting a heavy ABM defense of a widespread area. Thus all radar requirements of both sides appropriate to the ABM levels under consideration could be met.

The Soviets did not like this MARC idea. American concerns about possible expansion of limited ABM defenses were groundless. It was just not possible to create an area defense out of an NCA-level deployment. Their proposed geographical limit for the entire ABM system would preclude radar deployment for a widespread defense. In fact, while it was impossible to create a radar infrastructure for an area defense under their solution, they said that the U.S. proposal for three ICBM defense sites could be used to establish the basis for just such a defense.

They had no intention of thickening the Moscow defense. There was nothing to be concerned about in allowing any number of radars within the 200-kilometer radius. Financial considerations would limit both sides. But this, we said, would be the case without any SALT agreement.

The purpose of MARCs, we explained, was to assure against the possibility of a heavy local ABM defense. If either side could have an indefinite number of radars anywhere within a 200-kilometer circle, the sides would not have confidence that a thick defense of an important area was not intended. A thick defense of a substantial percentage of the population, industry, and military potential of a side could have strategic significance in itself and could be a step toward a nationwide defense. There seemed to be little difference in the general objectives of the sides, we suggested again, and our proposal would give maximum assurance against thick defense. I wondered aloud why the U.S.S.R. believed it needed four hundred times as much real estate to deploy radars for a capital defense as the United States considered adequate.

It was hardly practical, claimed the Soviets, to try to establish a thick defense of one area. It would not have a significant effect on the strategic relationship. And it would require an increase in the number of ABM launchers and interceptors, which would be a violation of the treaty. At the same time, they did not mean that one side could use the whole permitted area for radars or create an unlimited system of ABM radars. The Soviet Union simply wanted to retain flexibility in the construction of its allowed ABM system. The number of ABM radars depended on technical solutions each side would choose. The number deployed at an NCA site would be the number needed to insure the functioning of 100 interceptors. Future improvements as well as present equipment should be taken into account.

Soviet experts thought the MARC proposal seemed to represent an American attempt to prescribe a particular course that the other side must follow in their ABM radar development and deployment.

This Soviet position against tying designers' hands was repeated often, in several contexts, in the remaining months of the negotiation. Their case against our proposed controls often appeared to be tactically motivated, to support an interest in an agreement in general terms while delaying concessions until a more critical stage. Some Americans thought that the Soviets might be disposed to question U.S. proposals as probably designed to permit the United States to achieve or maintain technological advantages. They might fear that the United States, in proposing restraints such as MARCs, believed it could develop technology to build around these constraints while the Soviets could not. Perhaps a Soviet technological inferiority complex was a factor at this stage of the radar dickering.

I tried to get Semenov to consider radars of central importance. We had moved to meet them halfway by not insisting on listing specific radars and by advancing the concept of MARCs. I still hoped there could be a free dialogue on radars. Semenov did not think it desirable to pay too much attention to specialists since their methods would tend to fix existing positions. He was surprised that the Americans attached so much importance to this question. Each side should solve the radar problem in its own way, depending on locations to be defended. With this approach the question of what constituted a modern radar system would not arise at all, and it would be easier to find an ABM solution. I pointed out that the United States had moved from a technical prescription on radars toward a more political solution. Indeed one Soviet had called the MARC concept a political intervention into a technical problem!

We were not making any more progress on the question of restraints on other large phased-array radars (OLPARS) than on ABM radars. Our specific proposal to restrain OLPARs was that the sides not "deploy without prior mutual agreement phased-array radars having a product of power (in watts) and aperture (in square meters) greater than 1 million."

The absence of any provision for large phased-array radars was a major defect in the Soviet draft ABM treaty. An OLPAR is a non-ABM radar, but we insisted that account had to be taken of its potential. The one million power-aperture product criterion was reasonable because it would cover only those radars with an inherent potential to track many objects at distances of thousands of kilometers. All phased-array radars over that level had some inherent ABM tracking capability. Mutual agreement on OLPAR deployment thus would have a special significance in assuring that a potential radar base for a thick defense of a significant region or even a nationwide defense of a country was not created.

They said that we had recognized that OLPARs were not related to ABM systems. They were therefore beyond the framework of the talks—as defined in the May 20, 1971, understanding. Non-ABM systems should not be covered in an ABM agreement. Any attempted conversion to an ABM function would be discovered by national means of verification. The basic Soviet assumption was that national technical means of verification could determine the purpose of radars. There was no reason for establishing the power-aperture product criterion proposed by the United States since this would put a brake on the development of radars for other purposes, for example, air defenses. Large radars were also one element of national technical means of verification, and a side should also remain free to deploy and improve early warning radars independent of an ABM limitation.

We noted their contention that non-ABM radars could be distinguished from ABM radars and argued that the two major characteristics of radars with an inherently high ABM potential were their phased-array antennae and their high power-aperture product. This was the basis of our OLPAR proposal. Was it not correct that the principal observable characteristics of a radar were its location, orientation, size and type, power level and signal characteristics? Did the Soviets have in mind other characteristics? These questions were not answered.

The latest anti-aircraft missile system around Leningrad and Moscow—the SAM 5—was originally thought by some U.S. analysts to be an ABM system. It now seems to have been designed to defend against the B-70—the bomber which the United States never built. A Soviet delegate remarked informally that he understood that the United States had once thought this Soviet SAM system was an unsuccessful ABM system which had been converted to anti-aircraft purposes after its inadequacy had been discovered. Though the United States was wrong initially, he asserted, it had now concluded correctly that the system had been originally deployed for anti-aircraft purposes. This showed that the purposes of a system could be determined by national means. When his American counterpart commented that it had taken some years to determine whether this system was for ABM defense, the Soviet official said that the necessary sensors to pick up electronic emissions did not exist when this system was built.

After a long time our radar arguments appeared to be having some effect. The Soviets agreed to two provisions. First, compromise language on SAM upgrading was worked out. The parties agreed "not to give missiles, launchers, or radars, other than ABM interceptor missiles, ABM launchers, or ABM radars, capabilities to counter strategic ballistic missiles or their elements in flight trajectory, and not to test them in an ABM mode." This covered all non-ABM radars.

A second agreed undertaking was "not to give ballistic missile early-warning radars capabilities of performing an ABM role, not to test them in an ABM mode, and also not to deploy such radars in the future except at locations along the periphery of their national territories and oriented outward." Soviet acceptance of this language was conditioned on the United States not insisting on numerical limitations or having a veto on future Soviet radars.

These developments struck me as substantial Soviet concessions. I had not expected that the Soviets would be willing to take such a precise commitment as to the location and orientation of their early warning radars. This represented a new degree of precision in the negotiation.

The stalemate on MARCs and on limiting the number of OLPARs continued.

The Soviets could not accept constraints on their air defense systems because such systems were allegedly capable of being used in an ABM role. The proposed OLPAR limitation, they said, would limit modernization of Soviet defenses against bombers in spite of agreement that anti-aircraft defenses were not covered in SALT. It could also interfere with development of non-military radars. They just could not agree to this.

Semenov remarked to me privately that taking into account the length of the borders, the geographical situation of the Soviet Union, and the presence of third countries, his government could not fail to be concerned over its anti-aircraft defenses. Radars for air defense were extremely important. Any attempt in SALT to impose limitations on them would be tantamount to placing a very heavy load onto a most fragile negotiating structure. Another Soviet said that because the U.S.S.R. must have air defenses against numerous threats, not only from the United States but also from third countries, it must be able to deploy air defense radars in large numbers. If one were to attempt to give all these air defense radars the capabilities of ABM radars, the entire Soviet population would have to go without trousers for the next five years.

The Americans countered by saying that the proposed constraints affecting non-ABM radars were restricted to limiting their ABM potential. It was important to reduce to a minimum uncertainties about ABM capabilities. It was admitted by one American that, while our proposals did not involve any great restraints on air defenses, it was possible there could be some marginal effect. But we were convinced that any such effect was far less important than would be the result of creating a radar base for a thick or nationwide ABM defense system, a risk that was present in the Soviet proposals with their absence of limits on large ABM-capable radars. You can be sure the Soviets pounced on this, describing it as a "significant admission." Whether the extent of the restraint on their anti-aircraft systems would be large or small was a subjective judgment where the sides might differ, and the Soviet side could not agree to any limitations on air defenses. It was a matter of principle. Moscow would not accept the power-aperture product criterion or any other specific numerical restraint.

The Soviets held that our OLPAR provision was unnecessary as well as undesirable. They had now agreed not to deploy a national or regional ABM defense or the radar base for such a defense, not to upgrade non-ABM radars, and to restrain the location and orientation of early warning radars. Any actions in conflict with these provisions would constitute a violation of the treaty. Accordingly the remaining specific U. S. OLPAR proposal was unwarranted.

We were told many times that the Soviets would address the MARC concept further. But it was a long time before they did. They apparently were prepared to consider the MARC concept for national capital defense if the United States accepted their proposed deployment circle (now reduced to 150-kilometer radius) and dropped the power-aperture product criterion for OLPARs.

We said that the two problems were quite different. We believed it necessary both to limit the location and number of ABM radars *and* to prevent unconstrained proliferation of other large phased-array radars with ABM potential.

The Soviets confirmed this offer of a MARC for OLPAR trade-off. They would accept the general concept of MARCs if we would drop our call for controls on OLPARs. We asked when they would discuss the number of MARCs. A Soviet informally said that the number of MARCs they could agree to would be within the range of numbers referred to in previous informal discussions—from four to ten. Not very enlightening.

Soviet acceptance of MARCs was further conditioned. It applied only to a national capital defense ABM system and not to ABM sites to defend ICBMs. We had proposed a total of four MARCs for two ICBM defense sites, the same number proposed for capital defense. The Soviets proposed that the United States retain ABM components at one ICBM field while the U.S.S.R. would defend in addition to Moscow one half as many ICBM launchers as would be protected in the American ICBM field. This concept contained only a general qualitative restraint on radars for ICBM defense: they should be appropriate to the defense of ICBM silo launchers, that is, designed so as to have no capability to support a defense of objects other than ICBMs. The American perimeter acquisition radar (PAR) and missile site radar (MSR) then under advanced construction, although not specially designed for the defense of ICBM silos, would be allowed as exceptions. Otherwise, there was no need to limit the number of ABM radars specially designed for ICBM defense and located in permitted deployment areas.

The Soviets apparently now realized that any likely ABM treaty would permit them to defend some ICBM silos. Since they had not yet designed an ABM system for that purpose, Moscow evidently wanted to avoid any radar restrictions that might cramp its design flexibility.

We tried to extract specifics about this new Soviet idea. All we got was confirmation that the U.S.S.R. was proposing that the number of radars for ICBM defense not be numerically restricted and that their design capacity be held below a certain unspecified level. I asked at one meeting whether the Soviets had in mind specifying numerical restraints on ICBM defense radars or just a general criteria that such components should not have capabilities other than for ICBM defense. The answer was that the American MSRs, although inappropriate to ICBM defense (but allowed as an exception), would give some idea of an allowed ceiling on ICBM defense radar capability. But the Soviet side did not believe there was any need to agree to limit the number of such radars because each side could adopt different solutions.

I commented that such a subjective arrangement would be hard to live with. What the Soviet had just said had lowered any hypothetical appetite I might have had for radar limits on ABM systems for ICBM defense, which were different from those for the defense of capitals.

Our estimate of radar negotiating possibilities now was that the Soviets would certainly not accept an American veto on new construction of OLPARs. But they might accept some sort of "best efforts" clause involving advance notification of new construction of OLPARs.

For national capital defense, the U.S.S.R. probably would accept six to eight MARCs.

The Soviets would continue to oppose MARCs for ICBM defense but would press for as yet unknown qualitative constraints.

How this radar puzzle was worked out will be left for Chapters 12 and 14, about the last weeks at Helsinki in May 1972. Radar arrangements were not completed until the last month of the negotiation when the Moscow deadline was pressing and the other major pieces of the SALT agreements were falling into place. The delegation then was able to complete the radar negotiation and achieve some effective controls on radars. Although the final product was far from our first proposals, the outcome shows that some qualitative arms control measures can be worked out through persistent negotiation.

CHAPTER
11

THE
SUMMIT APPROACHES

Vienna VI:
November 1971–January 1972

On October 12, two weeks after our return from Helsinki, President Nixon announced that he would visit the U.S.S.R. the following spring. This surely set a SALT deadline. The previous May the United States and the U.S.S.R. had agreed to try to reach ABM limitations "this year." A better estimate would have been "within a year." It looked to me like a tactical error for the President to commit himself so far in advance to visit the U.S.S.R.—when the main item on the agenda, SALT, was so far from solution. It seemed to put more pressure on the visitor than on the host, especially as the visitor would face a presidential election six months later. Our SALT bargaining power was not increased by this commitment to a summit. Difficult decisions would now have to be faced and nettles grasped in the national security community.

It appears that the President already had in mind a May summit meeting in Moscow when he said in July that he would visit China "at an appropriate date before May 1972." The Soviet SALT delegation probably knew in August or September that a summit was in the wind and that the pace of SALT would have to be speeded up. We read about it in the newspapers.

I wrote the President about his recent press conference statement that "neither major power can get a decisive advantage over the other, an advantage which would enable it to launch a pre-emptive strike which might enable it to engage in international blackmail." That conclusion should guide our continuing efforts in SALT. I then made the case against "poor mouthing" our strategic forces that I believe remains largely valid today.

I do not think that the United States is on a course leading to an inferior strategic position. In our proper concern about the implications of current Soviet ICBM and SLBM programs, we should not persuade ourselves that we are in imminent danger of slipping into a position of inferiority. And we should not "poor mouth" our capabilities publicly in a way which may shake the confidence of the American public, or our Allies—or the Soviets—in our deterrent.

There is an impression in some quarters that we were standing still while the Soviets built up their strategic offensive capabilities. As you will recall, the United States made a determination some years ago that to achieve greater targeting flexibility and assured penetration, the important factor was the number of independently targetable re-entry vehicles —not the number of launchers. When your Administration took office, we had 1,710 independently targetable re-entry vehicles. Today we have more than twice as many. By the end of 1975, we will have between 6,000 and 7,000.

Our ballistic missile submarines are technically superior to the Soviet's and geography and foreign bases give us a large advantage.

We have an active program for hardening the Minuteman force.

The U.S. strategic bomber force is far larger and technically superior to that of the Soviet Union.

We are developing and deploying improved airborne missiles.

Late in the 60's our planning assumed that we might have to penetrate as many as 8,000 Soviet ABMs. Now, the Soviets have offered to accept a limit of 100 ABMs.

Finally, as major hedges for the future, the United States has a B-1 bomber program under development and an ULMS[1] program which will give us a major capability to further modernize the nuclear submarine fleet.

In its totality the power of all U.S. strategic nuclear forces that the Soviets must face is inconceivable. Some small measure of this power, however, may be derived from considering one Poseidon submarine. It would require 1,200,000 World War II B-17 aircraft or 200,000 B-52's with conventional bombs to match the equivalent explosive power carried by one Poseidon submarine. This is more than four times the total high explosive dropped on Germany and Japan during World War II.

This submarine can deliver this explosive power to 160 targets—more than the total number of German and Japanese cities subject to strategic bombing during the Second World War. Yet the megatonnage deliverable by one boat is only a small fraction of one percent of the total deliverable by U.S. strategic forces. Each one of the 16 missiles in this boat can cause a number of explosions of substantially greater power than that of the Hiroshima blast. In several years there will be 31 Poseidon boats in the fleet.

I think that if, in appropriate ways, our Allies and our public were more keenly aware of the size and flexibility of U.S. strategic forces, as well as of current measures to improve them—all of which can be adequately discussed on an unclassified basis—they would conclude that you are on the right track in the SALT negotiations.

The mood in Washington seemed to be that we had talked all summer about ABM limitations and now it was time to get down to brass tacks about the interim freeze on the Soviet launcher build-up.

The Soviets favored as simple a SALT agreement as possible. They said it would be a major political development if the great powers struck a strategic bargain. Fine print was not necessary or

[1] Undersea long-range missile system, now included in the Trident program.

appropriate for such a solemn accord. The United States wanted specific undertakings. Loophole closing is a more pressing purpose of an American negotiator than of a Soviet. At times I wondered if the Soviets thought that the Americans were more interested in loophole closing than in the larger aim of working out fundamental undertakings.

I have seen criticism of the drafting of the SALT agreements. I suspect that the critics have never studied the agreements with care. The delegation did not succeed in closing all loopholes but it was not because we were unaware of them or because we did not try hard. You cannot by clever drafting overcome unwillingness of the other party to take commitments.

Secretary Laird was now growing grimmer about SALT prospects. He was said to have disapproved of the recent White House decision that our ABM offer be changed to allow the United States two rather than three ABM sites. Even though the Soviets had not started any new ICBM silos since the May 20 accord, he was suspicious that they would soon start up again. He was reportedly irritated that the White House had not proposed a provision permitting large-scale deployment of hard-site ABMs specially designed to defend ICBMs. Laird's unhappiness during SALT anticipated and may partially account for his later publicly expressed doubts that the agreements were being faithfully carried out. But despite the gloom and foot dragging in some quarters, the smell of a summit was in the air and the general expectation was that something or somebody would have to give.

The Soviets must have thought they had played a high card by not starting any new ICBM silos after the May 1971 agreement. As has been said, there was no way to tell if this reflected the topping out of their ICBM program or a special SALT-related decision to suspend it, but it appeared responsive to American criticism of their build-up. What more did we want? We wanted them to stop building SLBM submarines now that they had about the same number in operation and under construction as the United States had.

Why did the Soviets not want at this time to include SLBMs in the freeze? They must have calculated that parity with the United States at 41 submarines apiece would operate to their disadvantage. They needed larger numbers in order to neutralize four U.S. advantages.

First, U.S. submarines operate from forward bases in Europe, which permits their more efficient use. The only potential forward base for Soviet submarines, Cuba, was out of bounds by virtue of a still secret agreement made by Kissinger in 1970 as a result of the Cienfuegos crisis. In arguing about the advantage the United States had in forward basing, they probably knew that longer-range missiles then in development would overcome this asymmetry, but not for many years.

Second, U.S. submarines were superior in a number of operating characteristics.

Third, geography favored the United States, since the Soviet submarines have to make difficult transits between NATO countries to reach patrol stations in the Atlantic.

Finally, America's allies, Britain and France, had programs for nine Polaris-type submarines whose missiles would be targeted on the U.S.S.R.

Since any SALT freeze would not affect Britain and France the numbers of their submarines might be increased. The closest the Soviets ever came to suggesting that the United States might violate an agreement was a statement that a party to an agreement might evade its terms by helping build up allied strategic forces.

There were two time-related issues in the freeze negotiation— how long should it last and what provision should there be for its possible termination? These issues had also been complicated in the 1971 back-channel negotiation, where Kissinger had suggested a freeze duration of one and a half to two years and indicated that no special termination clause was needed other than the usual provision in arms control agreements that a party can terminate on short notice by citing that its vital interests would otherwise be prejudiced. I felt that the more informal and the shorter the freeze was, the better it would be for the United States. If the freeze were short, it was more likely that the Soviets would include SLBMs. A short freeze would also reduce the negative psychological impact of registering any Soviet numerical advantage in missile launcher numbers. Paul Nitze disagreed and a short freeze did not appeal to the White House. Perhaps an offen-

sive arms limitation treaty would take longer to negotiate than expected. If a freeze stopped Soviet programs, a longer-term agreement would be better. It got down to whether one thought the
freeze would be good, fair or poor.

The delegation was directed to continue to press for a freeze of
indefinite duration with a provision permitting either party to terminate if more complete limitations on offensive systems were not
reached by a date to be agreed upon. I once recalled to Kissinger
that he had told Dobrynin that we would not insist on such a termination clause. He doubted my statement but said that logic was
on the side of not having a special termination clause. Still, we
were required to press for it. But the Soviets must by now have
been used to discrepancies between Kissinger comments and the
delegation's proposals. They were careful in delegation exchanges
not to give offense to the White House by any specific reference
to the former.

Before leaving for Vienna, I again asked Kissinger to try to cut
down the optimism emanating from the White House and also
spoke about leaks which I believed were coming from the Administration. He heatedly denied that any leaks had come from the
White House but agreed with my concerns about the effect of
optimism on our bargaining power. Kissinger again assured me
that there would be no negotiations unknown to me. I told him
that I appreciated that the President might want to use other people for certain aspects of SALT, but, if so, I should not be kept
in the dark. I told him that if there were any more "unknown
negotiations" I would resign and I asked him to tell that to the
President. He again assured me that there would be no such
negotiations.

My state of mind just before returning to Vienna was reflected
in a letter to Kissinger of November 5. I urged that the President
stress to the delegation that the prospect of a Moscow summit did
not affect the previous SALT goal of reaching agreement in 1971.
Perhaps with a subconscious motive to keep open in extremis the
possibility of only limiting ABMs if efforts to work out the "certain measures" to constrain offensive arms failed, I wrote that a
SALT outcome that for all practical purposes would keep the
U.S.S.R. defenseless against missiles would improve security.
Now that a ban was ruled out, I argued for one ABM site for

each side. We should not liberalize our proposed radar restraints to get two ABM sites for the United States. If we were able to negotiate as a companion to the ABM treaty a moratorium on offensive launcher build-ups, it should be seen as a first installment on subsequent more comprehensive offensive limitations. I touched on the possibility of a fallback position calling for a Soviet unilateral declaration of intention to restrict SLBM programs if we did not succeed in including SLBMs in the interim freeze. This was a point I was to come back to several times as the summit approached. I also wrote that the United States should avoid premature committal to a new submarine construction program. There might even be difficulty finding targets for the 7,000 to 9,000 warheads soon to be in the American strategic arsenal. As the United States already had a fully adequate retaliatory force, we should only build in the future what was needed to meet strategic requirements and not simply to match the other side's forces launcher for launcher. While pressing on the Soviets our concern about their missile launcher build-up, we should avoid giving Congress or the public any impression that the United States was becoming strategically inferior. "I do not think we are or will permit the United States to be in such an inferior posture unless we ourselves create such a posture by 'poor mouthing' our immense and redundant strategic forces which are even now being subsequently upgraded. The facts are that during SALT the USSR had increased the number of its missile launchers by about 20 per cent. The U.S. had more than doubled the number of its independently targetable warheads and its programs call for doubling that number in a few years."

The President's instructions for Vienna VI were simple. The basic position was as at Helsinki. Concentrate first on the interim freeze and "insist" that the Soviet delegation do the same. Here again, the White House staffer who chose the word "insist" must have had little knowledge of international negotiation. The President was specially interested in a sublimit on Soviet large missile launchers for SS-9s. We were to develop a "precise understanding" of what would be allowed under "modernization and replacement." Apparently the White House had developed a new appreciation of the importance of this term. Compare this guidance with the understanding in the Nixon-Kosygin exchange of May 1971 that the freeze on strategic offensive weapons would not preclude possible modernization and replacement.

We were to make a strong effort to include SLBM submarines in the freeze. If that was achievable only by adjustments in the United States proposal, the delegation was to recommend alternatives.

Work was also to start on drafting a joint text for the interim freeze agreement.

This kind of guidance clearly foreshadowed flexibility. How different was the instruction on ABMs. There was no alternative to the American "two or one" site proposal. The delegation was not even to do any scouting out of possible compromises. We could explore alternative radar and geographic limitations. And we were to explain to the Soviets a new American proposal that a side which originally chose to defend its capital could switch to defense of an ICBM field and vice versa. The delegation was to press for a special right to withdraw from the ABM Treaty if by a certain date the temporary freeze agreement was not superseded by a treaty limiting offensive arms. We were to make clear that some restraints on offensive arms must coexist in parallel with limitations on ABMs.

Pushed by the six-month-old momentum of the May 20 accord and now pulled by the prospect of a summit meeting six months away, the delegations returned to Vienna on November 15.

Semenov's opening presentation was mild and general. Mine was much more direct. Right at the start I stressed the importance of making progress on the full scope of the objectives set forth on May 20. It was important that measures to freeze offensive deployment programs now be given priority attention. The growth of Soviet strategic land- and sea-based missile launchers—which appeared to be aimed at the attainment of a far larger number of such launchers than currently possessed by the United States— had caused concern. It was hard to reconcile this build-up with any concept of equality. We believed that the equal aggregate levels that we had proposed in August 1970 were adequate to provide for the strategic requirements of the two countries. Our missile forces remained at the ceiling then proposed—the Soviet forces now substantially exceeded it. Continuing the offensive build-up seemed inconsistent with the Soviet position that reaching an ABM agreement would facilitate agreement on offensive limitations.

At our first private talk I read a statement which I had suggested to the White House.

"I have been personally instructed by President Nixon to advise you at the start of SALT VI as follows: The U.S. will estimate USSR intentions about the overall SALT negotiations by its willingness now to engage in serious exchanges about the full coverage of the offensive measures referred to in the May 20th understanding. The purpose of the SALT offensive measures referred to in the May 20th understanding was to limit the number of launchers of the two sides. The U.S. views with profound concern the continued widening by the USSR of the present numerical inequality in offensive ballistic missile launchers to its unilateral advantage."

Semenov asked if the United States was pulling away from the May 20 accord. I assured him we were not. Priority should now be given to negotiating the offensive freeze. Semenov resisted this proposition but said that a middle way could be found. I replied that no progress could be made on ABMs until the United States was enlightened as to the Soviet position on offensive measures.

Incidentally, after all my efforts at the President's direction to impress on Semenov concerns about the continuing Soviet build-up, I was flabbergasted to read a report of a conversation the President had with Foreign Minister Gromyko in the fall of 1971. He reportedly told Gromyko that he had noticed that the Soviets were continuing their build-up of offensive launchers. He said we did not object to that. We would be doing the same in a similar situation.

At this discussion Gromyko said he thought the recent Soviet ABM proposal was a good one. He wondered whether any detailed study had been given it and whether the President had been involved in it. Gromyko described it as "not bad as proposals go."

Semenov was thinking about the Moscow summit meeting. It was the central question that he wanted to raise. The Soviet side believed that the forthcoming state visit of President Nixon to the

Soviet Union and his talks with the Soviet leadership could serve the cause of developing Soviet-American relations and facilitate the solution of important international problems. It was with this in mind that the Vienna phase of SALT should be approached. Here was a strong hint of Soviet deadline diplomacy which could be practiced now that the President had agreed to be their spring-time guest.

I urged that we not go on reading speeches at each other. He defended this formal procedure, saying that the questions we were discussing were not by any means simple. We must carefully weigh many times over what we said to each other. (Although this would have been good advice for the SALT backchannel, I think the Soviets preferred the Kissinger type of "high politics" negotiating.) He suggested that we meet in a "troika" which would include himself, Academician Shchukin and General Trusov. We might call this a "mini-miniplenary."

One Soviet remarked that his delegation considered this round as appropriate for a discussion of offensive measures. He said that debates in Moscow on offensive measures had been intense and complex. There were those who felt it was necessary to make the most elaborate computations, taking into account not only numbers and quality of various weapons systems but also their disposition in relationship to the geographical asymmetries between the two countries. This official added that he thought such computations might be important in computing the relationships on a particular war front in the context of conventional arms such as tanks and artillery pieces, but in the strategic nuclear field there was a considerable area in which such differences were of no strategic importance. One could drown in details. And these elaborate computations depended on the instructions that had been programmed into the computer. The argument was really controlled by simple arithmetical computations that people could make at the table. I was inclined to agree.

We gained some insights into Moscow's decision-making processes for SALT. The Soviets had had no real vacation in the interval between Helsinki and Vienna. When their delegation returned from Helsinki they had devoted themselves to preparing a report on the Helsinki phase. On their side there was no organization to make decisions on substance during the negotiating phases. When the Soviet delegation was back in Moscow there were joint meetings of two groups, one in the military chain of command and the other within the Ministry of Foreign Affairs. These groups prepared issue papers for "the higher echelons." One Soviet said that he viewed the resumption at Vienna as being a rest after the exertions of the Moscow phase.

I reported to the President. The "sequence" issue was finally laid to rest. Referring to the May 20 understanding, Semenov had stated that the Soviet leadership had come to the conclusion that an understanding on both complexes of questions could be reached simultaneously. It was appropriate to engage in simultaneous discussion of both questions. They would try to meet us halfway. Semenov stressed that this decision was not the result of any arguments I had been making. I assumed he was trying to avoid the impression that the Soviets were being pressured into offensive measures discussion.

It had taken six months since the May 20 agreement to get a common interpretation on "sequence." The Soviet delegation at long last started to present views about the freeze. On November 23 they proposed that the obligation of the freeze be not to begin construction of land-based launchers after a certain agreed date. Launchers then under construction could be completed. He claimed that there already was agreement that a "freeze" would not affect the possibility of modernizing and replacing strategic offensive systems. A primary Soviet negotiating task for the next six months would be to water down or eliminate proposed American conditions that would crimp Soviet modernization programs which we now know called for deployment of several new classes of ICBMs.

Submarine missile launchers were still excluded. To give us a whiff of what talk of SLBM inclusion would lead to, Semenov raised the forward-based system issue once again. He said the composition of strategic offensive armaments must include any types of nuclear delivery systems whose geographic location enables them to strike targets on the territory of the other side. As a result "above all" of differences on FBS, we had failed to come to agreement on the overall problem of limiting strategic weapons. Freezing ICBM silo launchers was consistent with the present stage of the negotiations. But extending the freeze to other types of strategic offensive armaments would raise the same difficulties encountered earlier. ICBM silo launchers were such a major component of all strategic offensive armaments that an understanding about freezing them together with a treaty on ABMs was quite sufficient to ensure favorable conditions for further negotiations on limiting strategic armaments.

Two days later the Soviets tabled a proposed freeze in the form of an exchange of letters for signature by the heads of government. It called for a halt of construction starts of ICBM silos on July 1, 1972, or the date when the SALT agreements went into effect, whichever was later. The freeze was to last one and a half to two years. Modernization and replacement were not to be limited.

But they still opposed including SLBMs in the freeze. And Semenov privately and surprisingly said that the Soviet position was not based on an interpretation of the May 20 understanding. He repeated the bogeyman argument that attempts to include SLBM would revive the FBS argument. FBS and SLBMs were linked and both issues should be deferred for later negotiation. SLBMs, they argued, were just another type of mobile missile. SLBM submarines had different strategic significance depending on whether they were based in national territory or at overseas bases. So deployment restrictions must enter into consideration of SLBM limitation. Semenov again proposed withdrawal of SLBM submarines and attack carriers from agreed-upon areas. This was a tactical move, related to our constant pressing for SLBMs, but the Soviet position on the strategic value of forward basing would in the end be partially sustained. We heard again that SBLMs were related to FBS because the total megatonnage the U. S. FBS could deliver was greater than the megatonnage of Soviet SLBMs. A rather ingenious new argument was made that, since the freeze was to be coexistent with ABM limitation, and since U. S. ABMs protected only ICBMs, then only ICBMs should be in the freeze!

But gradually there seemed to develop some disposition on the Soviet side to include SLBMs. They informally said that it would be difficult for them to make a proposal. Any compromise initiative would have to come from us. In general, Soviets do better at reacting than at proposing specific arms controls. For a time the U.S. delegation was somewhat intrigued by the attention some Soviet officials paid to the fact that the United States proposed to freeze not only SLBM launchers but also construction of new missile submarines, saying that the U.S.S.R. could never agree to include submarines in a temporary freeze. The implication was that they might agree to a freeze limiting numbers of SLBM launchers if they could modernize their SLBM submarines by replacing older ones. We were to pursue this idea the next year.

A key issue in working out the interim freeze was what would be permitted under "modernization and replacement." We noted the absence of any reference to the U.S.-proposed freeze on launchers for very large missiles (MLBMs). The absence of an MLBM freeze could permit increases in the number of MLBM launchers through conversion of smaller ICBM launchers. In addition, a prohibition on increasing the depth and diameter of ICBM launchers was essential for verification of a freeze on MLBM launchers. It was important that an increase in numbers of MLBM launchers not come about through exercise of a right to modernize and replace.

The importance of modernization and replacement under the interim freeze was recognized by both sides. Even in their 1970 Basic Provisions the Soviets had provided that there be no limitations on modernization and replacement. While as a general proposition we favored a right to do some modernizing, an unlimited right would not be consistent with a ceiling on MLBMs. If in the name of modernization the Soviets could convert a silo launcher for a smaller ICBM such as the SS-11 into a launcher for an MLBM, any sublimit on MLBMs would be meaningless. Hundreds of SALT hours were spent in the last six months trying to get a precise understanding of what would be allowed under modernization and replacement. We did not succeed.

This had long been a major negotiating aim of the United States. The two comprehensive approaches tabled at Vienna in April 1970 included a precise definition of MLBMs, as missiles having a volume greater than seventy cubic meters (about the size of a Soviet SS-11), and included provisions that ICBM launchers could not be modified in externally observable ways and that retrofit of current launchers with missiles not previously deployed would be limited to missiles whose volume did not exceed seventy cubic meters. The August 4, 1970, proposal had provided that any silo launcher modified in externally observable ways would be counted under the MLBM launcher subceiling.

As was the case with some other issues, previous White House negotiating had not improved the delegation's bargaining power. I have already described how during the back-channel negotiation leading to the May 20 accord Kissinger had been asked if there would be any limitation on modernization under the freeze. He assured Dobrynin that there would be none.

After the May 20 accord the delegation was directed to negotiate somewhat different modernization and replacement provisions. The July 27, 1971, draft agreement, which remained the basic American freeze proposal until the closing days, provided that modernization of ICBM launchers would be permitted. But there was an important condition. There should be no increases in the depth or interior diameter of ICBM launchers, changes which would be observable by us. MLBMs, whose launchers would be limited to those externally completed by December 31, 1971, were again defined as missiles with a volume greater than seventy cubic meters.

When the delegation pressed for these limitations, Semenov said the May 20 accord was controlling. I knew what he meant. This was another case of locking the stable door after the horse was gone. Semenov recalled that the question of modernization and replacement had been decided in the May 20 understanding and that we were not called on to revise it. We were engaged in negotiations about quantitative limitations and one side should not try to use the negotiations to get qualitative limitations. He argued that there was an internal contradiction between our effort to limit changes in silo dimensions while purporting not to limit modernization. There was.

I agreed that the words "modernization and replacement" had appeared in the May 20 exchanges but argued that their meaning was not clear. I recalled that the previous March, when I had taxed Semenov with the renewed Soviet ICBM build-up, he had said it was modernization. It would make nonsense of the freeze if the sides could add to the number of launchers supposedly frozen by labeling the construction as modernization. So it was very important to have a clear understanding of what was meant by "modernization and replacement." He said he would like to remove this misunderstanding which he was now hearing for a second time. The previous year he had been referring to more than modernization and I should take a look at the form in which he had made his statement. I would then have a better understanding of what he had said. I did but the better understanding escaped me.

On December 3 the Soviets made what they billed as "a new major positive contribution to the development of the negotiations." They were prepared to agree that the freeze applied to light as well as heavy land-based ICBM silo launchers and that, if necessary, the two sides could assume an obligation not to convert from light launchers to heavy launchers in the process of modernization. There was less here than met the eye because they persisted in refusing to state their understanding as to what a heavy missile was. They said that, taking into account the importance of such an obligation by the sides, it was unnecessary to introduce any sort of definition which would include quantitative criteria. It was sufficient to proceed on the basis of the understanding of each side as to exactly which types of ICBMs these measures would cover. The sides had no doubt that national technical means of verification made it possible to distinguish light missiles from heavy ones with sufficient confidence, and no misunderstandings could arise in this regard.

Critics have written that the SALT negotiators were naïve in not foreseeing Soviet actions under the freeze. The record does not support this claim. On December 10, 1971, we made the following argument. The Soviet provision for an MLBM sublimit and for preventing conversion of silos for light missiles to handle heavy missiles was incomplete in several respects. Lack of an agreed definition of "heavy" missiles could lead to different judgments as to launchers for new missiles. During modernization, the U.S.S.R. might wish to deploy new missiles halfway between the volume of the SS-11 and the SS-9. Lack of a definition could lead to different views as to whether the new missiles were light or heavy and become a significant political issue between the governments concerning compliance. And at this time Garthoff stressed to Kishilov the importance of this statement and argued that an explicit limit and definition were necessary. Kishilov responded that he thought his delegation had gotten the message.

We returned to the "heavy" missile definition issue again and again, saying the lack of precise definition could lead to misunderstandings which could undermine the viability of an agreement. It was informally agreed that an SS-9 was a "heavy" missile and an SS-11 was a "light" missile. But an SS-9 is three times as large as an SS-11. A cutoff point at which a new missile placed in an old launcher would be deemed to be "heavy" was never identified. One Soviet official suggested that a benchmark to distinguish heavy and light missiles might be a comparison with the size of existing light missiles. This was a constructive suggestion and we then proposed it. It proved unacceptable.

The only launchers covered in the Soviet draft freeze agreement were underground silos for ICBMs. This would permit deploying ICBMs on so-called soft or mobile launchers—above ground—which would be a relatively easy way to avoid the effect of a freeze. Many of the Soviet older ICBMs were in soft launchers.[2] In a world without any SALT limits on ICBMs, it was highly unlikely that the U.S.S.R. would deploy more ICBMs in such a vulnerable configuration. But if there were ICBM limits which did not apply to soft launchers, the Soviets might just possibly use this loophole to deploy more ICBMs. So we wanted soft launchers to be frozen as well as silos. The Soviet delegation at first disagreed, saying that the freeze was intended only to constrain ongoing programs. Neither side was then deploying ICBMs in soft launchers and therefore it was not appropriate to include them in the freeze. This was one issue we felt sure would be resolved in our favor. It was.

The Soviets had no serious interest in keeping soft launchers out of the freeze and probably took this position for bargaining purposes. Mobile launchers were quite another thing. On these, the Soviets were doing development work. They might be a prime way to deploy ICBMs in the future if silos became vulnerable to destruction by U. S. ICBMs. Minuteman accuracy was improving as the Soviets well knew from reading the unclassified American literature. Mobile ICBMs' survivability would depend not on being hardened but on being a moving, if not an undetectable, target. Banning deployment of mobile ICBMs during an interim

[2] They are very vulnerable to an explosion, even at some distance away.

freeze might be used by the Americans as a precedent for banning them in the more complete agreement, which was expected to follow shortly. The Soviets said that limiting mobile ICBMs should be a subject for discussion in future negotiations. Their side believed that these negotiations would be of such limited duration that no changes in the strategic situation would occur while they were being conducted.

Negotiating the interim freeze was not made easier by the apparent and probably real ignorance of Soviet civilian delegates about the facts as to their own ICBM and SLBM deployments and rates of construction. One Soviet delegate said that he was not even entitled to ask his people how many missiles the U.S.S.R. had deployed. They relied on information published in the United States. Not knowing their own force levels, Soviet civilians had apparently calculated that the United States' SLBM freeze proposal would have left the U.S.S.R. in a position of SLBM inferiority. In fact, it would have allowed them a somewhat larger strategic submarine fleet.

With Washington authority, I advised that the Soviet SLBM force contained about 700 launchers operational and under construction. Some Soviets seemed incredulous. Some also incorrectly assumed that a large number of the launchers were on diesel and not nuclear-propelled submarines. Anticipating an issue which complicated the final SALT haggling in Moscow, one Soviet delegate asked if, under the U.S. proposal, the Soviets could decommission four diesel submarines, each with four SLBM launchers, and replace them with one nuclear submarine with sixteen SLBMs. We had no authority to answer.

Apparently civilians on the Soviet delegation had been told that the numbers of Soviet and American ICBMs were about equal. That could only be so by not counting ICBMs on soft launchers as well as a substantial number targeted on China. This was informally confirmed by a Soviet official. These Soviets may have thought that U.S.-expressed concern over the large and growing Soviet advantage in numbers of launchers was a form of negotiating pressure.

Some flexibility cropped up in the Soviet position in the first month at Vienna. It looked as if they were seriously trying to narrow differences. They retabled their freeze proposal as a formal agreement rather than an exchange of letters. They assumed the ABM limitation would be in the form of a treaty. While a treaty was my personal preference, I was not yet able to give Semenov assurance on that source. I looked to Washington for an early answer so that this question would no longer complicate the negotiation.

Using a space travel analogy, I told Semenov that for some time we had been under the influence of the field of gravity of one body. Now I had the feeling that we were entering the gravitational field of another. It seemed that once we were out of the first we had less resistance to overcome and we could use "small jets" at our disposal to make necessary course corrections in order not to miss our objectives. He liked the analogy.

The opening ABM positions at Vienna were leftovers from the long summer in Helsinki. The U.S. proposal was to make a choice—defend your capital with 100 launchers and interceptors, or defend two ICBM fields with 200 launchers and interceptors. The U.S.S.R. proposal was for each side to defend its capital with 100 launchers and interceptors, with the United States to have one additional site to defend a field of ICBM silos, and the U.S.S.R. to have an unspecified number of additional sites to defend an equal number of silos. Two hundred launchers and interceptors were to be allowed for ICBM silo defense. Each side quickly rejected the other's proposal.

The Soviets made a significant move late in November by calling for a ban on ABM systems for the defense of the territory of the country and for defense of an individual region, except as specifically provided by treaty. This willingness explicitly to forbid a nationwide defense against missile attack seemed to reflect acceptance of the "assured destruction" strategy. Its purpose probably was to do away with any need to spell out tight radar controls and to meet our requirement that future types of ABMs be banned because they might constitute a nationwide or regional defense. If the parties waived such territorial defense, the Soviets perhaps calculated that a specific ban on future-type ABMs would not be pressed. We did not agree with this reasoning but were pleased to have the proposal, which became an important plank in the ABM Treaty. We continued to insist on radar restraints and a ban on futuristic technology and also proposed that the new Soviet language be amended to extend its obligation to forbid creation of radar infrastructure needed for a widespread ABM system. They agreed.

Some Soviet officials floated the idea of a deferral option. While the latest Soviet formula would allow sites for them to defend ICBMs and for the United States to defend Washington, the parties might agree to defer construction of these additional sites. Soviet plenary statements had been especially tailored to permit such an interpretation. But by January we were told it was "too late" for a deferral arrangement. In any event Washington showed no interest.

A month after the start at Vienna the Soviet delegation came up with an ingenious, though unacceptable, ABM approach. Each side should have 150 ABM launchers, the United States to deploy them to defend one ICBM site, the U.S.S.R. to divide them between Moscow and defense of half as many ICBM silos as the United States would protect. Since the United States was not interested in defending its capital, the Soviet proposal did not include a site for defense of Washington. The Soviets argued that we had stressed so much the stabilizing effect of ICBM defense that we should have no objection to the Soviets defending some ICBMs. The U.S.S.R. would defend only one ICBM field containing less than half the number of silos to be defended by the Americans at Grand Forks, North Dakota.

This proposal permitting them two ABM sites to our one seemed more like a "tit for tat" way of demonstrating how they felt about the U.S. "two or one" proposal than a serious offer. While clearly unacceptable it had some interesting implications. It was a departure from their principle of homogeneity (that each side must protect the same kind of facilities). It also cut in half the earlier Soviet proposed number of permitted ABM launchers and interceptors. And with this proposal came a new qualitative limitation; the ABM components for defense of ICBMs must be of a kind "appropriate for defense of silos." Later it was said that as an exception the United States could keep the ABM components then under construction at Grand Forks (which had originally been designed for area defense purposes). This unusual Soviet venture into the complex realm of qualitative controls was not followed up. Perhaps it was a feint to try to drive us off a position favoring ICBM defense and toward the Soviet preference for defense of capitals.

The Soviet delegation had argued at length that the United States "two or one" proposal was unequal. We recommended that it be equalized by including a right to switch from one type of deployment to the other. After initially disapproving of the "switch" idea, the White House authorized it. But the idea proved of no interest at the time. In 1974, when it was agreed to have only one ABM site apiece, a right to switch was included.

As the negotiating pace stepped up to meet the summit deadline our meetings grew smaller. Now exchanges took place at different levels with greater frequency. Consider the following sample of an informal exchange, greatly abbreviated, with S the Soviet and A the American.

S. The Soviet latest ABM offer is a basis for reaching agreement.

A. How about the United States "two or one" proposal?

S. If you defend ICBMs, we must have the right to defend ICBMs.

A. What happened to the notion of one site apiece?

S. You would defend ICBMs, we would defend Moscow. That would lack homogeneity. Now if one and one meant both would defend their capitals that would be different. But you are not interested in defense of Washington— and three and three is not possible either.

A. Are you suggesting two and two?

S. [With a smile.] I made no proposal.

A. What about agreeing to defer a second site?

S. Maybe, on an informal basis.

A. How will the whole negotiation come out?

S. Two and two, of course. [As it did.]

The Soviets had been doing all the running at Vienna. In an effort to inject some flexibility into our position, I wired Washington that the Soviets had accepted our proposal that the freeze be in the form of an agreement rather than an exchange of letters. They had agreed that there would be no new ICBM silos built

ʼunder the modernization and replacement license. They had agreed not to substitute launchers for heavy missiles for launchers for light missiles (but had not agreed to define them). They had hinted that their proposed freeze commencement date of July 31, 1972, might be subject to change. They had confirmed that there had been no new starts of ICBM silos since the May 20 accord. They had proposed taking a commitment against any nationwide ABM deployment. They had accepted the American proposals for restraints on early warning radars and a ban on SAM upgrade. They had shown flexibility on some drafting problems.

But Washington was not yet ready for concessions. The President must have figured that the Chinese-American rapprochement had the Soviet leaders concerned and might nudge them along toward more acceptable SALT arrangements. I assumed that one dividend expected by the White House from the Kissinger return trip to Peking in late October to prepare for the President's visit in February 1972 was a heightened Soviet interest in SALT. Probably some American SALT moves were deferred until after the President's China trip in anticipation of a more receptive Kremlin atmosphere. I question whether these Chinese trips really had much effect on the Soviet SALT mentality. And I began to wonder whether the President really wanted to have the SALT agreements entirely worked out before Moscow. That would have deprived the summit of some suspense and drama and lost him an opportunity to demonstrate his skill as a negotiator.

Sir Winston Churchill said, "We arm to parley." The Pentagon fully subscribed to that doctrine. A SALT bargaining tactic which still is in use is to brandish the defense budget to remind the Soviets of what an open competition might be like if SALT failed. In fact, the very existence of SALT seemed an assist to weaponeers who for some time had been meeting public, congressional and even White House resistance to new strategic programs. The idea of a new generation of submarine-launched ballistic missiles known as the undersea long-range missile system to replace the Polaris/Poseidon systems was then being backed by the Navy. New submarines would be needed when Polaris reached the end of its "hull life," beginning in the mid to late 1980s. This new submarine system is now designated Trident. A perceived negotiating need to face the Soviets with an oncoming pluperfect missile system as a "persuader" or "bargaining chip" accelerated Trident by some years.

The defense budget for fiscal year 1973 for the first time in some years called for increased funding for the strategic forces. A 16 per cent increase of $1.2 billion was asked, the largest part for Trident—$942 million, up from $105 million the previous year. Secretary Laird, disturbed about SALT, called for acceleration of this program so that the first submarine would be commissioned in 1978 instead of 1981 as previously planned. He said, "The continuing Soviet strategic offensive force build-up, with its long-term implications, convinced us that we need to undertake a major new strategic initiative." Here was another step in the process of bargaining chipmanship that has made SALT a cause of increases in certain strategic weapons. It was, to say the least, unusual to start a shipbuilding program to replace a class of ships still being modernized (by installing MIRVed Poseidon missiles). More than a few critics questioned whether such an accelerated Trident schedule was necessary, how much more it would cost, and whether these new boats would be additions and not replacements. These questions are still being asked.

Although I was not consulted about the likely effect of defense budget increases on the Soviet SALT position, in general I took the line that appropriations should depend on military requirements unvarnished with calculations as to their possible effect on Soviet SALT positions. I felt that the original tempo for Trident was adequate, because the Poseidon MIRV program was not yet completed. There was no sign that existing American submarines were becoming vulnerable to Soviet anti-submarine warfare capabilities. I saw no evidence that this acceleration would have any effect on the negotiation. It was just a case of increased military spending because an arms control negotiation was in train. There are others. Ten days after the SALT I agreements were signed, Secretary Laird was to tell a House subcommittee that "Just as the Moscow agreements were made possible by our successful action in such programs as Safeguard, Poseidon and Minuteman III, these future negotiations to which we are pledged can only succeed if we are equally successful in implementing such programs as the Trident system, the B-1 bomber, NCA defense, site de-

fense, SLCM, and accelerated satellite basing of strategic bombers."

In early December an eleven-month crisis in South Asia over
the status of East Pakistan, now Bangladesh, erupted into a four-
teen-day war between Pakistan and India. Throughout the year
the Soviet Union and the United States had maneuvered to
influence events on the subcontinent. U.S. policy was to try to
persuade the Indian government to acquiesce in a negotiated settlement and Washington attempted to signal both New Delhi and
Moscow that the United States was not prepared to accept total
defeat for Pakistan or its dismemberment. After a visit by a Soviet Deputy Foreign Minister, the Indian External Affairs Minister had told a parliamentary committee that India could count
on the U.S.S.R. for total support in the event of conflict with
Pakistan.

Both superpowers sent naval forces into the Indian Ocean and
Bay of Bengal. A U.S. task force, including the nuclear carrier
Enterprise, arrived on December 15, one day before the hostilities
ended. The Soviets initially had reinforced a small flotilla of de-
stroyers in the Indian Ocean. Then they dispatched two missile
cruiser task groups from Vladivostok. The U.S.S.R. also vetoed
three American-sponsored UN Security Council resolutions calling for a cease-fire and negotiations. The SALT negotiating partners found themselves with a real crisis which might lead to military confrontation.

On December 13, I received an urgent message from the White
House saying that it was important that the U.S. delegation maintain a cool and somewhat more reserved attitude toward their Soviet counterparts in view of the situation in South Asia. This
demeanor should be adopted immediately and maintained until
further notice. The President left it up to me how to implement
this instruction.

At the next meeting the delegates adopted what they considered
an appropriately chilly demeanor. We had no way of knowing if
the Soviets felt it. I mentioned to Semenov that the South Asia
situation could have negative implications for Soviet-American
relations and SALT. He referred to the agreed "no linkage" pol-

icy and said there were other contacts between our governments to handle questions like that.

I reported the exchange to Washington. It provoked a signal from the White House that the President was "alarmed" that I had raised this linkage with Semenov. I was asked to refrain from further discussion of the matter but rather to initiate a stalling posture without attributing the shift in any way to events in South Asia. This was not difficult since the U.S. position had been in neutral for some time. I expressed regret and asked Kissinger why the President had been alarmed. There was no answer. Some weeks later he advised that "alarmed" was perhaps not the right word. The crisis over, we dropped the chill and got back to "serious and businesslike" conduct of the talks. I question whether having negotiating delegations adopt postures of this sort to reflect a Washington attitude is a very useful technique.

As Christmas approached, the question of a recess gave rise to a squabble. I had planned on the delegation's returning to Washington to permit people to be with their families for the holidays. A number had been away from home in the aggregate for one out of the past two years. Semenov reacted very negatively.

He said that our recesses sometimes had not been long enough for Smith, who had found himself in a position where for the first two or three weeks of a negotiating round he had been unable to develop his position because the work in Washington had not yet been completed. I replied by saying I couldn't understand how Semenov was so well informed about the reason for the timing of U.S. proposals. I thought that it was the business of each side to decide for itself when to present positions and in fact recesses in the past had nothing to do with that timing. I said his remarks were inappropriate.

Semenov felt that the session should continue without break. If I insisted on suspension, he would forward the proposal to Moscow with negative views attached. Probably his harsh line reflected his view of the tempo required by the May summit deadline. When I pointed out that a recess would permit consultations in Washington, he undiplomatically expressed doubts that they would take place during the holidays. I was puzzled and amused at this generation of more heat in discussing a holiday recess than any substantive question. I finally had to enlist the President's support and the delegation went home briefly for the holidays.

Before returning to Vienna, I discussed the state of play with President Nixon. He seemed to be in a negative frame of mind about Soviet policy, which I thought natural just after the recent Indian crisis. He stressed the strong tendency developing in Washington to distrust Soviet motivations. He referred to the anti-SALT effort of a conservative group called the American Security Council which had important financing. A number of senators had expressed worries to him about SALT. I again urged the importance of adding congressional advisers to the delegation. The President speculated that Senators Stennis and Cooper would be good candidates. Nothing came of it. He was reluctant to make any final decision on the ABM site question because it would leak and "the fat would be in the fire." I assumed he meant the congressional fire. I asked him if the Indian episode had affected his thinking about SALT. He felt we should proceed on our chosen course. But clearly world events were linked and he expressed some doubt that one could have confidence in the U.S.S.R. in SALT if it was aiming to outmaneuver us in other areas.

The second phase of this Vienna round lasted only four weeks. The Soviet delegation realized that we did not intend to budge from the "two or one" ABM position, and the sides spent the rest of their ABM time at Vienna working on other than site questions. We were finally authorized to advise the Soviets that the ABM limitation could be in the form of a treaty.

The ABM futuristics question was now resolved to our satisfaction. The Soviets urged that including unknown matters (like future ABM technology) in a treaty would create endless arguments and suspicions. Such an important document must be precise. As for my citing the Outer Space and Seabeds Treaties as precedents, their obligations were much more general than ABM limitations and dealt with weapons of mass destruction. The sides could not discuss questions not known to anyone. Our task was to limit deployment of known ABM components. The ABM Treaty would be of unlimited duration and the sides were agreed on provisions for amendments and periodic reviews. Systems that might be developed using other than current types of ABM components could be discussed in the Standing Consultative Commission. Accordingly, they considered the proposed futuristics provision not suitable for inclusion in the treaty.

I argued that in that event there would be a tendency on both sides to design systems that were not limited. I was sure Semenov would recall the experience with the naval limitation treaties of the 1920s and 1930s. Naval architects had gone to work to design around them. Semenov asked if I had in mind circumvention of the treaty. I said that technically this would not be circumvention, but more like a license to find ways of doing things that were not prohibited. I had once heard President Eisenhower say that wars have a dynamic of their own. I believed that weapons design also had a dynamic of its own. It was in the interests of both countries to outlaw future ABM systems before they were deployed.

An agreed interpretation was finally worked out.

In order to insure fulfillment of the obligation not to deploy ABM systems and their components except as provided in Article III of the treaty, the parties agreed that in the event ABM systems based on other physical principles and including components capable of substituting for ABM interceptor missiles, ABM launchers, or ABM radars are created in the future, specific limitations on such systems and their components would be subject to discussion in accordance with Article XIII and agreement in accordance with Article XIV of the Treaty.

Under Article III of the treaty the sides agreed not to deploy ABM systems or their components with two exceptions, both of which only permit ABM systems which use launchers, interceptors and radars. Thus, taking the agreed understanding together with Article III, systems employing possible future types of components to perform the functions of launchers, interceptors and radars are banned unless the treaty is amended. This statement was initialed by Semenov and me on the day the SALT agreements were signed. As an initialed common understanding, it is as binding as the text of the ABM Treaty.

At the delegation's recommendation, the U. S. SLBM position was now changed to freeze launcher numbers only. New submarines could be constructed as long as SLBM launchers did not exceed the number on the freeze date. Washington may have considered this change not only as added inducement to the U.S.S.R. to freeze SLBM launchers, but also to assure that the freeze could not be interpreted as restraining in any way our Trident submarine program. Once we had agreed that the Soviets could continue to build some submarines, I thought the way was clear for SLBMs to be included in the freeze. But it was some time before that happened.

Faced with continued Soviet refusal to include SLBMs, the delegation, with General Allison dissenting, recommended to Washington that it explore with the Soviets the idea of providing for a right to substitute SLBM launchers for ICBM launchers that would be decommissioned. This so-called one-way freedom-to-mix concept had been in United States proposals for a comprehensive treaty limiting both offensive and defensive arms. It was dropped when the lesser goal of an interim freeze on offensive arms was established by the May 20 accord. General Allison believed that it would tend to solidify the idea of unequal aggregates for the two sides, with prejudice to our ability to meet expected future Soviet claims to have more strategic launchers than the United States because of America's forward-based systems. He believed it would hurt United States chances of negotiating equal aggregates for strategic forces in the follow-on negotiations. If this substitution idea was to be pushed, he felt it should be based on equal aggregates even during the freeze. The problem with Allison's approach was that it was not negotiable. Washington did not reply but this substitution idea was shortly to be accepted when Kissinger again tried his hand at SALT negotiating.

On January 6, I suggested to the White House that I explore, on a non-committal basis, Soviet interest in an interim freeze with each side holding to the aggregate number of ICBM and SLBM launchers which were operational or under construction on a date to be agreed, with a one-way freedom to mix from land-based to sea-based launchers. At a Verification Panel meeting on December 23, Paul Nitze reported that Secretary Laird had said he would agree to this approach even though the Soviet aggregate would substantially exceed the United States aggregate. Kissinger advised that the President's view was that non-committal explorations get to be committal very quickly, but if I kept this in mind, he did not object to my exploring an interim freeze of this nature. In order to avoid confusion, Kissinger asked me to send this suggestion to Washington through normal channels, so that I could be instructed formally. Before Washington formally authorized the exploration, however, the session at Vienna had ended. The Joint Chiefs at this time opposed any freeze that would result in unequal numbers because it would be a bad precedent. Guidance for the next Helsinki phase did not authorize exploration of this concept.

I privately told Semenov that I favored a short-term freeze level for Soviet SLBMs at about the same as the U.S. level. I said that the United States would hardly be in a position to accept a freeze which would leave us in a numerically inferior position in both systems of strategic missiles. Semenov must know that objections would be raised in Washington, not only in the White House but in Congress where there were many strong supporters of SALT. I foresaw great difficulties in accepting a freeze in which the U.S.S.R. could within a year build up to a total of fifty submarines while the United States would be left with forty-one. Failure to achieve progress on SLBMs would tend to strengthen the position of those who were skeptical about SALT.

I pointed out that there were forces building up to accelerate new American programs. That was why I was anxious to get back to Washington with clear evidence that the Soviet side was really interested in leveling off its build-up of launchers. I urged Semenov to look at our concern over their missile programs in a historical perspective. I had the feeling that the time for strategic arms limitations was growing short. For the past twenty years I had been watching this competition. The United States had made some mistakes in structuring its forces, just as the Soviet side had made some mistakes. In part, on our side, this had been based on ignorance of the true state of Soviet armaments. Sometimes we had taken at face value what Soviet leaders had said about their forces. Then had come the "missile gap" and later the build-up of the Moscow ABM system. We had felt that we would need many more offensive arms to overcome an ABM defense. Now we were faced with the prospect of another spiral, owing to the continuing build-up of Soviet forces.

Even such pro-arms control men as Senators Hubert Humphrey and John Sherman Cooper were now concerned about this build-up. It was natural to expect Secretary Laird to express concern but when Senator Cooper did it was an important signal. It was an exacting process to try to understand the implications of all these programs. It went far beyond any attempt to reach agreement on the basis of interpreting the May 20 understanding. For all these reasons, I urged Semenov to look at the situation from a broader perspective. It seemed to me that engaging in a renewed competition in offensive missile launchers represented an absurdity at a time when both sides had more than enough.

He responded that he was a Marxist who adhered to the historical approach to events. From this approach, both of us were using the same method but we were reaching different conclusions. I said that if Marx could have anticipated creation of nuclear weapons, he as well as other historians would have changed many of their views. I recalled to myself the earlier comment of one Soviet to the effect that Marx regrettably had no knowledge of the physical sciences.

Before leaving Vienna and with authority from Washington, I privately advised Semenov that there was some flexibility in the U.S. position on the starting date for the freeze. This would permit the U.S.S.R. to start construction on some additional submarines. Semenov merely observed vaguely that "some problems" have a tendency to be self-solving, which I took to be a positive observation.

During the January 1972 session in Vienna, I received the following from Kissinger: "A number of news men including Joe Kraft and Chalmers Roberts have reported that the SALT Delegation is under the impression that they have to stall until the President's trip to Peking. You who know better than anyone that this is totally untrue should make every effort among the members to dispel this impression." I briefly replied, "Will do," and added, "Kraft and Roberts don't get any information from this Delegation."

It was clear by now that the SALT leaks were coming out of Washington and not from the SALT delegation in Helsinki or Vienna. The massive press attendance at the SALT opening round in Helsinki in 1969 had dwindled almost to zero when it became apparent that the only information to be given out there was that the meetings had been serious and businesslike.

A few weeks after this Vienna session ended, the following letter was received from the President.

Honolulu White House

February 19, 1972

Dear Gerry:

I was shocked to read a report in the NEW YORK TIMES about an ABM compromise, which I understand from reports here came from a source with ACDA.

It is imperative that you impose total discipline on your associates and staff, so that leaks and "inside dope" stories of this type will be stopped. They can only have the effect of compromising our negotiating position.

On my return from China I would like to have a recommendation from you as to how you can stop this kind of leak in the future.

/s/ RICHARD NIXON

I was struck by the fact that the President could take time from his China preparation for what seemed like a secondary matter. This leak was not as harmful as others. It had given only a fragmentary and inaccurate picture of the state of the negotiation. I wondered what friend of mine had given the President the "reports" that a source in ACDA was to blame.

I replied, "I believe you know how seriously I take the question of leaks in connection with SALT. I have hammered away at this subject to the staff of this agency for the last two and one half years. I think our record has been excellent. Therefore, I am especially disturbed that you have received reports that the New York Times article in question came from a source within ACDA. I trust that to help ACDA's investigation of this matter I will be advised of the nature of these reports." I never was.

At my last conversation with Semenov at Vienna, I had said that the Soviet approach to the MLBM question was putting a very heavy burden on national means of verification, requiring them not only to ascertain facts but also to make judgments. We could ask our national means of verification whether they saw missile launchers. They would respond yes. We could ask if a given launcher was for a heavy missile. A computer would then ask: What is a heavy missile? We would be forced to say that we did not know. I hoped that at the next phase of SALT we could get agreement on a definite criterion.

By the close of this round on February 4, some progress had been made. To summarize—the Soviet delegation had made it clear that an agreed freeze on ICBMs was acceptable. They accepted the U.S. proposal that the freeze be reflected in a formal agreement. They agreed to a prohibition on the relocation of ICBM silos and an obligation not to convert launchers for "light" ICBMs into launchers for "heavy" ICBMs. A Special Working Group had agreed on some language of a Joint Draft Text for the interim freeze. Agreement had been reached to prohibit ABM defense of the territory of either nation or creation of a base for such a defense; to prohibit ABM defense of a region except as the treaty permitted; and to ban deployment of futuristic components for ABM systems unless the treaty were amended. Differences had been narrowed on radar controls although serious issues remained.

Some progress had been made, although not on the central issues of ABM levels, SLBMs, and replacement and modernization. Each side was still putting off final commitments until efforts had been exhausted to gain preferred positions. The summit deadline was still far enough away—some three months—to permit holding back from final moves that might prove painful to important groups on both sides. But the expectation of both delegations was that their governments would now make adjustments necessary to permit conclusion of agreements either before or during the Moscow summit in May.

By February 1972 we had come a good way from the statements made during the Kissinger-Dobrynin back-channel talks a year earlier that the United States could accept a freeze which did not include SLBMs, which would last one and a half to two years, which placed no limits on modernization and replacement; and which did not provide a special right to withdraw from the

ABM Treaty if the follow-on negotiations for offensive weapon limitation failed. Now we were pressing for including SLBMs, for an indefinite freeze duration, for sharp limitations on modernization and replacement and a special withdrawal clause. In fact, these were among the remaining key issues.

LAST ROUND IN HELSINKI

March–April 1972

When we resumed at Helsinki late in March 1972 for the seventh and final round, the major open issues on the ABM Treaty were still how many sites would be permitted and where they would be; how many launchers and interceptors would be allowed; and the radar restraints discussed previously. On the offensive side, would SLBM submarines and their launchers be included in the freeze; would there be an effective ceiling on heavy missile launchers; when would the freeze start; and how long would it last?

Before the President issued guidance for the final round, I wrote him that ABM levels placing the lowest possible ceilings on Soviet ABMs would be to America's benefit. I thought the U.S.S.R. was still willing to settle for one ABM site. We should not press for a higher ABM level in the absence of a clear showing of U.S. military advantage. Funds for a second U.S. site would be better spent on other strategic programs. I predicted that if we had to go for a second site it would be Washington, which would not be favored by the Congress (which proved to be the case). I believed the Soviets would accept a "one for one" proposal permitting a subsequent switch from Grand Forks to Washington (which turned out to be the follow-on arrangement worked out in 1974). Secretary Laird was still pushing for an ICBM defense option giving both sides a right, after a short time and in the absence of agreement to the contrary, to deploy interceptors and radars in unlimited numbers at one ICBM defense site. My message to the President also questioned the wisdom of giving the Soviets such a blank check and expressed doubt that the Senate would ratify a treaty containing such an open-ended feature.

Main White House interest in the spring of 1972 was to include Soviet strategic submarines and their launchers in the freeze. Our strategy for the first three weeks was to try to use our ABM bargaining power to this end. I doubt that the Soviets' eventual agreement to include submarines was induced by our agreeing to their deploying ABMs to defend ICBMs. Two years later the Soviets agreed to give up this right to a second ABM site. All of this suggests that negotiating about ABMs in 1972 was mostly posturing as the sides tried to make up their minds as to what sort of offensive freeze arrangements would be to their best advantage.

At a National Security Council meeting on March 17, I set out the Helsinki guidance I thought we should have. Lest the whole SALT negotiation collapse over the SLBM issue, I stressed that first SALT agreements would be valuable even if they did not include SLBMs. I again asked to be kept informed if other negotiating channels were used.

Just before leaving for Finland the principal delegates met with the President. He directed me to suggest privately to Semenov that if the U.S.S.R. would agree to include SLBMs the United States would change its ABM position to take into account Soviet interest in defending some ICBMs. The President continued to believe that the key to SALT was U.S. willingness to restrain its ABM program if the Soviets would limit their offensive launcher build-up. His instructions were for us to try to get everything settled at Helsinki. He was not anticipating any SALT negotiations at Moscow. But that was not the way it worked out.

Many of us working on SALT were concerned over the prospect of a summit negotiation. I suppose the Soviets were also aware of the risks. However, if negotiation of SALT at the summit proved necessary, they might consider that it could work to their advantage, especially if focused on a small number of major unresolved questions. In 1960 there had been speculation that the abortive Eisenhower-Khrushchev Paris summit might have helped to elect President Kennedy. The Kremlin might calculate that Nixon, facing a national election, was under pressure not to return empty-handed, the more so in view of his year-old public statement, "There will be a SALT agreement."

The delegation's guidance was to press at the outset for the offensive freeze. We were to make clear that the American final decision on ABMs would be heavily influenced by the scope of the freeze. If Semenov showed interest in the President's SLBM-ABM trade-off proposition, I was authorized to propose a new set of ABM options: either capital defense and one ICBM defense site, or two ICBM defense sites, with a maximum of 100 launchers and interceptors at each site.

The previous U.S. freeze proposal had called for a cutoff of new launcher starts as of July 1, 1971, a date now well behind us. So we were to propose that no new ICBM silos or SLBM submarines be started after the date the freeze agreement was signed. In view of Soviet opposition to express provisions in the agreement against (a) changes in ICBM silo dimensions and (b) defining heavy missiles as those with a volume greater than seventy cubic meters, we were to propose agreed interpretive statements limiting increases in the depth or diameter of ICBM silos and defining heavy missiles as those of a size greater than the Soviet SS-11. We were to continue efforts to include in the limitations mobile ICBMs and those on soft launchers (above ground). The duration of the freeze, unless replaced by a more complete follow-on agreement, should be five years. This was thought by some to be a concession from the earlier U.S. position calling for a freeze of indefinite length to the Soviet position calling for one and a half to two years.

At the first plenary meeting, March 28, I had a sad report. "I would like at the start to record with sorrow the death during the post-Vienna recess of a principal United States SALT delegate, Ambassador Llewellyn E. Thompson, who spent much of his life's energies in trying to improve relations between our two countries." Tommy Thompson was a great diplomat and a good friend. He had been involved in SALT since the first effort during the Johnson Administration. He had come out of retirement to help the Nixon Administration. His extended service in the U.S.S.R., his lively understanding of Soviet motivations and large negotiating experience made his a great contribution to the delegation's work.

My opening presentation made clear that SLBMs were now the key issue. In view of the continuing Soviet build-up in numbers of SLBM launchers, the position of the U.S.S.R. that it would be inappropriate to include SLBM launchers was the most serious obstacle to reaching agreements. We labeled our new freeze date as "a significant change" and a "substantial step" reflecting many months of construction on Soviet submarines started since the previously proposed cutoff date of July 1, 1971.

After the plenary, Semenov remarked that the concluding phase of a negotiation was always very delicate. I said that I had read somewhere that Foreign Minister Gromyko once said that the last twenty minutes of a negotiation were the most important. I hoped these last twenty minutes would be accomplished here in Helsinki rather than in Moscow, that he and I could work out matters here and not get our leaders involved in negotiating on highly technical matters during the summit. Semenov replied that Gromyko's remark had been made by a minister who usually took part in negotiations which did not last as long as SALT. He would say it was the last twenty days that would be decisive. While the delegations were to be regarded as preparatory bodies, of course, and the adoption of final decisions and documents would take place at a higher level, he agreed that it would be useful for us to prepare the issues in such a way that our highest authorities would not find it difficult to reach final decisions. That did not turn out to be the case.

I explained how our ABM decisions would be heavily influenced by the terms of the freeze. If the Soviet side could meet our considerations in regard to submarine missile launchers, we would be able to move to meet what I understood to be Soviet interest in ABM protection of ICBM sites. Semenov responded that he believed we should move in all directions and that we could succeed in preparing all the necessary materials. I said I was authorized to give him specifics of a new position on ABMs which should meet a number of Soviet concerns, but only if the Soviet side met this key issue of submarine-based launchers.

Linkage of ABM levels to SLBM inclusion was then quickly rejected. Semenov said he understood my interest in discussing what should be covered in an interim agreement. In his view, however, we should not tie issues together in a knot or resort to "packaging." Over the next few weeks he continued to maintain that it would be quite enough to have a freeze only on ICBM launchers while we continued to negotiate for comprehensive offensive limitations.

I have said that I doubted that this offer of flexibility on ABMs had substantial effect on Soviet thinking about SLBMs. But each delegation now fully realized that an ABM treaty satisfactory to both could be quickly negotiated if the SLBM question was resolved. By this time it also must have been fairly clear to the Soviets, as it was to us, that the negotiation would result in both sides having the right to deploy ABMs at two sites. There no longer seemed any chance for an ABM ban and one site apiece seemed ruled out because it would have to be for capital defense, which the United States had repeatedly refused. There was no real leverage left in this issue of ABM levels. We had extracted about all we could reasonably expect for agreeing to limit our domestically unpopular ABM program. In fact, the new position left the implication that we might agree to some kind of ABM treaty even if SLBMs were not included. A Soviet official asked what ABM levels we would propose in that event. He got a curt reply. We had no alternative ABM position based on that assumption.

Other ABM issues including a provision for withdrawal from the treaty were important but secondary. For a short while, as we waited for the Soviet response, the delegation stood on the U.S. proposal of August 20, 1971, offering a choice between defense of two ICBM sites or defense of the national capital. The Soviets quickly reaffirmed their December 15, 1971, proposal for one American site to defend ICBMs at Grand Forks and two Soviet sites, one for Moscow and the other to defend half as many ICBM silos as the United States would defend. The Soviets complained that the U.S. side had never commented on this proposal. So we proceeded to leave them in no doubt as to its unacceptability.

The Soviets on April 7 made a new ABM proposal—that both

sides defend their capitals and some ICBM silos with a total of 225 launchers and interceptor missiles. The United States would have a Washington defense and one site to defend ICBMs while the U.S.S.R. would have two ICBM defense sites in addition to an ABM system around Moscow. This Soviet proposal had a deferral provision. For three to five years, the United States would defer the Washington deployment and the U.S.S.R. would defer its ICBM defenses. There would also be some unspecified limits on the range of interceptors deployed for ICBM defense to prevent them from being used to defend a whole region.

The Soviet delegates now parroted American arguments that defense of ICBM silos would contribute to stability. They said that we had convinced them of the need for ICBM defense, but it was not the number of sites that contributed most to deterrence but the number of ICBM silos to be defended. They needed two ABM sites for ICBM defense since their practice, for geographic reasons, was not to deploy as many ICBM silos in one field as did the Americans.

Some observers have said that American arguments in favor of defense of ICBM silos did in fact convert the Soviets to favor such a defense. I doubt it. This was on a par with a Soviet observation that in 1969 the Nixon Administration had made so much of the need for defense against a light attack from China that the Soviets began to think of their Moscow defense system in those terms. The Soviets were searching more for an appearance of ABM equality than for an ABM force for defense of ICBM silos that would be of real military significance. This seems borne out by the fact that only two years after the ABM Treaty was concluded the Soviets agreed not to deploy any ABMs to defend ICBM silos. As we jockeyed around the ABM site issue, I thought there might be something to the informal observation of a Soviet that the details of the ABM Treaty did not matter much since the ABMs allowed would be unable to defend either country against large-scale attack.

Needless to say, the idea of the U.S.S.R. having more ABM sites than the United States was just as uninteresting to us as our earlier unequal ABM proposals had been to the Soviets. I told Semenov that he must think I was very persuasive if he estimated that I could sell the Administration and the Congress a proposal which would provide three ABM sites for the Soviet Union and only two for the United States. I would not sound very convincing if I were to tell the President that it was a good idea, immediately after entry into force of the ABM Treaty, for us to stop construction of our second ABM site at Malmstrom Air Force Base while the Soviet Union could immediately begin construction of its second site. And it was difficult to see how the new Soviet proposal satisfied their own principle of equality. Semenov replied that the fault evidently was his, in that he had been unable to convince me that this proposal was constructive. He wanted to emphasize that we were evidently using different methods of calculation: the U.S. side counted ABM sites, while the Soviet side was counting the number of ICBM silos protected by ABMs. He argued that the latter method was more in keeping with the objective of deterrence. After all, he said, an ABM base in itself could not fulfill the function of deterrence, as did protected ICBM launchers.

We then turned again to radar restraints. A possible compromise on OLPAR restraint had been under discussion informally. To meet the Soviet objections to setting a numerical ceiling of one million watt-meters squared, the agreement might use as a criterion the missile site radar (MSR), the smaller of the two American system radars having a power-aperture product of two to three million watt-meters squared.

A Soviet introduced this subject at a meeting on April 4. He stated that constraints on radars for non-ABM purposes, especially air defense, were unacceptable. The Soviet delegation could not agree to numerical criteria in the form of a power-aperture product, or adoption of a list of characteristics, or even a comparison with U.S. radar to be used for limiting ABM radars. To meet U.S. considerations, the Soviets had agreed not to test non-ABM radars in an ABM mode. This would be adequate to preclude circumvention of constraints on ABM radars.

Nitze replied that the United States had reviewed its position on OLPARs. This had convinced us of the importance to both sides of insuring that the deployment of such radars was appropriately restrained. We were prepared to consider an interpretive statement rather than a provision in the agreement, but resolution of the OLPAR issue in some form was a sine qua non for agreement.

The Soviets informally handed over the following draft interpretive statement on OLPARs on April 8.

> Deployment by each party of phased-array radars having a potential (a product of mean emitted power and antenna area) equal to or exceeding the potential of the smallest modern ABM phased-array radar of the respective parties now deployed within Modern ABM Radar Complexes would not be made . . . except for the purposes of tracking objects in space or for utilization as national technical means of verification.

We said that if this referred to the Soviet radar under construction near Chekhov, it was at least ten times more powerful than an American MSR. Indeed, any standard for the U.S.S.R. different from that for the United States would not be acceptable. While the Soviets seemed to be moving in the right direction, the draft was unacceptable. It might be acceptable if the Soviets deleted the phrase "of the respective parties." Then the American MSR would be the standard for both sides. The Soviets replied that it had taken a great deal of difficult consultation in Moscow to reach the present text. MSR was too low in power to be the criterion for OLPARs. There obviously was a good deal of bargaining ahead.

About this time Semenov asked for more information about the hint of a possible change in the United States ABM position. I repeated that if the Soviets would agree to include SLBM launchers in the freeze we were prepared to modify our ABM position to take account of the Soviet interest in defending ICBMs. If Semenov was interested, I could provide more detail quite soon. Semenov replied that each side had to be interested in matters of interest to the other side. He would be a poor negotiator if he failed to pay attention to everything I had to say on one subject or another. Of course, to hear did not mean to agree, but it did mean to know.

On the basis of this conversation, Washington authorized presentation of an ABM proposal calling for two sites on each side, either to defend the capital and one ICBM field or to defend two ICBM fields. There had as yet been no sign of movement by the U.S.S.R. on offensive freeze issues. The notion that we could leverage a better freeze agreement with ABM moves had not worked. Now we went simply on the assumption that SLBM launchers would somehow be included. That was an explicit condition of our new ABM offer tabled on April 11. At least we were moving in the right direction with a proposal for two ABM sites for each side. Four days later Semenov flew to Moscow for consultations with his "highest authorities." Before leaving, he told me that only levels and the character of sites were left in the ABM negotiation. I added that very serious radar control problems remained.

We continued to argue the importance of a definition of what constituted a "heavy" ICBM. The sides could not expect national technical means to distinguish heavy from light missile launchers if the difference was not defined. The United States had proposed a provision that all missiles greater than seventy cubic meters in volume be classed as heavy. An agreed interpretive statement might be suitable to handle this problem. The United States could also accept a non-quantitative definition of a heavy missile as one with a volume greater than the Soviet SS-11, or the largest light missile currently deployed by either side. We assured the Soviets that we were prepared to explore any other alternatives they might have in mind and the sides should agree to ban increases in the depth or interior diameter of ICBM launchers. Such a prohibition would not impede normal modernization procedures such as silo hardening. And we were prepared to consider alternative formulations for handling this concern.

On April 4, Semenov replied that there was no need to introduce additional details on missile volume or silo depth and diameter. Such details could only complicate reaching agreement. The subject of the obligation (ICBM launchers) was clear and did not require additional delimitation since modernization and replacement would be accomplished within the framework of the obligations assumed.

Turning to soft and mobile ICBM launchers, Semenov said that expansion of the types of systems to be frozen could cause complications and delay agreement. In light of the May 20, 1971, understanding, it was hardly feasible to consider all offensive systems. There was no need to discuss land-based mobile launchers. Soft launchers could not be a cause of concern since the sides had long since stopped adding soft launchers. He understood that the United States did not intend to renew deployment of such systems. That exhausted the question. The Soviet side believed that a freeze on fixed land-based ICBM silo launchers was sufficient for this phase and that agreement should be concluded on that basis.

We said that, if the Soviets did not intend to deploy mobiles, why not include them in the freeze? If they did so intend, the introduction of a new ICBM system during the freeze would raise a serious issue. We would consider this contrary to the purpose of the freeze and soft ICBM launchers should also be included.

The Soviets proposed a duration of three years for the interim freeze, labeling this a "major move." It wasn't, and we continued to press the case for a five-year duration. It was argued that the shorter Soviet duration might lead to a lapse of the freeze before a follow-on treaty could be reached. The follow-on negotiations would aim to conclude an agreement in the shortest possible time, but refractory issues postponed by the May 20, 1971 accord remained.

The U.S. proposal for a special withdrawal clause in the ABM Treaty allowing a side to terminate if an agreement providing for more complete offensive limitations was not reached within five years remained on the table. The Soviets continued to object, saying that the sides agreed that the ABM Treaty would be of indefinite duration with withdrawal possible under a supreme national interest escape clause. The spirit of the May 20 understanding as well as the already agreed Joint Draft Text provisions contemplated that the ABM Treaty would be an independent document. Including a provision making the duration of that treaty dependent on reaching understanding on offensive arms was unfounded.

For two weeks after the start of this Helsinki round the Soviet delegation did not address the SLBM launcher question in any detail. Then one day my ears pricked up when a Soviet delegate said that it would be "sufficient" to have an interim freeze on ICBMs to accompany an ABM treaty. Before that, the Soviets had used the word "appropriate" in making this point. I asked Semenov if the choice of the word "sufficient" had been made advisedly, to hint at a change in the Soviet position. He said he would send me a copy of the paper the official had been reading from. After the interpreters left he said in Russian, "You have good antennae." At last the Soviets might be moving on SLBM inclusion! Hopes were raised that a freeze agreement was now in sight. On reporting the episode to the White House, I cautiously estimated that the Soviets wanted to keep the SLBM question "at least in neutral."

But for some days the Soviets continued to argue often and at length against including SLBM launchers. As the world's greatest land power, they were willing not to construct more launchers for land-based ICBMs. This represented a major step. The issue was very complex. Submarine capabilities depended not only on numbers of submarines and launchers but on geographic considerations. The U.S. chief of naval operations, Admiral Zumwalt, had recently cited certain U.S. geographical advantages. Forward bases for American submarines were a significant advantage. Another part of this complicated equation were the strategic submarines of America's NATO allies, Britain and France. On this score the Soviets cited Secretary of Defense Laird as to the allies' contribution to America's overall strategic defense posture. And a side could build additional submarines for its allies and thus circumvent a freeze. This last argument, I thought, was more of a sideswipe at our constant efforts to close loopholes than a real Soviet concern, especially since the freeze was to be only for a short term. The Soviet delegation continued to demonstrate dexterity in arguing that SLBM limitations should be postponed for the follow-on negotiation for a comprehensive offensive treaty.

Semenov and I met for a three-hour working dinner on the evening of April 10. After some leisurely small talk he asked why I did not think that a freeze limited to ICBM silo launchers would not create a more favorable psychological atmosphere for further negotiation on more complete limitations on offensive arms and create greater confidence between our two countries, thereby facilitating the solution of greater tasks before us. The best answer I could give was that we would have to tell our people that the Soviet Union had a numerical advantage in areas that we proposed to freeze, and approximate equality in the field that would not be frozen. The fact was that the Soviet Union had a large advantage in numbers of ICBMs and also now had slightly more launchers on submarines in operation and under construction than the United States. It was difficult for our people to understand why the Soviet Union should be free to continue to build up numbers of SLBMs.

If we looked further ahead, in a few years one might see U.S. shipyards producing submarines again and our people would be saying that this had not been a good arrangement. If they felt that way about the first important arms negotiation between the Soviet Union and the United States, that would not bode well for further agreements. I would like to make a good start because, as Semenov would agree, the real promise of our negotiations was what we could do in a second and third and fourth arms control agreement. We were reaching for a new relationship between our two countries, and yet there was a possibility that we would only work out an agreement that would subsequently turn sour, just as some marital arrangements do in spite of good prospects at the beginning.

Semenov thought there was a misunderstanding. The Soviet Union was the greatest land power in the world, and it was precisely land-based ICBM silo launchers that the Soviet side proposed to freeze. That was a significant step, and it would be a major factor in building confidence between our two countries and guiding us toward the solution of other problems. We had little more than a month's time left before the meeting between our highest authorities. If we were to link questions on which the sides could find agreement with those which were not agreed, we would find ourselves running out of time and we would not be able to work out the agreements for President Nixon's visit to Moscow. Things could fall apart.

Later, after Semenov repeated for the third time that it was most significant for the greatest land power in the world to limit its ICBMs, I rejoined that this reminded me that I had been reading recently that the Soviet Union was also a great sea power. Perhaps the best evidence of that latter fact would be provided if the Soviet Union agreed to a freeze on sea-based as well as land-based strategic offensive arms.

After hearing these Soviet SLBM arguments for some time, I sent along some views to the White House. The Soviet "neutral-negative" attitude toward including submarines in the negotiating moratorium continued to be puzzling. I said I had just about concluded that the U.S.S.R. would not agree to include SLBMs in a formal freeze. At best, they might agree at the summit to some kind of declaration about restraint in submarine construction while the offensive arms negotiation proceeded. Here I was wrong.

On April 8 after extended consultation with the other delegates I wrote Kissinger that the factor blocking an ABM settlement was our wanting to defend ICBMs in two fields while the Soviets could defend fewer ICBMs in only one field. The Soviets could easily calculate that the second site at Malmstrom would do little or nothing for us militarily. In all likelihood they estimated that we had in mind laying the groundwork for a widespread system. The signal I got from the latest Soviet ABM proposal was that this U.S. (two-site) ICBM defense option was very hard, if not impossible, for them to take. If the United States could see its way clear to opting for Grand Forks plus Washington, I believed the ABM log jam would be broken. I suggested enlarging the area of permitted ABM deployment sites to allow the Soviets to cover a number of silos comparable to those covered at Grand Forks. I asked the White House for authority informally to probe for Soviet interest. This was authorized two days later on a "highly tentative personal" basis.

Once it was understood that the Soviet Union did not deploy as many silos in an ICBM field as the United States and it was accepted that the Soviets would insist on protecting as many silos as the United States, it did not prove difficult to resolve the problem. The area of an ABM site could be increased to cover more than one Soviet ICBM field, by redefining it as a circle having a radius of 150 kilometers instead of 70 kilometers as proposed earlier. It was an important development when we recognized this way to deal with the different ICBM deployment practices of the two nations and the need to protect equal numbers of ICBMs with an equal number of ABM sites.

In these discussions about protecting ICBMs, we found ourselves tangled in metaphysics. The Soviets argued that, if defensive missiles were deployed in an ICBM field, all the silos in that field would be considered to be protected regardless of the number of anti-ballistic missiles deployed. A Soviet said that although 100 ABMs could not protect 150 silos, they could protect any 100 of the 150. It was thus not a question of the degree of protection and it would be unrealistic to say that the other fifty were getting no protection at all. I tried to reduce this to the absurd by asking, if a side deployed all but one of its missiles to defend its capital and only one to defend its ICBM silos, would it be fair to say all of the silos in the defended field were protected? There was no answer.

On April 14 we sent new recommendations to Washington. There had been forward movement on a number of issues, but important questions remained. On SLBMs, earlier indications that there might be a change in the Soviet position had not been borne out. The prospect seemed poor for a Soviet SLBM move short of the summit, if then. We were not yet facing a choice of settling for an ABM treaty plus an ICBM freeze, or no SALT deal. The delegation advised that negotiations on ABM levels should continue to be contingent on including SLBMs and that the Soviet attitude on SLBMs should be tested once more.

On ABMs, we urged that Washington be the second ABM location, dropping the second site at Malmstrom, and we asked for authorization to modify the size of the ICBM defense area. We believed that the Soviets would agree to two ABM sites for each side, the national capital plus one ICBM defense site. While recognizing the advantages of allowing a choice with regard to the second site, the delegation believed this would be more complicated and difficult to negotiate. The delegation believed Grand Forks plus Washington to be in the U.S. interest.

The delegations took a weekend excursion to Lapland on April 15–16. Beginning on Sunday afternoon and continuing on Sunday evening during a two-hour flight back to Helsinki, Kishilov, Grinevsky and Garthoff had an informal but important exchange on ABM issues. With Semenov in Moscow, my activity on the Lapland trip was limited to having a picture taken with a reindeer!

The Soviets said the whole ABM negotiation was complicated by the U.S. insistence on having two sites to defend ICBMs. The knot could be untied if the United States would agree to have its second site at Washington. Garthoff expressed a personal view that, if SLBMs were included in the freeze, such an arrangement was not ruled out. The Soviets said that even if the United States agreed to have only one ICBM defense site it would be necessary that the Soviets defend the same number of ICBM silos as the United States. Garthoff stressed the importance of having the number of sites equal and of the Soviet site for ICBM defense being in the non-European part of the U.S.S.R. to avoid its being the nucleus for a nationwide system. He advised the Soviets that their ICBM fields in that area were such that equality of numbers of ICBMs defended could be met with one circular ABM site of 150 kilometers radius. It was apparent that these Soviet officials knew nothing about the location of their ICBM fields. The talk turned to numbers of ABM interceptors and launchers. After considering various alternatives, it appeared that both sides were thinking in the same general range of numbers—probably 100 interceptors and launchers per site. This question should be manageable.

On the subject of radar controls, the Soviets said that radar constraints for defense of ICBMs looked like the toughest problem. The Soviets could agree to MARCs for the defense of capitals, but MARCs would be too restrictive for an ICBM defense system, which on the Soviet side had not yet been designed. Each side should be entitled to have an unlimited number of ABM radars specially designed for defense of ICBM silos. Garthoff disagreed. The number of radars for ICBM defense should neither be unlimited nor even a high number. How many did the Soviets think might be needed? At first they were evasive, then Grinevsky said perhaps one radar for each interceptor! Garthoff observed that, while it was theoretically possible to build and design an ABM system using that many radars, it was not necessary and we could not agree to it. Kishilov and Grinevsky repeated that their ICBM defense had not even been designed and that they needed freedom of action. But, said Garthoff, the purpose of SALT was to find agreed limitations on freedom of action. At the ABM levels we were then discussing, overall strategic stability would not really be affected by small differences in number of silos protected, or differences in ABM components.

The flight was over. This conversation was afterward called "the Tundra talks."

Semenov returned to Helsinki on April 21. We met for an hour that evening. He had conferred several times at the highest level. He read a statement: the question of SLBM launchers in connection with a possible agreement on certain measures with respect to strategic offensive weapons was presently under serious study in Moscow. I noted its positive nature. His instructions were to prepare both agreements for signing in Moscow. I confirmed that those were also mine.

We then talked about an ABM approach calling for one capital defense site and one ICBM defense site for each side—the probe the White House had authorized several days earlier. Numbers were not mentioned. We merely referred to the Tundra talks.

I said that the Tundra talks had been an effort to feel for a rapprochement in positions. If the substance of what I was getting at was of interest to Semenov, and I believed it was a possible and sensible approach, I would try to get my authorities to adopt it. There was no new U.S. position. This was a personal effort to feel out the possibilities. I recalled that Semenov had once said that it was sometimes necessary to take a slight risk and get somewhat ahead of one's authorities. I thought this conversation was a good example of a calculated risk. I would like to hear whether he believed this would be a useful line to pursue.

He replied that during SALT he had resorted to such a method many times (which I didn't recall to be the case), and had resorted to it productively. The substance of what I had mentioned was undoubtedly of interest to him. While he understood my reservation that the Tundra conversation had been informal, it would be interesting for the Soviet side to learn its concrete content.

I stressed that the matters discussed did not represent the views of the authorities in Washington at this time. But it seemed to me that, given interest on both sides, I could be persuasive with Washington. One of the important elements of the case in persuading my authorities would be an understanding of what the Soviet side's position was. Our specifics were well known to them.

Armed with a better understanding of their position, I believed I would be in a position to be successful in Washington. Semenov could help in this respect by showing me his hand, so that I could get a reaction. Washington quite naturally had awaited his return from Moscow to see what had happened there. If I went back to Washington and reported that I did not know any more now than I had known a week before, that would hardly be productive.

Semenov interrupted to ask could we or could we not discuss this ABM alternative? I was bound to reply that at the present time I would not be able to discuss that alternative in a formal meeting of the delegates. I had tried to make this clear. I would be prepared to discuss it privately, I thought even that evening, although Semenov evidently was not yet ready to go into substance. He suggested that we meet the next day. It would be better to discuss these matters then, because after his trip he would need some time to collect his thoughts and study the record of the Tundra talks.

We resumed the next afternoon. I asked what was new in Moscow. His authorities were seriously preparing for the state visit of President Nixon. In all his experience he could not recall any other visit when the scale of preparations was as large.

He repeated that the SLBM question was under serious study. Here was a sure sign that the Soviet position was changing. He next read and handed over two written interpretive statements for the ABM Treaty, on OLPARs and on banning multiple ABM warheads. A quick reading showed that they represented positive steps. I reserved our position until I had a chance to study them closely.

The revised Soviet interpretive statement that Semenov brought back from Moscow accepted the American MSR as an OLPAR ceiling: "Deployment by each party of phased-array radars having a potential . . . equal to or exceeding the potential of the smallest modern ABM phased-array radar now deployed . . . would not be made. . . ." Semenov said that he understood OLPARs to be a major question, that the U.S. side attached great importance to it, and so had the Soviet side in terms of "untying knots." One difficult remaining point was the U.S. requirement for consultations about the deployment of radars smaller than the ceiling. We finally dropped that requirement.

Another important qualitative limitation in the ABM Treaty

was now agreed on. Although technically possible, neither side had developed ABM launchers for multiple interceptor missiles. To limit ABM systems as much as possible, we had proposed banning multiple launchers. This was accepted by the Soviets. The ABM Treaty states that "Each Party undertakes not to develop, test, or deploy ABM launchers for launching more than one ABM interceptor missile at a time from each launcher, nor to modify deployed launchers to provide them with such a capability, nor to develop, test, or deploy automatic or semi-automatic or other similar systems for rapid reload of ABM launchers." The delegations then proposed refining this restraint to also ban the development of multiple warheads for individual interceptor missiles. Semenov now was proposing an agreed statement. "The Parties understand that Article V of the Treaty includes obligations not to develop, test, or deploy ABM interceptor missiles for the delivery by each ABM interceptor missile of more than one independently guided warhead." Here were good examples of controlling technology before it was developed and of the feasibility of putting limitations on the qualitative characteristics as well as the numbers of weapons systems. Too bad a similar ban on multiple warheads for offensive missiles could not have been agreed upon.

Semenov said he would like to know how I personally viewed a possible compromise solution of the ABM sites question. He would like to be able to look at this question in its totality. Obviously he wanted to confirm some details touched on in the Tundra talks.

I said that, while Garthoff's authorization to explore possible approaches had been unofficial, I would not have approved without calculating what might be possible. I had fair confidence that if the Soviet side could also throw some light on unsettled areas, such as they now had with the draft interpretive statements, I would be able to convert this informal exploration into a formal position. If this was a sufficient platform for continuing the exchange, I would be glad to go over the approach in more detail. Semenov said this would be good. On the understanding that I was speaking personally, I finally outlined the new ABM approach. There could be a capital and an ICBM defense site on each side (within a circular area having a radius of 150 kilometers). Radar would have to be located in MARCs at both types of site. I suggested that we could consider increasing somewhat the

LAST ROUND IN HELSINKI

number of MARCs. Keeping the two sites widely separate was an important consideration. I thought we could agree on the numbers of interceptors and launchers. The Soviets had in mind 75 for Moscow defense and 150 for defense of ICBMs, while we had proposed 100 interceptors and launchers for each mission. In closing I added that all of this was in the context of including SLBMs in the freeze. I again asked for more information about the Soviet ABM position. All Semenov would say was that Soviet views would be presented as soon as possible. But he said he understood that the ball was now in his court.

I had earlier written Kissinger about the timing of possible changes in the U.S. positions, and also stated that if there were any parallel negotiations in the SALT sphere I trusted that I would be kept currently and fully informed. "As I said in 1970, it can be not only demeaning but dangerous to have two-track diplomacy with one of us in the dark." Kissinger replied a few days later, "As I have told you on many occasions, and as I have consistently practiced, you will be kept fully informed if anything develops here." If I had been more suspicious, I would have noticed that he didn't say when I would be informed!

We did not know that the White House and the Kremlin were once again in the stream of the SALT negotiations. After some exchanges between the capitals, Kissinger had slipped secretly into Moscow on April 20 and did some SALT business directly with Leonid Brezhnev. I learned of Kissinger's trip late on Monday, the twenty-fourth, when I received a copy of a two-sentence announcement to be released by the White House at noon the next day.

Between April 20 and April 24, Dr. Henry A. Kissinger, Assistant to the President for National Security Affairs, was in Moscow to confer with the General Secretary of the Central Committee of the CPSU Brezhnev and Foreign Minister Gromyko. The discussions dealt with important international problems as well as with bilateral matters preparatory to the talks between President Nixon and Soviet leaders in May.

I was instructed that this wealth of privileged information was for me alone and should not be shared with anyone on either delegation.

CHAPTER
13

BULLSHIT

I was then recalled to Washington with General Allison and Paul Nitze. We arrived on Wednesday, the twenty-sixth of April, and in the car from the heliport I was advised that Secretary Rogers wanted to see me immediately. He told me of Kissinger's trip to Moscow. He did not like the procedure or the product. I then went to see Kissinger, who told me that the subject of SALT "had come up" in his talks at Moscow and that he had raised the issue of SLBMs. Brezhnev said that until recently the Soviets had been negative on this issue but they had restudied it. They discussed the matter further. Brezhnev then gave Kissinger a paper containing a Soviet SLBM proposal as well as one giving their ABM views. Kissinger gave me copies.

Brezhnev's ABM paper was only four sentences in length and covered the same ground I had discussed with Semenov on April 22. It recognized as "expedient" that ABMs be limited to the capitals and one area for defense of ICBM silos. The United States ICBM site would be at Grand Forks, North Dakota. The ABMs would be deployed in circles with a radius of 150 kilometers containing a maximum of 100 launchers and interceptors at each site.

Brezhnev's SLBM paper was longer. It referred to previous exchanges in the White House-Kremlin channel and then stated that a freeze on modern SLBM submarines and their missile launchers would be very significant. They occupied a special place in the composition of strategic offensive weapons. Their "consideration" should not overlook differences in the geographies of the two sides as well as the strategic missile submarines of our NATO allies and the U.S. submarine bases in Europe. These offered important strategic advantages to the American side, and under these conditions the number of submarines and their ballistic missiles at the disposal of the sides could not be equal. The U.S.S.R. agreed that the United States and its allies should have during the freeze up to 50 modern submarines with up to 800 SLBM launchers (including 41 U.S. submarines with 656 launchers). The Soviet Union could have 62 modern submarines carrying not more than 950 launchers. (For comparison it is well to recall existing guidance for the American delegation—no new submarines to be started after the freeze was signed.)

The Soviet proposal also provided in general terms that during the freeze the number of older ICBM launchers would be reduced and the sides could modernize and replace older submarines with new submarines under the ceilings.

The Brezhnev paper repeated that there was a strategic "disbalance" (sic) in the location of the strategic submarines of the sides. The Soviets believed that the whole of this problem, and primarily the issue of dismantling U.S. submarine bases outside the territory of the United States, should be appropriately resolved in the course of subsequent negotiations. And the Soviet Union reserved the right to a corresponding increase in submarines if the U.S. NATO allies exceeded the number then operational and under construction.

The Brezhnev proposal concluded with two brief sweeteners. The Soviet Union could take an obligation not to start new construction of fixed soft ICBM launchers. And Moscow believed it possible to have an interim offensive freeze of five years, as proposed by the United States.

Again there had been no preparations for this negotiation in the National Security Council machinery, no building blocks or Working Group consideration, no Verification Panel meetings or consultations with allies. It is not known what if any Kissinger's instructions from President Nixon had been. Secretary Rogers advised me that this mission to Moscow had been related to Vietnam and that Kissinger had no authority to negotiate about SALT. Be that as it may, SALT once more was taking what appeared to the delegation to be a random lurch in an unprepared direction. It must be assumed that Kissinger kept the President fully and currently informed of his exchanges with Brezhnev. I believe all other American officials were informed only after the event. Those of us working on SALT were left to ponder the origins and meanings of these proposals.

Here are some questions that I should then have asked but did not. Who proposed that the Soviets could build up to 950 launchers on 62 submarines during the freeze? Was this a Brezhnev or a Nixon or a Kissinger proposal? Were these numbers the end product of a bargaining process or were they the first figures tabled? Were they based on a calculation of the current rate of Soviet submarine construction projected for five years? Some SALT officials later noted a curious coincidence that a then current U.S. intelligence paper containing low, medium and high estimates of the Soviet strategic submarine program projected at the high end of this range a Soviet fleet in 1977 of 62 submarines with about 950 launchers.

I pointed out some of the difficulties involved in the proposed submarine and launcher arrangement. I asked to study the interpreter's notes of the Moscow conversations. None were available. A Soviet interpreter had been used. I asked if there were memoranda of the conversations. Kissinger said that "eventually" there would be. I never saw them. Kissinger seemed elated at this turn of events. I had the impression he felt the Brezhnev papers were a major breakthrough. He said the SALT agreements were now "practically guaranteed." He had told Brezhnev that the two papers represented positive moves. He asked how I thought we should now proceed. I said that I assumed the Brezhnev SLBM proposal clearly was not the last word. As was usually the case when I talked with Kissinger, he had other pressing preoccupations. This time his mind was on the Vietnam war. The conversation lasted barely fifteen minutes. I sensed that the Brezhnev-Kissinger arrangement was a fait accompli.

I later saw Secretary Rogers again. With him was U. Alexis Johnson, then the Undersecretary of State for Political Affairs (and later chief of the U. S. SALT delegation). After reviewing the Soviet SLBM offer, the Secretary said he did not like its psychological effect. I observed that we might be better off without an SLBM freeze. First we should try to improve the Soviet offer and only if we did not succeed consider whether or not to refuse it.

Two days later, Friday, April 28, the Verification Panel met, under Kissinger's chairmanship. I was asked to state what ABM guidance the delegation wanted. I recited the terms of the two-sites-apiece approach which I had already put to Semenov informally and which was tracked by the Brezhnev ABM paper. It seemed tacitly assumed that this would be our guidance. At our private meeting, Kissinger had said that the President liked the SLBM deal better than the ABM one, because the latter involved switching the second U. S. ABM site from Malmstrom to Washington, but he thought the President could be persuaded since all the agencies were for the change.

Reportedly, a Working Group paper had been prepared estimating a range of future Soviet SLBM levels, in which conveniently the numbers 950 launchers and 62 submarines were in the middle of the range. Discussion of an SLBM freeze was desultory. As I recall, Kissinger described the Soviet proposal but did not table the paper. I said that although we could perhaps accept the general principle of the Soviet proposal, with the knowledge that it could lead to the ceilings set out in the Brezhnev paper, we should not accept any explicit numerical ceilings on submarines and launchers that froze us in a position of significant inequality, that included British and French nuclear forces, or that prejudiced our future position on the FBS question. I tabled a draft proposal which I thought improved on the Brezhnev formula. It called for an aggregate missile launcher freeze including both ICBM and SLBM launchers and specifying no numbers. Submarine launchers could replace ICBMs decommissioned. On glancing at this draft, an irritated Kissinger ended the meeting. I was advised later by General Haig that the President thought my approach would be "underhanded."

Kissinger called me as soon as I reached my office to say he was astonished that I would table such an alternative approach after he had disclosed the Brezhnev paper to me. I replied that, if for no other reason than negotiating tactics, we should start from a harder position than the Brezhnev proposal if we were to end up with something worthwhile. He cooled off somewhat. Kissinger must have been annoyed that I was trying to change the Moscow arrangement. Perhaps he believed that I was bucking the proposal merely because it had been passed to him rather than presented to the delegation. I think he was surprised that as an arms control official I had not jumped at it.

Secretary Rogers now asked me to prepare a letter for him to the President advising that the Brezhnev proposal not be accepted. I was to include a last paragraph urging that, to avoid confusion, further negotiations be handled in one channel—at Helsinki. I put a draft to the Secretary. He decided not to send it. I do not know why.

A second Verification Panel meeting was held the next morning, Saturday, April 29. Before it started Kissinger said to me, "I'll deliver the Joint Chiefs and DOD. I worked on Moorer [chairman of the Joint Chiefs of Staff] all week." This time copies of the Brezhnev papers were passed around. The freeze proposal was a complex document, but after only a few minutes' reading the Secretary of Defense's representative said he thought it constituted a very good basis for an agreement. This seemed a case of remarkable ability to absorb, at a glance, a complicated proposition—or confirmation of the advance persuasion by Kissinger. Admiral Moorer's reaction was more cautious. He thought that, while we could agree with an SLBM outcome based on the paper, we should not accept its principles. The one consideration outweighing all others in this meeting was that, regardless of whether or not a SALT offensive missile freeze was agreed, the U.S.S.R. would have a substantially larger number of missile launchers than the United States before the end of the sixty months during which the freeze might last. The attention was concentrated on what the situation would be without the freeze. There was no way that the United States during this period could increase its strategic submarine fleet. The first boat of the new Trident class, even on the recently accelerated schedule, was not due to be commissioned for six years. The Brezhnev proposal commended itself to a majority of the Verification Panel because it offered some chance that the Soviet margin would be less with the arrangement than without it. The fact that the Soviets would be reducing old but heavy ICBMs as they built up their SLBM force was an added attraction.

I questioned whether we should accept an SLBM freeze on terms which to many would look so unequal. I couldn't help but point out how the passage of SALT time, spent in a foolish quest for an ABM arrangement proposing to give us four sites to the Soviets' one, had permitted the Soviets to build additional launchers, and I recalled the proposal to "Stop Where We Are" which I had made three years earlier. These bits of nostalgia did not improve the atmosphere. But other panel members remained convinced that it would be better to have an SLBM freeze on these terms than none at all. I predicted somewhat facetiously that a famous columnist would play hell with any such agreement. Kissinger quickly said, "No, he won't!" which led me to think that perhaps ground preparation had not been limited to Verification Panel members.

The next step was to consider a reply for the President to Brezhnev. Knowing that the official who prepares drafts can influence the outcome of issues, especially where there are differences of opinion, I volunteered to draft a reply. It started by stating that, although the United States could not agree to certain considerations in the Brezhnev paper, the general approach was acceptable. No numbers were mentioned in my draft, but it was "recognized" that this approach could lead to the Soviet Union having the number of submarines and SLBM launchers mentioned in the Brezhnev paper.

The more I thought about such a high SLBM ceiling for the Soviets, the less I liked it. The next morning I telephoned Kissinger and suggested that the reference in the draft reply which implicitly accepted the Soviet ceilings be stricken. Kissinger agreed. Events seemed to be taking a better turn.

The National Security Council met with President Nixon on Monday morning, May 1. He asked if a submarine freeze was an essential part of an interim agreement. Admiral Moorer and Secretary Laird argued forcefully that it was. Secretary Rogers was against accepting the Brezhnev approach, both on principle and because of the numbers, arguing with a vehemence I had never heard him use with the President before. In turn, I said that if the Brezhnev approach could be narrowed down to simply permitting replacements during the freeze, we could accept that concept. I did not like to see the specific numbers approved. Kissinger, answering Rogers, said that the proposed reply should suit him, since Smith had drafted it. Before the NSC meeting started, I had been handed an envelope containing the proposed reply and noticed that the introductory clause, "While we cannot agree with certain considerations expressed in the paper given to Henry Kissinger in Moscow," had been eliminated. I told the President that an important reservation had been removed from my draft. When I told him what had been stricken, the President said, "Bullshit." He would be glad to hear from me on matters of substance but this reference to a change in language was irrelevant. I pointed out that there were a number of principles in the Brezhnev paper which if not rejected could cause trouble in the future, but to no avail and the meeting ended.

I was puzzled by the violence of the President's reaction. I later surmised that the reply then being considered in the National Security Council had already been delivered at least in draft to Dobrynin. Haig told me after the meeting that the introductory clause had been stricken because the Soviets (Dobrynin?) had advised that it would have been very poorly received in Moscow. I later learned that the President had then decided to strike the introductory clause and have the omitted thought passed to the Soviets as an "oral note." The reason, I was told, was to give it emphasis! A strange way to underline a thought—to substitute an oral for a written transmission. As we filed out of the Cabinet Room, Kissinger heatedly observed to me that Secretary Rogers' and my positions at the meeting had been "unbelievable." Now that he had gotten a SALT agreement we were trying to block it.

I returned to the State Department with Secretary Rogers and he said we should prepare a Nixon approach and not work from the Brezhnev approach. I said I understood that the Brezhnev paper had already been accepted in principle. I thought it was too late to adopt a new approach. Rogers tried without success to reach Kissinger to confirm this. I had to leave to catch the plane back to Finland. Later the Secretary told me he had seen the President and asked him why he had "razzed" Smith, who was trying to get the best arrangement possible for the United States. He reported that Nixon was so angry he could only sputter.

In Helsinki on May 3, I wrote a memorandum for the file about the Washington visit.

> From all this I draw the following surmise. Kissinger, having taken it upon himself to negotiate the submarine launcher matter in Moscow, probably led Brezhnev to believe that his proposal was acceptable. Acceptance in principle was then passed to the Soviets before the meeting with the President. Rogers' argument against the approach must have put the President in an uncomfortable position. The President's personal excision of the first clause, perhaps without full understanding of its importance, led to his anger at me when I pointed out the importance of this language. . . . Throughout all the meetings it must have been a source of discomfort for Kissinger to have State and ACDA voicing objections, or at least dragging their feet, on the Brezhnev proposal, while the military and Defense Department were approving of it— at least on the basis of its being a less bad alternative.

My feelings about this latest development in SALT were mixed. I was glad that SLBMs were to be included in the freeze but not with the terms of their inclusion. I would have been even more chagrined to have known that the Soviets were going to interpret the Brezhnev paper differently than we did. I was especially concerned about the bad political effect of formally registering a future Soviet advantage in submarines and SLBM launchers on top of their de facto numerical advantage in ICBM launchers. I also felt that we probably were not going to get as much financial support from the Congress for the Trident program as we planned and that Trident's prospects would be worse if there were a freeze on SLBMs than if there were no freeze. I was flabbergasted that Kissinger once again had gone off on his own and by-passed the delegation and other government officials with SALT responsibilities. I was surprised by the President's harsh reaction to my efforts to keep some maneuvering room for the American position. It seemed to reflect some unknown factor, some loss of confidence in me, perhaps hostility. I was determined that this was the last time I would be put in such a position. But I was also determined to make the best of the situation the delegation now faced.

FINAL
HELSINKI DAYS

May 1972

On May 1 the White House announced that the President was sending me back to Helsinki with new instructions which could lead to an agreement. According to Press Secretary Ziegler, these instructions were based on conclusions drawn by the President after there had been a number of confidential meetings with Brezhnev. My new instructions constituted "a major advance" that would broaden the scope of the offensive freeze.

I met with Semenov May 3. The summit was two and a half weeks away. I told him that I understood that our authorities had been in contact with each other. While certain considerations had been expressed which we could not accept, I believed there was agreement in principle to a "replacement approach" in connection with including SLBMs in the freeze. The U.S. side would have a formula consistent with this approach ready in a matter of hours. On the ABM matter, I was instructed to advise him that the approach I had outlined to him on a personal basis the previous week was now confirmed as our official position. Semenov said he would listen with great pleasure to the considerations I had been instructed to present. We agreed to have an informal meeting of delegates that afternoon to provide the Soviets with drafts of the SLBM freeze arrangement and of the new ABM provisions.

Semenov and I confirmed our understanding that the documents we were preparing were for signature during President Nixon's visit to Moscow. I asked Semenov how long he thought we would remain in Helsinki. In Vienna we had talked about stopping the first week in May. That date had already passed. I had also heard mention of the fifteenth and the nineteenth. Our objective was clear, Semenov answered. When we reached it, our work would be finished and, of course, we would have to do so before the Nixon visit.

The May 3 afternoon session lasted only fifteen minutes. I gave Semenov a draft treaty article for the new ABM levels. It called for two sites on each side, one capital defense site and one ICBM defense site, each with 100 interceptors and launchers and 6 MARCs within a circular area having a 150-kilometer radius. Locations of the ICBM defense sites would be east of the Urals for the U.S.S.R. and west of the Mississippi for the United States. I expressly conditioned the ABM proposal on reaching a freeze agreement which included SLBM launchers. Semenov made no comment. He said he thought it would be advisable to wait until he and his colleagues had had a chance to study these drafts.

I then gave him some new language for the freeze.

> The Parties undertake to limit submarine-launched ballistic missile (SLBM) launchers to the number operational or under construction on the date of signature of this interim agreement, except that additional SLBM launchers may be constructed as replacements for equal numbers of older heavy ICBM launchers, under agreed substitution and dismantling procedures. [Later we would incorporate the Brezhnev-Kissinger SLBM ceilings in a protocol which was an integral part of the Interim Agreement.]

The Interim Agreement would remain in force for a period of five years unless replaced by a treaty limiting strategic offensive arms. If such a treaty were not achieved within a five-year period, the Interim Agreement could be extended by mutual agreement. Appropriate provisions for missile launcher substitution and dismantling procedures would be needed. The U.S. side would soon propose such procedures, and also an agreed statement of what constituted "operational" and "under construction." Semenov again deferred comment and the meeting ended.

It will be noted that this delegation formula differed from the White House position in that it would freeze the number of launchers only and not the number of submarines. This variance was promptly signaled to Washington. The delegation had trouble with the dual limits that Moscow had proposed and that Washington had accepted. We thought it would be preferable just to have a limit on launchers. We had found during the negotiation that some problems in limiting SLBM launchers would be more manageable if there were no limit on the number of submarines. We believed that any ultimate treaty on offensive arms should limit launchers only and it would be a bad precedent to limit both launchers and submarines in the interim freeze. I also thought there would be some advantage in not explicitly registering a large Soviet advantage in number of submarines in addition to SLBM launchers. Since we did not know whether the U.S.S.R. planned to put twelve launchers on new submarines or sixteen or even twenty-four, I argued that with a limit just on launchers the number of submarines the Soviets could have was not calculable. Admittedly this went not to substance but to the image which would be projected by the freeze. But the strategic balance has a large psychological component. I was still scrambling to improve the Kissinger-Brezhnev arrangement, or at least, if not successful, to make it look better.

Our May 3 SLBM proposal included missile launchers on all classes of Soviet missile submarines. And it required immediate replacement—that is, that "older, heavy ICBM launchers" of the Soviet SS-7 and SS-8 types and American Titans be dismantled if additional SLBM launchers were constructed, starting from the first new missile submarine after the agreement was signed. During the rest of the SLBM freeze negotiations at Helsinki, the delegation's aim was to negotiate the tightest terms possible. Specifically, we wanted to assure that the Soviets would not get a free ride, by building some new submarines without decommissioning older launchers, or by retaining their older G- and H-class submarines on top of the proposed ceiling of 62 modern submarines. (The U.S.S.R. deployed 20 Golf-class submarines

(Gs) with old SLBMs and 2 so-called testbeds with 10 launchers. These submarines had diesel engines and carried a total of 70 launchers. There were also 9 Hotel-class older nuclear-powered submarines (Hs) carrying a total of 30 launchers. These submarines were left over from the Soviet SLBM force of the early 1960s. The first Soviet Yankee-class submarines (Ys), with a modern nuclear propulsion system and carrying 16 SLBM launchers each, were deployed in 1967, the same year the last Polaris submarine joined the American fleet.) Our White House guidance was clear. Each new launcher on which construction was started after the freeze date had to substitute for an existing launcher. If the freeze agreement as finally worked out at Moscow had met that condition, it would have been somewhat better.

The Soviet delegation seemed to have two objectives in the final SLBM exchanges: to defer scrapping older ICBM launchers for a time while its submarine construction program continued; and to limit the freeze to modern Y-class submarines and exclude the older G- and H-class boats. The Soviet purposes were exactly the opposite of ours. Since the offensive freeze was not to restrain American strategic programs in any way, we had little bargaining power in this aspect of SALT, except for the massive but not very credible threat to break off the whole negotiation. It is not surprising that the U.S.S.R. accomplished more of its final purposes than we did.

About five-thirty on the morning of Monday, May 8, I was wakened by a White House message: Air and naval action against Haiphong and other ports in North Vietnam was commencing. My first sleepy thought was, "Here goes the ball game." We had been so close to limiting strategic arms, and now that damnable war in Vietnam, which had destroyed so many other values, was to kill off the best chance since World War II to improve Soviet-American relations. The White House message spelled out tactics for that day's plenary session, probably the last for some time. If the Soviets raised the issue of Haiphong, we were to note their comments and avoid debate. We were to proceed with business as usual. If the Soviet delegation adopted disruptive tactics or walked out, I was to express regret coupled with willingness to proceed. I did not go back to sleep.

The United States delegation was far from relaxed as the Soviets filed into the United States Embassy in Helsinki that morning. We shook hands all around as usual and the conference proceeded in normal fashion. There was no mention of Vietnam, not a frown, just serious, businesslike and affable exchanges. I was puzzled, until it dawned on me that the Soviets had not yet been informed of the American action.

Our astonishment in the morning was more than matched that evening at a reception in the Soviet Embassy. Here we were, bombing the capital of their socialist ally and mining its chief port, where Soviet ships were at anchor and tied up to docks. What should be said at such a social occasion by hosts and guests? The war was not mentioned. The silence about Vietnam was deafening. The hospitality seemed warmer than ever. Apparently SALT was to take priority. This was linkage in reverse. If this extension of the Vietnam war was not to prejudice SALT, what could? We went back to work confident that the Soviets really wanted SALT agreements.

As the summit neared and likelihood of reaching agreements increased, I facetiously asked Semenov whether the ABM agreement would be called the Semenov-Smith Treaty or the Smith-Semenov Treaty. Without cracking a smile he said, "It will be called the Brezhnev-Nixon Treaty."

During these days he stressed several times the fact that the SALT negotiation now had engaged the Politburo's attention and it was important to make progress while such a condition lasted. This struck me as curious. Our trouble was not in getting the White House's attention but in getting it to make the right decisions.

The ABM Treaty fell into place quickly after the number and type of sites were agreed. The Soviets tabled draft ABM language at a meeting on May 6. It incorporated the essentials of our draft of May 3, including the proposal for a six-MARC radar restraint for the national capital sites. The Soviet text also adopted our proposal for lead-in language designed to ban any ABM systems except those specifically permitted by the treaty. This language would mesh with the agreed interpretive statement that deployment of any future types of ABM systems using components other than launchers, interceptor missiles and radars would re-

quire amendment of the treaty. The Soviet text differed from the
U.S. position on two points. There was no provision for a minimum separation distance between the capital and the ICBM defense sites, and there remained a problem with proposed radar restraints for ICBM defense.

In proposing that the U.S.S.R. have two ABM sites, we were
concerned that these not be so close that overlapping radar and
interceptor coverage could provide a potential base for a regional
defense system, which in turn might become a springboard for a
nationwide system. In the U.S.S.R. some ICBMs are deployed not
far from Moscow and would be protected to some extent by the
Moscow ABM site. If the Soviets were also to defend other
ICBMs, we argued that they should be in an ICBM field east of
the Ural Mountains. It was no problem for us to specify that the
defended U. S. ICBM area would be west of the Mississippi River.
True to their allergy to specificity, the Soviet delegation rejected
this proposal. They maintained it was an unnecessary restriction on
their freedom of action regarding a defense system yet to be designed. The Soviet May 6 draft, while accepting a limit of six
MARCs for the ICBM defense area, would have permitted any
number of ABM radars of unlimited size within these MARCs
and, more importantly, an unlimited number of smaller ABM
radars anywhere in the ABM site. The day after we received
their counterproposal Paul Nitze stated in a meeting that such
an extensive radar base would be entirely inconsistent with the
proposed level of 100 launchers and interceptors. The United
States could not accept provisions permitting deployment of such
an extensive radar base. The Soviet delegation continued to insist
that the treaty should not prescribe any technical approach to
deployment of ABM systems in defense of ICBM launchers. Several Soviets stressed the requirement for equality. The Soviet
Union must have a right to have two large phased-array radars
comparable to the U.S. perimeter acquisition radar (PAR) and
missile site radar (MSR) under construction at Grand Forks.
And a large number of additional small radars might be needed.

On May 12 the delegation suggested to Washington and informally to Soviet representatives a Nitze-drafted compromise on
ICBM defense radars using a combination of qualitative and nu-

merical restraints[1] rather than a MARC limitation. Within the ABM defense circle of 150-kilometer radius, the sides would be allowed one radar comparable to the U. S. PAR and one comparable to the MSR. The delegation advised Washington that this arrangement was preferable to the ten MARCs for which we now had Washington authorization. The Soviet delegation indicated it could agree. We advised Washington that we planned to proceed on this basis. That evening Garthoff at my instruction informally presented Kishilov and Grinevsky with a text incorporating these terms.

But we were not yet out of the radar woods. We learned by telephone that the arrangement was meeting opposition in Washington and might not be approved. Some officials were suspicious that the 18 additional radars were a much larger number than appropriate for support of 100 launchers and missiles. The next morning, the thirteenth, Garthoff advised the Soviets that difficulties were arising and that they should have in mind the possibility that Washington might not support this radar approach. The Soviets were shocked. Grinevsky acknowledged that the text had been submitted on an ad referendum basis but said his delegation had nonetheless assumed prior Washington approval. If Washington sustained the objections to the compromise they had worked out, he did not see any further basis for a radar solution.

The delegation that afternoon sent Washington another recommendation for the "two plus 18" solution, arguing the strategic and political reasons why we supported it as the most realistic alternative. The next day Kissinger concluded a message on another subject with a White House approval of the "two plus 18" proposition. However, I was to take a firm position that this deal was totally dependent on agreement that the ICBM defense site would be east of the Urals. There was great relief at a delegates' meeting Tuesday, May 16, when I announced that the ABM text we had passed to the Soviet delegation on May 12 was acceptable to Washington.

We still had some OLPAR and non-ABM radar problems. A few days after Semenov at an April 22 meeting had delivered a revised interpretive statement limiting future large phased-array

[1] A ceiling of 18 ABM radars for ICBM defense was proposed.

radars (OLPARs), the delegation advised Washington that we should give the Soviets an indication of what the power-aperture product or potential of the American missile site radar (MSR) actually was. Besides being the proposed OLPAR ceiling, we were then proposing this level as the limit on the 18 smaller radars for ICBM defense. We were told to state officially that the potential of the MSR was between two and three million watt-meters squared ($2-3\times10^6$).

On May 1, while I was in Washington, Semenov told Garthoff privately that the potential of the MSR was greater than the United States had indicated, saying he had this information from the press but declined to provide a reference. Unofficially, he said it was known that the maximum power of the MSR was 50 million watt-meters squared! The Soviet delegation instructions were to agree to a level of 50 million. Garthoff vigorously objected to that, both as the MSR's potential level and that such a level be the standard for OLPARs.

On May 10 the Soviet delegation stated formally that the MSR was not acceptable as the standard for a ceiling on OLPARs. The Soviets now maintained that, in earlier proposing the smallest phased-array radar currently deployed, they had not considered the MSR as yet deployed. The delegation advised Washington that we should not agree to an OLPAR power-aperture product ceiling higher than three million. By explicitly agreeing to allow larger phased-array radars, it would be harder for us to object to Soviet radar deployments which might cause concern. In these final days at Helsinki considerable irritation was generated over OLPAR restraint. We complained that since April 22 we had believed that there was agreement on using the MSR potential as the OLPAR standard. Not so, they said, but they continued to believe that a mutually acceptable solution could be found.

The Soviets proposed on May 14 what they called a "decisive compromise" on OLPARs, proposing a standard of 10 million watt-meters squared. We were told there had been great difficulty in getting acceptance in their delegation for this standard. It was a rock-bottom figure, arrived at after the most careful consideration and probably not satisfying the views of all their experts. We continued to press for three million. The OLPAR issue was one of the last to be resolved at Helsinki.

Toward the end of the ABM negotiation the Soviet delegation had become skittish about referring to the U.S.S.R.'s national capital as one of the permitted ABM deployment sites. Semenov recalled that during an early phase of American ABM deployments there had been difficulties over why one American city should be defended and not another. (The facts were just the opposite—controversy over the Johnson Administration's Sentinel ABM program, the predecessor of the current program, reflected an aversion by communities selected to be hosts for ABM deployments!) We continued to insist that the agreement specify national capital deployments. When one American asked, "Is this because Leningraders and Kievans would be disturbed that only Moscow is to be defended?" he was told, "People are people." I think the most likely reason for the desire to avoid singling out Moscow for protection and special status was given by a Soviet official who said it was based on concern lest there be objections from the capitals of the other Soviet republics. The Soviets shortly thereafter dropped this objection.

Their delegation continued in the final days at Helsinki to oppose an agreed statement that their ICBM defense site be located east of the Ural Mountains, saying it was a matter of prestige. There were those on the Soviet side who thought it improper for Americans to dictate the location of the U.S.S.R.'s defenses. They argued that the first article of the ABM Treaty was a full guarantee against attempts to deploy an ABM defense of the whole territory of a country or even to create a basis for such defense. This was supplemented by obligations to limit ABM deployments to two different areas, including definite limitations spelling out a circle of 150-kilometer radius for each area and constraints on the radar potential for ICBM defense. It was clear, they said, that these commitments would not permit creation of a base for a territorial defense system regardless of the geographic location of the ABM defense of ICBMs. There were other indications, however, that this matter could be compromised. Shortly before the summit, Kishilov and Garthoff worked out an alternative formula calling for a minimum separation distance of 1,300 to 1,500 kilometers (the distance from Moscow to the Urals). The Soviet delegation then advised that they would recommend favorably to Moscow a figure of 1,300 kilometers. Confirmation of this "separation" solution was then deferred until the summit, perhaps to give the top leaders some part to play in concluding the ABM Treaty.

Some of the Soviet delegation continued to press for agreement to defer the second site. But they wanted us to make a formal proposal. Deferral would mean that the Soviet Union would have no defense of ICBMs and the United States would. Their sense of the appropriate was to leave this initiative to us. Apparently Semenov's instructions were to accept a deferral proposal if made.

I favored deferral of second sites, believing that it would add some aspects of a freeze to the ABM agreement since the sides would, at least for a time, be limiting themselves to sites already under construction. And this freeze would be at equal levels. I advised Washington that deferral would amount to a de facto ABM freeze and would minimize somewhat the apparent difference between the treatment proposed for defensive limitations and the offensive freeze. Washington, probably calculating that a deferral provision would make Senate ratification of the ABM Treaty slightly more difficult, and perhaps to make an inexpensive gesture to military sentiment, would not authorize a deferral proposal. On May 17, I told Semenov that we had no interest.

In fact, as mentioned earlier, neither side started to build its second ABM system. Two years later, at the 1974 Moscow summit, agreement was reached on a protocol to the ABM Treaty that terminated the right of the sides to have a second ABM site.

The Soviets made a number of moves, which they regarded as marking a major step forward. Besides presenting draft ABM language differing from the U.S. position on only two points (location of ICBM defense sites and ICBM defense radar restraints), they tabled a provision including soft ICBM launchers in the freeze and the U.S.-proposed date for the freeze to begin. They agreed to a five-year duration for the Interim Agreement. And they tabled an interpretive statement on increases in silo dimensions.

The Parties understand that in the process of modernization and replacement there will be no substantial increase, observable with the aid of national technical means of verification, in the external dimensions of land-based ICBM silo launchers currently in the possession of the parties.

This was the first time the Soviets had attempted to move to meet our proposed provision for not increasing the depth or diameter of ICBM silos.

On heavy missiles, the Soviets now said that the obligation not to convert land-based launchers for light ICBMs into launchers for heavy ICBMs, taken together with this commitment not to increase substantially the external dimensions of ICBM silo launchers, dealt with the whole problem. There was no need to define heavy and light missiles.

We said no—it was still necessary to have a clear common understanding of the difference between heavy and light ICBMs, whether in the agreement or in an interpretive statement. We both knew about existing missiles, but a definition was needed to deal with future missiles. While a provision against substantially increasing the dimensions of silo launchers was important, it was no substitute for a definition of a heavy missile.

We also asked what they meant by "no substantial increase" in silo dimensions—qualified by the clause "observable with the aid of national technical means of verification." We could not agree that an obligation be defined in terms of how well verification techniques operated. We recalled past Soviet objections to the word "substantial" when the United States had used it in connection with the non-transfer problem. It was natural for ideas to migrate, replied Semenov. The Soviets maintained that it was not possible to quantify precisely what the word "substantial" meant, but they thought both sides understood what it meant. It would always be possible to raise any questions in the Standing Consultative Commission.

As the summit approached and we continued to press for a definition of heavy missiles, the Soviet delegates usually fell back to their tired argument that heavy missiles had features distinguishing them from other types of missiles. I repeated that we did indeed know what the Soviet side now called a light missile, but the problem was in the future. The Soviets had SS-11s and SS-9s. Would a missile with a volume between these two classes be considered light or heavy? The only reply was that national means could distinguish between light and heavy and could show whether any increase in the former was substantial enough to bring it into the category of heavy.

A Soviet indicated informally what the trouble was on the question of silo dimensions and heavy missiles. They did not want to foreclose possibilities for the future. Missile designers or silo designers wanted flexibility to resolve problems. For that reason, the Soviet delegation could not accept a precise definition of the word "substantial" as we had proposed.

His American interlocutor said we could understand it if they had in mind modernizing their SS-11s with a new version that did not differ significantly in size from the existing version. If they had in mind a totally new missile, intermediate in size between a current light and heavy missile, this was a different matter.

A Soviet informally indicated they had one or two missiles under development as replacements for the SS-11. He hinted that the work was more advanced than mere design. He would not even say that certain tests had not been made. The designers of each side might wish to MIRV in different ways. The way in which the Americans MIRVed missiles might require less size. But it was not their intention to approach the halfway mark between the volume of their current light missiles and heavy missiles.

On May 16 the delegation advised Washington:

> The Delegation has sought repeatedly in SALT VII at all levels an agreement on a definition of "heavy" in connection with non-conversion of light to heavy. . . . If, as appears to be the case, the Soviets are resisting volume limits so as to be assured that they can modernize SS-11s with modernization and replacement missiles larger in volume than the current version and evidently already well along in development, any criterion which denies them this right will be just as unacceptable as the 70 cubic meter criterion.

A Soviet official under instructions said on May 20 that the Soviet side could not agree to define heavy missiles as those having a volume greater than seventy cubic meters, or larger than the SS-11, the largest light missile that either side deployed. Definitions of heavy missiles, he said, were superfluous for an interim agreement.

We advised Washington that it now appeared unlikely that we could move the Soviets from their position. Our guidance authorized a fallback to a unilateral statement on silo dimensions, but not on the definition of a heavy ICBM. But the only feasible solution now seemed to be a unilateral statement.

On May 7, Semenov had presented in very general terms an approach to SLBM limitations. He repeated the "considerations" in the Brezhnev paper. The U.S.S.R. had now decided in principle to include submarines, but agreed levels had to take account of U.S. forward submarine bases and allies' submarines, and therefore the numbers could not be equal for both sides. The Soviets intended to reduce older ICBM launchers during the freeze. It was also necessary to provide for replacement of older submarines with new ones. He said the question of liquidating U.S. forward submarine bases "must" receive an appropriate solution in the follow-on talks. (The word "must" was soon changed to "will," probably to avoid a claim that the Soviet delegation was using the same language of *diktat* which earlier they had objected to so vigorously when the English word "requirement" had been rendered by an interpreter into the Russian word for "demand.") If the U. S. NATO allies increased the number of their SLBM submarines during the freeze, the Soviet Union reserved the right to a corresponding increase.

The next day Semenov elaborated, stating that each side had undertaken to limit modern SLBM submarines and launchers to agreed levels on the principle of insuring equal security and not providing unilateral military advantages, and also with due regard to factors affecting the strategic situation. Within the limits of these levels, the modernization and replacement of older SLBM submarines by new SLBM submarines would be permitted. To create more favorable conditions for the follow-on negotiations and to strengthen trust between the parties, they would reduce ICBMs by dismantling older ICBM launchers.

We said that the process of replacement was the key to the SLBM freeze. If the Soviets wanted to produce additional modern submarines and launchers beyond the number in operation and under construction, it would have to decommission an equal number of older launchers. If this was a correct understanding of the situation, the language that Semenov had just proposed was too vague. There must be a definite connection between the process of increasing the SLBM force and reducing the ICBM force.

Eight days before the summit was to begin and after what seemed like an unnecessarily long wait for the Soviet interpretation of the SLBM accord, we finally received their proposal. They said it was a major step to agree in principle to include SLBMs. Here is their text.

> The Soviet Union agrees that for the period of effectiveness of the interim "freeze" agreement the USA have 41 modern submarines with a total number of 656 ballistic missile launchers on them. The Soviet Union during the same period will have a total number of not more than 950 ballistic missiles on modern submarines. In the Soviet Union this number of launchers will be deployed on modern submarines which are operational and under construction as of the date of signature of the Interim Agreement, as well as on submarines which will be constructed additionally. In the Soviet Union commissioning of additional launchers on submarines, over and above 48 modern submarines operational or under construction, will be carried out in replacement of ICBM launchers of old types constructed before 1964.

This Soviet proposal came as a shock. I pointed out that the Soviets were proposing a U.S. limit on both submarines and missile launchers, but only a limit on launchers for themselves. This would prevent the United States from increasing the number of its submarines by three if it replaced its 54 "older" Titan ICBM launchers. The Soviets were not accepting our proposal that only SLBM launchers and not submarines be frozen. Semenov said that this text "reflected" the U.S. draft—this was only partially true. He confirmed that it would not give the United States the right to trade in Titan ICBMs for new SLBMS.

Most surprising was the implied claim that they then had 48 modern submarines operational and under construction. This was the first time we had heard the number 48. U.S. intelligence estimates were that the Soviets then had 41 to 43 submarines opera-

The Semenovs and the Smiths at a reception beginning SALT in Vienna, March 15, 1971. Courtesy, USIS Vienna

Hotel Kalastajatorppa (Fisherman's Cabin) where the U.S. SALT delegation stayed during the Helsinki rounds

Assisted by Kishilov and Garthoff, Semenov and Smith sign the communiqué ending another round of SALT talks

The signing ceremony in St. Catherine's Hall, the Kremlin, May 26, 1972

The signing of the Instruments of Ratification, October 3, 1972 (L-R: *Dobrynin, Gromyko, Nixon, Rogers, Smith*). Courtesy, the New York Times.

Smith takes his leave on January 4, 1973. Courtesy, White House Photo

tional and under construction. (We later determined by technical means that the correct figure at that time was 42.)

I countered that our proposal of May 3 would permit the Soviet Union to reach the levels it was seeking. Under their approach, older launchers could be retained until the Soviet side reached a level of 48 boats, while under our proposal replacement would be required for any launchers additional to those operational and under construction at the date of signature. The Soviet proposal would also permit their reaching the 950 launcher level on "modern submarines" while retaining approximately 100 additional launchers on older G- and H-class submarines, whereas the U.S. approach would include in the 950 ceiling the number of launchers then on older submarines.

I doubted the accuracy of the Soviet figure of 48 modern submarines operational and under construction. Semenov replied that the United States and its NATO allies had 800 launchers on modern submarines, and the United States also had forward submarine bases. For these reasons the figures he had given seemed realistic and should be mutually acceptable. While the Soviets ostensibly were not claiming explicit compensation for U.S. forward submarine bases and the submarines of our allies, Semenov in effect admitted that the number 48 included a factor for this purpose. We also learned that the Soviets now had in mind a "side understanding," based on their belief that we might want to avoid formal disclosure of these terms in the Interim Agreement. Semenov said that political considerations need not be registered in the agreement. I advised Washington that I did not believe this was the final Soviet SLBM position. I would forward alternative approaches looking to negotiating an acceptable agreement.

On this same day, the fourteenth, Kissinger wired saying he was puzzled as to why I was not trying to get the Soviets to limit the numbers of both submarines and launchers. He thought the limits of 62 and 950, which were in my instructions approved by the President, would impose on the Soviets greater constraints than just a launcher limit. He felt that without a submarine limit the Soviets could get up to 66 during the freeze, with the 48 boats they now claimed plus nearly 18 new submarines in lieu of 209 old ICBMs. I was surprised that he was apparently accepting the

Soviet claim of 48, even if only to make this argument. I wondered if he was taking at face value the Soviet claim to have 48 boats operational or under construction? In any event it looked as if the delegation would have to stick to the letter of the presidential instructions.

I made one last try to persuade the White House that the delegation's approach of just limiting launchers was better. All the delegates felt that the proposal was consistent with our instructions and would offer substantial advantages over explicit ceilings on the number of submarines. A formal registration of a Soviet-American 62:41 ratio for submarines would cause greater political difficulties than an agreement about launcher levels from which one could not tell how many of what type submarines (12- or 16-launcher) would be built during the freeze. Having only a launcher limit offered a better chance to get a Soviet commitment that G- and H-class boats must be used for replacement, while on its face a limit of 62 *modern* submarines would leave the Soviets free to retain and perhaps re-equip their older submarines with modern missiles. And we assumed that in the follow-on negotiation we would be dealing only with launchers (which proved to be the case), and an interim freeze limiting submarine numbers as well as launchers would be a bad precedent.

The White House was unpersuaded. At a meeting on Tuesday, May 16, I had to walk the cat back and make a new proposal that the freeze be on both submarines and missile launchers.

This proposal had another new element. To require immediate replacement and neutralize the Soviet claim to 48 modern submarines, we devised and incorporated with Washington approval replacement thresholds for SLBM launchers beyond which new launchers would be replacements and require dismantling of older launchers. A threshold figure of 740 for Soviet launchers was based on an estimate that the Soviets had 640 launchers on 42 (not 48) modern nuclear submarines (Y-class and a variant now called the Delta class) plus 100 launchers on older G- and H-class boats. Replacement would have to begin shortly after the freeze agreement was signed.

Semenov did not hide his feelings. He expressed astonishment that the position of one side on such a major question could so easily be changed at such a critical stage of the negotiations. It was difficult for him to believe that the positions unfolded by the sides were presented in a manner that was not controlled. The switch could hardly make a good impression in Moscow. I replied that I was surprised he considered this a bad turn of events. We were now proposing what Brezhnev had originally wanted, a limit on the number of submarines as well as on launchers. It had been clear that we were operating on an ad referendum basis. I did not understand Semenov's comment that we were operating here entirely as guided agents under continuing instructions from our authorities. But I felt somewhat sheepish about this switch back to what all the American delegates felt was a poorer formula.

The next day, May 17, during a private meeting, Semenov provided a Soviet text for including SLBMs in the Interim Agreement. "The Parties undertake to limit for the period of operation of this Interim Agreement the total number of ballistic missile launchers on modern submarines to levels mutually agreed for each Party." He was instructed to propose that this understanding be in the form of an exchange of letters between our authorities which would be a component part of the Interim Agreement.

I advised him that there were strong opinions in Washington that the Interim Agreement should stand on its own without side understandings. Semenov then read what he termed a "statement of the Soviet side."

Taking into account that modern ballistic missile submarines are presently in the possession of not only the U.S., but also of its NATO allies, the Soviet Union agrees that for the period of effectiveness of the Interim 'Freeze' Agreement the U.S. and its NATO allies have up to 50 such submarines with a total of up to 800 ballistic missile launchers thereon (including 41 U.S. submarines with 656 ballistic missile launchers). However, if during the period of effectiveness of the Agreement U.S. allies in NATO should increase the number of their modern submarines to exceed the numbers of submarines they would have operational or under construction on the date of signature of the Agreement, the Soviet Union will have the right to a corresponding increase in the number of its submarines. In the opinion of the Soviet side, the solution of the question of modern ballistic missile submarines provided for in the Interim Agreement only partially compensates for the strategic imbalance in the deployment of the nuclear-powered missile submarines of the U.S.S.R. and the U.S. Therefore, the Soviet side believes that this whole question, and above all the question of liquidating the American missile submarine bases outside the U.S., will be appropriately resolved in the course of follow-on negotiations.

He said it was understood by the Soviet side that the United States was not prepared to join in making such a statement. It was, therefore, a unilateral statement setting forth the Soviet point of view. I replied that I thought that our position had been made clear in communications between our authorities. We rejected these considerations and considered them irrelevant to any bilateral agreement between us.

The Kissinger-Brezhnev arrangement on SLBMs provided for the sides retiring older ICBM launchers during the freeze, but the Soviets did not have in mind that the United States could replace its 54 older Titan ICBMs. (They had been retained in our force structure as a bargaining chip, to see if some concession for their retirement might be obtained.) We claimed the right to replace them with three submarines carrying 16 SLBM launchers apiece. The U. S. Navy had no interest in such a switch. It made no sense to build three additional Poseidon submarines of the current class during the five-year freeze period (presumably 1972 to 1977) when the new Trident class of strategic submarines was being developed with the first boat to be commissioned in 1978. Even if it had made sense to build three more Poseidons, there were no shipyards available. The right to replace Titans had no practical value.

But the Soviets did not want the United States even to have such a right. Under these circumstances, I thought that it might make Soviet acceptance of our SLBM provisions somewhat more likely if we stated that the United States did not intend to exercise this replacement option. Washington authorized such an initiative some days later. I raised this possibility with Semenov. He seemed interested. I advised him that some statement of U.S. intention not to replace Titans with SLBMs might be part of an otherwise acceptable arrangement.

In our last few days at Helsinki the Soviet delegation continued to give considerable emphasis to an explicit American assurance that, if the agreement provided a reciprocal right to replace old ICBMs with SLBMs, we would not exercise it. One Soviet said what really bothered him about the revised U. S. SLBM provisions of May 16 was the implication that we intended to replace the Titans. On a number of later occasions we had to correct Semenov and his colleagues by repeating that, while the United States had no plans to build new submarines during the freeze and replace the Titans and we might make a statement to that effect if all other provisions of the agreement were satisfactory, this did not mean that we would give up this right. Replacement rights under the Interim Agreement must apply equally. Eventually the Titan replacement question was left for the Moscow summit.

The claimed number of 48 Soviet submarines operational and under construction, beyond which the Soviets would dismantle older ICBM launchers, proved very slippery. I continued to press Semenov. Were they now claiming they had 48 modern submarines? That would call into question the reliability of national means of verification. This line of argument had the desired effect of implying an eleventh-hour challenge to the Soviet position against any need for on-site inspection. Semenov fudged the issue. At first he repeated that the difference could be accounted for because America's allies had strategic submarines which must be counted in the balance. Then he insisted that the number 48 had originated with us.

I queried Washington. Kissinger was adamant. Forty-eight had not come from there. We could not accept 48 as the replacement threshold. That was good news. Otherwise the Soviets could continue to build submarines for some time without decommissioning older ICBM launchers.

One Soviet advised that the number 48 had no direct or indirect relationship to third-countries' forces. It was to be taken as the number of modern SLBM submarines operational or under construction in the U.S.S.R. as of the expected dates of signature. The Soviets either were confused or wanted to confuse us on this issue.

We thought that possibly the term "modern" as used by the Soviets included the H-class boats which, while older than the Y-class, were nuclear-propelled. When asked a few days earlier what was meant by "modern," Kishilov had said it meant Y-class, adding that a modern submarine was one that had nuclear propulsion. Garthoff asked again. Was a modern submarine one that had nuclear propulsion? Now Kishilov said he did not know. He also did not know if the H-class was to be considered modern. Semenov ended this guessing game on the nineteenth, when he advised that a "modern" submarine was a nuclear-powered submarine which became operational after 1965. That excluded the H boats.

Semenov and I met on May 18. I had searched the record but could not find any use by us of the number 48. My difficulty with this number was that, if the H-class submarines were not included in it, then it would mean that our national technical means of verification could not support the proposition that the Soviet Union had 48 modern submarines operational and under construction. This struck me as a serious threat to our confidence that national means of verification were adequate. That was why I was pressing for clarification of this number 48.

I reminded him that he had often said in these negotiations how important it was not to indicate in any way that national means were inadequate to verify the arrangements we were trying to work out. I raised this matter in all seriousness. If we were not able to identify the beginning levels of the freeze by national means, how could we determine the point at which the final levels would be reached? How could we be sure that construction stopped when the ceiling was reached? Semenov flatly said that national means of verification were not affected by this matter.

He would repeat with all responsibility that what we were talking about here did not affect by one iota the adequacy of national means. He saw that Smith "was approaching the tree of agreement in such a way that the poor thing could just barely withstand his shaking."

The next evening Semenov said he would answer my question. This number 48 had not initially been cited by the Soviets. I should not believe that it contained secret meaning for the Soviet side. I responded that I did not recall at any time having cited such a number. Or had it been cited by someone else? Semenov said he did not know. Perhaps there had been a breakdown of U.S. communications. I remarked that the main thing I wanted to be sure of was that my memory had not broken down, and I understood Semenov's reply to indicate that it had not. He said he had a high opinion of my memory.

Semenov finally and flatly said that, while replacement would begin with the forty-ninth submarine, the proposal did not constitute a claim that the U.S.S.R. had 48 modern submarines in operation and under construction at that time. Soviet delegates still maintained that the number 48 came from American sources. The only explanation of this obscure episode is that, as one Soviet official reportedly said at the Moscow summit, they wanted assurance (presumably during the April exchanges between Brezhnev and Kissinger) that they could have five or six more submarines "as an offset." An offset to what was not disclosed—perhaps U.S. forward submarine bases. Kissinger, the report has it, replied, "No, the 950 takes care of that." If this was the reason for the Soviet claim, Kissinger's assurances that the number 48 did not come from Washington could still have been correct. It is likely he never used or even heard the number 48 during his April talks. Perhaps he forgot what could have been a passing reference to an offset of five or six more submarines, assuming as he read Brezhnev's formal proposal for Soviet ceilings of 62 and 950 that this took care of the "offset" issue. The Soviets might have thought that Kissinger had agreed that a replacement threshold of 48 boats was part of the offset. In any case, they decided to push 48, at least for bargaining purposes.

On May 19, I sent along to the White House impressions of where we stood in Helsinki. The SLBM freeze matter was in some confusion. We had been told informally that the Soviets did not know what the situation was regarding Soviet SLBM submarines, did not know the meaning of "modern" submarine, did not know the meaning of "under construction." Under these circumstances, our short-term tactic was to advise the Soviet delegation that their proposal was incomprehensible to us and therefore we were hard put to try to negotiate some mutually acceptable solution. The only move that I would suggest was that, if the Soviets would agree that the United States had the right to convert the 54 Titans to SLBMs, they might be given some high-level assurance that we did not intend to exercise that right. I advised that we should stand on our position that the U.S.S.R. could have up to 950 missiles on 62 boats only if they replaced a number of older launchers equal to new launchers built. I thought it would be hard to find a persuasive rationale for the United States agreeing to their building additional boats and launchers without replacing existing launchers. In knowledgeable circles, such a "free ride" would be seen as acquiescence in the Soviet FBS thesis. It was hard for me to conceive of the Soviets considering such a bonus as anything else. Perhaps there were considerations bearing on this of which I was unaware.

I reported that the other main sticking point in the freeze agreement was the Soviet continued refusal to agree to a definition of a "light" or "heavy" ICBM. This foreshadowed the development of a new Soviet missile somewhat larger than the SS-11. I wired that "A unilateral statement by us may have some slight deterrent effect on any such new Soviet program, but I wouldn't put a very high estimate on the value of such deterrence."

I thought that the ABM Treaty would be well received. I expected that we would hear more from Semenov about a deferral of the second site. "I believe you know that I think we should have made our deferral decision positively—but I do not propose to enter the lists on this one any more." In closing I noted that I had received a White House message indicating I should be in Moscow on the twenty-fifth of May.

As the Moscow deadline approached both capitals became impatient with their SALT delegations. Kissinger wired on the nineteenth that Moscow had made a strong démarche through the President's special channel that the U.S. delegation was moving too slowly. The President was most anxious to expedite the talks in every reasonable way, with a view toward reaching final agreement not later than Wednesday, May 24—now only five days away. Kissinger as usual was being kept well informed by Dobrynin. He reported that Moscow was giving a similar jolt to its delegation. The President hoped that we would be able to move promptly within existing guidance to resolve remaining obstacles, which the Soviets had listed as their base figure of 48 submarines, mobile ICBMs, a definition of heavy missiles, and ABM site separation. Kissinger advised me to make an additional effort to determine the meaning of the number 48. He recognized that a free ride for the Soviets on H-class submarines would be a problem. (Here was a signal that the White House in extremis would drop its position that the G-class boats must also be decommissioned if the Soviets were to reach the 950 launcher-62 submarine ceilings.) The White House also now authorized the Titan conversion matter to be handled as I had suggested.

It was obvious that not all disputed issues would be resolved before the summit meeting. In Washington President Nixon told a press conference that there was a "possibility" of agreement at the coming summit provided that remaining bottlenecks could be broken. Some of these were very difficult problems that could be resolved only by a decision at the top. He added that the discussion of these problems with Brezhnev would lead to agreement.

My central concern remained that the Soviets claimed that replacement should start only with their forty-ninth boat. This free ride struck me as completely unacceptable. I knew of no way to justify such a bonus for them and recommended to the President that it not be accepted. I suggested that some form of summit declaration regarding restraint on SLBM programs of the two sides during the freeze period was a possible fallback position.

May 20, Saturday, was a busy day. We met with the Soviet delegation in the morning to make a unilateral statement about mobile ICBMs.[2] I had planned to delay this move until at least the next day because of the unyielding Soviet positions on SLBMs, heavy missiles, mobile ICBMs and the ABM site separation distance, but this schedule was changed by the message that the President wanted us to move promptly.

Since an ABM treaty was close at hand, we finally dropped the U.S. requirement for a special withdrawal provision in the event of failure of the follow-on negotiations for a treaty to limit offensive arms. Instead we put the Soviets on notice in a unilateral statement that if such failure occurred our supreme interests could be jeopardized, thus constituting a basis for terminating the treaty. Semenov said that my statement would be brought to the

---

[2] ". . . I have been instructed to inform you . . . that the U.S. would consider the deployment of operational land based mobile ICBM launchers during the period of the interim agreement as inconsistent with the objectives of that agreement."

attention of the Soviet leadership. He declared that the U.S.S.R. also attached great importance to concluding a more comprehensive agreement on strategic arms. The sides' positions coincided in this respect. He welcomed our dropping the special withdrawal clause. That would make the ABM Treaty a "stable" document.

I made one more effort to reach agreement on SLBMs before the summit began. Stressing that I was not speaking under instructions, I told Semenov that I thought I could get approval for a reformulation of the U.S. position along the following lines. If no reference was made to 48 submarines and it were understood that any hull sections entering construction halls after the date of signature of the agreement would only be for submarines carrying SLBM launchers replacing other SLBM or older ICBM launchers, we would not insist on specifying a Soviet replacement threshold of 740 launchers. We could also agree to an explicit statement that new SLBM submarines could replace older SLBM submarines. We would be willing to provide in an appropriate separate form assurance that during the freeze the United States would not have operational more than 41 SLBM submarines.

Semenov said he would immediately put this new formulation to Moscow. That was the last I heard of it.

In reporting the day's happenings to the White House, I suggested a top-level "counter démarche" to the Kremlin, pointing out that the United States was now making all the running. The Soviet statements on "heavy" ICBMs and the ABM site separation issue had been entirely negative in the session that morning. This U.S. démarche might endorse the informal SLBM position I had put to Semenov, perhaps indicating that this was the position on which the President would be willing to close at Moscow. But the prospect of the Moscow summit taking over the negotiations was already overhanging Helsinki. I received no reaction from Washington.

I did not then fully appreciate that the important part of the Interim Agreement negotiation had in effect been finished when President Nixon accepted the Brezhnev-Kissinger arrangement that the Soviets could build up to 62 submarines and 950 launchers during the freeze. All the rest of the discussion was over secondary issues, some of importance, but in no way comparable to the questions of launcher and submarine ceilings. Militarily it made little difference if the Soviets did or did not have 100 old SLBM launchers in addition to the 950 launchers on 62 modern submarines. The G-class diesel submarines were obsolete. The H-class nuclear submarines were by no means a first-line force. The SS-7- and SS-8-type ICBMs probably would soon be phased out in any case. The strategic balance would not be affected if the Soviets delayed replacement of these older launchers. But psychological factors of not inconsiderable weight were at stake, as the Soviets seemed to believe, and while the negotiations were going on at the summit the delegation would continue to advise a hard line to get the best-looking SLBM freeze possible.

The White House party left Washington May 20 en route to Moscow with a stopover in Salzburg, Austria. The next day Kissinger sent me two messages. The first indicated that the summit negotiators would maintain a firm position on the provisions of the SLBM freeze. We could not accept 48 modern submarines as the Soviet base point, if they insisted that this should include only Y and later classes. It was imperative for congressional reasons that there be some retirement of H and G classes involved in the Soviets reaching a level of 62. For this reason, the Soviet replacement threshold should be about 41 to 43 submarines, which corresponded to the real situation. Kissinger's second message requested an up-to-date assessment of where matters stood, to be available upon his arrival in Moscow Monday afternoon.

I replied that the delegation was trying to work out an agreed statement about locations for a Soviet ICBM defense site east of the Urals, or in the non-European part of the U.S.S.R., or at least 1,500 kilometers from the national capitals. The delegation did not favor a unilateral statement on ABM site separation. If necessary, the outcome should be left for the summit.

An agreed statement restricting increases in ICBM silo dimensions might still be reached. The delegation continued to press for a definition of a heavy missile but had concluded that the Soviets were unlikely to agree. A possible outcome might be an agreed statement on silo dimensions and whatever unilateral statement the United States might want to make on what constituted a heavy ICBM.

On SLBMs, the delegation would that morning give the Soviet delegation new texts for the SLBM freeze provisions, which included all types of Soviet SLBM launchers in the 950 ceiling. We were proposing a general article freezing SLBMs in the Interim Agreement, to be supplemented by a formal, signed protocol setting out the details. The protocol set out the ceilings for SLBM launchers and modern submarines operational and under construction: not more than 710 SLBMs and 44 modern submarines for the United States; not more than 950 SLBMs and 62 modern submarines for the U.S.S.R.

Because this protocol did not contain threshold numbers after which additional SLBM launchers would be deemed replacements and require dismantling of older ICBM or SLBM launchers, it would have required replacement to begin promptly because of our proposed interpretation of "under construction" as meaning that submarine hull sections put into construction halls after the signature of the agreement would be considered as being for replacement submarines.

The Soviets still favored an exchange of letters about details. The delegation was pressing for an agreed definition of SLBM launchers "under construction." The Soviet delegation would not agree and offered no alternative. We believed the Soviets were keeping flexible on this definition while negotiating SLBM levels.

About midmorning Kissinger advised that I should persist in the effort to get an agreed formulation on heavy missiles. But he also asked for a draft unilateral statement to which we might fall back. I sent the following draft:

> The United States would consider any ICBM having a volume significantly greater than that of the largest light ICBM now operational on either side to be a heavy ICBM. The U.S. proceeds on the premise that the Soviet side will give due account to this U.S. understanding.

After further unsuccessful negotiating on this issue at the Moscow summit, the delegation was instructed to make this unilateral statement on May 22.

Perhaps it should have struck me as strange that the delegations were apparently expected to continue to negotiate in Helsinki even while their principals were talking SALT in Moscow. A better blueprint for confusion could hardly be imagined. I cabled the Moscow White House that the delegation assumed it would be conducting negotiations through Wednesday, May 24. This was getting to be more like a military operation than a diplomatic process.

There was an important working session in Helsinki on Monday the twenty-second, involving Garthoff, Kishilov and Grinevsky. They negotiated a package of solutions for three remaining issues. While the Soviets still opposed an agreed definition of heavy ICBMs, they now accepted a compromise statement limiting increases in the size of silo launchers. "The Parties understand that in the process of modernization and replacement there would be no significant increase in the dimensions of land-based ICBM silo launchers." In tentatively agreeing to this statement, Garthoff made it clear that it did not meet our concerns about defining a heavy missile and explicitly reserved the United States position on this score.

The second part of the package settlement was Soviet agreement to an acceptable formulation on OLPARs. "The Parties agree not to deploy phased-array radars having a potential (the product of mean emitted power in watts and antenna area in square meters) exceeding three million, except as provided for in the Treaty, or except for the purposes of tracking objects in outer space or for use as national technical means of verification." We had come a long way from the Soviet proposal for 50 million.

There was also a compromise agreed interpretive statement on dismantling and replacement procedures. "The Parties understand that dismantling and/or destruction of ICBM launchers of older types constructed prior to 1964 and ballistic missile launchers on older submarines being replaced by new SLBM launchers on modern submarines will be initiated at the time of the beginning of sea trials of a replacement submarine, and will be completed in the shortest possible agreed period of time. Such dismantling or destruction, and timely notification thereof, will be accomplished under procedures to be agreed in the Standing Consultative Commission." This statement still left unsettled the thorny issue of what would be considered a replacement submarine as well as which older submarines would have to be replaced if the Soviets were to build up to 62 during the freeze.

These developments were reported to the Moscow White House shortly after nine o'clock Monday evening. The next day negotiations began at the Moscow summit.

CHAPTER

15

THE MOSCOW
NEGOTIATIONS

*"What mighty contests
rise from trivial things."*

POPE

The Moscow summit phase is still somewhat murky. It was inevitable that confusion would result when a new group of officials picked up the threads of a negotiation that had been under way for two and a half years. No complete record of the Moscow exchanges was made available to me in spite of several requests. It may well be that no full record exists—on the U.S. side —since again American interpreters were not used. The usual and best basis for a negotiating record, interpreters' verbatim notes, were not available to the American side. A bare summary of the agreements reached was provided us by the White House after the return to Washington.

The following account is taken from communications I received from and sent to the Moscow White House party, as it styled itself, oral reports after the Moscow phase ended, and material published by the White House. Out of the Moscow murk comes a picture of a rather confused group of officials, on both sides. The Moscow negotiations retraced some matters already agreed upon at Helsinki; concessions were made to American views and then withdrawn; matters of not great significance were blown up in importance; long-distance telephone and telegraphic advice was solicited and given between Moscow, Helsinki and Washington, and the Politburo engaged in long sessions wrestling with technical matters probably far from the range of normal experience of its members. After President Nixon had some early sessions with the Soviet top leadership, it seems that Foreign Minister Gromyko headed up the Soviet group, a man whose negotiating philosophy is suggested by his statement noted above that "It is the last twenty minutes of a negotiation that counts." Minister Smirnov, head of the Military-Industrial Commission which oversees missile and other defense manufacturing, played an important role. The American representatives then were Kissinger and two of his non-technical aides from the National Security Council staff.

The delegation at Helsinki had not known for sure whether the President wanted some SALT items left open for him to work out with the Soviet leadership. Back in March the President had said at a press conference that the sides were "still very far apart on some fundamental issues." He added that Smith had been instructed "to do everything he could to attempt to narrow those differences." But the President also said he did not think that an agreement would be worked out before his forthcoming Moscow trip. We were still under pressure from the White House to reach agreement on as many points as possible, but my hunch was that the President welcomed the opportunity to wind up SALT himself.

I wondered why the Soviet and American SALT delegates were excluded from the Moscow phase. The Soviets had a practice in SALT of imitating the Americans. I suspect that if American delegates had shown up in Moscow, Soviet delegates would have also been there. A Soviet remarked informally at the outset of the last Helsinki round that he expected Semenov and Smith to attend the summit and finish the negotiation in Moscow. Perhaps the President felt that he would have more flexibility if SALT delegates were absent. Probably he assumed that Kissinger knew all about SALT anyway. Whatever the reasons, it was a case of negotiations being too important to be left to the negotiators.

A week before the summit it seemed likely that some issues could only be resolved at Moscow. My guidance was to stand ready to attend a signing ceremony there. The delegation was to continue work with the view toward having a final agreement not later than Wednesday, May 24. On May 16, I called General Haig at the White House to ask if this meant that, if there were SALT negotiations at Moscow, I was not to participate. Haig estimated that possibility to be non-existent. He said that only one other delegate besides myself should attend the signing ceremony. I reminded him that the President had said earlier that he wanted all SALT principal delegates to be present. The President had changed his mind. If that were the case, I said, it was up to the White House to make the decision as to which agency to offend, the State Department, the Defense Department or the Joint Chiefs of Staff. The President directed that Paul Nitze and General Allison should attend with me. I thought this exclusion of Ambassador Parsons, who had made an important contribution to SALT, was an extreme example of heartlessness. With plenty of room in the airplane and I assumed in the Kremlin, I could only think that the President wanted to minimize the delegation's image at the Moscow signing. He couldn't afford to exclude the Pentagon. Garthoff was the only other member of the delegation to go to Moscow. He was needed for last-minute work on documents. The White House staff seemed leery of SALT people. "Don't bring your wives" was one of our last logistical instructions.

The SALT issues which the delegations had not been able to settle were all quite technical, a fact which even a close reader of this chapter may find exasperating. What would be permitted in the way of modernization and replacement under the freeze? When in the course of new launcher construction would older launchers have to be dismantled? But these issues had to be settled if there were to be SALT agreements. It was thus left to the top American political official and his national security aide to work out technicalities with the Soviet leadership, which included Minister Smirnov, whose technical knowledge to say the least exceeded that of President Nixon and Kissinger and the two NSC staff advisers.

Obviously, the President of the United States should make central decisions affecting strategic arms limitations—should the country enter a negotiation, should it agree to limit strategic arms, should it agree to limit only defensive arms or should there be parallel constraints on offensive arms, how many ABM sites should the United States negotiate for, should the constraints on offensive arms include SLBMs? But it seemed out of keeping for President Nixon to negotiate about what constituted a significant increase in the dimensions of a concrete silo, what was the appropriate cutoff point between a light and a heavy ballistic missile, or when and what kind of a missile launcher must be decommissioned if replaced by a new launcher. These were the main subjects of concern at Moscow. It is hard to avoid a conclusion that there was some pretense about the nature of these Moscow negotiations. They were tense. They lasted well into the night. But they concerned secondary, not central issues. Kissinger was to say later that most of the Moscow phase was spent on "esoteric aspects of replacement provisions and not about the substance of the agreement."

The provisions of the ABM Treaty had all been agreed on at Helsinki, save for one relatively minor matter involving the minimum distance that was to separate the two permitted ABM locations in order to prevent overlapping radar and interceptor coverage having some area defense potential. And that issue would be resolved at Moscow by adopting a formula worked out previously at Helsinki.

It had already been agreed that there would be no ICBM launcher construction starts after the freeze was signed. In fact, there had been none for the past year. The levels of submarines and launchers for the interim offensive freeze had already been worked out by Kissinger and Brezhnev in Moscow in April. The Soviet ceilings would be 950 missile launchers on 62 submarines. The Brezhnev April paper had specified U.S. ceilings at the existing force level of 656 launchers on 41 submarines; the United States was to have a right to increase these to 710 launchers on 44 submarines. Older launchers were to be decommissioned during the freeze if new SLBM launchers were built.

The remaining issues involved what throughout SALT had been called "modernization and replacement." The delegation had sought assurances that Soviet modernization programs would not result in a continuing build-up of their heavy ICBM (MLBMs) force through conversion of launchers for light missiles into launchers for heavy missiles. This involved the question of how much larger replacement missiles could be. The Soviets had agreed at Helsinki not to convert launchers for light missiles into launchers for heavy missiles, but they adamantly refused to define "heavy." Once again we found that it is easier to agree to limit numbers of weapons systems than to limit their characteristics. One difficulty here was that we were now attempting to agree only on a short-term negotiating freeze, not a comprehensive treaty of indefinite duration, and for verification reasons it was to cover missile launchers, not the missiles themselves. If missiles were not limited, getting an agreed definition of one type of missile would be a hard and, in the event, impossible task.

Another modernization and replacement issue involving ICBMs which the President and the Soviet leadership worked on was what increases in the size of existing silo launchers would be permitted during the freeze. They apparently were unaware that this issue had already been settled at Helsinki, on a basis authorized by Washington, that there would be no "significant" increases in launcher dimensions. Eventually negotiators at Moscow were to add some precision to this provision by agreeing that "significant" meant that silo increases could not exceed 10 to 15 per cent. But some ambiguity remained as to whether the 10 to 15 per cent referred to one or all dimensions of a silo.

The real center of the negotiating storm at Moscow involved SLBM modernization and replacement issues. We have seen that, before the summit started, it had been agreed that new strategic submarines with SLBM launchers could be built, up to the 62–950 and 44–710 ceilings. Submarines started after the freeze became effective had to replace older missile launchers. The difficulty was to agree on when a submarine was started. The remaining questions for the summit involved older launchers to be replaced and when they would have to be decommissioned. The question of when replacement was to start depended on several factors.

First, how many modern SLBM submarines did the Soviet Union then have in operation and, more importantly, how many did they then have "under construction"? It had been agreed that submarines under construction could be finished without requiring decommissioning of older submarines. The Soviets were apparently claiming they had 48 modern submarines operational or under construction, while, as Kissinger disclosed at a Moscow press conference, United States intelligence estimated the number at some 41 to 43. At Helsinki we had tried and would continue till the end to try to reach agreement on a definition of "under construction" that would have required the Soviets to decommission older launchers very soon after the freeze went into effect. Our formula would have started the decommissioning process with the first submarine hull sections to enter construction halls after the agreement was signed. Under this definition it would have made no difference whether one assumed that the Soviets had 41 or 43 or 48 submarines.

A second factor determining when decommissioning would start at issue in Moscow was whether or not older Soviet submarines of the G and H classes were to be included in the freeze. The United States maintained that they should be included; the Soviets wanted to exclude them.

Another submarine issue was the Soviet position that the United States should not exercise its right to replace its 54 older ICBM launchers, the Titan IIs, with new launchers on three new submarines; that is, whether the U.S. ceiling would be 41–656 or 44–710. The U.S. position was that, while we had no plans to exercise this right, the agreement should contain this right.

We were advised that President Nixon talked with the Soviet leadership about SALT on Tuesday afternoon, May 23. They returned to the subject at a second session which lasted well into the evening. After the Moscow phase was finished it was reported to us that these negotiations were highly successful. Nixon was told there would be no increase in the volume of Soviet missiles or silo launchers. All their G- and H-class submarines were rusty and outmoded and would soon be scrapped. Additional Soviet SLBMs would be only for replacement of older launchers from the date of signing of the Interim Agreement. Contrary to what the Soviet delegation had said at Helsinki, there was no need to mention 48 submarines in the agreement as the threshold at which replacement must start. It was heatedly argued by the Soviet side that our proceeding with the U. S. Trident submarine program would be inconsistent with the freeze. Apparently the Soviet leadership did not at all like the prospect of an agreement which limited the

Soviet SLBM force while the Americans started construction of Tridents. It was reported that a number of Politburo meetings were devoted to this issue. The matter was then dropped. It was agreed that the second Soviet ABM location would be more than 1,500 kilometers from Moscow.

Strange to say, only this last "concession" survived the final forty-eight hours of SALT. Even this would be shaved to 1,300 kilometers, which was the lower end of the range the delegations had agreed to at Helsinki several days before.

Back in Helsinki, I was somewhat surprised by Kissinger's first report. The President had talked about SALT that afternoon. His message was being sent during a break in talks. In regard to the heavy missile definition issue, the Soviets were prepared to drop the word "significant" between "no" and "increase" in a proposed interpretive statement. The Soviets asserted they had no intention of increasing the size of their missiles. Kissinger asked me to comment by FLASH reply regarding the acceptability of this proposition. This was a rather confusing concession. It appeared that the Moscow negotiators were mixing up the silo dimensions and the missile volume issues. I had often read about the fog of war. This was the fog of negotiation.

I replied that I did not understand the situation. The Soviets had been adamant in Helsinki against defining heavy missiles. The missile volume issue was related to but separate from the silo dimensions issue. A solution on silo dimensions had been reached in a package arrangement worked out by the delegations in Helsinki and previously reported to the Moscow White House. As part of the package, the Soviets had accepted the long-sought American OLPAR restraint and had agreed to a satisfactory statement on certain replacement and dismantling procedures. The solution of the silo dimensions issue was in the form of an agreed interpretive statement: "The Parties understand that in the process of modernization and replacement there would be no significant increase in the dimensions of land-based ICBM silo launchers." Omitted from this interpretive statement was a definition of a heavy missile on which we had not reached agreement but had reserved our position and as authorized by the White House planned to make a statement the next morning: "The United States would consider any ICBM having a volume significantly greater than that of the largest light ICBM now operational on either side to be a heavy ICBM. The U.S. proceeds on the premise that the Soviet side will give due account to this consideration." This was the situation at Helsinki. We had an agreement about silo launchers but none about missile volume. Of course, if the U.S.S.R. was now willing to make a commitment not to increase the size of its missiles—and it involved no concession on our part—we should accept. Even a unilateral Soviet statement that they had no intention of increasing the size of their missiles would be first rate. I pointed out that the Soviets at Helsinki would suspect that we had pocketed their earlier package concessions and then sought and received an additional concession at the highest level. I concluded by reminding Kissinger that we already had intelligence indications that the Soviets planned to do just what they now were reported as saying they would not do, increase the volume of their missiles. I added, "I am sure you must have found their statement extremely surprising in light of intelligence indications to the contrary."

This was puzzling, and that the President of the United States would get into such technicalities, important though they were, struck me as peculiar, if not dangerous. These first discussions on SALT appeared based on unawareness by our boss of the Helsinki record. Evidently one or both sides did not understand the differences in substance and status between the heavy missile and the silo dimension issues. The "no significant increase" interpretive statement was for silo dimensions, not missile volume. And U.S. intelligence was aware that the next generation of Soviet ICBMs then in advanced development would be larger in volume than the missiles they would replace. Whatever the reason, this first summit statement of Soviet intentions was incorrect. Why didn't Kissinger or others in the White House party pick up this misunderstanding? We had sent three cables reporting the status of the silo dimension and the heavy missile definition issue. The President and Kissinger perhaps had been too busy to read these reports. Kissinger probably did not have time to check with his staff before sending off his report to Helsinki during the break in the talks. This fumbling start did not bode well for the summit.

Wednesday, May 24. I learned at 9:00 A.M. that the negotiations in Moscow about possible constraints on ICBM modernization had evolved during the night. Kissinger wired that the talks had continued late. The Politburo that morning was considering a proposed agreed statement to the effect that during the process of modernization and replacement of ICBMs there could be no significant increase in the size of the silo launcher or the volume of the missile, with the word "significant" further defined to be no more than 10 to 15 per cent. This was probably the weirdest part of the entire Moscow negotiation. Although I received this information with the caveat not to share it with anybody until I heard further from Kissinger, I passed on its substance to the other principal delegates. And it was well I did. General Allison immediately pointed out that under the proposed formula the United States would have to halt its Minuteman III program, in which 550 single-warhead Minuteman I missiles were being replaced with MIRVed Minuteman III missiles. The Minuteman III missile had "significantly" larger volume than the Minuteman I. I did not realize it at the time, but the Moscow negotiators were about to stumble into a partial MIRV ban. The proposed formula would also have forbidden Soviet MIRVed missiles then under development.

I rushed a message to Moscow headed DELIVER IMMEDIATELY EVEN IF DR. KISSINGER IS IN MEETING. I advised that if this formula was mutually binding it would prevent continuance of the present program converting Minuteman I to Minuteman III which was scheduled to continue until 1974. The delegation's proposed solution avoided that impact on U.S. programs and seemed much better. It will be recalled that the purpose of the American proposal to limit increases in the size of silo launchers and to define heavy missiles was to prevent increased numbers of Soviet MLBMs from being deployed under the guise of modernization replacements for existing smaller ICBMs. The delegation had earlier proposed to define a heavy missile as one having greater volume than "the largest light ICBM now operational on either side," which was the Soviet SS-11. This formula would still permit significant increases in U.S. ICBMs while stopping the build-up of Soviet ICBMs. It was this solution that seemed much better than one which prohibited a 15 per cent increase in missile volume.

Not knowing whether my message would be delivered quickly

enough, I telephoned the Moscow White House. The only member of the party available was the chief of protocol, Ambassador Mosbacher. I did my best to explain to him the effect the provision under consideration would have on the U. S. MIRV program. Ambassador Mosbacher was the greatest yachtsman in the United States but he had little acquaintance with ICBMs. I finally said that it was most important not to accept anything until Kissinger received my message. I still am not sure whether Mosbacher knew what I was getting at, but he must have been impressed by my urgency. A Kissinger aide called back, saying they had my message from Mosbacher but couldn't understand it. They thought they were trying to get the definitions precisely as I had recommended. The ensuing conversation was not made easier by the fact that we were talking over an open line which I assumed Soviet intelligence agents were listening to. I advised him not to use the specific numbers (10 to 15 per cent) to define "significant" as it applied to missile volume. He asked if the delegation wanted a smaller or a larger number. I said, "No number." The one they were trying to use would have a negative impact on American programs. We were better off without a number. I left it that my next telegram would reach the Moscow White House shortly. They should then understand what I meant.

I again wired Kissinger, spelling out exactly how the formula under consideration would affect Minuteman III. I suggested that if at Moscow he could get agreement that there would be no significant increase (a) in the size of ICBM silo launchers or (b) in the volume of missiles *beyond that of the largest light ICBM currently deployed by either side,* and then define "significant" as no more than 10 to 15 per cent, the formula would be a great improvement.

Not surprisingly, the U.S. negotiators in Moscow were in the end unable to get an agreed limitation on increases in missile volume. Not surprisingly because both the original Moscow formula and my suggested amendment would have prevented deployment of the new Soviet ICBMs then being developed. I could only assume that after reviewing the Helsinki message Kissinger withdrew American support for the formula he had reported to be under Moscow consideration. And Soviet experts must have brought to the attention of their leaders what the formula the Politburo was considering would do to their new missile programs. The Politburo probably then disposed of this issue rather quickly. It would have been the major irony of SALT and of arms control history if the leaders had inadvertently stumbled into MIRV controls and a large cutback in their strategic arms plans. Some people may say we should have kept quiet at Helsinki!

The next I heard about missile volume was in Kissinger's report next morning on the President's "extensive talks" Wednesday night. "There was no give on missile volume and it was left that we would make a unilateral statement." Wednesday afternoon, Kissinger wired that my messages on the missile volume formula had been "most helpful." He added this poignant passage: "You should understand that we are operating in a situation where we never know from hour to hour with whom we are meeting or what the topic will be. I will inform you as soon as we have something." That struck me as a blueprint for how not to conduct a negotiation of any sort.

On the aircraft on which we returned from Moscow to Helsinki, Paul Nitze drafted a short memorandum entitled "The Last Twenty Minutes of a Negotiation Are the Most Important." It included guidelines for getting the best out of those twenty minutes. First, "Arrange for the negotiations to be conducted at several levels. Then try to pocket the optimum for your side arising at any one of the levels. Subtechniques include: (a) General statements at top subsequently withdrawn at a lower level; (b) Introduction, without prior notice, of added starters at an intermediate level, to swing situation in your favor; *e.g.,* at political meeting, introduce "expert" prepared to use his special knowledge to your advantage under circumstances where those on other side not in a position to contradict him." Secondly, "arrange to have top negotiations in your capital. Have their Delegation split between Kremlin, Spasso House and Rossiya Hotel. Use your interpreters for both sides. Have no typewriters nor Xerox machines available when needed. Give other side as minimum secure communications facilities as possible."

Both Helsinki delegations now were kept in suspense We were to find out later that the Soviets received no information at all about the Moscow talks until the day the agreements were signed. For once we were the better informed. Semenov remarked that it was a good thing that our leaders were discussing these matters, even though he had instructions to conclude agreements in Helsinki. I confirmed that I had the same guidance. He went on to say he had no new instructions on the SLBM question, that the Soviet side considered the number 48 important, that contrary to my earlier claim this figure did not put in question the efficacy of national technical means of verification. It was apparent that the Soviets continued to be sensitive to our argument that the Soviet claim to 48 submarines called into question the adequacy of national means of verification. The Soviet position remained that additional SLBM launchers on modern submarines would, beginning with the forty-ninth submarine, be replacements for older types of ICBM or SLBM launchers. This fell short of an outright claim that they then had 48 under construction and operational. But it was not very far short. I then offered a strictly personal and uninstructed view that it might be possible even at this late date to change the form of the detailed SLBM provisions. Here I was trying to lay groundwork for a possible fallback. Although I did not say so, I had in mind that if at Moscow a formal agreement to freeze submarines and launchers could not be agreed on the sides could make declarations of their intentions regarding SLBMs during the freeze period. By this time I preferred a less formal way of registering what would be a substantial potential Soviet numerical advantage in strategic submarines.

I also read and handed him a text which I introduced as a "statement of the U.S. side."

> The United States side has studied the "Statement of the Soviet Side" of May 17 concerning compensation for submarine basing and SLBM submarines belonging to third countries. The United States does not accept the validity of the considerations in that statement.

Semenov said he understood our position. We could consider the Soviet statement a unilateral one. I repeated that the U.S.S.R. statement was not acceptable. Semenov replied that if there had been agreement the statement would have been bilateral. He was sorry the sides could not reach agreement on it but he thought that this situation could hardly change in the short time remaining.

By Wednesday afternoon, May 24, the only issue left at Moscow involved the SLBM freeze details—when would the decommissioning process start and would older Soviet submarines be included in the freeze? I had made clear my concern about the SLBM terms which Kissinger had brought back from Moscow the previous month. This was not because their implementation during a five-year interim period would affect the military balance significantly, but rather because it seemed unwise formally to register such a large potential submarine numbers differential in the Soviets' favor, especially if after this Moscow meeting negotiations were to continue looking toward offensive arms limitations based on equality. I had expressed concern on this score in the Verification Panel, and to the President in the National Security Council. If the Soviets were to have such a significant increase in their SLBM force, I hoped it would not be with the explicit blessing of a formal arms control agreement. I gathered that my views had not been welcomed by the President.

I became even less satisfied with the SLBM arrangement when it was clarified in May by the U.S.S.R. position that it would not start decommissioning older launchers until it had finished its forty-ninth modern submarine. As we approached the summit I was still urging Kissinger to consider a less formal way than an agreement to try to get some restraint on the Soviet SLBM program. I would have preferred limiting the formal agreement to ICBMs, with parallel declarations of intent to exercise some restraint regarding strategic submarines while the negotiations continued for an offensive arms treaty to match the ABM Treaty. In any event, if a formal agreement was to include submarines I felt the United States should make no further concessions.

The Moscow negotiation on the submarine freeze was as confusing to us in Helsinki as it probably will be to the reader. There were now two positions. The delegation wanted all three classes of Soviet missile submarines—Ys, Gs and Hs—included in the freeze, and we wanted the Soviets to decommission older launchers as soon as construction was started on an SLBM submarine after the freeze was signed. The Soviets apparently wanted to be able to reach the agreed freeze ceiling of 950 launchers on

62 modern submarines without decommissioning older strategic submarines, and they did not want to start decommissioning older ICBM launchers for some time after the freeze started. The American delegates watched as best they could at long distance as the Moscow negotiation unfolded. The eventual compromise reached at Moscow was to include in the freeze the older class of nuclear submarines (Hs) of which there were 9 with 30 launchers but not the diesel G class, and to set an arbitrary threshold number of 740 Soviet launchers (operational and under construction) after which new SLBM launchers had to be replacements requiring reductions in launchers for older ICBMs and launchers on H-class submarines. In retrospect, it does not seem so very important. I now think we at Helsinki somewhat exaggerated the significance of the need for immediate decommissioning and inclusion of the diesel G-class submarines. But in pressing my positions, I thought I was doing what the President wanted—to have the views of his chief arms control adviser before he made final decisions. During the Moscow negotiation Kissinger repeatedly characterized this advice as "very helpful." I hope that subsequent reports that President Nixon felt I was trying to frustrate his SALT efforts were not true.

On Wednesday afternoon I wired Kissinger—the first of what turned out to be a number of fairly sharp exchanges over the next thirty-six hours. A good ABM treaty and a fair ICBM freeze were now in sight. I believed that he was aware that I had some reservation about the SLBM deal. I was concerned that what would appear in certain quarters to be an inequitable submarine arrangement could sour the whole SALT outcome. In any event, I advised that the President not accept any SLBM freeze that did not call for compulsory decommissioning from the start of the freeze. Rather than settle for anything less, I would limit the SALT arrangements to an ABM treaty plus an ICBM freeze. This would still be a significant arms control accomplishment. Even taking into consideration present expectations, I believed there would be broad public support for a position in which we had tried our best to freeze SLBMs but the Soviet offer was unacceptable. We would push hard in the second SALT negotiation for overall offensive limitations including SLBMs. Meanwhile, we would press on with strategic programs that we deemed necessary and that were not frozen. I asked that these considerations be put to the President. What I did not know then was that on that Wednesday afternoon, as later reported in Moscow to one of the American delegates, the Soviets were taking the position that they would not agree to any interim freeze unless submarines and launchers were included! After many months of refusing to include submarines, the Soviets were now making their inclusion a sine qua non for an interim agreement. That said something about Soviet satisfaction with the submarine freeze levels agreed on in the previous month.

This long Wednesday came to a close with another message from Kissinger shortly after midnight. It stated the obvious but in a disconcerting manner. The situation in Moscow did not warrant my traveling there the next morning. I should plan to stay in place until the agreements were wrapped up. Meetings were being held during the night and I would be advised of developments. So I stayed "in place" as SALT continued in the Kremlin through most of the night.

Thursday, May 25. I was awakened about four o'clock by a FLASH message from Kissinger for immediate reply. The cable reported that the President had had extensive talks on SALT Wednesday night. The only ABM Treaty business transacted in Moscow was now settled. As proposed by the United States in Helsinki the sides' two ABM sites would be separated by no less than 1,300 kilometers. The United States would make a statement that its ICBM defense location would be at Grand Forks. Kissinger's message said this was acceptable if I agreed. The Soviets would table this position in Helsinki. The idea that I would not accept something that the President and the Politburo had agreed on was somewhat bizarre, and this Kissinger deference was a novelty. Perhaps he was leaning over backward to avoid any duplication of the recently aborted missile volume episode.

The Soviets at Moscow had provided a text of an agreed statement on decommission procedures. They would also table that in Helsinki, and we were to answer them there. Apparently there was a limit to the technicalities that the President and Kissinger wanted to get involved in. The delegations had already agreed ad referendum on a jointly drafted compromise statement on dismantling and destruction procedures. When the new Soviet dis-

mantling statement was received from Moscow it was identical
with the agreed Helsinki draft.

On Wednesday night the Soviets also had provided a text on
the ICBM silo dimensions issue. It will be recalled that the delegations at Helsinki had already agreed on the following: "The
Parties understand that in the process of modernization and replacement the size of land-based ICBM silo launchers will not be
significantly increased." The new Soviet draft, except for the
omission of the word "significantly" before "increased," was the
same as that agreed upon at Helsinki. Kissinger reported that it
had, however, been agreed at Moscow that the U.S. side could
choose between this later formula or the earlier Helsinki statement that had included the word "significantly." In that event
"significantly" would be defined as 10 to 15 per cent. Kissinger
magnanimously, or because he was no longer fully confident of
his technical judgment, wired that the choice was up to the delegation. The President required my statement of preference for a
meeting scheduled for ten o'clock that morning.

Kissinger also reported that most of the talk had been about
submarines and particularly an effort on his part to obtain immediate beginning of decommissioning. He reported that the Soviets
had promised an answer at 10:00 A.M. to the threshold figure of
740 SLBMs, which the delegation had proposed as a base. Apparently Kissinger's staff had not followed the arithmetic of this
part of the negotiation because he asked me to provide an immediate answer as to how the 740 figure achieved immediate
decommissioning.

A reply was dispatched at 6:45 A.M. Thursday morning. Since
the figure of 1,300 kilometers was within the range we had proposed, I endorsed it. This was subsequently elaborated by Kissinger in a press conference. He said a 1,500-kilometer figure was
originally accepted by the Soviets. Then when the working crew
worked it out it turned out that 1,300 was a better figure for
reasons that were too technical to go into. The President then
proposed 1,300. I was not advised as to who was on this "working crew" or what the technical reasons were.

On the question of allowed increases in silo dimensions (not
missile volume), we elected the version which did not include the
word "significantly," advising that it was clearly preferable. But

the next day we were to be informed that the other version had been agreed upon at Moscow. No explanation was given. I guess it was another case of, having been given a choice, we made the wrong choice—just one in a series of Moscow curiosities! Another possible explanation based on an informal report from one of the participants in the Moscow phase is that Kissinger checked with Washington as well as Helsinki and got differing advice. Perhaps Washington (read the Pentagon) felt that you never could tell when some increase in silo dimensions might be useful. It looked like a case of Soviet willingness to accept a stricter qualitative constraint than the United States.

I advised Kissinger that we now planned to make the unilateral statement about heavy missiles as directed by the Moscow White House in the form which had been forwarded to Moscow on May 22. This was the statement which earlier I predicted would perhaps have "some slight deterrent effect . . . but I wouldn't put a very high estimate on the value of such deterrence."

I then explained how the figure of 740 launchers had been derived. Estimates were that the Soviets then had 41 to 43 Y-class submarines with 608 to 652 launchers operational and under construction. Adding 100 launchers that were on G- and H-class submarines made a total of 708 to 752 SLBM launchers. Seven hundred and forty was a relatively safe arbitrary figure up toward the high side of this range (and, in fact, corresponded exactly with a later estimate of 42 Y class with 640 launchers, plus 100 on the G and H classes!). In view of the already agreed ceiling of 950 launchers, a 740 threshold would require the Soviets to decommission all 209 older ICBMs as well as all older submarines if they were to build up to the 950 SLBM ceiling (950 minus 209 equals 741 rounded to 740). However, at the risk of complicating an already confused situation, I had to remind Kissinger that, although this threshold number of 740 launchers had appeared in an earlier U.S. draft (May 19), a later U.S. proposal of May 22 had not referred to it. This later Helsinki formulation would have required immediate decommissioning regardless of the actual Soviet SLBM launcher numbers operational and under construction at the date of signature of the agreement and was clearly the best basis for an SLBM arrangement. The reader may properly feel put upon in being faced with this abundance of numbers. But that's the way it was in Moscow in May 1972, and it is important that these events be seen as they occurred if repetition of these disorganized days is to be avoided.

By midafternoon the Soviet Helsinki delegation had said nothing about the new silo dimension text their authorities had proposed in Moscow. The main action in Helsinki was the continued effort to reach an agreed interpretation of the term "submarines under construction," a wasted effort as we soon learned. The Soviets seemed loath to get involved in any more interpretations. Time was on their side and running out. I wired Kissinger that we were stymied since the Soviet delegation had no instructions. If appropriate, I suggested he point out the Helsinki situation to the Soviet leadership so that we could get on with the process of closing out in Helsinki that night, if expectations were for signing the agreements the next day. It was no use. Kissinger replied that, as they understood it, the Politburo had been in session all day and they were thus as stymied as we were. They would continue to keep us fully abreast of developments.

By this time tempers were short. The negotiation that we had so carefully developed for several years had been taken out of our hands—or had it? Some matters were still being discussed at Helsinki. Some other matters were being referred by Moscow to Helsinki. Things were going on in Moscow that we either did not know about or did not understand. The white nights of late May in the high latitude of Helsinki competed with Kissinger's telegrams to kill sleep. Was this the necessary labor pain accompanying the birth of new international law?

Shortly after 10:00 A.M. (11:00 Moscow time) I received from Moscow a Soviet draft text on the submarine issue. The state of SALT play can best be judged by Kissinger's procedural advice which accompanied it. "We will tell them to propose it to you, but need your views soonest." This was parallel negotiation with a vengeance. The language of the new text looked promising.

> The Parties undertake to limit submarine-launched ballistic missile launchers and modern submarines with ballistic missiles to the number operational and under construction on the date of signature of this agreement, and also to launchers and submarines constructed additionally, provided that their

construction will be carried out in a manner prescribed for the sides as replacements for equal numbers of launchers for ICBMs of older type constructed before 1964, or launchers of older submarines.

This read as if the Soviets had accepted our immediate replacement concept. I advised Kissinger that the Soviet draft appeared to stem from our text of May 22 and seemed to meet its substance.

Kissinger telephoned on Thursday evening to say that the Soviet position was not as I had understood from the language of their new text. They did not interpret the immediate replacement language as I had. Gromyko had something different in mind for the "manner prescribed for the sides" for replacement. Kissinger asked my views. I wired that I was not sufficiently clued in to the Moscow exchanges to give categorical advice. I did not understand the reason for the apparent switch in that morning's reported position. In these circumstances, I could only advise the President to hold to the present U.S. position through the night. I added parenthetically that the difference between the U.S. and the U.S.S.R. positions now appeared to be 60 old launchers on 20 diesel submarines, plus two additional test facilities having 10 launchers. If the President later found it necessary to adjust the U.S. position, he might consider the following line. If the Soviet position was that 60 old launchers on 20 diesel submarines would make the difference between a major strategic arms limitation agreement or no agreement; and if he therefore were to agree that these diesel boats need not be included in the freeze; and if the Soviets would agree to have no more than 20 diesel-powered strategic submarines (plus the two test facilities) during the freeze and not to place modern SLBM launchers on any of them; and if they further agreed that any replacements for these diesel boats must be counted under the 950–62 ceilings; the United States could agree with the Soviet proposal. Coming back to the immediate replacement question, I said that such an adjustment should be based on the understanding that any additional modern SLBM submarine started after the date of the signature of the agreement would count as a replacement submarine and must be accompanied by the dismantling of either an old nuclear-propelled submarine (H class) or an appropriate number of older ICBM launchers. Kissinger replied that these latest views were very helpful.

On rereading my message, I began to have doubts. I wired Kissinger again to advise a harder position. After mulling over further the omission of the diesel submarines, and given the intelligence estimates and the definition of "under construction," I saw no way to meet simultaneously all three of the following conditions: (a) levels for the Soviets of 62–950 (which had already been agreed); (b) the Soviet aim to exclude the diesel submarines; and (c) the U.S. need for a rational explanation of an agreed replacement formulation that would not be a clear admission of a free ride for the Soviets. I knew this new advice would not be well received. It provoked a sharp response, vintage Kissinger. He much preferred my earlier telegram. Could I explain how 60 missiles of 300- to 700-mile range, barred from modernization in diesel submarines that have to surface to fire, representing less than 3 per cent of the total Soviet force, could represent a free ride? What were we giving up that we had intended to do? The Soviets in turn would have a ceiling on their SLBMs, a ban on modernization of the diesel class, and lost 240 launchers. If the Soviets refused to accept the compromise, Kissinger wanted someone to explain how our security was enhanced when we then confronted the G class, the H class, 240 more launchers, and a larger number of SLBMs. My advice on the G-class launchers obviously had angered the Moscow White House. Kissinger told me on the phone that everyone in Washington approved of the line he was pressing for and that only I was objecting to it. A quick check with Phil Farley, acting director of ACDA, disclosed that he had not been consulted.

Friday, May 26. Early this morning news came in from Moscow explaining how the Soviets wanted to handle the replacement issue. Kissinger advised that meetings on SALT had been occurring sporadically between the President's meetings on other matters with the Soviet leaders. He sent along a text which Gromyko had just handed him of a protocol to the Interim Agreement spelling out details of the SLBM freeze. The first clause set out ceilings for the United States of 710–44 and for the U.S.S.R. of 950–62 SLBM launchers on modern submarines The second clause used the base figure we had proposed of 740 Soviet SLBMs as a replacement threshold.

Additional submarine-launched ballistic missile launchers up to the above-mentioned levels for the USA in excess of 656 nuclear submarine-launched ballistic missile launchers and for the USSR—in excess of 740 nuclear submarine-launched ballistic missile launchers, operational and under construction, may become operational as replacements for equal numbers of launchers for ICBMs of older types constructed before 1964 or of ballistic missile launchers of older submarines.

In the ensuing discussion, the Soviets had made clear that all H-class missiles were included in the 740 total. But the 20 G-class diesel submarines with their 60 launchers had been excluded from the replacement threshold and ceiling for SLBMs by the use of the modifier "nuclear" before the word "submarine." "Nuclear" stands out underlined in blue ink on the copy of the telegram I received in Helsinki. I doubt that anyone recalled then that back in 1970, when a more comprehensive arrangement was still being negotiated, the Soviets had agreed that launchers on diesel submarines would be included.

Kissinger reported that he had proposed additional language based on my earlier message. "Deployment of modern submarine-launched ballistic missiles on any submarine, regardless of type, will be counted against the total submarine-launched ballistic missiles permitted for the US and the USSR." This point, which was covered in the final agreement, prevents the Soviets from installing launchers for modern SLBMs on the G-class diesel boats over and above the ceiling of 950 launchers. That was a minor plus. But it would have no effect whatever on the immediate replacement question. If our estimates were correct that the U.S.S.R. then had 638 to 682 SLBM launchers on Y- and H-class nuclear submarines, operational and under construction, the Soviets could deploy from 58 to 102 launchers on three to six new submarines not then under construction before they reached the replacement threshold of 740 launchers on nuclear submarines. By adopting the U.S.-proposed base figure of 740 but successfully excluding from it launchers on G-class submarines, the Soviet negotiators in Moscow subtly postponed the requirement to trade in older launchers for a good part of the freeze period.

Kissinger ended his first message of this last day of SALT I by saying that he believed the issues discussed in our early telegrams could be settled between us and the Soviet delegation. He said that a signing was not likely until Sunday. I had not the foggiest idea of what he meant about early telegrams which contained issues that we could settle in Helsinki. Obviously, nothing important could be settled in Helsinki while the summit talks continued.

I had wired him on May 23 that a Soviet delegate had asked about an assurance that the United States would not exercise its right to replace 54 old Titan ICBMs with SLBMs on new submarines. The possibility of such an assurance was known by a number of members of the U.S. delegation. I advised Kissinger that I thought an assurance that could be made public might be called for. The next I heard of the Titan matter was early Friday morning when Kissinger passed on a Gromyko text which contained the language, "The US side will take an obligation in a written form not to construct additionally three submarines in excess of 41. The text of the undertaking shall be agreed with the Soviet side." I then had wired that I thought the best Titan formula would be a unilateral statement that "the US in practice does not have plans for nor does it intend to exercise the right during the five-year freeze." If the Soviets pressed for a more firm commitment with regard to Titans, I thought we would be better off not to have this "right" at all. The final Kissinger message also said that the Titan replacement question would not be included in the protocol and would be handled in other channels. I was later informally told that a message had been given to the Soviets on this matter but I was not told its contents. Kissinger subsequently explained at a press conference on July 22, 1974, that "the President thought it desirable to tell the Soviet Union what would become apparent within a matter of weeks anyway, namely that we had no intention of exercising the conversion right from Titan missiles to submarines during the period of the Interim Agreement." It has been reported that this took the form of a letter.

At 4:45 A.M. on May 26, I sent a final message to Kissinger in a last unsuccessful attempt to influence the SLBM outcome. I knew from the tone of his last report that agreement would be reached at Moscow soon—perhaps it already had been. But immediate replacement might be salvaged from the Gromkyo formula even while excluding the G-class diesel boats. I repeated my doubts about retaining an understandable rationale for a submarine freeze with a 62–950 Soviet ceiling excluding the G-class submarines. If Soviet submarines were to be under a freeze all of them should be included. But I thought the Gromkyo formula as amended by the Kissinger additions seemed better than no SLBM freeze if certain conditions were met: (a) the President had concluded that the public and congressional relations problem was manageable and that the rationale was adequate for the Soviets to have 62–950 plus the G class, and (b) if the Soviets would decommission older missiles from the start, thus getting a right to build their last 60 or so launchers before reaching 950 without replacing anything (which might be justified because the non-compensatory phase would be in the latter part of the freeze period, which might not be reached because of prior successful negotiation of a follow-on agreement, and because the Soviets might elect to retire the G-class boats). I assumed that the Soviets would agree to accept the language they had tabled the previous day. This was important because it called for immediate decommissioning. There should be no reference to 740. An explicit 740 base line would be inconsistent with the requirement for immediate replacement. It was also important to avoid a gap between our intelligence estimates at date of signature and the Soviet opening freeze number. Another short night was finished!

About noon on May 26, Kissinger reported that tentative agreement had been reached on outstanding issues, subject to editing by the delegations in Helsinki. The President and Brezhnev hoped very much to sign an agreement not later than 8:00 P.M. that day. I should arrive in Moscow by 6:30 P.M. Minister Semenov was welcome to ride in the U. S. Air Force plane which had been standing by to take the American delegates to Moscow. If any substantive points still deeply concerned me, I was to contact Kissinger at once. I wonder what would have happened if, with about seven hours left to do the editing, hold a final meeting of the delegates, and make the flight to Moscow, I had taken up this suggestion and proposed substantive changes. The expression "You must be kidding" came to mind when I read this contrived record of how Kissinger valued the delegation's judgment. And after two and a half years of SALT, this unreasonable speed was made necessary because the Soviet leadership reportedly was now insisting that the agreements had to be signed that day. Saturday or Sunday would not do. The Soviets' reasons for this urgency were not made clear. Perhaps they wanted to close out the negotiations before President Nixon had second thoughts. Perhaps it was to prevent those pesky Helsinki people from pointing out mistakes.

The Soviet draft texts of the previous day had been accepted, with the one American amendment (which the delegation had proposed) providing that, if modern missile launchers were put on the old G-class diesel submarines, they would have to be included under the ceiling. There would be an agreed statement that the size of land-based ICBM silo launchers would not be "significantly" increased, with the further agreed interpretation that the word "significantly" meant 10 to 15 per cent. It has been reported that the texts of instructions to the two delegations for these final agreements were checked in Moscow to see that the Russian and English versions were identical. Kissinger later told a press conference this was "the first time that the instructions on the Soviet side and the American side were absolutely identical to make sure there wouldn't be any hang-up because of misinterpretation." But this is fiction. The telegram I received stated that "Semenov will have Russian texts which we have not, repeat not, checked here." The message said that my help was much appreciated. "The President is very proud of accomplishment and your contribution." Before the day was over I had reason to question the second sentiment.

After the negotiation was over we saw a written report as to how the last phase of the Moscow talks had gone. All day Thursday, the twenty-fifth, there had been a Politburo meeting. In the evening Gromyko advised Kissinger that further discussion was necessary. The next morning Kissinger and his two aides met with Gromyko, accompanied by Smirnov. Gromyko said their ABM site for ICBM defense would be more than 1,300 kilometers from Moscow. Kissinger said that President Nixon had been told that 1,500 kilometers was acceptable. Gromyko replied that the delegation at Helsinki had agreed to 1,300.

Gromyko said there would be no significant increase in silo dimensions. Kissinger said that President Nixon had been told that no increases in either Soviet missile volume or silo dimensions would be necessary during the freeze. Gromyko said that Kissinger had misunderstood.

Gromyko proposed a replacement threshold for SLBMs of 740 launchers. Kissinger said that President Nixon had been told that all the G- and H-class submarines would have to be scrapped if the Soviets were to build up to the 950–62 ceilings. Gromyko said the Hs could be included in the 740 but the Gs would not be included, that they might or might not be scrapped. Kissinger recalled that the Soviet leadership had said that replacement would start from the very beginning. Smirnov said that they had been assured that they could have five or six more submarines as an offset. Kissinger said that the agreed ceiling of 950 already reflected that offset. Smirnov said that in any event they had more than 740 launchers in Y-class submarines alone, that they had operational or under construction submarines with 768 launchers. They would agree to start replacement after the seven hundred and fortieth launcher. And Gromyko said that it was essential to reach agreement about submarines. They would not agree to a freeze unless it included submarines on these terms.

Shortly thereafter, at eleven o'clock Friday morning, the Americans in Moscow were advised that Soviet leadership wanted to sign the agreements that day. The Gromyko provisions were then agreed. Perhaps Kissinger was right in saying later that every concession at Moscow was made by the Soviets. But the report given to us hardly supports that conclusion.

About 2:30 P.M. I was informed that President Nixon and Secretary Brezhnev had definitely decided to sign the agreements at eight o'clock that night. Brezhnev's signing instead of Nikolai Podgorny, the head of state, was an indication of the importance placed on these agreements for the U.S.S.R. as well as for Brezhnev's personal fortunes. Kissinger's last message sounded somewhat hilarious to me. "Don't be bashful about making suggestions to the other side because our impression is that they will accept anything reasonable within the basic framework of the agreement." It scarcely gybes with the later Kissinger press conference statement already cited that this was "the first time that the in-

structions on the Soviet side and the American side were absolutely identical to make sure there wouldn't be any hang-up because of misinterpretation." And this advice was less than six
hours before the agreements were to be signed some four hundred
miles away.

In spite of our having been kept away from Moscow and the
fact that our views, when solicited, had been only partially accepted, we felt that the agreements—especially the ABM Treaty
—were solid accomplishments. Although appearances may cast
the delegation in the role of bucking what the Moscow White
House had been trying to do, that was not the case. At Helsinki
our aim was to get the best settlement possible. We knew from
months of struggling with these issues what negotiating difficulties
the President and Kissinger were up against in trying to get
agreement on the interim freeze. We were well aware of the fact
that, in the case of the "freeze" on offensive systems, since only
Soviet programs were to be restrained U.S. leverage was not
great. But we also knew that since the Soviets had not suspended
the negotiation over the bombing and mining of Haiphong they
put a very high value on SALT.

Could a better settlement have been reached? The only
significant issue in my judgment that was considered at Moscow
was the definition of a heavy missile. Any definition that the
United States would have agreed to would have stopped several
important Soviet ICBM/MIRV programs. I believe now that
there was no chance that the Soviets would have agreed to stop
those programs in order to get an interim freeze under which U. S.
MIRV programs would proceed. When the President did not succeed in this aim, he had the implicit choice to end SALT (including abandoning the ABM Treaty) or to make the best of it by accepting a freeze that left the heavy missile definition issue
unresolved. I think he made the correct choice. In fact, this was
so clearly indicated that I doubt that he even thought of any other
course.

The fact that the Soviets succeeded in deferring the time when
they were required to start scrapping older launchers was of little
significance for the strategic balance. And the exclusion of the
G-class diesel submarines was of even less. These submarines
were not of the first line. Since he had tried to get the G-class

submarines included, I did not take seriously Kissinger's press conference statement that gave the impression that the G-class exclusion was our idea. "We wanted to prevent the U.S.S.R. from trading in a weapon which we were certain they would have to retire in any event for a modern weapon." That was clearly a rationalization. But an ingenious one.

Before we left Helsinki Garthoff, Grinevsky and Kishilov beavered away for several hours putting the Moscow texts into final form. It was well into the afternoon before the delegations were ready for the Helsinki closing session, a miniplenary at which Semenov and I read into the record various agreed and unilateral interpretations of the two agreements. Semenov handed me a copy of a "statement of the Soviet Side" of May 17 claiming a right to more SLBM submarines and launchers if Great Britain or France increased their fleets of missile submarines. I asked why it was necessary to reintroduce that document. He replied that he wanted it recorded as of May 26. I then reread my rejection statement of May 24. I next read a statement that the ABM sites would be separated by no less than 1,300 kilometers. Semenov accepted it. I stated that the term "significantly increased" in the silo launcher dimensions provision meant 10 to 15 per cent. Semenov said that corresponded to their understanding. I read into the record a U.S. statement of our understanding of a heavy ICBM. Semenov noted that this had been the subject of lengthy discussions and no common understanding had been reached, "therefore the understanding reached between the two parties in the Interim Agreement was valid." In effect this left the matter up in the air. Then it was decided that the formal portion of the meeting would be resumed on the flight to Moscow for the purpose of initialing the interpretive statements and the session was recessed to permit a hasty departure.

There was some confusion at the airport. The Soviets, hearing that the U.S. aircraft (which had been standing by for several days) was a somewhat antiquated propeller plane which would take several hours to make the trip, had chartered a Finnair Caravel and proposed that we fly with them. I declined and repeated the invitation that they fly with us. Since there was work still to be done and I made quite clear that I would not change my mind, we all boarded the American plane. Initialing the agreed interpretations was quickly accomplished, and the ABM Treaty and Interim Agreement were placed on a table. We all had a glass of beer. Whereupon we ran into turbulent air and I had visions of delivering two beer-soaked parchments to our principals. I do not recall whether we put the beer or the documents in a safe place. Perhaps both. It had been an extraordinary piece of work to put the two documents in final form for signing. They were all but letter perfect. But on the plane a final close reading disclosed several insignificant lapses from protocol. There was now no time to make corrections. This was done the following day so these agreements had to be signed twice.

Beer or no beer, this was an exuberant group of flying negotiators. The climax of three years of hard work overcame any specific reservations the Americans might have had about the interim freeze. We all realized the drama of this airborne conclusion of our long efforts and thought it would be a good idea to record our thoughts in the airplane's guestbook. Here is what we wrote.

A day we should all remember with the greatest satisfaction—it may well be the day on which was started one of mankind's great adventures.

It seems specially fitting that members (and Chiefs) of the Soviet Delegation and the American Delegation are flying together to Moscow with great trophies of our long hunt together for a start—and a very good one—on control of strategic arms. May we soon have more such trophies to bring back to our capitals.

GERARD SMITH

This is a happy moment in my life to be flying to Moscow on this airplane with an awareness of a fulfilled obligation and looking forward to a historic event—the signing by the leaders of our two States of the important agreements on the limitation of strategic weapons.

V. S. SEMENOV

Every man must want to do his best. The worse will come of itself. All's well that ends well.

P. S. PLESHAKOV

We the Delegations have sought to assure that today marks a watershed and a beginning. Our peoples and history will judge our efforts.

ROYAL B. ALLISON

I have a feeling of completed work of great significance, which, I hope, will last as a bright memory for my whole life.

A. N. SHCHUKIN

From the beginning we agreed that nothing was agreed until all was agreed. Today we achieve the reward of two and one half years patient and constructive work to bring that about. I feel that only those of us who were a part of it will ever fully know what was involved.

PAUL H. NITZE

After what has been said above, to which I subscribe, this aircraft should be preserved as a historical monument.

K. A. TRUSOV

On arriving at the Moscow airport I was handed the following message by a State Department officer:

Secretary Rogers asked me to tell you, before he left for dinner, that you should be sure to attend the press briefing in connection with the 11:00 P.M. signing. Subsequently and as plans evolved, I learned that arrangements have been made for you to go directly from the airport to the Embassy for the 10:00 P.M. backgrounder.

But just after receiving this message I was escorted by some Soviet officials to a car. They told me I was wanted at the Kremlin. I objected, saying that I was due at the press conference. After repeated assertions that I was expected at the Kremlin, I got in the car with Semenov. Driving in, I only half listened to his descriptions of the places of interest along the way. It had been a hard day and my mind came up with no satisfactory explanation for my conflicting instructions about the press conference. I concluded it was a normal mix-up on the fringes of a summit conference.

The sight of the American flag spotlighted above the Kremlin was extraordinarily cheerful. But my reception was not. No one knew why I had been called there. The few American security officers standing around the President's quarters seemed never even to have heard of SALT. I decided to try to find the press conference. It was to be held in the embassy snack bar. When I got there it had not yet started as Kissinger was still at a banquet being given by the President for the Soviet leadership. I paced up and down a dark alley outside the bar, trying to keep my temper. Except for the beer, I had had nothing to eat or drink during this day which had started about 3:00 A.M. Here I was in the Soviet capital for the signing of SALT agreements on which I had worked so long and I felt like an alley cat looking for a scrap to eat while the great men dined in state. This was some ending for the "most momentous negotiation ever entrusted to an American Delegation." (I learned later that I hadn't been the only delegate in a holding pattern. General Allison and Paul Nitze were stranded at the airport for some time before they could arrange a ride to their hotel. I was told that for some reason the Soviet authorities had not permitted American delegation cars to meet the flight.) Finally Kissinger arrived.

He must have been surprised to see me. I expect he thought I was safely parked at the Kremlin waiting for the signing ceremony. I told him what I thought of my Moscow reception. He then opened the press conference by saying that "Ambassador Smith of course, who has conducted the negotiations and brought them to this conclusion, is in the best position to go through the details of the agreement." I then set out in general terms the provisions of the ABM Treaty and the interim freeze. Press questioning soon focused on the specifics of the submarine limitations which Kissinger had negotiated and their relation to U.S. intelligence estimates about the Soviet strategic submarine force.

QUESTION: "What about the submarines, the question of figures? Is this figure of 42 Y-class submarines an accurate one, that they will be allowed to complete, and we with 41?"

SMITH: "I don't know about this figure of 42 submarines. I have seen all sorts of speculations about Soviet submarines but it is perfectly clear that under this agreement, if the Soviets want to pay the price of scrapping a substantial number of other important strategic weapons systems, they can build additional submarines."

QUESTION: "What submarines do they have under construction now? I think you are evading the point on the number of submarines that will be frozen at under this treaty."

SMITH: "I am purposely evading the point because it is an intelligence estimate that I am not in a position to give out."

QUESTION: "How many old submarines with three obsolete launchers on them would they be able to convert?"

SMITH: "I would have to answer that in the same way: I am not in a position to describe the breakdown of the Soviet fleet between old and new submarines."

QUESTION: "You are leaving open the possibility of a very large Soviet superiority in the SLBM field."

SMITH: "I am leaving open the possibility that you are facing an indefinite period of time. We don't know how long it will last. If we negotiate a treaty within a year, then the Soviet submarine level, if they elect to follow this route, will be one thing. If it is two years, it will be another. There is no doubt that under this arrangement they could at a high price increase their submarine fleet."

QUESTION: "The question is whether the Soviets will be able to complete their construction of Y-class submarines and modernize their older submarines to become new Y-class submarines and if they do all of this and pay the price, as you said, of retiring the SS-7 and SS-8 missiles, what is the advantage to them to retire the missiles, for example, and keep these submarines? Do they have a significant advantage if they do that?"

SMITH: "I cannot tell you what the factors making up their force planning are. All I can do is explain the provisions of these treaties. Now what the Soviets will do with the rights under this arrangement is something that we cannot know."

ZIEGLER: "We have time for just one more question. We are running short of time. Dr. Kissinger has one comment to make."

QUESTION: "We have had only ten minutes of questions."

ZIEGLER: "The entire delegation and Dr. Kissinger will be available at the press center later tonight."

KISSINGER: "Since I am not quite as constrained or don't feel as constrained as Ambassador Smith, lest we build up a profound atmosphere of mystery about the submarine issue, I will straighten it out as best I can. The base number of Soviet submarines is in dispute. It has been in dispute in our intelligence estimate exactly how much it is, though our intelligence estimates are in the range that was suggested."

QUESTION: "Forty-one to forty-three?"

KISSINGER: "I'm not going to go beyond what I have said. It is in that general range."

He went on to discuss possible levels of the Soviet submarine program during the freeze. Later he jokingly said, "If I get arrested here for espionage, gentlemen, we will know who is to blame."

Back at the Kremlin, I found myself next to Kissinger as President Nixon's and General Secretary Brezhnev's pens were scratching away on the documents. He whispered, "What were you trying to do, cause a panic?" I didn't know what he was talking about. My press conference statements did not warrant any such histrionics. I put it down to his fatigue. But Kissinger did not want any more help with the press from me—even though, as he had said about one hour before, the reason we were briefing the press was because of the work of the SALT delegation! As the President left the Kremlin, Herb Klein, head of White House communications, advised me that the President did not want me to take part in the reconvened press conference. I asked if he were sure that this was the President's decision. Klein said yes, he had just checked with Kissinger. I sensed that this was probably a case of the President's name being used without his knowledge, but the Kremlin's St. Catherine's Hall did not seem like a good place to appeal the decision.

Allison and Nitze had no car assigned to them. They walked from the Kremlin to their hotel. At least I was driven to Spasso House, where Ambassador Beam and his wife were relaxing after the President's dinner. Pianist Van Cliburn also was a guest at the embassy. We had a nightcap. As I turned in, I was told that my suitcase had been lost at the airport. It was just not my day.

I was wakened in the middle of the night with the interesting but not very useful advice that my suitcase had been found. About six-thirty in the morning the telephone rang again and a voice in Russian asked me if I would care to go sightseeing. It was Semenov, who had word that the SALT delegation was leaving Moscow about nine-thirty that morning. I accepted with alacrity and we were soon driving around Red Square, which even at that hour was jammed with people obviously excited about President Nixon's visitation. I was still tired from the events of the previous days and in my half-awake condition absorbed little of what I was seeing. Aside from the Kremlin and Red Square my only recollection is having seen the central headquarters of the Communist Party.

Then Semenov asked if I would care to see his apartment. My wife, who had been there for a dinner given by Madame Semenova, had described it to me and I jumped at this chance to see a part of the life of Soviet officialdom seldom exposed to foreigners. He lives in a gray stone apartment house occupied, as I understood it, by high-level officials of the Party and the government. We were greeted by a fine-looking *babushka* whom I took to be a member of the family. Semenov showed me around the apartment with obvious pride in his objets d'art, which included a number of excellent modern Russian paintings, a number of pieces of Empire furniture, a well-stocked small library. It was the first time we had no interpreters in two and a half years of private talks and I had to work hard to keep the Russian conversation going. He then brought out a decanter of red wine which he told me had been produced at his dacha some miles outside of Moscow. We solemnly drank to each other's health. By this time it must have been seven-thirty in the morning and he then drove me back to the American Embassy.

Although we were to work together again for a short time in November and December of 1972 at Geneva when the SALT II negotiations made a rather desultory start, I felt that that morning in Moscow marked the beginning of the end of my active participation in SALT. I was grateful to Semenov for having struck a final note of warmth and hospitality at the end of a long, hard SALT road.

16

AFTERMATH

Back home that night on the Eastern Shore of Maryland, I started to develop a different perspective on the negotiation—and especially on the Moscow phase. I felt neither elation nor much sense of resentment at the White House having "hogged" the final days of SALT. The goal of years of work had been reached under circumstances for which even a generation of working in government had not prepared me. Banner headlines announced the Moscow accomplishments of the White House; the labors of the SALT delegates were ignored. Well, the agreements were signed. That was the main thing. The image of a Kremlin topped by a floodlighted Star-Spangled Banner drifted through my imagination and I realized SALT was finished for me.

General Haig advised the next morning that I was expected to brief the congressional leaders on the agreements. Since I was less than fully briefed myself, I demurred, arguing that such briefings should wait until the White House party's return. Haig passed this advice on to Kissinger, who agreed. Perhaps this explains why, when the congressional leaders were briefed, none of the SALT delegates were asked to be present.

The Moscow precedent of keeping the delegates out of sight was followed on the Washington return. A State Department official returning from the White House asked me what was going on. He had just heard a staffer there turn down a request from a leading Sunday television talk show that I be interviewed. I had no answer. When the President addressed the Congress on SALT I was unable to get a ticket for my wife to sit in the gallery. I did receive a request from Charles Colson asking if I would sign an article for *Foreign Affairs* magazine which the White House would arrange to have written. I endorsed that over to Kissinger, asking what he, as a scholar, thought of the suggestion. It was one communication I was pleased not to have answered.

It took some time for the White House to spell out definitively what the submarine arrangements were under the freeze. As quickly as a paper was issued to the bureaucracy, some sharpshooter would point out an inconsistency and a new version would be drafted. The fifth try seemed to hang together fairly well and formed the basis for the congressional presentation.

Since White House staff do not appear formally before congressional committees, the castoff SALT delegates were re-enlisted for this function. If ever the deficiencies of two-track negotiation were shown up, it was during these congressional hearings, especially those in which Senator Jackson had his day in court. He went right for the jugular—the Moscow negotiations about which the SALT delegation had not even seen memoranda of conversation—if they existed. We did our best to describe these exchanges, so much of our knowledge of which was almost hearsay.

The congressional vote in favor of the agreements was overwhelming. Even Senator Jackson voted affirmatively after engineering an amendment the thrust of which was criticism of the freeze as unequal. It contained a minatory piece of congressional advice to the President to negotiate for equal levels in the future. It was acceptable in important quarters of the Congress only because the White House let it be known that it favored the amendment. I questioned General Haig as to why the Administration in effect was thus vomiting on its own much-vaunted SALT freeze agreement. His reply was hard to believe. It had to be done to assure Jackson's vote in favor of the new Trident submarine program. I recalled that Jackson had been the foremost supporter of nuclear submarine programs. This amendment was hard for those to take who at White House direction had just finished defending that freeze against Jackson's attacks, a freeze they had had so little hand in negotiating.

Jackson apparently believed that the unequal freeze arrangement was the result of undue influence of "arms controllers" in ACDA and the State Department—against whom he believed the military representative on the delegation had not stood firmly enough. His influence with the White House was substantial. Two members of the SALT delegation seemed to be special targets of Jackson's displeasure. Raymond Garthoff received the State Department's highest award, the Distinguished Honor Award and Gold Medal, for his fine work at SALT. He was then exiled to non-operational responsibilities with the Inspector General. One of the top Soviet experts in the Foreign Service whiled away four of his best years checking on whether embassies around the world were being efficiently operated.

General Allison was abruptly advised early in 1973 by the chairman of the Joint Chiefs of Staff that he would no longer be on the SALT delegation. After being offered what he deemed an unsuitable assignment for an officer of his experience, he retired from the Air Force, but not before asking Senator Jackson why he, Jackson, had thus ended a distinguished military career. Jackson did not deny responsibility. He charged Allison with having joined "those disarmers" in ACDA and of failing to press the military position with vigor—accusations which had no bases in fact. He indicated that he disagreed with Allison's professional judgment on the prospective vulnerability of U. S. ICBMs under SALT conditions. Allison's judgment seems to have been proved correct by subsequent events; Jackson's views that before 1977 the ICBMs could be intolerably vulnerable have not. That vulnerability is seen as still in the future—and a mobile ICBM system is being programmed to correct it. Working in arms control is a dangerous business but one in which expert and courageous military advice is badly needed. The Allison example is not likely to encourage top military officers to take on arms control responsibilities.

As soon as my responsibilities for the congressional phase were finished I advised Kissinger that I was going to resign, stating that if the President wished I would defer leaving until after the first session of SALT II, which was due to start late in November.

This offer was accepted. For a few weeks in November and December the SALT delegations resumed their talks in Geneva. It was obvious that both sides were marking time.

On advising Secretary Rogers of my plans, he said he did not blame me and suggested that I write him of my decision to leave government, saying it was important to make a record lest people in the White House claim that I had been fired. Until then I had been innocent of this aspect of the mores of the Nixon White House.

In January 1973, on taking my final leave of the President, he referred to the "hectic" days in Moscow, gave me a glass ashtray, and we parted in a not unfriendly fashion. The shadows of Watergate were already gathering around him.

A number of my SALT associates left the government as part of the purge that ushered in the second Nixon administration. The government lost a great accumulation of experience and knowledge unique in government. My deputy Philip Farley, although asked to remain, decided that it would be demeaning to continue after so many of his associates had to leave. His premature retirement marked a clean sweep of top arms control civilians. Of the seventeen people in ACDA's top positions in 1972, only three were left by 1974. In 1973 the ACDA budget was cut by a third and it lost 50 of its 230 employees. As one of those involved puts it, somebody had to hold the bag for criticism of the agreements, and there were only two candidates—the White House or ACDA.

During his press conference at Moscow, Kissinger on being asked the meaning of certain words in the freeze agreement said, "Well, some of the more profound minds in the bureaucracy, which is not necessarily saying a great deal, [laughter] have addressed this question." But this bureaucracy was indispensable to the SALT negotiation and it has been given little credit for its essential role. I would like to pay tribute to these maligned SALT individuals. Without them there would have been no success.

The problem of double-track negotiation evaporated when Kissinger was both Secretary of State and for over two years continued to be Special Assistant to the President for National Security Affairs. He could be sure then that nobody in the White House was negotiating behind his back about SALT or anything else.

By the end of 1976 none of the original SALT delegates remained in government. Hearsay has it that many of the Soviet officials were promoted for their SALT efforts. The Soviet military adviser General Ogarkov is now the top military officer of the U.S.S.R. Asymmetry exists even here.

Several years ago I received a birthday gift from Semenov. It was a loaf of black bread from Moscow of a type which we had often broken together during SALT.

Bread and salt.

CHAPTER

17

RETROSPECTIVE

Before evaluating the SALT record let us take a glance back
to an earlier strategic arms negotiation, the Washington Naval
Limitation Conference of 1921–22,[1] which many of us passed by
quickly in studying American history. It sheds interesting light on
SALT.

Forty-eight years before SALT started, in November 1921, the
Harding Administration engaged in a negotiation aimed at avoiding naval competition among the United States, Great Britain and
Japan. France and Italy also participated. While these nations
were potential rivals, there had been no recent hostility and there
were no deep ideological differences. They were former allies who
only three years before had won a world war together. The negotiation lasted only twelve weeks with six plenary meetings.

During SALT little attention was paid to this naval negotiation
of the twenties. We assumed that things were so different in the
nuclear era that there was little if anything to learn from the past.
The strategic weapons then under consideration were tiny compared to those in SALT, although important to the military bal-

[1] For much of the material in this chapter, I am indebted to *Toward a
New Order of Sea Power* by H. M. Sprout (Princeton University Press,
1943).

ance of the day. Under the terms of the Washington Naval Limitation Treaty of 1922, Japan could have ten battleships having a total of eighty 14-inch guns and sixteen 16-inch guns. One salvo from this battle line threw 6,800 pounds of explosives. Now a single warhead, one of the 160 or more carried on the sixteen missiles in each Poseidon submarine, can deliver an explosive force equivalent to 80 million pounds of TNT. One submarine carries a total TNT equivalent almost two million times that of the explosives that could be delivered by a ten-battleship salvo.

One finds in the record of the Washington Conference a number of old SALT friends. There were moratoria proposals, linkage, calls for bargaining chips and negotiating from strength, telegrams intended for congressional eyes, public and congressional pressures against military programs—even forward bases and secrets kept from the United States military. *Plus ça change . . . !*

I had tried at SALT to imitate the most striking psychological move of this Washington Conference, urging President Nixon to adopt Secretary of State Charles Evans Hughes's device of calling right at the start for a full stop to all construction of strategic arms. It seemed simple logic that the best way to reach strategic arms limitations was to stop building strategic arms. SALT did not work out that way.

As for "linkage"—in 1919, President Wilson was working on the British leadership to support his project for a League of Nations. A provisional naval agreement was reflected in a secret exchange of memoranda between Colonel House and Lord Robert Cecil. Britain would support the League of Nations, and in return Wilson agreed to consider postponing work on battleships already authorized but whose keels had not yet been laid down, and not to go ahead with the naval construction program then before the Congress. This was called a maritime truce. It could also be described as an interim freeze. Its conversion into a more formal arrangement was prevented by the collapse of Wilson's health and the Senate's rejection of participation in the League of Nations.

This negotiation by a White House confidant of the President was not unlike certain SALT episodes. It was carried out without the knowledge of American naval advisers. Some weeks were to pass before members of the naval staff on the American Peace Commission in Paris learned that the Commander-in-Chief, contrary to their professional advice, had entered into this preliminary arms control accord. This was not the only case of professional military advisers being kept in the dark.

And linkage was involved in the final settlement of February 1922. The Naval Limitation Treaty was part of a cluster of agreements designed to improve political relations between the signatory nations. Along with the capital ship limitation and restrictions on the use of submarines and poison gas, there was a four-power pact recognizing rights in Pacific possessions, a treaty reaffirming the integrity of China and the open-door policy, as well as several ancillary agreements, nine in all. The 1972 SALT agreements were also part of a cluster of agreements—involving arrangements about trade and cooperative initiatives in space, the environment, health, science and technology.

Negotiating from a position of strength was acknowledged doctrine in the period leading up to the Washington Conference. We were still catching up with Britain in capital ships, and it was thought, especially in the Navy, that only when parity was reached would we have a favorable bargaining position.

Both the Wilson and the Harding administrations regarded ongoing strategic programs as essential bargaining chips to persuade the foreign nations concerned to accept agreed limits on their strategic systems. Secretary of the Navy Josephus Daniels reported that President Wilson had said that "nothing would so aid him in the peace conference as congressional authorization of a big navy." It was widely reported and weakly denied that Wilson had cabled from Paris that failure to pass the naval construction bill of 1920 would be fatal to his negotiation.

President Harding favored building "the most powerful navy in the world, not only as a guarantee but assurance to American citizens of the sincerity of the administration when it proposes changed international relations and the reduction of armaments." In 1921 an appropriation of $90 million for naval construction was justified by the Administration because early completion of the capital ship program would hasten rather than retard progress toward universal reduction of armaments.

As in the SALT period, these calls for arms programs to bargain with conflicted with a popular inclination to curtail armaments. The United States in 1921 had a number of battleships under construction and the Congress was being asked to authorize still more. In 1970 the Congress was being asked to authorize more ABM sites. In 1921 a wave of what was called anti-navalism spread over the United States, finding its focus in strong congressional sentiment against what promised to be an arms race of indefinite length with Britain and Japan. A similar wave of revulsion against ballistic missile defenses swept the United States in 1969 and 1970. The strategic arms debates of half a century earlier were on a par with arguments made in 1970 and 1971 that failure of Congress to vote for the ABM program would terminate any Soviet interest in a treaty limiting ABMs—and with executive anxieties in those years that a popular inclination toward unilateral disarmament would spoil any chance to negotiate mutual limitations on strategic arms.

In 1921, as in 1969, the United States had forward bases at Guam, Wake and the Philippines. The Japanese were well aware of their strategic significance. In the event of war in the western Pacific these forward bases would greatly enhance U.S. naval capabilities. The Japanese had no interest in limiting their strategic naval forces if these American bases could be fortified. Our willingness to take a commitment in the 1922 agreement not thus to increase their wartime utility paved the way for limits on numbers and armaments of capital ships. American naval authorities learned of this key concession only after it had been made.

In answering critics of this concession on forward bases, Admiral Pratt, one of the leading naval advisers to the American delegation, pointed out that, although the United States had controlled and been free to fortify these insular possessions for almost a generation, no such decision had been made. Even after the treaty prohibition had lapsed in 1936, the United States neglected to strengthen these bases. Some SALT critics have focused on the restraints put on America's ability to deploy ICBMs as large as the U.S.S.R.'s. When free to do so before 1972, the United States had shown no interest. Even during the SALT freeze the United States could have significantly increased the size of its ICBMs but has not done so. This self-restraint seems wiser than the earlier instance.

By 1969 the United States' world posture had changed. Requirements for deterring world-wide nuclear war were quite different from deterring naval hostilities in the western Pacific. We had security guarantees outstanding to many nations of which our forward bases were concrete evidence. We had no inclination to retract them in order to reach agreement about Soviet-American strategic arms levels. In SALT I our unwillingness to have our forward-based systems taken into account was used by the U.S.S.R. to block a treaty limiting offensive strategic arms.

There was some cynical comment that the 1922 battleship limitations were acceptable only because it was already recognized that the battleship era was coming to a close. In the summer of 1921 an old German battleship, the *Ostfriesland,* had been sunk in an aerial bombing test. It is true that a few farsighted observers at that time realized that submarine and naval air power were likely to play a leading role in future hostilities at sea. The 1922 limitations on aircraft carriers were quite permissive, and there were no limitations on submarine construction. Some critics of SALT I have suggested that the ABM limitations merely reflected the low regard in which this technology was held by the military of both nations. That is far from demonstrable.

Somewhat surprisingly, some top American military officials approved of the naval limitation talks. General Pershing said that he favored the limitations "to prevent us from plunging headlong down through destructive war to darkness and barbarism." General Tasker Bliss agreed. Not so surprisingly, however, this enthusiasm for naval arms control came from army officers. Many naval officers whose systems were to be limited did not share this enthusiasm.

The United States military seemed to have done somewhat better in SALT than in the Washington Conference. There they were willing to live with a capital ship ratio of 5-5-3 for the United States, the United Kingdom and Japan—on the assumption that the United States could retain ships displacing one million tons in the aggregate. They were even willing to reduce this figure to 800,000 tons if Japan's share was reduced from 3 to 2½. But they conditioned support for these positions on American freedom to develop naval bases anywhere in the world. In the event, the treaty in no way met these conditions. Total capital ship tonnage permitted the United States was 525,000 tons. The agreed ratio was 5-5-3, but the United States gave up its right to fortify naval bases in the western Pacific. American naval officers were not the only ones disregarded. Reports at the time indicate that disgruntlement with the conference was prevalent in all five of the navies that felt the sting of limitation.

Several times in SALT, I urged the President to ask the congressional leadership to designate members to be advisers to the SALT delegation. Nothing came of it. I assumed that the White House did not welcome the prospect of legislators being privy to this very private negotiation. At the Washington Naval Conference things were different. Our delegation included Henry Cabot Lodge, chairman of the Senate Foreign Relations Committee, and Oscar W. Underwood, ranking minority member.

At both the Washington Naval Limitation Treaty and at SALT, agreements were welcomed with political hyperbole. Secretary Hughes at the end of the Naval Conference said, "We are taking perhaps the greatest forward step in history to establish the reign of peace." And President Harding said, "The faith plighted here today, kept in national honor, will mark the beginning of a new and better epoch in human affairs." At the close of SALT, President Nixon's speech writers indulged in rhetoric which could have been adopted from this earlier record, e.g., "Last Friday in Moscow we witnessed the beginning of the end of that era which began in 1945. We took the first step toward a new era of mutually agreed restraint and arms limitations between the two principal nuclear powers . . . let us seize the moment so that our children and the world's children live free of the hatreds that have been the lot of mankind through the centuries. . . . Then the historians of some future age will write of the year 1972, not that this was the year America went up to the summit and then down to the depths of the valley again, but that this was the year when America helped to lead the world up out of the lowlands of constant war and onto the high plateau of lasting peace."

What does the record of the interim naval limitations treaties have to say for what one can expect from the SALT agreements? Results were ambiguous. In after years the impression grew that the naval treaties had been a failure because they did not prevent World War II. However a good case can be made for their having been a modest success. The Second World War was not caused by arms competition in capital ships. The stoppage of capital ship construction programs reduced defense budgets markedly. Overall defense expenditure in the United Kingdom and the United States did not reach pre-treaty levels until 1938. But the same results might have been obtained without the limitations because of anti-armaments pressures in both countries. Some of the savings were channeled into construction not limited by treaty, for example, cruisers, foreshadowing expensive programs such as cruise missiles now being pursued in the backwash of SALT. A case can be made that the naval limitations weakened the American and British will to face up to Japan in the 1930s, resulting in the wartime disasters of the early 1940s. Here again it will be recalled that, after Japan denounced the treaties and the United States was at liberty to fortify the Pacific islands, it did not elect to do so.

It seems difficult to draw clear lessons about SALT from the record of the Washington naval limitation, but the simple similarities are striking. Negotiations for strategic arms limitations inevitably involve heavy doses of international bargaining and domestic politicking. And too much should not be expected from partial arms limitations. The results will not be all good or all bad. This is a valuable perspective.

CHAPTER

18

THE SALT I
AGREEMENTS

President Nixon said after the Moscow summit, "When we consider what the strategic balance would have looked like later in the seventies if there had been no arms limitation, it is clear that the agreements forestalled a major spiraling of the arms race, one which would have worked to our disadvantage." There was some basis for this claim. But it also reflected the natural tendency of a politician approaching an election to magnify the significance of his accomplishments, especially in bringing off arms agreements after years of failure by his predecessors. These agreements promised to attract millions of voters, and beyond that mundane consideration lay the blessedness promised to the peacemaker—heady stuff for the former youth from Whittier, California, or for anyone else in the world.

Despite the aura of jubilee generated by the White House on the Moscow return, the SALT outcome fell short of earlier hopes. The treaty limiting ABM systems would have been better had it completely banned this newcomer on the strategic scene. The offensive freeze has had only a modest effect on Soviet strategic programs. It did not do much to relieve the overall offensive force threat. It let MIRVs run free. Moscow did not interpret the new Soviet-American relationship as ruling out Angolan, Afghan, and other adventures. This is not the place to consider the relation between SALT II's non-ratification and the Afghanistan invasion.

SALT was far from a failure, however, just because it did not lead to a pacific Soviet Union, content with its 1972 models of strategic weapons and abandoning its self-appointed world mission to nudge along the course of history by covert and not so covert applications of force in developing countries. SALT may not affect central historic trends. But it can make for a somewhat safer world.

Strategic arms negotiations between equals may succeed or fail but they are not won or lost. Negotiating for strategic arms limitation is a far cry from labor or business negotiations to which many of us are accustomed. It is more like negotiating to bring Christian churches together. It is not a matter of one man's skill. It does not depend on which side employs the best stratagems. It has nothing to do with a shrewd Yankee's successful horse trading or city slickers taking advantage of country yokels. Strategic arms negotiating is a form of politics—international politics. It is a facet of the constant interaction between the United States and the U.S.S.R.

In the 1950s the Soviet Union seemed to pursue a tactic of political aggression by conference. Negotiation was at one end of a spectrum, at the other end of which lay a fairly undressed threat of force. The Soviets still seem to see negotiation, including SALT, as part of a broader policy of getting their way in the world. It is made up of a continuous spectrum of activity, from projecting a clear image of forces in being, armies and air fleets in Afghanistan, Eastern Europe and along the Chinese border (and even a brigade in Cuba) and navies now in all the world's oceans, to propaganda and subversion, and ultimately to conferences and negotiations. While the United States also engages in all these types of activities to make its way in the world, Americans tend to look at arms control negotiations as part of a separate process, a discontinuity, something entirely different from other national security activities, as a goal which if reached will mean the end of a time of struggle. The Soviets are more realistic. We should follow their example. SALT should be pursued for limited purposes to reduce the risks of war and the costs of security.

This can be done with advantage to both sides. But it is chasing illusions to think that once strategic arms are limited to some more reasonable level our security will be assured. Kremlin leaders work on no such premise. This asymmetry in fundamental national assumptions is as much or more to be avoided as asymmetries in strategic power.

Contrary to cynical expectations, SALT resulted in solid areas of agreement. It proved that Soviet-American strategic arms limitation was possible. Just as the American demonstration during World War II that a nuclear chain reaction could be sustained made Soviet weaponeers' jobs somewhat easier, so the SALT demonstration that curbs on strategic arms can be negotiated should ease difficulties in achieving further controls. The first olive is out of the bottle.

The ABM Treaty is by far the most significant of the two agreements. It is a comprehensive, precisely drafted contract to govern ABM relations of the superpowers into the indefinite future. It rules out a race in defensive missile systems which threatened to be a major new and dangerous form of arms competition. It put to rest serious concerns that the U.S.S.R. could quickly mount large-scale defenses to neutralize the deterrent effect of American retaliatory forces. It put an end to the expensive and unpopular U. S. ABM program. It should keep future generations of ABMs that American and Soviet weaponeers may conceive of in the infancy of research and development. Without the ABM Treaty, it is most likely that one or both nations would have tried to mount widespread defenses against ballistic missiles, which in turn would lead to higher levels of offensive systems. And the treaty should reduce to a minimum American concerns that the Soviets might convert some part of their nationwide anti-aircraft missile systems to an ABM role. The SAM upgrade problem no longer gets so much attention.

The ABM Treaty severely constrains an entire area of the strategic arms competition. It dealt with systems which, for the most part, had not yet been deployed. Safeguard and Galosh were early-generation technologies of dubious effectiveness. Both sides retained under the treaty a right to deploy ABMs at a second site. Neither side did so and these rights were ended by agreement in

1974. The prospective threat of great instability from ABMs seems to have passed. In the long reach of history, if the nuclear era is to have any long future, it will seem like a surprisingly sensible thing that the superpowers did in 1972—in agreeing not to duplicate in the defensive field the foolish, costly, dangerous escalating competition that they had been slaves to for over twenty years in the offensive weapons field. That was the great prize of SALT I.

With hindsight it now appears that the ABM Treaty would have been advantageous even if unaccompanied by the freeze. If the SALT II treaty limiting offensive arms is not ratified, there will be pressures to annul the ABM Treaty. They should be strongly resisted. Its benefit to the United States is independent of the nature and extent of the Soviet offensive threat (although we argued the contrary during SALT I in an effort to get limitations on offensive systems). As this threat increases, especially to our fixed land-based ICBMs, the appropriate U.S. reaction is to deploy less vulnerable launchers, either on land or at sea, or in the air—rather than to defend vulnerable ICBMs with ABMs. Denouncing the ABM Treaty in order to permit defense of American ICBMs would open the door to Soviet ABM deployments which would reduce the retaliatory potential of all American strategic ballistic missiles, SLBMs as well as ICBMs. Such ABM deployments would be destabilizing and likely would result in higher levels of strategic forces on both sides. We should keep the ABM Treaty even if further limitation of offensive arms eludes us.

SALT opportunities were lost. There was a chance to outlaw ABMs entirely. We pulled away when this prospect seemed to brighten. Now we are in a fair way to accepting tacitly a unilateral ABM ban by putting our remaining Grand Forks site "in mothballs." The Soviets have not built up their Moscow system to the size permitted by the treaty. Too bad the sides did not agree to an ABM ban!

The ABM Treaty has received little attention. Most interest has focused on limits on offensive arms. I would give the interim freeze much lower marks. Why was a freeze acceptable at the end of the negotiation after a substantial increase in Soviet launchers but not acceptable at the beginning, as some of us proposed to the President? Probably the Soviets would not have been willing to freeze launcher numbers in 1969 or 1970 unless the United States had been willing to suspend MIRV deployments. But a negotiating freeze proposal should have been made right at the start. It was poor background for the talks to have Soviet launcher numbers increasing while ours stayed level. Two and a half years were allowed to pass, a good deal of which was spent by the White House pressing for an unrealistic ABM settlement allowing the United States an apparent substantial advantage. The unequal situation that the freeze registered may in part have been of our own making.

The Nixon Administration refused the Soviet proposal for an ABM Treaty standing alone (a position which I had backed). Soviet agreement to some sort of a freeze was our condition for agreeing to an ABM Treaty. The freeze in effect meant that the SALT negotiation could continue for up to sixty more months in an effort to reach limitations on offensive arms to match the ABM Treaty.[1] During that time the parties would hold down the aggregate levels of their land- and submarine-based missile launchers. The interim freeze was no more than a negotiating moratorium. It should be understood as such. The sooner it is replaced by broader, more equitable and lasting limitations, the better.

The freeze was resorted to and comprehensive offensive limitations set aside because of disagreement as to whether American forward-based systems were strategic. We refused to admit that these systems, although having some strategic capability, gave any special advantage for which the Soviets should be compensated. Under White House guidance the delegation argued that the United States did not derive any net strategic advantage from these systems. We maintained that they were balanced off by Soviet intermediate-range missiles targeted on Western Europe and their large numbers of medium bombers. Then, in justifying the freeze, this argument was rather surprisingly reversed by the White House, when it pointed to forward-based systems as compensating for the Soviet advantage in launcher numbers under the freeze. A cynical turn of mind would suggest that the Soviets did

[1] In fact the freeze was extended by mutual agreement and in September 1980 the parties still continue to honor it.

get compensation for our forward-based systems in the form of a substantial though hopefully short-term numerical launcher advantage. The U.S.S.R. has clearly signaled that it will again raise the forward-based systems issue if strategic force reductions are to be negotiated.

A better justification for accepting a launcher freeze at unequal levels was that this Soviet numerical advantage was tolerable under a short-term negotiating moratorium because of U.S. advantages in numbers of warheads and in strategic bombers, and also because the United States could not in any event "catch up" in launchers during the next five years. We were getting ready to construct the Trident submarines, which would tend to restore equality to the strategic submarine balance. During the freeze Trident would be considered as a replacement program. But after 1977 if the freeze were not extended or if additional limitations on offensive systems were not agreed on, Tridents could be deployed in addition to the Polaris/Poseidon fleet. In the interim freeze the United States was buying time for two alternative contingencies: either negotiation of equitable and more lasting limitations on offensive arms or an increase in the number of our submarine-based launchers. That was not a bad idea. Why didn't we say so more directly? That would have made the unequal freeze look better. The Soviet leadership was well aware of this fact. Reportedly at Moscow they complained strenuously about the effect of this American double option.

The freeze was a curious device, an agreement which affected only Soviet programs. You could not expect the Soviets to agree on provisions for this short-term arrangement as specific as those in the ABM Treaty. Although there have been some constructive developments in Soviet programs—no new ICBM silo starts and some launchers decommissioned—it cannot be demonstrated that this resulted from the agreement and would not have occurred anyway. The agreement served one important political purpose. It evidenced the success of American policy against having an ABM treaty alone. But still it was something of a fig leaf to cover the nakedness of our inability to get broad and lasting limitations on offensive arms to match the ABM Treaty.

The freeze may be considered more an intelligence disclosure by the Soviets of their future programs than a limitation on those programs. This was of no small value. A driving force in the strategic competition has been uncertainty about future Soviet programs. In permitting us to enter into the ABM Treaty with knowledge of what the maximum number of Soviet offensive launchers would be in 1977, the freeze performed a significant function. If Soviet programs had called for ICBM and SLBM levels higher than in the freeze agreement, or if the Kremlin in the absence of a freeze might have decided to continue the build-up of strategic launchers beyond original plans, then the freeze was important both as a brake on Soviet missile launcher programs and as a prerequisite for continued SALT efforts.

Could a single overall SALT offensive and defensive limitation treaty have been reached? At Vladivostok in November 1974, only two and a half years after the SALT I agreements, a general accord was reached, in principle, limiting and not just freezing offensive launcher numbers, including heavy bombers and launchers for MIRVed missiles. And in 1979 an offensive arms limitation treaty was agreed on. This suggests that the possibilities for a comprehensive offensive and defensive limitation treaty may not have been exhausted by the spring of 1971 when the first Nixon-Kosygin SALT accord was signed. But both sides still are hedging their full commitments to limit offensive strategic arms. SALT II, if ratified, would last only about as long as the term of the 1972 freeze.

There is no more objective witness to what the Nixon Administration thought of the two SALT agreements than Secretary of Defense Laird. On June 6, 1972, he told the Senate Armed Services Committee, "Our security will be enhanced. We have applied brakes to the momentum of Soviet strategic missile deployments. We have adequate means of verification." But Laird conditioned his approval on the assumption that "Congress will support the strategic programs we have proposed and will propose." This signal that the SALT agreements meant no letup in the offensive strategic arms competition came as a surprise to people who believed that the era of confrontation was over and an era of negotiation begun. This dose of cold water, coming so soon after the President's jubilant rhetoric, began a somewhat bittersweet legacy. We saw the same phenomenon in pressures for large increases in defense funding as the price of support for SALT II.

SALT I, as President Nixon had feared, spawned some divisions in this country. The most serious involve different opinions about Soviet compliance with the freeze. It is worth noting that some original critics of the freeze in 1972 are now doubters about Soviet compliance. Since their initial criticism was that the agreement favored the U.S.S.R. and prejudiced the United States, one may wonder why they now believe the Soviets are violating an agreement supposedly so much in their interest!

The most significant assertion of non-compliance was that the U.S.S.R. has violated either the letter or the spirit of the interim freeze by replacing "light" SS-11 ICBMs with the new MIRVed SS-19 missile which by our definition is a "heavy" missile having a volume larger than contemplated by the agreement. It is true that the Soviets have not conformed to the U.S. unilateral definition of a heavy missile. But the Soviet Union has not violated the agreement. Ungrounded U.S. expectations are responsible for this particular disillusion. The Soviet delegation had repeatedly refused to accept our proposed definition. They told us informally that they would be deploying new MIRVed missiles of a larger volume in their SS-11 silo launchers. After signing the SALT agreements, Brezhnev advised President Nixon that the Soviet Union would proceed with its missile modernization program as permitted by the agreement. In view of this record, the Soviet ICBM replacement activities under the freeze are not as surprising as the White House's assurances in June 1972 that there were adequate safeguards in the agreement against substitution of heavy missiles (presumably as we had defined them) for light ones.

The real issue here is not American naïveté, poor drafting or Soviet violation of the letter or spirit of the freeze but whether the talks should have been broken off over the failure to agree on a definition of the term "heavy." I think not. We had a number of SALT objectives other than holding down the size of Soviet missiles during the freeze. Most important was the ABM Treaty. We had little bargaining power on the heavy missile issue, since we were trying to fix constraints on ongoing Soviet programs that would not also affect our own.

As with any other lawmaking process, SALT has its loophole problems for both sides. When some things are proscribed, energies and interests tend to flow into permitted areas. Since the freeze was so largely a matter of quantitative constraints on launchers, qualitative improvements have taken on special interest. It has been claimed that the Soviets are taking advantage of "loopholes" in the freeze. So are we. These are not loopholes but areas not under control. With a freeze arrangement that to some looked disadvantageous to the United States, new impetus was given in certain quarters to the possibilities of making effective strategic delivery systems out of cruise missiles which had been largely abandoned when ballistic missiles became practical in the late 1950s. Strategic cruise missiles were not covered in the 1972 agreement. In 1970 the U.S. delegation had proposed their limitation. The Soviets accepted the proposal that intercontinental cruise missiles be banned. But when efforts to reach a broad agreement covering offensive systems were suspended in 1971, cruise missile limitation was dropped, and we are now developing strategic cruise missiles and the Soviets likely will follow our lead. The momentum of this development may present an insurmountable block to the possibilities for controlling these new delivery systems.

Jan M. Lodal, a former National Security Council official who dealt extensively with SALT after the 1972 agreements, recently made a pungent assessment of Soviet SALT compliance. "Events since SALT I do not support the view that the Soviets are cheating, that they are unreasonably pushing the limits of the agreements, that they are attempting to use loopholes to their advantage, or that our verification capabilities are inadequate. Rather, the record demonstrates the strength of our verification capabilities, that we are willing to raise questions related to compliance promptly, and that the basic terms of the agreements are being observed."

Just as it is fashionable in some quarters to think Soviets are "ten feet tall" when it comes to weapons, so some American folklore has it that Soviets are superior negotiators and that Americans always come out second best. This is not true. The Soviet Union made significant concessions to American positions, by agreeing on quite detailed limitations including qualitative controls, in spite of its traditional preference for broader, political-type agreements, and on verification provisions that establish new precedents in international law. Moscow pressed hard for an ABM treaty not directly linked to constraints on offensive arms. It did not succeed. The Soviets pressed long and hard for ABMs to be limited to defense of capitals. They were not so limited. They agreed to ban the deployment of future ABM systems and multiple warheads for ABM interceptor missiles. They wanted only loose restraints on ABM radars. In the end they agreed to relatively strict restraints, not only on ABM radars but also on other radars with some ABM potential. They resisted provisions to prohibit the upgrading of SAM anti-aircraft missiles but finally agreed to them. They pressed hard for including forward-based systems in the agreement. FBS were not included. The Soviets pressed for an agreement about "provocative attack." None was reached. They proposed pledges of "no first use" of nuclear weapons and a limitation of submarines and aircraft carriers to certain zones. These initiatives were not successful. Moscow accepted after many objections a specific, public, rather lengthy and formal Interim Offensive Agreement, including some limits on SS-9 launchers and a prohibition on ICBM silo relocation, for a much longer term than they originally wanted.

The U.S.S.R. evidenced in SALT a solid interest in strategic arms control. Soviet officials were serious and businesslike, and they worked hard to reach the unprecedented 1972 agreements. Polemic was kept to a minimum. Moscow passed up two prime propaganda opportunities: in the April 1970 Cambodia incursion and the eleventh-hour bombing of Hanoi and mining of Haiphong Harbor two years later. This evidence should not be forgotten.

Most SALT critics pass over the first two agreements that came out of the SALT process—one on accident control, the other on upgrading the Hot Line. While not central to the purposes of limiting strategic arms, these agreements could be invaluable aids in the safe and successful management of possible future crises.

Overlooked also by those whose disposition is critical are the substantial gains for international law in Soviet acceptance of the legitimacy of the use of certain national means of verification, especially satellites in outer space to monitor arms control agreements.

Another constructive product of SALT I is the Soviet-American Standing Consultative Commission. Its general purpose is to make the agreements more viable, by clearing up ambiguities which were expected to crop up as the agreements are implemented—and so it has. It has operated well for years, permitting a serious dialogue on a technical level. Ambiguities have somewhat soured the SALT relationship, but they would have caused worse trouble had it not been for this clarifying function of the Consultative Commission.

The pre-SALT Soviet-American strategic relationship had been not unlike two boxers in a ring—one muscle-bound, the other partially blind—going through the motions of warming up for a fight, practicing punches and engaging in footwork with occasionally a roar from the crowd. And they had not talked very much to each other in an effort to avoid a fight. The SCC is being used now, in good part, to try to clear up ambiguities in the implementation of the first two SALT agreements. It has a larger potential. If talk is a prime tool of international politics, here is an ever ready instrument for talking things out, not just about clarifying the past, but also about how to steer clear of future dangers. In past years the United States has often tried to signal the Kremlin, through speeches, budgetary actions and private communications between Washington and Moscow, about its interest in mutual restraint and its concern about certain Soviet moves. This has been a somewhat random process without clear results. The Consultative Commission could be used for this purpose, permitting a degree of precision and continuity not possible in ad hoc communication.

Fortunately there remains a strong popular preference for setting strategic force levels, by international agreement rather than by the pressures of an uncurbed arms competition. This preference is based in part on a hope that arms controls can save economic resources. Many consider SALT a disappointment on this score. Large ABM Treaty savings may in good measure be offset by the costs of accelerating the Trident submarine program, cruise missile programs, and the incremental costs of other SALT bargaining chips and hedges.

In fact, SALT I did result in considerable savings and proved that financial benefits can be realized through arms control. The negotiation cost the taxpayers about $6 million. Net SALT savings in the 1973 defense budget alone were about $800 million. Estimated longer-term SALT savings from not having a four-site ABM program were $11 to $13 billion. A generally unrecognized SALT bonus has been large savings in scaling down air defense programs of the United States. Former Secretary of Defense Schlesinger recognized the illogic of maintaining large anti-aircraft defenses after we had agreed, in effect, to be defenseless against missile attack. So far the Soviets have not moved in this direction, perhaps in part because they have Chinese bombers to cope with but mainly because the American bomber threat to the U.S.S.R. is so much greater than theirs to the United States.

Nations' commitments are not enforceable anywhere. They are statements of intention to do or refrain from doing something. The very fact of a nation's being willing to make such statements can be as important as their contents. The aims of a negotiation like SALT are not limited to agreeing on specific terms. The general principles of an agreement can be more significant than its specific provisos. So the SALT fact that both sides have stated their intentions in the ABM Treaty to refrain from building significant ABM defenses and thus remain defenseless against missile attack was more significant than the specific limitations. And that the sides agreed that for five years their aggregate offensive missile launcher numbers would remain at about the 1972 levels was more important than the specific provisions of the freeze.

The ultimate test of any agreement is whether the parties would be better off without it. Would the United States, and the rest of the world's nations, be better off now if the superpowers had failed to agree to preclude an ABM-generated escalation in the nuclear arms competition and to remain defenseless against missile attack? Would they be better off without the freeze commitments? It is easy to nitpick specific language in the agreements and the accompanying statements but the majority of Americans answer this question affirmatively and support efforts to negotiate arms limitations.

CHAPTER
19

LESSONS LEARNED

The first SALT experience was valuable in providing lessons on how the United States should go about future arms control negotiations. Here are some guidelines for the future.

At the preliminary Helsinki round in 1969 we tabled a set of illustrative elements to stimulate a dialogue. This was a useful technique. But after the negotiation had started the United States tabled a number of what appeared to be proposals but were called "approaches," thus keeping the President free to repudiate them if that appeared prudent. But negotiations are not seminars. Only those positions should be tabled that the United States can live with.

The United States tabled a number of alternate ABM limits, thus giving the Soviets a plausible claim that a choice had been offered. When their pick did not suit our policy, confusion, delay and embarrassment resulted. We should avoid giving the other side a chance to pick and choose. We should defer making any offer until sure that it is in the American interest.

For many months in 1971 and 1972 the United States pressed for an ABM agreement based on inequality—only to agree in the end on two ABM sites for each side. We should avoid wasting time on obviously inequitable propositions—especially when that time is being better used by the other side.

A great deal of the principal delegates' time was spent in the oral presentation of formal papers. The SALT negotiating process could be substantially speeded up if this unnecessary step was eliminated. While plenary statements are necessary for a complete negotiating record, nothing is gained by their oral presentation.

Several covert back-channel negotiations deemed necessary by the President to break SALT deadlocks led to confusion and discontinuities in the U.S. negotiating posture. Twice the White House reached agreements with the Soviets, the bases for which were not understood by the delegation. We have seen that in April 1972, in the course of Kissinger's trip to Moscow, a long-held United States position for a freeze on submarines and their launchers at approximately equal levels was changed. And not much effort was made to enlighten the bureaucracy, which was then called on to convert general accords into specific agreements. I suspect that the Soviet delegation was also confused by this random process of high-level and somewhat erratic participation in a negotiating process that depended for progress on a painstaking process of developing and recording common understandings about complicated concepts.

A main thrust of this book has been to describe two methods of conducting strategic arms talks. While Presidents surely should be free to choose differing methods, representatives and procedures for negotiations, if plural approaches are adopted special care should be taken in their coordination to prevent confusion if not worse. The front channel should at least be aware that parallel negotiation is under way. Preferably the official primarily responsible for the front channel should be advised in general terms of the negotiating aims of the back channel.

And no matter how able a presidential confidant may be, he cannot produce best results while simultaneously negotiating, as Kissinger was, a number of important issues. Interventions by the highest level of government are obviously sometimes necessary to remove jams that usually develop in negotiations. But such emergency moves should not evolve into second negotiations.

Back-channel negotiations at times were conducted partially through the agency of Soviet interpreters. The American negotiator could only assume that what the Soviet negotiator had said in Russian was being accurately rendered in English— and what he said in English was being accurately conveyed in Russian. Traditional diplomatic practice is to avoid any such dependence on an agent of the other side. Any American who does not speak and understand Russian like a native should use an American interpreter in all Soviet-American arms control negotiations involving the use of Russian.

In the absence of an American interpreter's verbatim notes, one cannot prepare the fullest possible record of negotiating exchanges. In a number of cases no record was made available to SALT officials as to what transpired in the back channel. As SALT is, hopefully, a continuing process, unavailability of significant portions of the record can be a substantial handicap. Back-channel exchanges should be as fully recorded as those in the front channel and should be made available to top officials responsible for SALT negotiations.

The SALT I negotiation was successful but I think a better result would have emerged if under the President's direction the delegates had remained responsible for the entire negotiation. It is not, as Lloyd George said, that one general is better than another, but that one general is better than two, particularly when one is trying to outmaneuver the other. And there is a kind of Gresham's law in a plural approach to negotiations. It becomes increasingly difficult to resolve issues at lower levels.

The United States always carried the burden of pressing for verification commitments. This gives the U.S.S.R. somewhat greater leverage on other aspects of an agreement which are of special interest to it. This fact of Soviet-American life suggests that the United States should avoid past procedure of first reaching an agreement in general terms, what the British would call a "Heads of Agreement," which in good part commits the United States to reach subsequent agreement on the "fine print." The May 20, 1971, and the Vladivostok accords are examples. With the negotiations thus structured, there is pressure on the United States to be less sticky on verification points that do not appear as central issues. Put another way, the Soviets, in the absence of such an agreement in principle, might be more disposed to concede on other points in order to reach agreement on basic limitations than if the agreement on basic limitations had already been reached in principle.

Lust for a summit affected the SALT negotiation in several ways, at least in timing, perhaps in substance. From the start of his administration in 1969 President Nixon aimed for a summit meeting with the Soviet leadership—the centerpiece of which would be a SALT agreement. The Soviets apparently went along with this general scenario. When plans for a summit in 1971 did not pan out, the Soviets had little incentive to reach an early agreement. Time was not working in favor of the United States. The Soviets were adding launchers to their strategic forces— launchers which were the objects to be limited in SALT. The agreement finally reached in 1972 could have been reached in 1971 when the Soviet SLBM launcher numbers were lower. We should try not to link summitry and arms control negotiations.

Negotiations of issues of great technical complexity were conducted by the President of the United States and some confusion resulted. Negotiating about strategic arms at the summit was not invented by President Nixon. In 1961, President Kennedy met with British Prime Minister Macmillan at Nassau to agree on the extent of United States aid for the United Kingdom strategic submarine program. President Kennedy later told me, "We didn't know the meaning of the words we were using." That experience as well as SALT offer powerful arguments against direct presidential involvement in negotiating the details of strategic arms arrangements. If the reader has persisted this far, I trust that he will agree. Technical issues should be handled at lower levels. If they cannot be resolved there and must be considered at the highest level the President should be assisted by technically competent and experienced officials.

In a number of cases the sides, after failing to reach agreement, placed on the record unilateral interpretations of the language of certain provisions in the agreements. Although unilateral statements may in some instances be useful, for example, as statements of a side's future intentions, SALT experience suggests that they can be harmful. When in the execution of an agreement one party does not meet the terms of the other's interpretation, questions about proper fulfillment of the agreement may well arise. If unilateral statements are used interpretively in an effort to impose constraints beyond the agreement, it should be recognized that they are only unagreed proposals that may well have been refused for reasons that foreshadow the very activity sought to be prohibited. It seems better not to make any unilateral statement about unagreed limitations. Some argue that unilateral statements should be made only when the United States would terminate the agreement if the Soviets engage in activity inconsistent with them. But in such cases it might be better not to conclude an agreement. Conversely, if the agreement is in our interests without the provision, it is better not to try to establish unilateral standards for compliance.

Through frequent frank and full briefings by the principal delegates, Congress was kept currently informed of all aspects of SALT except the back-channel exchanges. This process was supplemented by occasional informal visits to the negotiating front by interested members of the Senate and House. But the degree of congressional interest and understanding of SALT issues was not high. A better procedure would be to ask the congressional leadership to designate congressional advisers for the SALT delegation. I understand that during the negotiation of SALT II there was a great deal of congressional participation in the negotiations.

It is executive branch folklore that information given the Congress soon appears in newsprint. That was not our experience. After briefing of congressional committees on over forty-five occasions I recall only one leak from that source. We stressed the importance of privacy. We were candid and forthcoming. It seemed to work well.

In peacetime diplomatic activity there will always be competing claims for privacy and publicity. Conflicting efforts on behalf of these two desiderata led to some demoralization in the Washington SALT community and an extreme presidential reaction aimed at discovering sources of leaks and preventing their recurrence. I cannot document any episode where a leak, no matter how contemptible an action by the official concerned, directly prejudiced the negotiating outcome. Indirectly, leaks led to negotiating techniques which should be avoided in the future.

The SALT I record was good on consultations with allies. War deterrence is just as important to them as to the United States, even though the greatest part of the responsibility rests with the

United States. Never before have so many nations placed their central security in the hands of another nation. In SALT, they in effect gave powers of attorney to the United States to guard their strategic interests by assuring that any agreed strategic balance would be as secure as or more secure than the pre-SALT equilibrium. At the start it was not at all clear how America's allies, especially in Europe, would react to Soviet-American arrangements affecting their strategic relations. Even before the negotiation started the North Atlantic Council reacted nervously to the Johnson Administration report that the superpowers might concert on ways to handle "conflict-fraught" situations. That sounded too close for comfort to the sort of Soviet-American condominium that some European strategists had anticipated for years. It was a significant but underappreciated SALT accomplishment that all countries of the North Atlantic alliance gave clear endorsement to the SALT agreements. It reflected the deep and continuous consultations which the SALT delegation had maintained to the best of its ability with the North Atlantic Council all during the negotiation. (On those segments of SALT secretly negotiated by the White House, I suppose the allies felt much as the SALT delegates felt about the lapses in otherwise excellent consultation.) In addition to NATO, Japan, Australia and New Zealand were also kept fully informed of all important SALT developments known to the delegation and fully supported the final agreements. This unique consultation record went a long way to meet the allies' inherent sensitivities about the United States negotiating alone with the Soviet Union on matters of the highest importance for their national security.

The most difficult problems in arms control are with systems that can perform more than one function. This was the case especially with FBS, which though originally designed in good part for tactical missions can carry out not insignificant strategic missions. The SAM upgrade problem arose from a belief that anti-aircraft systems could be effective against ballistic missile re-entry vehicles. Some radars designed for space or early warning missions could also be useful in ABM defense. An ABM defense of Moscow could also defend ICBM silos in nearby fields. SS-11 missiles targeted on Western Europe could also strike targets in the United States and the difference between the alleged peripheral role of the Soviet Backfire bomber and its apparent intercontinental capability plagued SALT II. Such gray-area systems deserve special attention and extraordinary ingenuity will be needed to cover them adequately.

There is a kind of Parkinson's law of international negotiation. If there is a deadline, even if it is well in the future, and if an agreement is in the cards, it will be reached just before the deadline. A deadline may well mean a delay. The fact that the interim freeze could last five years set up a likelihood that it would last that long. It has lasted longer. The U.S.S.R. had proposed a short informal freeze arrangement, with an exchange of letters. The White House, I believe at the urging of the Defense Department, insisted on a formal agreement with a duration five times longer than the one year the Soviets would have settled for. Psychologically, it would have been better to cast this freeze, registering a substantial Soviet advantage in missile launcher numbers, in the less formal and shorter-term arrangement proposed by the Soviets. Although this would have lessened its intelligence value, it could have led sooner to comprehensive offensive arms limitation.

There is a tendency in arms control as in most other human affairs to put off hard issues for the future. Thus the complete banning of nuclear tests has for years been approved in principle but left for future negotiations. The SALT freeze left comprehensive limitations on offensive arms for another day. Control was deferred until too late for a MIRV ban. The Vladivostok Accord treated reductions in strategic forces in the same way. Mutual reductions are favored, but only in the future. With a relatively minor exception the SALT II treaty confirms this. The explicit Soviet-American commitment to negotiations for reductions gives no great assurance that early reductions are in the cards. As we have just seen, cruise missiles are a current example of the effect of putting off arms control possibilities. In SALT I, both sides appeared initially to favor preventing cruise missile systems from becoming a part of the strategic arms competition before either side was seriously committed to them, but this opportunity was forfeited when the negotiations turned away from comprehensive offensive limitations.

The major failure of SALT I was that MIRVs were not banned. That more than anything else set back the cause of strategic arms control. Only during the opening months was there a chance to stop MIRVs, before they were deployed on American missiles, several years before the Soviets even tested them and some five years before they began to deploy them. As the Soviet missile launcher numerical advantage increased in 1970 and 1971, the chance for a MIRV ban quickly receded.

We should learn from this failure. If restraining measures are not taken early in the development of new weapons systems, control becomes much more difficult. The Johnson Administration perhaps missed a last clear chance to avoid MIRV missiles on both sides by not deferring or stretching out the developmental testing of MIRV systems until the degree of Soviet interest in banning them could be established. The superpowers are now approaching a similar situation in strategic cruise missiles. Unless their development can soon be stopped the prospect for their control will be poor.

With a MIRV ban out the window, there went the possibility of preserving the relative invulnerability of American ICBMs into a longer future. As we watch very large Soviet MIRVed missiles being deployed and calculate what they could do to our ICBMs, we should wonder whether a greater effort to ban MIRVs would not have been in our interest. As we realize how little the freeze actually restrained the Soviet programs, we may legitimately question if we should not have been willing to restrain some American program in order to get more substantial restraints on the Soviets. Here again the finger points to MIRV, which was then our only deployment program in prospect.

The blame, I think, should be shared by both sides. Seven years later, the Soviets agreed to limit the number of launchers for MIRV missiles. A complete ban would have made for a more stable strategic balance and perhaps would have been less difficult to verify. Maybe MIRV controls slipped away from SALT because the negotiations at the outset were in a state of incubation. The next time such a fundamental strategic weapons development appears, we should remember the failure to control MIRVs and the success in controlling ABMs.

The future challenge is to make SALT irreversible. But as the Arab saying goes, "It takes two hands to clap." Both Soviets and Americans must see that it is in their security interests to keep the first agreements and build on them. They must push on or risk a slide back into the approaches to belligerency.

St. Luke wrote, "Salt is good but if the salt has lost its savor wherewith shall it be seasoned? It is fit neither for the land nor yet the dunghill, but men cast it out."

Let us continue, while the light lasts, to keep the savor in SALT.

APPENDICES

APPENDIX 1

*Two Alternative Approaches
for Comprehensive Limitations*

• Common to both the C and D packages were provisions for (1) a limit of 1,710 on intercontinental ballistic missile launchers with (2) a subceiling of 250 launchers for modern large ballistic missiles (MLBM), the Soviet SS-9 ICBMs; and (3) a freeze at current levels on other strategic launch vehicles—intercontinental heavy bombers, medium- and intermediate-range ballistic missiles (MR/IRBMs), and submarine-launched cruise missiles (SLCMs).

• Also common to both options—for defensive arms, we were to propose a limit of one ABM site for each side to defend its national command authority (NCA). Both options C and D had as an alternative a complete ban on ABMs. President Nixon directed us to present only the NCA alternative.

• The first comprehensive approach, C, included a prohibition on the flight testing and deployment of MIRVs. It called for on-site inspection to verify that no MIRVs were being deployed. Option D would not constrain MIRVs but provided for reductions of 100 ICBM launchers a year for seven years. After January 1, 1978, the agreed ceiling would be an aggregate of 1,000 ICBM and SLBM launchers.

• A number of so-called corollary constraints to help verify compliance were included, i.e., for offensive missile launcher limitations, there would be bans on relocation of ICBM launchers, on changes in their external configuration and on the construction of new MR/IRBM silos. Mobile ICBMs would be prohibited (a change from the Helsinki Illustrative Elements as the delegation had recommended).

• The ABM limitation included radar controls and a ban on upgrading anti-aircraft surface-to-air missile (SAM) systems to give them a capability against ballistic missile re-entry vehicles. Testing SAMs in an ABM manner would be prohibited.

• Both approaches also would establish a joint standing commission for consultations about compliance and about other aspects of implementation of an agreement.

• The delegation was to make clear that each alternative was a package for total acceptance or rejection.

APPENDIX 2

*First Memorandum to President Nixon
Regarding MIRV Ban*

Our MIRV flight testing program is reaching a crucial stage. Fifty-two flight tests in all are scheduled, with the first Minuteman III missiles scheduled to be operational at the end of fiscal year 1970, and the first Poseidon in January 1971, with actual deployment to be spread out over some years. Only 11 of these tests had been conducted in the nine months from the beginning of the test program in August 1968 through April of 1969. From now through November, the tests are scheduled to run at a rate of three a month. Even before the completion of these tests, MIRVs could on a crash basis be introduced into our missiles—or so the Soviets may think.

If, by the time SALT talks begin, we already have—or the Soviets think we have—substantially completed MIRV testing, any limitation of MIRVs will be difficult to achieve: While MIRV testing is observable by national means, the only way you can tell whether or not a missile has MIRVs is through on-site inspection.

The delay in initiation of SALT talks, combined with entry into a period of sustained and even accelerated MIRV testing, could therefore operate to reduce significantly the options, flexibility and leverage you have to make these talks productive.

One of the major options under study is a reciprocal leveling off in additional missiles, with introduction of MIRVs excluded on both sides. This is a complicated option, but it may be a key one. If the Soviets are to forego construction of more land-based hard-site ICBMs and SLBMs and *any* mobile land-based ICBMs, they could understandably ask for some quid pro quo from us. It is hard to see anything in our current programs but the MIRVs which we could offer.

If we press ahead in this period with an aggressive program of MIRV flight testing, we may appear to the Soviets to have passed the point of no return. To the Soviets as well as to our congressional critics, we may then seem vulnerable to the charge of having deliberately stalled on the negotiations to permit us to prove out our MIRVs and thus put them beyond the realm of negotiability.

The simplest way of preserving our options would be to stretch out U.S. MIRV flight testing. For example, the services might be directed to conduct not more than one more Minuteman III and one more Poseidon flight test between now and the establishment of the U.S. position on SALT, with whatever guidance that decision may contain regarding subsequent testing. The action would have the advantage of leaving us maximum freedom of maneuver. By not actually suspending tests in advance, we would avoid playing our trump card prematurely and keep it for the best moment in the negotiations.

A second possibility would be to propose an immediate moratorium on all multiple warhead testing—both of U.S. MIRVs and Soviet MIRVs. This would be dramatic, require a quid pro quo from the Soviets, and place the United States in a favorable position before world opinion. However, this course could in itself complicate the negotiations and might risk limiting our flexibility of choice.

APPENDIX 3

Second Memorandum to President Nixon Regarding MIRV Ban

I understand that in Washington consideration is being given to what, if anything, I would say on MIRV—the one important subject which remains officially unmentioned here. The delegation is sending its views through normal channels.

. . . If it were to our advantage—and there are a few sensible people who think it would be—to have no mention of MIRV at Helsinki, this may be doable while still having MIRV on the work program for the next phase under some appropriate euphemistic label.

. . . I do not recommend leaving MIRV in this state for the following reasons.

. . . First, it would not be consistent with the general guidance to me in your letter of July 21st: "If the Soviet leaders operate on similar premises (which we do not know and which their current military programs give some reason to doubt), there could be, I believe, a prospect of reaching an understanding with them whereby, in the first instance, limits would be placed on the quantitative and qualitative growth of strategic forces. It will be your task to obtain evidence that will assist me in making a determination whether such a prospect is real and what the elements of such an understanding could be." Soviet MIRVed SS-9s appear to present the greatest qualitative growth potential for the USSR. No exploration of Soviet MIRV views here would therefore not appear responsive to this guidance. Second, some pro-MIRV-ban politicians would likely deem such skirting of what they consider a central problem to be curious, and inconsistent with what they may believe they have been led to expect. This may make a later careful approach to SALT more difficult, and also might further stimulate pressures for a *unilateral* U.S. move. And the general U.S. image of seriously seeking strategic arms controls may be somewhat tarnished if, as is likely, some politicians/columnists vent exasperation at our MIRV silence in the press. Third, an exploratory operation that did not penetrate the MIRV area at all will perhaps leave in unnecessary uncertainty the information base for next steps in the U.S. SALT decision process. Fourthly, the conspicuous absence of any raising of MIRV might unnecessarily cause unfortunate estimates of U.S. intentions in Moscow.

. . . I am *not* suggesting reconsideration at this time of my moratoria proposal presented at NSC meeting last month. I *do* recommend that I be authorized to tell Semenov that the possibility of a MIRV ban/limitation in any agreement should be discussed at an early point in the next stage and to ask for present Soviet views on MIRV control.

. . . Except for the MIRV issue, I think the Helsinki exploration/probe had fulfilled its purpose and will hold up—even to critical cross-questioning. I cannot say the same for the present record on MIRV.

APPENDIX 4

Program for Interim Agreements

We should try to obtain as broad a SALT agreement as is verifiable and negotiable. It was premature to conclude that the USSR is unwilling to negotiate an offensive/defensive agreement.

Our approach should be to try to negotiate a simplified version of the August 4 proposal. The August 4, 1970, proposal had three main objectives: (1) a low limit on ABM systems; (2) limits on aggregate numbers of offensive missile launchers and heavy bombers; and (3) a limit on the number of modern large ballistic missile launchers. I outlined for Secretary Rogers some modifications of the August 4 proposal, intended as a description of quid pro quo tradeoffs and step-by-step negotiations which I thought would produce an acceptable outcome.

For the offensive provisions, the main modifications would be to increase the aggregate total from 1,900 to an equal agreed number between 1,900 and 2,100, dropping the 1,710 subceiling for missile launchers, and changing the MLBM sublimit within the aggregate ceiling from 250 for each side to the number operational and under construction as of an agreed date. Modification of the sublimit on MLBMs to permit implicitly the current Soviet total of about 300 was not significantly different from the 250 limit, from the point of view of U.S. security, and should increase negotiability, and dropping the U.S. quota for MLBMs (which would be the effect of limiting them to those operational and under construction) would not affect any planned U.S. systems.

For ABMs, although I thought the U.S. should stand by its alternative offers for either a ban or an NCA level, we should now press for an ABM ban. An ABM ban would be more negotiable than an NCA level and it would be advantageous to the U.S. in terms of verifiability, ease of definition, economics, public appeal, and its effect upon the strategic arms competition.

The objectives of the August 4 proposal could safely be met without a number of the detailed corollary constraints now in the U.S. proposal. In most cases, these corollary constraints would prove almost as effective if used unilaterally as "indicators" of proscribed activities.

The agreed limitations should be in the form of a treaty. But, if necessary, we might propose an "interim understanding," say for three years, to allow time to negotiate a treaty. The interim understanding might be along the following lines. Each nation would agree it would not be the first to exceed the present levels of its heavy bombers and strategic missile launchers and during the term of the preliminary agreement would not substitute one type of launcher for another. Each nation would agree promptly to start demolishing ABM facilities and not to be the first to start deploying an ABM system thereafter. Alternatively, if an ABM ban was not acceptable to the USSR, the United States could agree, for the period covered by this interim agreement, not to start new construction at additional Safeguard sites if the USSR would agree not to start additional ABM deployments.

APPENDIX 5

President Nixon's Letter
Regarding ABM Ban

At this point in our negotiations with the USSR I am persuaded we are within reach of an equitable agreement if we can reinforce the momentum created by the joint decision of May 20. Two years ago, we had all hoped that the Soviet side could be brought around to a comprehensive arms control agreement. The Soviets were aware of our interest in a complete ban on ABM systems and reductions in offensive systems. Our record on these issues is clear. But in matters affecting so directly their vital interests it is understandable that the Soviet leaders have preferred to move to an initial agreement of limited scope.

Thus, the understanding of the May 20 agreement was that we would now make a major effort to agree this year on some limitations on ABMs together with some limitations on offensive systems while deferring some issues for a second stage. That decision, I believe, represented a major political commitment by the Soviet leaders and was based on a general understanding that both sides could not expect to achieve all of their objectives in one agreement.

In reviewing the record leading to that agreement and taking into account your most recent contacts, it is my conclusion that pressing for a complete ban on ABMs would risk jeopardizing the understanding already achieved with the USSR. This is all the more true because if we went to a zero ABM proposal we would have to ask for more sweeping offensive limitation than seems immediately negotiable. Our objective should be to consolidate gains we have made, and translate our mutual commitment into a viable agreement.

Accordingly, I have decided that we should continue within the framework of the May 20 understanding that the USSR will not be required to dismantle its ABM system in order to reach an agreement. Similarly, the Soviets should also recognize that we will not dismantle our system, as long as the agreement envisaged is to be limited to only a part of our offensive arsenals.

This mutual recognition of current realities forms the basis for an agreement. The latest Soviet offer, while not yet acceptable, does indicate some movement from their rigid formulas for a Washington-Moscow defense. It encourages me to believe that hard bargaining on the key issues will lead to a breakthrough.

Thus, I am very reluctant to introduce a complete ban as our preferred solution and thereby move the negotiations back into the realm of comprehensive agreements. Nor do I want to create any pretext for the USSR to reopen the question of a completely separate ABM agreement.

Your Soviet counterparts, however, should be made aware of the seriousness with which we consider the second stage of these negotiations. If we can take a major step now, we can create the mutual confidence that is a prerequisite to broader arms control. It is in this light that I hope you will impress on the Soviet negotiators that in the second phase of negotiations, we will set as our goal a ban on ABMs and a reduction in offensive systems. The crucial step toward this goal is the agreement you are now negotiating.

APPENDIX 6

ABM *Treaty*
with Agreed Interpretations
Common Understandings
Unilateral Statements

TREATY
BETWEEN THE UNITED STATES OF AMERICA
AND
THE UNION OF SOVIET SOCIALIST REPUBLICS
ON THE LIMITATION OF ANTI-BALLISTIC MISSILE SYSTEMS

The United States of America and the Union of Soviet Socialist Republics, hereinafter referred to as the Parties.

Proceeding from the premise that nuclear war would have devastating consequences for all mankind.

Considering that effective measures to limit anti-ballistic missile systems would be a substantial factor in curbing the race in strategic offensive arms and would lead to a decrease in the risk of outbreak of war involving nuclear weapons.

Proceeding from the premise that the limitation of anti-ballistic missile systems, as well as certain agreed measures with respect to the limitation of strategic offensive arms, would contribute to the creation of more favorable conditions for further negotiations on limiting strategic arms.

Mindful of their obligations under Article VI of the Treaty on the Non-Proliferation of Nuclear Weapons.

Declaring their intention to achieve at the earliest possible date the cessation of the nuclear arms race and to take effective measures toward reductions in strategic arms, nuclear disarmament, and general and complete disarmament.

Desiring to contribute to the relaxation of international tension and the strengthening of trust between States.

Have agreed as follows:

ARTICLE I

1. Each Party undertakes to limit anti-ballistic missile (ABM) systems and to adopt other measures in accordance with the provisions of this Treaty.

2. Each Party undertakes not to deploy ABM systems for a defense of the territory of its country and not to provide a base for such a defense, and not to deploy ABM systems for defense of an individual region except as provided for in Article III of this Treaty.

ARTICLE II

1. For the purposes of this Treaty an ABM system is a system to counter strategic ballistic missiles or their elements in flight trajectory, currently consisting of:

(a) ABM interceptor missiles, which are interceptor missiles constructed and deployed for an ABM role, or of a type tested in an ABM mode;

(b) ABM launchers, which are launchers constructed and deployed for launching ABM interceptor missiles; and

(c) ABM radars, which are radars constructed and deployed for an ABM role, or of a type tested in an ABM mode.

2. The ABM system components listed in paragraph 1 of this Article include those which are:

(a) operational;

(b) under construction;

(c) undergoing testing;

(d) undergoing overhaul, repair or conversion; or

(e) mothballed.

Article III

Each Party undertakes not to deploy ABM systems or their components except that:

(a) within one ABM system deployment area having a radius of one hundred and fifty kilometers and centered on the Party's national capital, a Party may deploy: (1) no more than one hundred ABM launchers and no more than one hundred ABM interceptor missiles at launch sites, and (2) ABM radars within no more than six ABM radar complexes, the area of each complex being circular and having a diameter of no more than three kilometers; and

(b) within one ABM system deployment area having a radius of one hundred and fifty kilometers and containing ICBM silo launchers, a Party may deploy: (1) no more than one hundred ABM launchers and no more than one hundred ABM interceptor missiles at launch sites, (2) two large phased-array ABM radars comparable in potential to corresponding ABM radars operational or under construction on the date of signature of the Treaty in an ABM system deployment area containing ICBM silo launchers, and (3) no more than eighteen ABM radars each having a potential less than the potential of the smaller of the above-mentioned two large phased-array ABM radars.

Article IV

The limitations provided for in Article III shall not apply to ABM systems or their components used for development or testing, and located within current or additionally agreed test ranges. Each Party may have no more than a total of fifteen ABM launchers at test ranges.

Article V

1. Each Party undertakes not to develop, test, or deploy ABM systems or components which are sea-based, air-based, space-based, or mobile land-based.

2. Each Party undertakes not to develop, test, or deploy ABM launchers for launching more than one ABM interceptor missile at a time from each launcher, nor to modify deployed launchers to provide them with such a capability, nor to develop, test, or deploy automatic or semi-automatic or other similar systems for rapid reload of ABM launchers.

ARTICLE VI

To enhance assurance of the effectiveness of the limitations on ABM systems and their components provided by this Treaty, each Party undertakes:

(a) not to give missiles, launchers, or radars, other than ABM interceptor missiles, ABM launchers, or ABM radars, capabilities to counter strategic ballistic missiles or their elements in flight trajectory, and not to test them in an ABM mode; and

(b) not to deploy in the future radars for early warning of strategic ballistic missile attack except at locations along the periphery of its national territory and oriented outward.

ARTICLE VII

Subject to the provisions of this Treaty, modernization and replacement of ABM systems or their components may be carried out.

ARTICLE VIII

ABM systems or their components in excess of the numbers or outside the areas specified in this Treaty, as well as ABM systems or their components prohibited by this Treaty, shall be destroyed or dismantled under agreed procedures within the shortest possible agreed period of time.

ARTICLE IX

To assure the viability and effectiveness of this Treaty, each Party undertakes not to transfer to other States, and not to deploy outside its national territory, ABM systems or their components limited by this Treaty.

ARTICLE X

Each Party undertakes not to assume any international obligations which would conflict with this Treaty.

ARTICLE XI

The Parties undertake to continue active negotiations for limitations on strategic offensive arms.

ARTICLE XII

1. For the purpose of providing assurance of compliance with the provisions of this Treaty, each Party shall use national technical means of verification at its disposal in a manner consistent with generally recognized principles of international law.

2. Each Party undertakes not to interfere with the national technical means of verification of the other Party operating in accordance with paragraph 1 of this Article.

3. Each Party undertakes not to use deliberate concealment measures which impede verification by national technical means of compliance with the provisions of this Treaty. This obligation shall not require changes in current construction, assembly, conversion, or overhaul practices.

ARTICLE XIII

1. To promote the objectives and implementation of the provisions of this Treaty, the Parties shall establish promptly a Standing Consultative Commission, within the framework of which they will:

(a) consider questions concerning compliance with the obligations assumed and related situations which may be considered ambiguous;

(b) provide on a voluntary basis such information as either Party considers necessary to assure confidence in compliance with the obligations assumed;

(c) consider questions involving unintended interference with national technical means of verification;

(d) consider possible changes in the strategic situation which have a bearing on the provisions of this Treaty;

(e) agree upon procedures and dates for destruction or dismantling of ABM systems or their components in cases provided for by the provisions of this Treaty;

(f) consider, as appropriate, possible proposals for further increasing the viability of this Treaty, including proposals for amendments in accordance with the provisions of this Treaty;

(g) consider, as appropriate, proposals for further measures aimed at limiting strategic arms.

2. The Parties through consultation shall establish, and may amend as appropriate, Regulations for the Standing Consultative Commission governing procedures, composition and other relevant matters.

ARTICLE XIV

1. Each Party may propose amendments to this Treaty. Agreed amendments shall enter into force in accordance with the procedures governing the entry into force of this Treaty.

2. Five years after entry into force of this Treaty, and at five year intervals thereafter, the Parties shall together conduct a review of this Treaty.

ARTICLE XV

1. This Treaty shall be of unlimited duration.

2. Each Party shall, in exercising its national sovereignty, have the right to withdraw from this Treaty if it decides that extraordinary events related to the subject matter of this Treaty have jeopardized its supreme interests. It shall give notice of its decision to the other Party six months prior to withdrawal from the Treaty. Such notice shall include a statement of the extraordinary events the notifying Party regards as having jeopardized its supreme interests.

ARTICLE XVI

1. This Treaty shall be subject to ratification in accordance with the constitutional procedures of each Party. The Treaty shall

enter into force on the day of the exchange of instruments of ratification.

2. This Treaty shall be registered pursuant to Article 102 of the Charter of the United Nations.

Done at Moscow on May 26, 1972, in two copies, each in the English and Russian languages, both texts being equally authentic.

FOR THE UNITED STATES
OF AMERICA:

(signed) RICHARD NIXON

President of the United States
of America

FOR THE UNION OF SOVIET
SOCIALIST REPUBLICS:

(signed) L. I. BREZHNEV

General Secretary of the
Central Committee of the CPSU

AGREED INTERPRETATIONS,
COMMON UNDERSTANDINGS,
AND UNILATERAL STATEMENTS

1. AGREED INTERPRETATIONS

(*a*) *Initialed Statements.*—The document set forth below was agreed upon and initialed by the Heads of the Delegations on May 26, 1972:

AGREED STATEMENTS REGARDING THE TREATY BETWEEN THE UNITED STATES OF AMERICA AND THE UNION OF SOVIET SOCIALIST REPUBLICS ON THE LIMITATION OF ANTI-BALLISTIC MISSILE SYSTEMS

[A]

The Parties understand that, in addition to the ABM radars which may be deployed in accordance with subparagraph (a) of Article III of the Treaty, those non-phased-array ABM radars operational on the date of signature of the Treaty within the ABM system deployment area for defense of the national capital may be retained.

[B]

The Parties understand that the potential (the product of mean emitted power in watts and antenna area in square meters) of the smaller of the two large phased-array ABM radars referred to in subparagraph (b) of Article III of the Treaty is considered for purposes of the Treaty to be three million.

[C]

The Parties understand that the center of the ABM system deployment area centered on the national capital and the center of the ABM system deployment area containing ICBM silo launchers for each Party shall be separated by no less than thirteen hundred kilometers.

[D]

In order to insure fulfillment of the obligation not to deploy ABM systems and their components except as provided in Article III of the Treaty, the Parties agree that in the event ABM systems based on other physical principles and including components capable of substituting for ABM interceptor missiles, ABM launchers, or ABM radars are created in the future, specific limitations on such systems and their components would be subject to discussion in accordance with Article XIII and agreement in accordance with Article XIV of the Treaty.

[E]

The Parties understand that Article V of the Treaty includes obligations not to develop, test or deploy ABM interceptor missiles for the delivery by each ABM interceptor missile of more than one independently guided warhead.

[F]

The Parties agree not to deploy phased-array radars having a potential (the product of mean emitted power in watts and antenna area in square meters) exceeding three million, except as provided for in Articles III, IV and VI of the Treaty, or except for the purposes of tracking objects in outer space or for use as national technical means of verification.

[G]

The Parties understand that Article IX of the Treaty includes the obligation of the US and the USSR not to provide to other States technical descriptions or blue prints specially worked out for the construction of ABM systems and their components limited by the Treaty.

(*b*) *Common Understandings.*—Common understanding of the Parties on the following matters was reached during the negotiations:

A. LOCATION OF ICBM DEFENSES

The U. S. Delegation made the following statement on May 26, 1972:

> Article III of the ABM Treaty provides for each side one ABM system deployment area centered on its national capital and one ABM system deployment area containing ICBM silo launchers. The two sides have registered agreement on the following statement: "The Parties understand that the center of the ABM system deployment area centered on the national capital and the center of the ABM systems deployment area containing ICBM silo launchers for each Party shall be separated by no less than thirteen hundred kilometers." In this connection, the U.S. side notes that its ABM system deployment area for defense of ICBM silo launchers, located west of the Mississippi River, will be centered in the Grand Forks ICBM silo launcher deployment area. (See Initialed Statement [C].)

B. ABM TEST RANGES

The U. S. Delegation made the following statement on April 26, 1972:

> Article IV of the ABM Treaty provides that "the limitations provided for in Article III shall not apply to ABM systems or their components used for development or testing, and located within current or additionally agreed test ranges." We believe it would be useful to assure that there is no misunderstanding as to current ABM test ranges. It is our understanding that ABM test ranges encompass the area within which ABM components are located for test purposes. The current U. S. ABM test ranges are at White Sands, New Mexico, and at Kwajalein Atoll, and the current Soviet ABM test range is near Sary Shagan in Kazakhstan. We consider

that non-phased array radars of types used for range safety or instrumentation purposes may be located outside of ABM test ranges. We interpret the reference in Article IV to "additionally agreed test ranges" to mean that ABM components will not be located at any other test ranges without prior agreement between our Governments that there will be such additional ABM test ranges.

On May 5, 1972, the Soviet Delegation stated that there was a common understanding on what ABM test ranges were, that the use of the types of non-ABM radars for range safety or instrumentation was not limited under the Treaty, that the reference in Article IV to "additionally agreed" test ranges was sufficiently clear, and that national means permitted identifying current test ranges.

C. MOBILE ABM SYSTEMS

On January 28, 1972, the U. S. Delegation made the following statement:

Article V (1) of the Joint Draft Text of the ABM Treaty includes an undertaking not to develop, test, or deploy mobile land-based ABM systems and their components. On May 5, 1971, the U.S. side indicated that, in its view, a prohibition on deployment of mobile ABM systems and components would rule out the deployment of ABM launchers and radars which were not permanent fixed types. At that time, we asked for the Soviet view of this interpretation. Does the Soviet side agree with the U.S. side's interpretation put forward on May 5, 1971?

On April 13, 1972, the Soviet Delegation said there is a general common understanding on this matter.

D. STANDING CONSULTATIVE COMMISSION

Ambassador Smith made the following statement on May 22, 1972:

The United States proposes that the sides agree that, with regard to initial implementation of the ABM Treaty's Article XIII on the Standing Consultative Commission (SCC) and of the consultation Articles to the Interim Agreement on offensive arms and the Accidents Agreement, [1] agreement establishing the SCC will be worked out early in the follow-on SALT negotiations; until that is completed, the following arrangements will prevail: when SALT is in session, any consultation desired by either side under these Articles can be carried out by the two SALT Delegations; when SALT is not in session, *ad hoc* arrangements for any desired consultations under these Articles may be made through diplomatic channels:

Minister Semenov replied that, on an *ad referendum* basis, he could agree that the U.S. statement corresponded to the Soviet understanding.

E. STANDSTILL

On May 6, 1972, Minister Semenov made the following statement:

In an effort to accommodate the wishes of the U.S. side, the Soviet Delegation is prepared to proceed on the basis that the two sides will in fact observe the obligations of both the Interim Agreement and the ABM Treaty beginning from the date of signature of these two documents.

In reply, the U. S. Delegation made the following statement on May 20, 1972:

The U.S. agrees in principle with the Soviet statement made on May 6 concerning observance of obligations beginning from date of signature but we would like to make clear our understanding that this means that, pending ratification and acceptance, neither side would take any action prohibited by the agreements after they had entered into force. This understanding would continue to apply in the absence of notification by either signatory of its intention not to proceed with ratification or approval.

The Soviet Delegation indicated agreement with the U.S. statement.

2. UNILATERAL STATEMENTS

(a) The following noteworthy unilateral statements were made during the negotiations by the United States Delegation:

A. WITHDRAWAL FROM THE ABM TREATY

On May 9, 1972, Ambassador Smith made the following statement:

The U. S. Delegation has stressed the importance the U. S. Government attaches to achieving agreement on more complete limitations on strategic offensive arms, following agreement on an ABM Treaty and on an Interim Agreement on certain measures with respect to the limitation of strategic offensive arms. The U. S. Delegation believes that an objective of the follow-on negotiations should be to constrain and reduce on a long-term basis threats to the survivability of our respective strategic retaliatory forces. The USSR Delegation has also indicated that the objectives of SALT would remain unfulfilled without the achievement of an agreement providing for more complete limitations on strategic offensive arms. Both sides recognize that the initial agreements would be steps toward the achievement of more complete limitations on strategic arms. If an agreement providing for more complete strategic offensive arms limitations were not achieved within five years, U.S. supreme interests could be jeopardized. Should that occur, it would constitute a basis for withdrawal from the ABM Treaty. The U.S. does not wish to see such a situation occur, nor do we believe that the USSR does. It is because we wish to prevent such a situation that we emphasize the importance the U. S. Government attaches to achievement of more complete limitations on strategic offensive arms. The U. S. Executive will inform the Congress, in connection with Congressional consideration of the ABM Treaty and the Interim Agreement, of this statement of the U.S. position.

B. TESTED IN ABM MODE

On April 7, 1972, the U. S. Delegation made the following statement:

Article II of the Joint Text Draft uses the term "tested in an ABM mode," in defining ABM components, and Article VI includes certain obligations concerning such testing. We believe that the sides should have a common understanding of this phrase. First, we would note that the testing provisions of the ABM Treaty are intended to apply to testing which occurs after the date of signature of the Treaty, and not to any testing which may have occurred in the past. Next, we would amplify the remarks we have made on this subject during the previous Helsinki phase by setting forth the objectives which govern the U.S. view on the subject, namely, while prohibiting testing of non-ABM components for ABM purposes: not to prevent testing of ABM components, and not to prevent testing of non-ABM components for non-ABM purposes. To clarify our interpretation of "tested in an ABM mode," we note that we would consider a launcher, missile or radar to be "tested in an ABM mode" if, for example, any of the following events occur: (1) a launcher is used to launch an ABM interceptor missile, (2) an interceptor missile is flight tested against a target vehicle which has a flight trajectory with characteristics of a strategic ballistic missile flight trajectory, or is flight tested in conjunction with the test of an ABM interceptor missile or an ABM radar at the same test range, or is flight tested to an altitude inconsistent with interception of targets against which air defenses are deployed, (3) a radar makes measurements on a cooperative target vehicle of the kind referred to in item (2) above during the reentry portion of its trajectory or makes measurements in conjunction with the test of an ABM interceptor missile or an ABM radar at the same test range. Radars used for purposes such as range safety or instrumentation would be exempt from application of these criteria.

C. NO-TRANSFER ARTICLE OF ABM TREATY

On April 18, 1972, the U. S. Delegation made the following statement:

In regard to this Article [IX], I have a brief and I believe self-explanatory statement to make. The U.S. side wishes to make clear that the provisions of this Article do not set a precedent for whatever provision may be considered for a Treaty on Limiting Strategic Offensive Arms. The question of transfer of strategic offensive arms is a far more complex issue, which may require a different solution.

D. NO INCREASE IN DEFENSE OF EARLY WARNING RADARS

On July 28, 1970, the U. S. Delegation made the following statement:

Since Hen House radars [Soviet ballistic missile early warning radars] can detect and track ballistic missile warheads at great distances, they have a significant ABM potential. Accordingly, the U.S. would regard any increase in the defenses of such radars by surface-to-air missiles as inconsistent with an agreement.

APPENDIX 7

Interim Agreement and Protocol
with
Agreed Interpretations
Common Understandings
Unilateral Statements

INTERIM AGREEMENT
BETWEEN THE UNITED STATES OF AMERICA
AND
THE UNION OF SOVIET SOCIALIST REPUBLICS
ON CERTAIN MEASURES WITH RESPECT TO THE
LIMITATION OF STRATEGIC OFFENSIVE ARMS

The United States of America and the Union of Soviet Socialist Republics, hereinafter referred to as the Parties.

Convinced that the Treaty on the Limitation of Anti-Ballistic Missile Systems and this Interim Agreement on Certain Measures with Respect to the Limitation of Strategic Offensive Arms will contribute to the creation of more favorable conditions for active negotiations on limiting strategic arms as well as to the relaxation of international tension and the strengthening of trust between States.

Taking into account the relationship between strategic offensive and defensive arms,

Mindful of their obligations under Article VI of the Treaty on the Non-Proliferation of Nuclear Weapons,

Have agreed as follows:

ARTICLE I

The Parties undertake not to start construction of additional fixed land-based intercontinental ballistic missile (ICBM) launchers after July 1, 1972.

ARTICLE II

The Parties undertake not to convert land-based launchers for light ICBMs, or for ICBMs of older types deployed prior to 1964, into land-based launchers for heavy ICBMs of types deployed after that time.

ARTICLE III

The Parties undertake to limit submarine-launched ballistic missile (SLBM) launchers and modern ballistic missile submarines to the numbers operational and under construction on the date of signature of this Interim Agreement, and in addition to launchers and submarines constructed under procedures established by the Parties as replacements for an equal number of ICBM launchers of older types deployed prior to 1964 or for launchers on older submarines.

ARTICLE IV

Subject to the provisions of this Interim Agreement, modernization and replacement of strategic offensive ballistic missiles and launchers covered by this Interim Agreement may be undertaken.

ARTICLE V

1. For the purpose of providing assurance of compliance with the provisions of this Interim Agreement, each Party shall use national technical means of verification at its disposal in a manner consistent with generally recognized principles of international law.

2. Each Party undertakes not to interfere with the national technical means of verification of the other Party operating in accordance with paragraph 1 of this Article.

3. Each Party undertakes not to use deliberate concealment measures which impede verification by national technical means of compliance with the provisions of this Interim Agreement. This obligation shall not require changes in current construction, assembly, conversion, or overhaul practices.

ARTICLE VI

To promote the objectives and implementation of the provisions of this Interim Agreement, the Parties shall use the Standing Consultative Commission established under Article XIII of the Treaty on the Limitation of Anti-Ballistic Missile Systems in accordance with the provisions of that Article.

ARTICLE VII

The Parties undertake to continue active negotiations for limitations on strategic offensive arms. The obligations provided for in this Interim Agreement shall not prejudice the scope or terms of the limitations on strategic offensive arms which may be worked out in the course of further negotiations.

ARTICLE VIII

1. This Interim Agreement shall enter into force upon exchange of written notices of acceptance by each Party, which ex-

change shall take place simultaneously with the exchange of instruments of ratification of the Treaty on the Limitation of Anti-Ballistic Missile Systems.

2. This Interim Agreement shall remain in force for a period of five years unless replaced earlier by an agreement on more complete measures limiting strategic offensive arms. It is the objective of the Parties to conduct active follow-on negotiations with the aim of concluding such an agreement as soon as possible.

3. Each Party shall, in exercising its national sovereignty, have the right to withdraw from this Interim Agreement if it decides that extraordinary events related to the subject matter of this Interim Agreement have jeopardized its supreme interests. It shall give notice of its decision to the other Party six months prior to withdrawal from this Interim Agreement. Such notice shall include a statement of the extraordinary events the notifying Party regards as having jeopardized its supreme interests.

Done at Moscow on May 26, 1972, in two copies, each in the English and Russian languages, both texts being equally authentic.

FOR THE UNITED STATES OF AMERICA:	FOR THE UNION OF SOVIET SOCIALIST REPUBLICS:
(signed) RICHARD NIXON	(signed) L. I. BREZHNEV
President of the United States of America	General Secretary of the Central Committee of the CPSU

PROTOCOL

TO THE INTERIM AGREEMENT BETWEEN
THE UNITED STATES OF AMERICA
AND
THE UNION OF SOVIET SOCIALIST REPUBLICS
ON CERTAIN MEASURES WITH RESPECT TO THE
LIMITATION OF STRATEGIC OFFENSIVE ARMS

The United States of America and the Union of Soviet Socialist Republics, hereinafter referred to as the Parties.

Having agreed on certain limitations relating to submarine-launched ballistic missile launchers and modern ballistic missile submarines, and to replacement procedures, in the Interim Agreement,

Have agreed as follows:

The Parties understand that, under Article III of the Interim Agreement, for the period during which that Agreement remains in force:

The US may have no more than 710 ballistic missile launchers on submarines (SLBMs) and no more than 44 modern ballistic missile submarines. The Soviet Union may have no more than 950 ballistic missile launchers on submarines and no more than 62 modern ballistic missile submarines.

Additional ballistic missile launchers on submarines up to the above-mentioned levels, in the U.S.—over 656 ballistic missile launchers on nuclear-powered submarines, and in the U.S.S.R.—over 740 ballistic missile launchers on nuclear-powered submarines, operational and under construction, may become operational as replacements for equal numbers of ballistic missile launchers of older types deployed prior to 1964 or of ballistic missile launchers on older submarines.

The deployment of modern SLBMs on any submarine, regardless of type, will be counted against the total level of SLBMs permitted for the U.S. and the U.S.S.R.

This Protocol shall be considered an integral part of the Interim Agreement.

Done at Moscow this 26th day of May, 1972.

FOR THE UNITED STATES OF AMERICA:

FOR THE UNION OF SOVIET SOCIALIST REPUBLICS:

(signed) RICHARD NIXON

(signed) L. I. BREZHNEV

President of the United States of America

General Secretary of the Central Committee of the CPSU

Agreed Interpretations, Common Understandings, and Unilateral Statements

1. AGREED INTERPRETATIONS

(*a*) *Initialed Statements.*—The document set forth below was agreed upon and initialed by the Heads of the Delegations on May 26, 1972:

AGREED STATEMENTS REGARDING THE INTERIM AGREEMENT BETWEEN THE UNITED STATES OF AMERICA AND THE UNION OF SOVIET SOCIALIST REPUBLICS ON CERTAIN MEASURES WITH RESPECT TO THE LIMITATION OF STRATEGIC OFFENSIVE ARMS

[A]

The Parties understand that land-based ICBM launchers referred to in the Interim Agreement are understood to be launchers for strategic ballistic missiles capable of ranges in excess of the shortest distance between the northeastern border of the continental U.S. and the northwestern border of the continental USSR.

[B]

The Parties understand that fixed land-based ICBM launchers under active construction as of the date of signature of the Interim Agreement may be completed.

[C]

The Parties understand that in the process of modernization and replacement the dimensions of land-based ICBM silo launchers will not be significantly increased.

[D]

The Parties understand that during the period of the Interim Agreement there shall be no significant increase in the number of ICBM or SLBM test and training launchers, or in the number of such launchers for modern land-based heavy ICBMs. The Parties further understand that construction or conversion of ICBM launchers at test ranges shall be undertaken only for purposes of testing and training.

[E]

The Parties understand that dismantling or destruction of ICBM launchers of older types deployed prior to 1964 and ballistic missile launchers on older submarines being replaced by new SLBM launchers on modern submarines will be initiated at the time of the beginning of sea trials of a replacement submarine, and will be completed in the shortest possible agreed period of time. Such dismantling or destruction, and timely notification thereof, will be accomplished under procedures to be agreed in the Standing Consultative Commission.

(*b*) *Common Understandings.*—Common understanding of the Parties on the following matters was reached during the negotiations:

A. INCREASE IN ICBM SILO DIMENSIONS

Ambassador Smith made the following statement on May 26, 1972:

The Parties agree that the term "significantly increased" means that an increase will not be greater than 10–15 percent of the present dimensions of land-based ICBM silo launchers.

Minister Semenov replied that this statement corresponded to the Soviet understanding.

B. STANDING CONSULTATIVE COMMISSION

Ambassador Smith made the following statement on May 22, 1972:

> The United States proposes that the sides agree that, with regard to initial implementation of the ABM Treaty's Article XIII on the Standing Consultative Commission (SCC) and of the consultation Articles to the Interim Agreement on offensive arms and the Accidents Agreement,[1] agreement establishing the SCC will be worked out early in the follow-on SALT negotiations; until that is completed, the following arrangements will prevail: when SALT is in session, any consultation desired by either side under these Articles can be carried out by the two SALT Delegations; when SALT is not in session, *ad hoc* arrangements for any desired consultations under these Articles may be made through diplomatic channels.

Minister Semenov replied that, on an *ad referendum* basis, he could agree that the U.S. statement corresponded to the Soviet understanding.

C. STANDSTILL

On May 6, 1972, Minister Semenov made the following statement:

> In an effort to accommodate the wishes of the U.S. side, the Soviet Delegation is prepared to proceed on the basis that the two sides will in fact observe the obligations of both the Interim Agreement and the ABM Treaty beginning from the date of signature of these two documents.

In reply, the U. S. Delegation made the following statement on May 20, 1972:

> The U.S. agrees in principle with the Soviet statement made on May 6 concerning observance of obligations beginning from date of signature but we would like to make clear our understanding that this means that, pending ratification and acceptance, neither side would take any action prohib-

ited by the agreements after they had entered into force. This understanding would continue to apply in the absence of notification by either signatory of its intention not to proceed with ratification or approval.

The Soviet Delegation indicated agreement with the U.S. statement.

2. UNILATERAL STATEMENTS

(a) The following noteworthy unilateral statements were made during the negotiations by the United States Delegation:

A. WITHDRAWAL FROM THE ABM TREATY

On May 9, 1972, Ambassador Smith made the following statement:

> The U. S. Delegation has stressed the importance the U. S. Government attaches to achieving agreement on more complete limitations on strategic offensive arms, following agreement on an ABM Treaty and on an Interim Agreement on certain measures with respect to the limitation of strategic offensive arms. The U. S. Delegation believes that an objective of the follow-on negotiations should be to constrain and reduce on a long-term basis threats to the survivability of our respective strategic retaliatory forces. The USSR Delegation has also indicated that the objectives of SALT would remain unfulfilled without the achievement of an agreement providing for more complete limitations on strategic offensive arms. Both sides recognize that the initial agreements would be steps toward the achievement of more complete limitations on strategic arms. If an agreement providing for more complete strategic offensive arms limitations were not achieved within five years, U.S. supreme interests could be jeopardized. Should that occur, it would constitute a basis for withdrawal from the ABM Treaty. The U.S. does not wish to see such a situation occur, nor do we believe that the USSR does. It is because we wish to prevent such a situation that we emphasize the importance the U. S. Government attaches

to achievement of more complete limitations on strategic offensive arms. The U. S. Executive will inform the Congress, in connection with Congressional consideration of the ABM Treaty and the Interim Agreement, of this statement of the U.S. position.

B. LAND-MOBILE ICBM LAUNCHERS

The U. S. Delegation made the following statement on May 20, 1972:

In connection with the important subject of land-mobile ICBM launchers, in the interest of concluding the Interim Agreement the U. S. Delegation now withdraws its proposal that Article I or an agreed statement explicitly prohibit the deployment of mobile land-based ICBM launchers. I have been instructed to inform you that, while agreeing to defer the question of limitation of operational land-mobile ICBM launchers to the subsequent negotiations on more complete limitations on strategic offensive arms, the U.S. would consider the deployment of operational land-mobile ICBM launchers during the period of the Interim Agreement as inconsistent with the objectives of that Agreement.

C. COVERED FACILITIES

The U. S. Delegation made the following statement on May 20, 1972:

I wish to emphasize the importance that the United States attaches to the provisions of Article V, including in particular their application to fitting out or berthing submarines.

D. "HEAVY" ICBM'S

The U. S. Delegation made the following statement on May 26, 1972:

The U. S. Delegation regrets that the Soviet Delegation has not been willing to agree on a common definition of a heavy missile. Under these circumstances, the U. S. Delegation believes it necessary to state the following: The United States would consider any ICBM having a volume significantly greater than that of the largest light ICBM now operational on either side to be a heavy ICBM. The U.S. proceeds on the premise that the Soviet side will give due account to this consideration.

(b) The following noteworthy unilateral statement was made by the Delegation of the U.S.S.R. and is shown here with the U.S. reply:

On May 17, 1972, Minister Semenov made the following unilateral "Statement of the Soviet Side":

> Taking into account that modern ballistic missile submarines are presently in the possession of not only the U.S., but also of its NATO allies, the Soviet Union agrees that for the period of effectiveness of the Interim 'Freeze' Agreement the U.S. and its NATO allies have up to 50 such submarines with a total of up to 800 ballistic missile launchers thereon (including 41 U.S. submarines with 656 ballistic missile launchers). However, if during the period of effectiveness of the Agreement U.S. allies in NATO should increase the number of their modern submarines to exceed the numbers of submarines they would have operational or under construction on the date of signature of the Agreement, the Soviet Union will have the right to a corresponding increase in the number of its submarines. In the opinion of the Soviet side, the solution of the question of modern ballistic missile submarines provided for in the Interim Agreement only partially compensates for the strategic imbalance in the deployment of the nuclear-powered missile submarines of the USSR and U.S. Therefore, the Soviet side believes that this whole question, and above all the question of liquidating the American missile submarine bases outside the U.S., will be appropriately resolved in the course of follow-on negotiations.

On May 24, Ambassador Smith made the following reply to Minister Semenov:

> The United States side has studied the "statement made by the Soviet side" of May 17 concerning compensation for submarine basing and SLBM submarines belonging to third

countries. The United States does not accept the validity of the considerations in that statement.

On May 26 Minister Semenov repeated the unilateral statement made on May 24. Ambassador Smith also repeated the U.S. rejection on May 26.

APPENDIX 8

Accidents Agreement

AGREEMENT
ON MEASURES TO REDUCE THE RISK OF OUTBREAK OF
NUCLEAR WAR BETWEEN
THE UNITED STATES OF AMERICA AND
THE UNION OF SOVIET SOCIALIST REPUBLICS

The United States of America and the Union of Soviet Socialist Republics, hereinafter referred to as the Parties:

Taking into account the devastating consequences that nuclear war would have for all mankind, and recognizing the need to exert every effort to avert the risk of outbreak of such a war, including measures to guard against accidental or unauthorized use of nuclear weapons,

Believing that agreement on measures for reducing the risk of outbreak of nuclear war serves the interests of strengthening international peace and security, and is in no way contrary to the interests of any other country,

Bearing in mind that continued efforts are also needed in the future to seek ways of reducing the risk of outbreak of nuclear war,

Have agreed as follows:

ARTICLE 1

Each Party undertakes to maintain and to improve, as it deems necessary, its existing organizational and technical arrangements to guard against the accidental or unauthorized use of nuclear weapons under its control.

ARTICLE 2

The Parties undertake to notify each other immediately in the event of an accidental, unauthorized or any other unexplained incident involving a possible detonation of a nuclear weapon which could create a risk of outbreak of nuclear war. In the event of such an incident, the Party whose nuclear weapon is involved will immediately make every effort to take necessary measures to render harmless or destroy such weapon without its causing damage.

ARTICLE 3

The Parties undertake to notify each other immediately in the event of detection by missile warning systems of unidentified objects, or in the event of signs of interference with these systems or with related communications facilities, if such occurrences could create a risk of outbreak of nuclear war between the two countries.

ARTICLE 4

Each Party undertakes to notify the other Party in advance of any planned missile launches if such launches will extend beyond its national territory in the direction of the other Party.

ARTICLE 5

Each Party, in other situations involving unexplained nuclear incidents, undertakes to act in such a manner as to reduce the possibility of its actions being misinterpreted by the other Party. In any such situation, each Party may inform the other Party or request information when, in its view, this is warranted by the interests of averting the risk of outbreak of nuclear war.

ARTICLE 6

For transmission of urgent information, notifications and requests for information in situations requiring prompt clarification, the Parties shall make primary use of the Direct Communications Link between the Governments of the United States of America and the Union of Soviet Socialist Republics.

For transmission of other information, notifications and requests for information, the Parties, at their own discretion, may use any communications facilities, including diplomatic channels, depending on the degree of urgency.

ARTICLE 7

The Parties undertake to hold consultations, as mutually agreed, to consider questions relating to implementation of the provisions of this Agreement, as well as to discuss possible amendments thereto aimed at further implementation of the purposes of this Agreement.

ARTICLE 8

This Agreement shall be of unlimited duration.

ARTICLE 9

This Agreement shall enter into force upon signature.

Done at Washington on September 30, 1971, in two copies, each in the English and Russian languages, both texts being equally authentic.

FOR THE UNITED STATES
OF AMERICA:

FOR THE UNION OF SOVIET
SOCIALIST REPUBLICS:

(signed) WILLIAM ROGERS

(signed) A. GROMYKO

APPENDIX 9

Revised Hot Line Agreement with Annex

AGREEMENT BETWEEN
THE UNITED STATES OF AMERICA AND
THE UNION OF SOVIET SOCIALIST REPUBLICS
ON MEASURES TO IMPROVE THE USA-USSR
DIRECT COMMUNICATIONS LINK

The United States of America and the Union of Soviet Socialist Republics, hereinafter referred to as the Parties,

Noting the positive experience gained in the process of operating the existing Direct Communications Link between the United States of America and the Union of Soviet Socialist Republics, which was established for use in time of emergency pursuant to the Memorandum of Understanding Regarding the Establishment of a Direct Communications Link, signed on June 20, 1963,

Having examined, in a spirit of mutual understanding, matters relating to the improvement and modernization of the Direct Communications Link,

Have agreed as follows:

ARTICLE 1

1. For the purpose of increasing the reliability of the Direct Communications Link, there shall be established and put into operation the following:

(a) two additional circuits between the United States of America and the Union of Soviet Socialist Republics each using a satellite communications system, with each Party selecting a satellite communications system of its own choice,

(b) a system of terminals (more than one) in the territory of each Party for the Direct Communications Link, with the locations and number of terminals in the United States of America to be determined by the United States side, and the locations and number of terminals in the Union of Soviet Socialist Republics to be determined by the Soviet side.

2. Matters relating to the implementation of the aforementioned improvements of the Direct Communications Link are set forth in the Annex which is attached hereto and forms an integral part hereof.

ARTICLE 2

Each Party confirms its intention to take all possible measures to assure the continuous and reliable operation of the communications circuits and the system of terminals of the Direct Communications Link for which it is responsible in accordance with this Agreement and the Annex hereto, as well as to communicate to the head of its Government any messages received via the Direct Communications Link from the head of Government of the other Party.

ARTICLE 3

The Memorandum of Understanding Between the United States of America and the Union of Soviet Socialist Republics Regarding the Establishment of a Direct Communications Link, signed on June 20, 1963, with the Annex thereto, shall remain in force, except to the extent that its provisions are modified by this Agreement and Annex hereto.

ARTICLE 4

The undertakings of the Parties hereunder shall be carried out in accordance with their respective Constitutional processes.

ARTICLE 5

This Agreement, including the Annex hereto, shall enter into force upon signature.

Done at Washington on September 30, 1971, in two copies, each in the English and Russian languages, both texts being equally authentic.

FOR THE UNITED STATES
OF AMERICA:

FOR THE UNION OF SOVIET
SOCIALIST REPUBLICS:

(signed) WILLIAM ROGERS

(signed) A. GROMYKO

ANNEX
TO THE AGREEMENT BETWEEN
THE UNITED STATES OF AMERICA AND
THE UNION OF SOVIET SOCIALIST REPUBLICS
ON MEASURES TO IMPROVE THE USA-USSR
DIRECT COMMUNICATIONS LINK

Improvements to the USA-USSR Direct Communications Link shall be implemented in accordance with the provisions set forth in this Annex.

I. Circuits

(a) Each of the original circuits established pursuant to paragraph 1 of the Annex to the Memorandum of Understanding, dated June 20, 1963, shall continue to be maintained and operated as part of the Direct Communications Link until such time, after the satellite communications circuits provided for herein become operational, as the agencies designated pursuant to paragraph III (hereinafter referred to as the "designated agencies") mutually agree that such original circuit is no longer necessary. The provisions of paragraph 7 of the Annex to the Memorandum of Understanding, dated June 20, 1963, shall continue to govern the allocation of the costs of maintaining and operating such original circuits.

(b) Two additional circuits shall be established using two satellite communications systems. Taking into account paragraph I (e) below, the United States side shall provide one circuit via the Intelsat system and the Soviet side shall provide one circuit via the Molniya II system. The two circuits shall be duplex telephone band-width circuits conforming to CCITT standards, equipped for secondary telegraphic multiplexing. Transmission and reception of messages over the Direct Communications Link shall be effected in accordance with applicable recommendations of international communications regulations, as well as with mutually agreed instructions.

(c) When the reliability of both additional circuits has been established to the mutual satisfaction of the designated agencies, they shall be used as the primary circuits of the Direct Communications Link for transmission and reception of teleprinter messages between the United States and the Soviet Union.

(d) Each satellite communications circuit shall utilize an earth station in the territory of the United States, a communications satellite transponder, and an earth station in the territory of the Soviet Union. Each Party shall be responsible for linking the earth stations in its territory to its own terminals of the Direct Communications Link.

(e) For the circuits specified in paragraph I (b): —The Soviet side will provide and operate at least one earth station in its territory for the satellite communications circuit in the Intelsat system, and will also arrange for the use of suitable earth station facilities in its territory for the satellite communications circuit in the Molniya II system. The United States side, through a governmental agency or other United States legal entity, will make appropriate arrangements with Intelsat with regard to access for the Soviet Intelsat earth station to the Intelsat space segment, as well as for the use of the applicable portion of the Intelsat space segment. —The United States side will provide and operate at least one earth station in its territory for the satellite communications circuit in the Molniya II system, and will also arrange for the use of suitable earth station facilities in its territory for the satellite communications circuit in the Intelsat system.

(f) Each earth station shall conform to the performance specifications and operating procedures of the corresponding satellite communications system and the ratio of antenna gain to the equivalent noise temperature should be no less than 31 decibels. Any deviation from these specifications and procedures which may be required in any unusual situation shall be worked out and mutually agreed upon by the designated agencies of both Parties after consultation.

(g) The operational commissioning dates for the satellite communications circuits based on the Intelsat and Molniya II systems shall be as agreed upon by the designated agencies of the Parties through consultations.

(h) The United States side shall bear the costs of: (1) providing and operating the Molniya II earth station in its territory; (2) the use of the Intelsat earth station in its territory; and (3) the transmission of messages via the Intelsat system. The Soviet side shall bear the costs of: (1) providing and operating the Intelsat earth station in its territory; (2) the use of the Molniya II earth station in its territory; and (3) the transmission of messages via the Molniya II system. Payment of the costs of the satellite communications circuits shall be effected without any transfer of payments between the Parties.

(i) Each Party shall be responsible for providing to the other Party notification of any proposed modification or replacement of the communications satellite system containing the circuit provided by it that might require accommodation by earth stations using that system or otherwise affect the maintenance or operation of the Direct Communications Link. Such notification should be given sufficiently in advance to enable the designated agencies to consult and to make, before the modification or replacement is effected, such preparation as may be agreed upon for accommodation by the affected earth stations.

II. TERMINALS

(a) Each Party shall establish a system of terminals in its territory for the exchange of messages with the other Party, and shall determine the locations and number of terminals in such a system. Terminals of the Direct Communications Link shall be designated "USA" and "USSR".

(b) Each Party shall take necessary measures to provide for rapidly switching circuits among terminal points in such a manner that only one terminal location is connected to the circuits at any one time.

(c) Each Party shall use teleprinter equipment from its own sources to equip the additional terminals for the transmission and reception of messages from the United States to the Soviet Union in the English language and from the Soviet Union to the United States in the Russian language.

(d) The terminals of the Direct Communications Link shall be provided with encoding equipment. One-time tape encoding equipment shall be used for transmissions via the Direct Communications Link. A mutually agreed quantity of encoding equip-

5

ment of a modern and reliable type selected by the United States side, with spares, test equipment, technical literature and operating supplies, shall be furnished by the United States side to the Soviet side against payment of the cost thereof by the Soviet side; additional spares for the encoding equipment supplied will be furnished as necessary.

(e) Keying tapes shall be supplied in accordance with the provisions set forth in paragraph 4 of the Annex to the Memorandum of Understanding, dated June 20, 1963. Each Party shall be responsible for reproducing and distributing additional keying tapes for its system of terminals and for implementing procedures which ensure that the required synchronization of encoding equipment can be effected from any one terminal at any time.

III. OTHER MATTERS

Each Party shall designate the agencies responsible for arrangements regarding the establishment of the additional circuits and the systems of terminals provided for in this Agreement and Annex, for their operation and for their continuity and reliability. These agencies shall, on the basis of direct contacts:

(a) arrange for the exchange of required performance specifications and operating procedures for the earth stations of the communications systems using Intelsat and Molniya II satellites;

(b) arrange for testing, acceptance and commissioning of the satellite circuits and for operation of these circuits after commissioning; and,

(c) decide matters and develop instructions relating to the operation of the secondary teleprinter multiplex system used on the satellite circuits.

GLOSSARY

ABM—Anti-Ballistic Missile (System): A defensive weapon (system) to destroy offensive missile re-entry vehicles. There are three major components in contemporary ABM systems: interceptor missiles, launchers and radars. All three are limited by the 1972 ABM Treaty. ABM radars track incoming re-entry vehicles and also can guide defensive missiles to intercept and destroy them.

ACDA—United States Arms Control and Disarmament Agency.

Area Defense: Defense of a large geographic area, as compared to defense of a particular point.

Assured Destruction: The capability to inflict unacceptable damage on an aggressor even after absorbing his first strike attack. Mutual assured destruction is assured destruction capabilities possessed by opposing sides.

B-1: Proposed U.S. intercontinental bomber—subsequently canceled. (Three prototypes were built.)

B-52: U.S. intercontinental bomber, first deployed in 1955 and subsequently modernized. The United States had 450–500 B-52s deployed during the 1969–72 period.

Backfire: NATO designation for a new Soviet bomber with limited intercontinental capabilities, first deployed in 1974.

Ballistic Missile: Missile which flies to its target on an elliptical path outside the atmosphere. The missile is guided only during the initial powered phase of its flight, with the altitude, bearing and velocity setting the missile on a programmed course to an apogee and descent to its target.

BMEWS—Ballistic Missile Early Warning System: U.S. electronic warning network in Greenland, Scotland, and Alaska, deployed in the early 1960s to detect incoming Soviet missiles.

Checkhov: NATO designation for a large, modern phased-array Soviet radar which was under construction in the Moscow area during the SALT negotiation. It is capable of tracking incoming missile re-entry vehicles for the ABM defense deployed around Moscow.

CIA—United States Central Intelligence Agency.

Counterforce Strike: An attack on military capabilities, generally meaning an attack on an adversary's strategic forces.

Countervalue Strike: An attack on cities or industries.

Cruise Missile: A missile powered by rocket or jet engines which flies like an airplane at low altitudes to its target. The Soviet navy has deployed anti-ship cruise missiles with ranges as great as 450 miles since 1962. The United States is currently developing cruise missiles with greater range and accuracy for deployment in the early 1980s.

Delivery System: The vehicle such as aircraft, missile or submarine which delivers a weapon to its target.

Delta(D)-Class Submarines: NATO designation for Soviet ballistic missile submarine carrying 16 SLBMs, first deployed in 1973 as a follow-on to the Yankee-class missile submarines.

Deployment: Weapons and forces in place for military operations.

Deterrence: A strategy designed to persuade an adversary that the costs and risks of aggression clearly outweigh the possible gains.

Development: The process from laboratory research through engineering and field testing by which a new weapon system is designed for production.

Dog House: NATO designation for a large, phased-array type of Soviet radars. A Dog House radar tracks incoming offensive re-entry vehicles for the ABM defense deployed around Moscow.

First Strike: An initial strategic nuclear attack before the opponent has used any strategic weapons.

FBS—Forward-Based Systems: A term introduced by the U.S.S.R. to refer to U.S. aircraft based in third countries or on aircraft carriers which have the range to deliver a nuclear strike against Soviet territory.

Galosh: NATO designation for the Soviet ABM interceptors deployed around Moscow.

Golf(G)-Class Submarine: NATO designation for a first-generation Soviet diesel-powered ballistic missile submarine carrying 2 or 3 SLBMs, first deployed in 1960. The Soviets deployed about 30 G-class submarines during the SALT negotiation.

Hardening: Protection with concrete, earth and other measures so as to withstand the blast, heat and radiation effects of a nuclear attack. The term is most commonly applied to missiles housed in underground concrete silos mounted on steel springs and fitted with armored blast doors.

Heavy Missile: Large ICBMs, including Modern Large Ballistic Missiles and Older Heavy Ballistic Missiles. The 1972 Interim Agreement prohibits the conversion of launchers for light ICBMs or older heavy ICBMs into launchers for modern heavy ICBMs. The Soviets would not agree to a definition of "heavy" in SALT I, so the United States made a unilateral definition.

Hen House: NATO designation for a large, phased-array type of Soviet radars deployed on the periphery of the Soviet Union for early warning of missile and aircraft attacks.

Hotel(H)-Class Submarines: NATO designation for a first-generation Soviet nuclear-powered ballistic missile submarine carrying 3 SLBMs, first deployed in 1960. The Soviets deployed 10 H-class submarines during the SALT negotiation.

HSD—Hard Site Defense: An ABM defense designed specifically to protect ICBM silos or other hardened facilities from nuclear attack.

ICBM—Intercontinental Ballistic Missile: A land-based ballistic missile capable of a range in excess of 5,500 kilometers (3,400 miles).

Invulnerability: Protection of nuclear forces from destruction by a counterforce attack. Invulnerability measures include hardening, dispersal of nuclear forces at multiple staging areas, and mobility and concealment, the characteristics of ballistic missile submarines.

IRBM—Intermediate Range Ballistic Missile: A ballistic missile with a range of 1,500 to 3,400 miles.

JCS—Joint Chiefs of Staff.

Kiloton: A measure of the explosive power of a nuclear weapon equivalent to 1,000 tons of TNT. The atomic bomb detonated at Hiroshima had an approximate yield of 14 kilotons. The strategic nuclear weapons currently deployed by the United States and the Soviet Union range from about 40 kilotons to 10 or more megatons (a megaton is equivalent to one million tons of TNT).

Launch-on-Warning: The launching of missiles on the basis of detection and warning of an attack before the attacking warheads reach their targets.

Launcher: The launching equipment for a missile, such as an ICBM silo or erector platform or a missile tube in a submarine. The 1972 Interim Agreement limits missile launchers rather than missiles because launchers are much easier for national means of verification to detect and count.

MARC—Modern ABM Radar Complex: Under the ABM Treaty, a circular area of three kilometers in diameter in which ABM radars can be deployed. The MARC concept was introduced by the United States in July 1971 to meet Soviet objections against limiting ABM radars by specifying their number and type.

Minuteman: U. S. ICBM. The Minuteman I and Minuteman II versions, first deployed in 1963 and in 1965, have single warheads; 450 Minuteman IIs are currently deployed. The Minuteman III is a MIRVed missile which has replaced the Minuteman I version; 550 Minuteman IIIs were deployed between 1970 and 1975. Minuteman missiles comprise 1,000 of the 1,054 U. S. ICBM force; the remainder are older Titan missiles.

MIRV—Multiple Independently Targetable Re-entry Vehicles: Two or more re-entry vehicles carried on a single missile and capable of being independently targeted. A MIRVed missile uses a dispensing mechanism that maneuvers to send each warhead on a separate path to its programmed target. The U. S. Minuteman III ICBMs each carry three warheads, while the Poseidon SLBM missile can carry 8–14 warheads.

MLBM—Modern Large Ballistic Missile: Large ICBM of a type deployed since 1964. The United States introduced this category in SALT I to limit Soviet SS-9 ICBMs.

MRBM—Medium Range Ballistic Missile: A ballistic missile with a range of 600–1,500 miles. The United States has never deployed MRBMs, while the U.S.S.R. has deployed 500–600 older MRBMs, most of which are targeted on Western Europe.

MRV—Multiple Re-entry Vehicle: Two or more re-entry vehicles carried by a single missile but not capable of being independently targeted to separate targets.

MSR—Missile Site Radar: An ABM radar designed for the U. S. Safeguard program to provide terminal tracking and guidance for interceptor missiles.

NAC—North Atlantic Council: The Council is the permanent working group of the North Atlantic Treaty Organization, with representatives from each NATO member state. The Council meets regularly at NATO headquarters in Brussels, and was briefed by the delegation and other U.S. officials throughout the SALT negotiations.

NATO—North Atlantic Treaty Organization.

NTM—National Technical Means of Verification: Satellite reconnaissance and other intelligence-gathering systems under national control for monitoring compliance with agreed limitations.

Older Heavy Ballistic Missiles: A large ICBM of a type deployed before 1964, including the U. S. Titan and the Soviet SS-7 and SS-8 missiles.

OLPAR—Other Large Phased-Array Radars: Under the ABM Treaty, non-ABM-associated phased-array radars having a potential (the product of mean emitted power in watts and antenna area in square meters) greater than three million. Phased-array radars with this potential are capable of tracking large numbers of incoming re-entry vehicles for an ABM defense. The OLPAR concept was introduced by the United States in July 1971 to meet Soviet objections against limiting Hen House radars by specifying their numbers and types.

OSD—Office of the Secretary of Defense.

PAR—Perimeter Acquisition Radar: A powerful ABM radar designed for the U. S. Safeguard program to provide initial detection and long-range tracking of incoming offensive re-entry vehicles.

Parity: A condition in which opposing nations have approximately equal strategic military capability.

Penetration: The ability of offensive weapons to penetrate defenses and reach their targets.

Phased-Array Radar: A modern type of radar using an electronic scan antenna, which permits the radar to track many items simultaneously. The heavy traffic handling capability of a phased-array radar makes it more useful for ABM defenses than the older type of mechanical scan radar.

Point Defense: Defense of a limited geographical area or an individual target.

Polaris: First generation U.S. missile submarine system. The U.S. built 41 Polaris submarines between 1960 and 1967, with each submarine carrying 16 SLBMs. Ten Polaris boats remain operational, and 31 have been converted to the MIRVed Poseidon system.

Politburo: The executive body which acts as the authority for the Central Committee of the Communist Party of the Soviet Union between the biannual meetings of the Central Committee. The Politburo has 16 full and 7 alternate members, including top government officials as well as Party leaders. It is the most powerful decision-making body in the Soviet system.

Poseidon: Second-generation U.S. missile submarine system. Beginning in 1970, 31 of the 41 U. S. Polaris submarines were converted to Poseidons by modifying the structure of the Polaris boats to carry 16 MIRVed Poseidon SLBM missiles.

Pre-emptive Strike: An attack initiated in anticipation of an opponent's decision to resort to war, which is intended to prevent or reduce the effect of his attack.

Proliferation: Acquisition of nuclear weapons by states not previously possessing them.

RV—Re-entry Vehicle: The top section of a ballistic missile which carries the nuclear warhead and is designed to separate from the booster and re-enter the earth's atmosphere in the terminal portion of the missile's flight.

SA-5: NATO designation for a Soviet high-altitude surface-to-air interceptor missile which has been extensively deployed in the Soviet Union. The U.S. intelligence community debated for many years whether the SA-5 (also called the Tallinn missile for the capital of Estonia around which the missile was first discovered) was an ABM or an anti-aircraft missile, and this missile was the primary cause of the SAM upgrade issue in the SALT I negotiation. U.S. intelligence now believes the SA-5 was designed as an anti-aircraft missile for intercepting high-altitude bombers.

Safeguard: U. S. ABM system under development and initial deployment during the SALT I negotiations. Announced by

President Nixon in March 1969, Safeguard was a major modification of the previous Sentinel ABM system, in that it was to defend ICBM sites rather than population centers.

SAM: Surface-to-air interceptor missile for defense against air attack.

SCC—Standing Consultative Commission: A permanent U.S.-Soviet SALT commission established by the ABM Treaty "to promote the objectives and implementation" of the 1972 agreements. The SCC has met regularly since December 1972 to consider these matters.

Second Strike: A retaliatory attack in response to a first strike.

Sensors: Devices used to detect objects or environmental conditions, such as radars and optical systems for detecting and tracking missiles and aircraft.

Sentinel: The first U. S. ABM program, approved by President Johnson in 1967, which was to protect American cities against small-scale attacks and provide the potential for expansion into a thick defense against larger attacks.

SLBM—Submarine Launched Ballistic Missile: Ballistic missile carried in and launched from a submarine.

SLCM—Sea Launched Cruise Missile: A cruise missile launched from a submarine or surface ship.

SS-7/SS-8:   NATO designation for first-generation Soviet ICBMs which were deployed between 1961 and 1963. The Soviets had 209 operational SS-7s and SS-8s during the SALT I negotiation.

SS-9:   NATO designation for a large Soviet ICBM. The Soviets deployed 288 SS-9s between 1966 and mid-1971.

SS-11:   NATO designation for the Soviet ICBM which was the bulk of their ICBM force during the SALT I negotiation. The Soviets deployed 1,018 SS-11s between 1966 and mid-1971.

Strategic Power: A nation's military, economic and political power and its ability to control the course of military and political events. Nuclear weapons are considered strategic because their purpose is destruction of an enemy's political system, economic resources and military capacity.

Strategic Stability: An American concept of a stable strategic nuclear relationship between adversary states. *Crisis stability* refers to a strategic balance of forces in which neither side has an incentive to initiate the use of those forces in a crisis. *Arms stability* refers to a strategic force relationship in which neither adversary perceives a need to undertake major new weapons programs to avoid being placed at a strategic disadvantage.

Sufficiency: A doctrine for U.S. strategic forces which during the Nixon Administration called for an adequate second strike retaliatory capability, which would provide no incentive for the Soviet Union to strike first in a crisis, and which would not allow the Soviets to destroy greater urban and industrial resources than the United States could inflict on the U.S.S.R. in a nuclear war.

Tactical: Generally, relating to immediate battlefield operations (or operational means of pursuing a strategy).

Throw Weight: Maximum weight of nuclear warheads and re-entry vehicles which can be carried on the powered stages of a ballistic missile. Throw weight determines the number and size of warheads which can be carried by a missile.

Titan: An older, large U. S. ICBM. First deployed in 1962, the United States retains 54 Titan IIs in its ICBM force.

Triad: Term for the basic structure of U.S. nuclear forces, which consist of three elements: ICBMs, SLBMs, and bombers. Each element of the Triad relies on different means of survival against attack, so that the Triad greatly reduces the possibility of a successful pre-emptive strike against it and increases the deterrent effect of U.S. retaliatory forces.

Trident: New U.S. submarine missile system currently under development and production. Known as ULMS or Undersea Long Range Missile System during most of the SALT negotiation, the Trident submarines will be much larger than the Polaris and Poseidon boats and carry 24 instead of 16 missiles. The Trident missile will also have greater range than the earlier U. S. SLBMs.

The Navy plans to deploy at least 13 Trident submarines, with the first becoming operational in 1981.

Verification: Determining whether the parties to an arms control agreement are complying with its provisions.

Verification Panel: The senior committee in the Nixon National Security Council system responsible for U. S. SALT policies. The Panel was chaired by Henry Kissinger as the President's Assistant for National Security Affairs. Other members were the Director of the Arms Control and Disarmament Agency, the Deputy Secretary of State, the Deputy Secretary of Defense, the Chairman of the Joint Chiefs of Staff, and the Director of the Central Intelligence Agency. A Verification Panel Working Group with representatives of these agencies prepared and co-ordinated detailed analyses of specific SALT issues for the Verification Panel's consideration.

Vladivostok Accord: During a summit meeting at Vladivostok in November 1974, President Ford and General Secretary Brezhnev agreed on a framework for an offensive arms treaty to replace the 1972 Interim Agreement which would last until 1985. The parties agreed to an aggregate ceiling of 2,400 ICBM and SLBM launchers and intercontinental bombers, and a subceiling of 1,320 for MIRVed launchers. The Soviet Union implicitly dropped its claim that forward-based systems be included in offensive treaty limitations (which had been renewed in the SALT II negotiations preceding the Vladivostok meeting).

Warhead: Explosive mechanism carried by a missile or other delivery system.

Yankee(Y)-Class Submarine: NATO designation for a second-generation Soviet nuclear-powered ballistic missile submarine carrying 16 SLBMs. The Soviets deployed 34 Y-class submarines between 1968 and 1974.

INDEX

A

ABM, *see* Anti-ballistic missile;
   ABM Treaty of 1972;
   Grand Forks site
ABM Treaty of 1972, 3, 38, 42,
   43, 49, 51, 58, 95, 96, 155,
   261, 265, 270, 294, 356,
   357, 360, 367, 383, 388,
   400, 401, 402, 410, 419,
   420, 421, 432, 434, 436,
   455–59, 460, 461, 463,
   464
   common understandings,
      496–98
   initialed statements, 494–96
   location of ICBM defenses, 496
   mobile ABM systems, 497
   radar negotiations, 301–18
   Standing Consultative
      Commission, 497–98
   standstill, 498
   terms of, 487–93
   test ranges, 496–97
   unilateral statements, 499–501

Academy of Sciences (U.S.S.R.),
   151, 282
Accidents and Hot Line
   Agreements, 43, 280–98
   areas for consideration, 283–84
   four-point proposal, 282
   Joint Technical Group and,
      289–92
   need for, 280–81
   reaction to, 296–97
   signing of, 290, 295
   terminal points, 293
   terms of, 517–19
   Verification Panel
      recommendations, 287–88
   White House study, 281
   See also Hot Line
ACDA, *see* Arms Control and
   Disarmament Agency
Acheson, Dean, 40
Afghan crisis of 1979–80, 2, 454
Agnew, Spiro, 30
Agreement on the Prevention of
   Nuclear War (1963), 144

Air Force 2, 77
Alaska, 309
Albertina (museum), 70
Alekseyev, Colonel General
    Nikolai, 48, 49, 216
Alexander, Tsar, 53
Allison, Lieutenant General
    Royal, B., 39, 41, 42–43,
    47, 56, 61, 87, 161,
    181–82, 186, 216, 227,
    268, 283, 345, 370, 409,
    415, 435, 436, 439, 443
American Defense Satellite
    Communications System
    (DSCS), 293, 294
American Peace Commission,
    447–48
American Security Council, 343
Anderson, Dillon, 242
Angola, 454
Antarctica, 17
Anti-ballistic missile (ABM), 14,
    16, 27, 28, 30, 31, 42, 47,
    49, 261–63, 285, 370, 373,
    410, 433, 449, 450, 453,
    465, 470, 529
  back-channel negotiations, 222,
    226, 229, 230, 231, 234,
    235, 238, 245
  basic function of, 301–2
  final Helsinki negotiations, 379,
    380, 383–84, 387, 400,
    401
  Helsinki I talks, 79, 80, 86, 89,
    93–96, 101, 105–6, 107
  Helsinki III talks, 179, 182,
    188, 191–98
  Helsinki V talks, 247–50,
    252–72, 275, 276, 277,
    278
  Kosygin press conference on
    (1967), 32

last Helsinki round, 351–59,
    364–66
  MIRV ban proposal, 154, 155,
    156, 157, 163, 165, 166,
    169, 173
  purpose of, 19
  unwanted competition in, 32
  Vienna II talks, 124–26,
    129–32, 133, 144, 146–49,
    152, 153
  Vienna IV talks, 201–22
  Vienna VI talks, 319, 320,
    324–25, 327–28, 330,
    336–39, 343–44
  Washington policy planning
    and, 112–13, 116, 117,
    119
Apollo 13 mission, 57
Arbatov, Georgi, 191, 195
Area defense, 529
Armed Services Committee
    (House of
    Representatives), 112
Armed Services Committee
    (U. S. Senate), 112, 135,
    243, 459
Arms competition stability, 86
Arms Control and Disarmament
    Act of 1961, 243
Arms Control and Disarmament
    Agency (ACDA), 6,
    13–14, 38–39, 44, 49, 54,
    55, 62, 113–14, 118, 160,
    164, 171, 173, 222, 233,
    237, 348, 377, 426, 443,
    444, 529
Arms Control Subcommittee
    (Armed Services
    Committee), 243
Assured destruction capabilities,
    85, 529
Assured destruction strategy, 336

Atlas, 11
Atomic Energy Commission
(AEC), 6, 7, 13, 15, 171,
285
Atoms for Peace Conference of
1955, 8–9
Atoms for Peace program, 237
Australia, 470

B
B-1 intercontinental bomber, 2,
79, 133, 321, 340, 529
B-17 aircraft, 321
B-29 bombers, 93
B-47 bombers, 30, 93
B-52 crash of 1966 (in Spain),
296
B-52 intercontinental bomber, 2,
132, 133, 184, 529
Back-channel negotiations,
222–46, 323, 328
ABM and, 222, 226, 229, 230,
231, 234, 235, 238, 245
FBS issue, 225, 226, 227, 246
how May 20 accord was
reached, 225–33
ICBMs and, 222, 223, 227,
228, 229–30
Nixon and, 222–24, 226, 228,
233, 237, 238, 239
privacy and, 241–42
reaction to, 243–44
results of, 233–46
SALT security leaks, 236–41
SLBMs and, 223, 225, 228–29
use of Soviet interpreters,
466–67
White House draft (February
17), 229
See also Dobrynin, Anatoly;
Kissinger, Henry
Backfire, 530

Backstopping Committee, 43–44,
109
Ballistic missile, 530
Ballistic missile early warning
system (BMEWS), 309,
530
Bangladesh, 341
Bank of Russia, 66
Baruch plan of 1946, 19–20
Basic National Security Policy
(Eisenhower
administration), 10
"Basic Provisions for an
Agreement on Limiting
Deployment of ABM
Systems" (Helsinki III),
192–93
"Basic Provisions for Limiting
Strategic Armaments"
(Vienna II), 123
Beam, Ambassador, 439
Beecher, William, 253, 274
Beecher leak, the, 252–53
Berchtold, Count Leopold, 138
Biological Warfare Convention,
164
Bliss, General Tasker, 450
BMEWS, see Ballistic missile
early warning system
Board of Economic Warfare, 40
Bohlen, Charles "Chip," 12, 39
"Bomber bonfire" plan of 1960s,
30
Bowie, Robert, 10
Brest-Litovsk, Treaty of (1918),
77
Brezhnev, Leonid, 2, 144, 197,
369, 379, 380, 395, 402,
410, 429, 431, 438, 460
proposal on ABM and SLBM,
370–78, 391, 410
Brookings Institution, 50

Brown, Dr. Harold, 24, 39, 40, 60, 157–58
Budenny, Marshall Semën, 67
Bulganin, Nikolai, 12
Bundy, McGeorge, 18, 242

C
California Institute of Technology, 40
Cambodian incursion of 1970, 26, 136, 137, 152, 153, 196, 197; *See also* Vietnam War
Camp David, 10; *See also* Détente
Cat Ballou (motion picture), 61
Cecil, Lord Robert, 447
Central Intelligence Agency (CIA), 31, 54, 55, 114–15, 147, 173, 239–40, 530
Chekhov radar, 302, 306, 358, 530
China, 19, 20, 32, 94, 133, 142, 144, 250, 253–54, 291, 294–95, 319, 348, 356, 448, 454, 464
    hostility with U.S.S.R., 34, 35, 144
    Kissinger in, 253–54, 258, 294–95, 339
    nuclear program, 9
    rapprochement with U.S., 34
    Warsaw talks, 197
Chou En-lai, 253
Chukotsk Peninsula, 129
Churchill, Sir Winston, 339
Cienfuegos crisis, 323
Cliburn, Van, 439
Colson, Charles, 442
Committee on Lenin Prizes for Science and Technology, 47
Communications Link

Agreement, 280, 296, 297
Communist Party Congress (1971), 48
Communist Party of the Soviet Union, 15, 48, 67, 197
Comprehensive limitations, alternative approaches to, 477–78
Conference on Security and Cooperation, 77
Consultative Commission, *see* Standing Consultative Commission
Cooper, John Sherman, 10, 112, 343, 347
Counterforce strike, 530
Countervalue strike, 530
Crisis stability, 86
Cruise missile, 530
Cuba, 93, 323, 454
Cuban missile crisis of 1962, 31
Cutler, Robert, 242
Czechoslovakia, Soviet invasion of (1968), 20, 53, 104, 158

D
Daniels, Josephus, 448
D-class, *see* Delta(D)-class submarines
Dean, Gordon, 15–16
De La Cruz, Madame, 13
Delivery system, 530
Delta(D)-class submarines, 530
Democratic Policy Council, 206
Deployment, 530
De Sales, St. Francis, xi
Détente, 10, 34, 38, 219
Deterrence, 531
Development, 531
Dillon, Douglas, 13
Disarmament Conference, *see* Geneva Conference on Disarmament

Distinguished Honor Award (Department of State), 50, 443

Dobrynin, Anatoly, 20, 78, 80, 170–71, 176, 207–8, 212, 222, 226–31, 235, 237, 242–43, 248, 249, 250–52, 257, 259, 260, 267, 272, 273, 274, 276, 324, 332, 349–50, 376

Dog House, 302, 306, 531

Dulles, Allen, 61

Dulles, John Foster, 7, 9, 10–11, 14, 121

Dürer, Albrecht, 70

E

Eighteenth Congress of the Communist Party, 67

Einstein, Albert, 15

Eisenhower, Dwight D., 7, 9, 10, 14, 23, 80, 122, 237, 238, 344, 353
    attitude toward arms control, 17
    doctrine of sufficiency, 24
    Open Skies proposal, 12
    U-2 incident, 11–12, 282

Empedocles, 138

Engels, Friedrich, 71

England, *see* Great Britain

Enterprise (carrier), 341

Eugene, Prince of Savoy, 121

Eugen Onegin (Pushkin), 70, 143

F

Farley, Philip, 38–39, 43–44, 109, 222, 296, 297, 426, 444

FBS, *see* Forward-based systems

Federation of American Scientists, 206

Fields, W. C., 82

Finland Station, 60

First International Congress, 67

First strike, 531

Ford, Gerald, 171

Foreign Affairs (magazine), 442

Foreign Affairs Committee (House of Representatives), 112, 162, 205

Foreign Affairs Committee (U. S. Senate), 112

Foreign Policy Report of 1971, 178, 203, 235

Foreign Relations Committee (U. S. Senate), 9, 149, 161, 205, 451

Foreign Service Language School, 13

Forward-based systems (FBS), 90–93, 101, 155, 307, 330, 400, 462, 470, 531
    Helsinki III talks, 179, 182–84, 185–86, 187–88, 192, 194, 197
    strategic capability of, 128
    Vienna II talks, 123–30, 131, 146, 148

Foster, William, 44

France, 19, 20, 145, 291, 323, 361, 446

Franklin, Benjamin, 55

Frederick II, Emperor, 222

Futuristics limitation, 263–65

G

Galosh deployment, 32, 59, 255, 455, 531

Garthoff, Raymond, 49, 50, 58, 60, 71, 118–19, 307, 364–65, 366, 368, 385, 386, 387, 398, 405, 409, 443

G-class, *see* Golf(G)-class submarine

General Advisory Committee (Arms Control Agency), 116

Geneva Conference on Disarmament, 14, 49, 118, 130

Germany, 25, 81–82, 96, 97, 321

Glassboro summit meeting, 32

Goethe, Johann Wolfgang von, 69–70

Golf(G)-class submarines, 59, 381–82, 393, 394, 403, 412, 419, 420, 423, 426, 427–28, 429, 430, 431, 432–33, 531

Grand Forks, ABM site at, 262, 337, 351, 355, 363, 364, 370, 421

Gray, Gordon, 242

Great Britain, 19, 97, 309, 323, 361, 446, 448, 449, 450, 452

Grechko, Marshal, 46, 139

Greenland, 309

Grinevsky, Oleg, 48–49, 50, 58, 307, 364, 365, 385, 405, 433

Gromyko, Andrei, 10, 34, 70, 181, 233, 271, 280, 297–98, 327, 354, 369, 408, 425, 428, 429, 430–31

Guam, 449

H

Haig, General, 201, 202, 249, 257, 373, 376, 409, 441, 442

Haiphong, bombing of (1972), 26, 382–83

Haise (astronaut), 57

Hamlet (ballet), 189

Hardening, 531

Harding, Warren G., 446, 448, 451

Hard-site defense (HSD) system, 202, 205, 209, 532

Harvard University, 111

H-class, see Hotel (H)-class submarines

Heartbreak House (Shaw), 243

Heavy missile, 531

Hegel, Georg Wilhelm Friedrich, 69

Helms, Richard, 109, 239

Helsinki I (November–December 1969), 75–107, 126, 133
    China and, 96
    document guidance, 80
    end of, 105–7
    FBS issue, 90–93, 101
    Illustrative Elements device, 88–90, 93, 102
    opening session, 82
    press corps, 77–78
    reciprocal exchanges offer, 99
    strategic theory and, 85–87
    Verification Panel, 99–100
    work program, 101–3

Helsinki III (November–December 1970), 179–98
    ABM limitation and, 179, 182, 188, 191–98
    cruise missile issue, 189–90
    difference between U.S. and Soviet negotiating practices, 194
    FBS issue, 179, 182–84, 185–86, 187–88, 192, 194, 197
    Finnish press story, 181
    levels for limiting strategic offensive arms, 190–91
    Nixon's Formula, 186–87
    opening week, 180–81

results of, 195–98
second American plenary
    statement, 180–81
Soviet Basic Provisions on
    ABMs, 192–93
Soviet tactics, 183
U.S. aircraft incident, 181–82
Helsinki V (July–September
    1971), 247–79
Beecher leak, 252–53
beginning of, 250
Dobrynin–Kissinger
    back-channel negotiations
    and, 248, 249, 250–52,
    257, 259, 260, 267, 272,
    273, 274, 276
end of, 269
futuristics limitation, 263–65
pace of talks, 259–60
President's decision against
    ABM ban, 261–63
results of, 269–79
"sequence" issue, 250–52
Soviet ABM interests,
    265–67
tabling of ABM draft, 254–55
Helsinki (March–April
    1972—last round), 351–69
ABM issues, 351–59, 364–66
ICBM issues, 352–57, 359–66,
    368
radar constraints and, 357–58,
    367
SLBM launcher question, 351,
    352, 354, 360–61, 363,
    364, 366, 367
soviet "neutral-negative"
    attitude, 363
strategy, 352
Tundra talks, 365–66, 368
Helsinki (May 1972—final
    days), 379–406
ABM issues, 379, 380, 383–84,
    387, 400, 401
Haiphong bombing and,
    382–83
ICBM and, 380, 381, 384–89,
    391–93, 397, 400–5
Interim Agreement, 380–81,
    388–89, 392, 395, 397
Kissinger-Brezhnev
    arrangements and, 380,
    381, 396, 402
Nitze-drafted compromise,
    384–85
OLPAR issue, 385–86
"separation" solution, 387–88
SLBM provisions, 379–82,
    391–97, 399–400, 402–4
"statement of the Soviet side,"
    395–96, 433
"two plus 18" solution, 385
See also Moscow negotiations
Helsinki Work Program, 122,
    139, 146, 167, 281
Hen Houses, 305, 306–7, 308,
    309–10, 532
Herblock (cartoonist), 162
Herter, Christian, 10
Hiroshima, atomic bombing of, 6,
    44, 321
History of Diplomacy, A
    (Semenov), 46
Hitler, Adolf, 40
Homogeneity, Soviet principle of,
    267–68
Hotel(H)-class submarines, 59,
    381, 382, 393, 394, 398,
    400, 403, 412, 419, 420,
    423, 426, 431, 532
Hot Line, 6, 140, 207, 279, 462
revised agreement, 521–27
weaknesses, 281
See also Accidents and Hot
    Line Agreements

Hot Line Memorandum (1963), 293, 296
House, Colonel Edward M., 447
"How Much Is Enough?" (Quarles), 23–24
HSD, *see* Hard-site defense
Hughes, Charles Evans, 160, 447, 451
Humes, Mrs. Jean, 51
Humes, John, 51
Humphrey, Hubert, 163, 206, 347

I
ICBM, *see* Intercontinental ballistic missile
Illustrative Elements, 88–90, 93, 102, 130, 225
India, 9, 341
India-Pakistan War, 341
Industrial College of the Armed Forces, 43
Initial Strategic Arms Limitations Agreement, 151
Institute of U.S. and Canada Studies (U.S.S.R. Academy of Sciences), 191
Intelsat, 293
Intercontinental ballistic missile (ICBM), 2, 3, 11, 16, 17, 31, 32, 41, 42, 52, 284–85, 296–97, 370, 371, 375, 377, 443, 449, 456, 458, 459, 460, 462, 470, 472, 532
  back-channel negotiations and, 222, 223, 227, 228, 229–30
  final Helsinki negotiations, 380, 381, 384–89, 391–93, 397, 400–5
  Helsinki I talks, 79, 86, 87, 88–91, 94, 101, 105, 107

Helsinki III talks, 187, 188, 189, 192
Helsinki V talks, 247–49, 252, 255–57, 259–60, 262, 266–70, 272, 273, 277
  last Helsinki round, 352–57, 359–66, 368
  MIRV ban proposal and, 156, 157, 158, 160, 161, 162, 163, 165, 166, 168, 172, 175, 178
  Moscow negotiations, 410–16, 418, 420, 422, 423, 425, 427, 428, 432, 433
  radar constraints and, 307, 310, 311, 317
  Vienna II talks, 122–23, 124, 125, 128, 130, 134–36, 146, 148, 149, 150
  Vienna IV talks, 202, 203, 204–21
  Vienna VI talks, 320, 322, 326, 329–30, 332–39, 345, 349
  vulnerability problem, 27–29
  Washington policy planning and, 112, 114, 117, 118, 119, 120
Interim Agreement, 380–81, 388–89, 392, 395, 397, 412, 421, 434, 462
  program for, 483–84
  terms of, 503–6
Intermediate range ballistic missiles (IRBM), 88, 532
International Atomic Energy Agency, 9
Invulnerability, 532
IRBM, *see* Intermediate range ballistic missile
Irwin, John, 108–9
Italy, 446
Izvestia (newspaper), 205, 250–51

J

Jackson, Henry "Scoop," 7, 14, 112–13, 149, 207, 212, 243, 442–43

Japan, 6, 44, 321, 446, 449, 450, 452, 470

Jay, John, 54

JCS, *see* Joint Chiefs of Staff

Johnson, Lyndon B., 9, 14, 16, 18, 19, 20, 22, 29, 32, 39, 40, 41, 58, 159, 161, 168, 232, 353, 387, 470, 472

Johnson, U. Alexis, 372–73

Joint American-Soviet Draft Document on Accident Measures (Joint Technical Group), 292

Joint Chiefs of Staff (JCS), 10, 11, 27, 39, 41, 42, 54, 55, 62, 79, 86, 108, 114, 119, 205, 233, 239, 274, 303, 304, 346, 374, 409, 443, 532

Joint Draft Text, 270, 271, 279, 349, 360

K

Karjalainen, Foreign Minister, 82

Kekkonen, President, 66

Kennedy, John F., 14, 18, 40, 164, 353, 468

Kesselring, Field Marshal Albert, 61

Khrushchev, Nikita, 10, 12, 353

Kiloton, 532

Kishilov, Nikolai, 49, 50–51, 58, 71, 307, 333, 364, 365, 385, 387, 398, 405, 433

Kissinger, Henry, 1, 15–16, 18, 26, 33, 38, 40, 62, 198, 324, 368, 369, 380, 396, 410, 430–33, 436, 438, 439, 441, 442, 443

back-channel negotiations, 222–46, 248, 249, 250–52, 257, 259, 260, 267, 272, 273, 274, 276, 289, 323, 332, 349–50

Brezhnev proposal and, 370–77

in China, 253–54, 258, 294–95, 339

final Helsinki negotiations and, 397, 399, 400–1, 403, 404

Helsinki I talks, 84, 93

Helsinki V talks, 249, 250, 256, 259–60, 262, 269, 278

last Helsinki round and, 363, 368, 369

MIRV ban proposal, 156, 169, 174, 176, 177

Moscow meeting with Brezhnev, 369, 370, 372, 444, 466

Vienna II talks, 147, 148, 149, 151

Vienna IV talks, 201–2, 209, 211, 212, 216, 217

Vienna VI talks, 323, 328, 339, 342, 345–46, 347

Washington policy planning and, 108, 109, 110, 111, 112, 115

Klein, Herb, 438–39

Kollontai, Alexandra, 65–66

Konev, Marshal, 66

Koran, 69

Korean War, 6

Korniyenko, Georgi, 48

Kosygin, Aleksei, 19, 22, 32, 48, 136, 223, 233, 326, 459

Kraft, Joe, 347

Krimer, William, 70

Krock, Arthur, 237

Kuznetzov, 39

L

Ladder, Richard, 57

Laird, Melvin, 28, 29, 30, 42, 64, 79, 113, 135, 138, 139, 160–61, 180, 184, 188, 205, 206, 209, 223–24, 262, 322, 340, 347, 352, 361, 459

"Last Twenty Minutes of a Negotiation Are the Most Important, The" (Nitze), 417

Launcher, 532

Launch-on-warning, 532

League of Nations, 447

Lenin, Nikolai, 40, 56, 60, 66, 71, 77, 82, 100

Liberation (propaganda film), 60–61

Lighter delivery aircraft (LDA), 90–91

Limited Test Ban Treaty (1963), 49

"Linkage" concept, 25–26, 127, 303, 341–42, 355, 383, 447, 448

Livermore Laboratory, 7

Lloyd George, David, 467

Lodal, Jan M., 461

Lodge, Henry Cabot, 451

London Disarmament Conference of 1957, 9

Longest Day, The (motion picture), 61

Los Alamos, 7

Lovell (astronaut), 57

Luke, St., 473

Lynn, Laurence, 109

M

Macmillan, Harold, 468

McNamara, Robert, 18–19, 32, 68

McQuarrie, General, 181–82

Malenkov, Georgi, 15

Malmstrom Air Force Base, 247–48, 357, 363, 364, 373

Mao Tse-tung, 40

MARC, *see* Modern ABM radar complex

Marx, Karl, 71, 347

M*A*S*H (motion picture), 61

May, Clifford D., Jr., 292

Medium range and intermediate range ballistic missiles (MR/IRBMs), 88–89
  Helsinki I talks, 88, 89, 90, 91, 101, 107
  Helsinki III talks, 182, 184
  Vienna II talks, 138, 146, 150
  Washington policy planning and, 119

Medium range ballistic missile (MRBM), 533

Memorandum of Understanding of June 1963, 292

Military-Industrial Commission, 408

Millionshchikov, 163

Minashin, V. P., 292, 293, 294

Minuteman missiles, 11, 19, 28, 41, 86, 87, 94, 118, 122, 123, 130, 136, 172, 202, 203, 207, 214, 228, 256, 320, 533

Minuteman I, 79, 415, 533

Minuteman III, 79, 175, 340, 415, 416, 533

MIRV, *see* Multiple independently targetable re-entry vehicle

"Missile gap" issue, 29, 346

Missile site radar (MSR), 302, 358, 367, 386, 533

Mitchell, John, 109

Modern ABM radar complex (MARC), 310–13, 315,

316, 317, 318, 358, 365, 368, 369, 383, 384, 385
Modern large ballistic missile (MLBM), 11, 220, 249, 533
  Moscow negotiations, 410–11, 415
  Vienna II talks, 122, 123, 130, 150, 151
Molniya II satellite, 293–94
Molotov, Vyacheslav M., 66, 69, 121
Monnet, Jean, 72
Moorer, Admiral Tom, 41, 108, 374, 375–76
Mosbacher, Ambassador, 416
Moscow negotiations, 22, 407–40, 442
  decommission procedures, 421–22
  exclusion of Soviet and American SALT delegates, 408, 417–18, 432
  modernization and replacement issue, 410–15
  question of silo dimensions, 422–25
  results of, 432–40
Moscow-Washington Direct Communications Link, see Hot Line
MRV, see Multiple re-entry vehicle
MSR, see Missile site radar
Multiple independently targetable re-entry vehicle (MIRV), 16, 19, 27, 33, 41, 206, 214–15, 248, 274, 307, 340, 390, 415, 416, 417, 432, 453, 457, 459, 460, 471–72, 533
  ban proposal, 154–78
    ABM system and, 154, 155,

156, 157, 163, 165, 166, 169, 173
    case for, 157–60
    failure of, 156
    ICBMs and, 156, 157, 158, 160, 161, 162, 163, 165, 166, 168, 172, 175, 178
    memorandum to Nixon, 479–82
    on-site inspection issue, 167–72, 174, 176–77
    Pentagon opposition to, 168, 169–70
    public support for, 162, 168
    purpose of, 156
    SLBMs and, 156, 160, 163, 165, 168
    "Stop Where We Are" (SWWA) position, 160, 161, 163
  Helsinki I talks, 79, 89, 95, 102, 107
  justification for, 16–17
  purpose of, 154–55
  Vienna II talks, 122–23, 125, 133, 150, 153
  Washington policy planning and, 114, 116, 117, 118, 119
Multiple re-entry vehicle (MRV), 533
Murphy, Robert, 80
Murray, T. E., 6–7
Muskie, Edmund, 206
Mutual balanced force reduction (MBFR), 184–85
MX system, 2–3, 88

N
NAC, see North Atlantic Council
Nagasaki, atomic bombing of, 44
Napoleon I, 40, 53
National Command Authority (NCA), 131, 150, 152,

205, 211, 215, 217, 227, 229, 232, 234, 306, 312, 340
National Security Affairs, 18
National Security Council (NSC), 58–59, 108, 109, 110, 111, 112, 113, 117, 160, 169, 185–86, 209, 210–11, 212, 225, 256, 352, 371–72, 375–76, 408, 409, 419, 461
National Security Decision Memoranda (NSDMs), 80, 110, 239
National technical means of verification (NTM), development of, 30–31
NATO, *see* North Atlantic Treaty Organization
Nautilus (submarine), 7
Negotiators, The (Walder), 69
Nekrasov, Governor General, 82
New Testament, 69
New York *Times*, 149, 206, 237, 253
New Zealand, 470
Nitze, Paul H., 10, 40–42, 44, 47, 56, 57, 60, 308, 323–24, 357–58, 370, 384, 409, 417, 435, 436, 439
Nixon, Richard, 1, 2, 5, 6, 13, 21–22, 23, 25–26, 30, 34, 35, 39, 40, 41, 59–60, 64–65, 70, 72, 444, 451, 453, 457, 459, 460, 468
    back-channel negotiations and, 222–24, 226, 228, 233, 237, 238, 239
    Brezhnev proposal and, 372, 375–76, 377–78
    "bullshit" reaction, 376, 377
    criteria of sufficiency, 24
    decision against ABM ban,
261–63, 485–86
    decision-making responsibility, 114
    final Helsinki negotiations and, 380, 400, 401, 402
    Foreign Policy Report (1971), 178, 203, 235
    Helsinki I talks, 75–77, 78, 81, 82, 84, 93, 94, 97–98, 100, 104–5, 106
    Helsinki III talks, 179, 186–87, 194
    Helsinki V talks, 248, 253, 256, 261–63, 271, 272
    last Helsinki round and, 353, 354, 356, 362, 367
    MIRV ban proposal and, 154, 158, 161, 163, 164, 166, 168–71, 178, 479–82
    Moscow negotiations, 22, 408–10, 412, 420–22, 429–31, 432, 436, 438, 439
    Vienna II talks, 124, 126–27, 136–37, 144, 147, 149
    Vienna IV talks, 201, 202, 203–4, 208–9, 210, 212, 218
    Vienna VI talks, 319–20, 325, 326, 327, 342, 343, 348
    Washington policy planning and, 110, 112, 114–16, 117–18
Non-Proliferation Treaty (NPT) of 1968, 8, 20, 22, 44, 49, 68, 81, 124, 145
North Atlantic Council (NAC), 77, 109, 124, 150, 210, 244, 249, 296, 470, 533–34
North Atlantic Treaty Organization (NATO), 21, 97, 104, 133, 142, 144,

145–46, 244, 281, 323, 361, 371, 391, 393, 395, 470, 534

multilateral force (MLF), 144

NTM, *see* National technical means of verification

Nuclear testing moratorium of 1958–60, 122

Nuclear weapons, criminal actions with, 282–83; *See also* names of weapons

Nuclear Weapons and Foreign Policy (Kissinger), 15–16, 40

O

"Objectives and Principles" draft (1968), 20–21

Ogarkov, Colonel General Nikolai, 46, 48, 49, 181, 182, 283, 445

Older heavy ballistic missiles, 534

Old Testament, 69

OLPAR, *see* Other large phased-array radar

Open-door policy, 448

Open Skies proposal, 12

Oppenheimer, Robert, 16

Ostfriesland (battleship), 450

Other large phased-array radars (OLPAR), 310, 313–14, 315, 316, 318, 357–58, 367, 385–86, 413, 534

Outer space, 17, 31, 305–6, 343

Owen, Henry, 160

P

Packard, David, 108

Pakistan, 341

PAR, *see* Perimeter acquisition radar

Paris *Herald Tribune*, 53–54

Paris summit meeting (1960), 12

Parity, 16, 22, 141, 534

Parsons, James Graham "Jeff," 43, 44, 60, 270, 289–90, 409

Peaceful coexistence, policy of, 33–34

Penetration, 534

Pentagon, 10, 28, 41, 158, 190, 247, 260, 339, 409, 423

Perimeter acquisition radar (PAR), 302, 306, 310, 317, 385, 534

Pershing, General John J., 450

Petersen, Val, 51

Petrov, 67

Phased-array radar, 534

Philippines, 449

Pleshakov, Petr S., 48, 434

Point defense, 534

Polaris missile submarine system, 7, 96, 97, 145, 161, 163, 339, 382, 458, 535

Policy Planning Staff (Department of State), 40, 160

Politburo, 58, 191, 197, 226, 233, 383, 408, 415, 424, 430, 535

Pope, Alexander, 407

Poseidon missile submarine system, 7, 79, 161, 214, 274, 321, 339, 340, 396, 447, 458, 535

Pratt, Admiral, 449

Pravda (newspaper), 250

Pre-emptive strike, 535

Present Day Problems of Disarmament (U.S.S.R. Academy of Sciences), 282

Proliferation, 535

Public Information Center

(Department of Defense), 164

Pushkin, Alexander, 70, 143

Q
Quarles, Donald, 23–24

R
Rabi, I. I., 36
Radar controls (ABM system), 301–18
  importance of, 303
  last Helsinki round and, 357–58, 367
Reconnaissance capabilities, improvement of (U.S.), 30–31
Re-entry vehicles (RV), 16, 302, 303, 305, 535
Richardson, Elliot, 108
Rickover, Admiral Hyman, 7, 13–14
Roberts, Chalmers, 347
Rogers, William, 6, 24, 36, 39, 64, 78, 79, 104, 110, 118, 156, 159–60, 163, 197, 204, 236, 238, 240, 280, 297, 370–76, 377, 435, 444
Rostow, Walt, 242
Rostropovich, 141
Rusk, Dean, 18
Russian language, 6, 12–13, 56, 57, 181, 195, 244, 270, 430
Russo-Finnish War, 66
RV, see Re-entry vehicle

S
Safeguard ABM program, 95, 148, 149, 192, 211, 218, 340, 455, 535–36
SA-5 (Soviet high-altitude surface-to-air interceptor missile), 535
SALT necktie, 66
SAM, see Surface-to-air interceptor missile
SAM 5, 314
SCC, see Standing Consultation Commission
Scherrer, General, 181–82
Schlesinger, James, 11, 464
Scientific Council for the Propagation of Radio Waves, 47
Seabeds Treaty, 124, 164, 343
Sea-launched cruise missile (SLCM), 88, 101, 150
Second strike, 536
Selective direct observation (SDO), 134
Semenov, Vladimir S., 5–6, 7–8, 10, 39, 45–46, 48, 49, 50, 53, 55–56, 57, 60, 61, 65–72, 167, 168, 171, 175, 176–77, 222, 224, 237, 245, 307, 312, 370, 408, 418–19, 429, 430, 433, 434, 435, 439–40, 445
  Accident Agreement, 281, 284, 286, 288, 291, 294, 295
  final Helsinki negotiations and, 379, 380, 385, 386, 388, 391–92, 394–95, 398–401
  Helsinki I talks, 78, 80–82, 83, 84, 86, 88, 90, 91, 95–98, 99–103, 104, 106
  Helsinki III talks, 180, 181, 183, 184, 185, 188, 189, 192, 194–95
  Helsinki V talks, 251–52, 254, 255, 256–59, 262, 267, 274
  last Helsinki round, 354–62, 366, 367, 369

Vienna II talks, 123, 126, 127, 128, 130–31, 133–43, 150–51

Vienna IV talks, 207, 212–13, 216, 218–21

Vienna VI talks, 326, 327–30, 332, 336, 342, 344, 346, 348–49

Semenova, Mme. Lydia, 80, 439–40

Sensors, 536

Sentinel ABM program, 387, 536

Shaw, George Bernard, 243

Shaw, Jack, 43

Shchukin, Aleksandr N., 47, 60, 286, 308, 328, 435

SLBM, *see* Submarine launched ballistic missile

SLCM, *see* Sea-launched cruise missile

Smirnov, 408, 409, 430

Smith, K. Wayne, 109

Soviet Basic Provisions, 123–24, 127, 130, 131, 134, 144, 187, 189, 192–93

Soviet Cuban missile deployment, 184

Soviet-German Non-Aggression Pact (1939), 45

Soviet Strategic Rocket Forces headquarters, 75

Soviet ultimatum of November 1958, 10

Special Technical Group, 289–90

Special Working Group, 270

Sprout, H. M., 446

SS-7 (deployed between 1961 and 1963), 381, 403, 536

SS-8 (deployed between 1961 and 1963), 381, 403, 536

SS-9 (deployed between 1966 and mid-1971), 28, 59, 79, 86, 87, 122–23, 125, 130, 166, 206–7, 249, 325, 333, 334, 389–90, 462, 536

SS-11 (deployed between 1966 and mid-1971), 59, 189, 331, 333, 334, 353, 389–90, 391, 400, 415, 460, 470, 536

Stalin, Joseph, 40, 60, 66, 67, 71

Standing Consultative Commission (SCC), 344, 389, 405, 463, 497–98, 536

Stassen, Harold, 9

State of the Union message (1953), 15

Stennis, John C., 343

"Stop Where We Are" (SWWA) position, 160

Strategic Air Command headquarters, 75

Strategic Arms Limitations Talks (SALT) I
  Accidents and Hot Line Agreements, 43, 280–98
  aftermath, 441–45
  agreements, 453–64
  aim of, 8
  arrangements, 194–298
  back-channel negotiations, 222–46, 323, 328
  beginnings, 15–36
  breaches of security of information, 236–41
  Brezhnev proposal, 370–78, 391, 410
  compared to Washington Naval Conference, 446–52
  delegates, 37–72
  financial benefits from, 463–64
  glossary, 529–38
  Helsinki I, 75–107, 126, 133

Helsinki III, 179–98
Helsinki V, 247–79
Helsinki (final days), 379–406
Helsinki (last round), 351–69
lessons learned from, 465–73
major failure of, 471–72
MIRV ban proposal, 154–78
Moscow summit, 22, 407–40, 442
objectives, 20–21
preparation, 5–14
probings, 73–199
radar restraints, 301–18
retrospective, 446–52
U.S.S.R. goals, 33
Vienna II, 121–53, 179, 210–11
Vienna IV, 201–22
Vienna VI, 319–50
Washington policy planning, 108–20
working it out, 299–473
See also ABM Treaty of 1972
Strategic Arms Limitation Talks (SALT) II, 2, 30, 89, 90, 105, 156–57, 158, 171, 190, 263, 440, 443, 454, 456, 459, 460, 471
Strategic Arms Limitation Talks (SALT) III, 458
Strategic equality, Soviet goal of, 33–34
Strategic nuclear weapons, purpose of, 24
Strategic power, 536–37
Strategic stability, 537
Subcommittee on Defense Appropriations (House of Representatives), 23
Submarine-launched ballistic missile (SLBM), 86, 203, 459, 468, 536
    back-channel negotiations and,

223, 225, 228–29
    final Helsinki negotiations and, 379–82, 391–97, 399–400, 402–4
Helsinki I talks, 86, 88, 89, 101, 105
Helsinki III talks, 187, 189
Helsinki V talks, 247, 248, 272–76, 277
last Helsinki round, 351, 352, 354, 360–61, 363, 364, 366, 367
MIRV ban proposal and, 156, 160, 163, 165, 168
Moscow negotiations, 410–13, 418–20, 423, 425–29, 437
Vienna II talks, 125, 128, 130, 136, 145, 146, 149, 150
Vienna VI talks, 320, 322–24, 326, 329–31, 335, 344–46, 349, 350
Washington policy planning and, 119
Sufficiency, doctrine of, 24, 537
Surface-to-air interceptor missile (SAM), 32, 95, 101, 107, 128, 131–32, 133, 150, 151, 165, 172, 173, 193, 303, 305, 307, 455, 461, 470, 536
Swigert (astronaut), 57

T
Tactical, 537
Tallinn missile, see SA-5
Tenth Strategy for Peace Conference (1969), 162
Test Ban Treaty (1963), 17
Thompson, Llewellyn E., 12, 39–40, 43, 44, 48, 91, 121, 353–54
Throw weight, 537

Timerbayev, Roland, 49, 270, 289–90, 292, 295
Titan, 11, 381, 392, 396, 397, 412, 428, 537
Tolstoy, Leo, 76–77
Toward a New Order of Sea Power (Sprout), 446
Triad, 86, 537
Trident missile system, 2, 321, 339, 340, 377, 396, 412–13, 458, 463, 537–38
Trotsky, Leon, 77
Troyat, Henri, 76–77
Truman, Harry, 14, 15
Trusov, Lieutenant General Konstantin A., 49, 216, 328, 435
"Try Adds," 302, 306
Tsarapkin, Ambassador, 130
Tundra talks, 58, 365–66, 368
Twenty-fourth Congress of the Communist Party, 67, 197

U
ULMS (or Undersea long-range missile system), *see* Trident missile system
Underwood, Oscar W., 451
United Kingdom, *see* Great Britain
United Nations, 9, 49, 84, 271, 341
United Nations Charter, 191
U. S. Department of Defense, 28, 42, 45, 54, 55, 62, 63, 64, 114, 117–18, 135, 158, 164, 204, 262, 285, 374, 377, 409, 471
U. S. Department of State, 6, 7, 9, 10, 13, 14, 38, 40, 43, 44, 45, 50, 52, 54, 55, 62, 80, 108, 113, 118, 160, 173, 376, 409, 435,

441–42, 443
U. S. Strategic Bombing Survey, 44
U-2 incident (1960), 11–12, 282

V
Verification, 538
Verification Panel, 99–100, 108, 109, 111–12, 169, 173, 186, 225, 256, 261, 264, 287–88, 419, 538
Brezhnev proposal and, 371–74, 375
Kissinger's use of, 111
meetings of, 111–12
Verification Panel Working Group, 173, 287
Vienna Option, 62, 127, 146–47, 149–50, 175
Vienna II (April–August 1970), 121–53, 179, 210–11
alternative approaches for comprehensive limitations, 122–23, 477–78
bilateral agreement proposal, 141–44
"continuing dialogue," 133–34
"launch on warning" episode, 135–36
opening session, 121
Operation A, 126–27
SAM upgrade constraints, 131–32, 133
selective direct observation (SDO), 134
Soviet Basic Provisions, 123–24, 127, 130, 131, 134, 144
U. S. Initial Strategic Arms Limitations Agreement, 151–52
Washington policy planning, 108–20

Vienna IV (March–May 1971), 201–22
  Defense Department concerns, 204–5
  FBS issue, 201, 203, 210, 215, 219–20
  "four-to-one" approach, 215–17
  ICBMs and, 202, 203, 204–21
  radar controls, 216
  withdrawal of NCA offer, 218
Vienna VI (November 1971–January 1972), 319–50
  ABM positions, 336–39, 343–44
  back-channel negotiations and, 323, 324, 328, 332, 349–50
  freeze negotiations, 322–36, 339, 344–46, 347, 349, 350
  holiday recess, 342–43
  India-Pakistan War and, 341–42
  leaks, 348
  President's instructions for, 325–26
  press attendance, 347–48
  second phase, 343–49, 350
  Washington mood, 321–22
Vietnam War, 21, 25, 26, 52, 372, 382, 383; See also Cambodian incursion of 1970
Vladivostok Agreement, 171, 245, 459, 467, 471, 538
V-1 "buzz bombs" (World War II), 89
Vorontsov, Counselor, 162

W
Wadsworth, James J. "Jerry," 9
Wake Island, 449
Walder, Francis, 69
Warhead, 538
Warsaw Pact, 53, 104, 144
Warsaw talks, 197
Washington Naval Limitation Conference of 1921–22, 160, 446–52
  terms of, 447
Washington Post, 162, 296
Washington SALT planning, 108–20
  "building blocks," 115–16
  Kissinger and, 108, 109, 110, 111, 112, 115
  optional approaches, 116–20
Watergate, 444
Weiler, Lawrence, 49
Western Peace Plan, 10
Westmoreland, General, 149
Wheeler, General Earle "Bus," 11, 27, 41
Wilson, Charles E., 23
Wilson, Woodrow, 447, 448
World War I, 105
World War II, 22, 38, 60, 61, 66–67, 89, 105, 143, 155, 207, 321, 451–52, 455

Y
Yalta Conference, 122
Yankee(Y)-class submarines, 59, 382, 394, 419, 423, 426, 431, 436, 437, 538

Z
Zablocki, Clement, 112
Zaroubin, Ambassador, 9
Zero-level limitation, 131
Zhukov, Marshal Georgi, 80
Ziegler, 379, 438
Zumwalt, Admiral, 361

A NOTE ON THE AUTHOR

GERARD SMITH is a veteran of over twenty-five years of
government service, including posts in the Truman,
Eisenhower, Kennedy, Johnson, Nixon and Carter administrations. Shortly after his appointment as Director
of the United States Arms Control and Disarmament
Agency in 1969, he was chosen by President Nixon to
be the Chief U. S. Delegate to SALT I. He has written
about the SALT talks for several publications, including
the *Wall Street Journal* and the *Journal of Economic
Affairs*. Mr. Smith practiced law in Washington, D.C.
with the firm of Wilmer, Cutler, & Pickering. He also
has served as President Carter's Special Representative
and Ambassador-at-Large for Non-Proliferation Negotiations. Mr. Smith lives in Washington, D.C.